Full Pews and
Empty Altars

Social Demography

Series Editors
Doris P. Slesinger
James A. Sweet
Karl E. Taeuber
Center for Demography and Ecology
University of Wisconsin–Madison

Full Pews and Empty Altars

*Demographics of
the Priest Shortage
in United States
Catholic Dioceses*

Richard A. Schoenherr
Lawrence A. Young

with the collaboration of
Tsan-Yuang Cheng

The University of Wisconsin Press

The University of Wisconsin Press
114 North Murray Street
Madison, Wisconsin 53715

3 Henrietta Street
London WC2E 8LU, England

Library of Congress Cataloging-in-Publication Data
Schoenherr, Richard A.
    Full pews and empty altars : demographics of the priest shortage
in United States Catholic dioceses / Richard A. Schoenherr and
Lawrence A. Young with the collaboration of Tsan-Yuang Cheng.
    460 p.   cm. — (Social demography)
    Includes bibliographical references and indexes.
    ISBN 0-299-13690-6   ISBN 0-299-13694-9
    1. Catholic Church — United States — Clergy — History — 20th
century.   2. Catholic Church — United States — Clergy —
Statistics.   I. Young, Lawrence A. (Lawrence Alfred), 1955–   .
II. Cheng, Tsan-Yuang.   III. Title.   IV. Series.
BX1407.C6S36   1993
251 — dc20   93-22427

For
Judith Ann Woods Schoenherr
Daren Curtis and Ruth Wilson Young

Judith Ann

a lot,

now,

forever

Richard

Christmas

Contents

Figures

Tables

xi

Preface

The Roman Catholic church faces a staggering loss of diocesan priests in the United States as it moves into the 21st century. There is little chance of reversing this trend in the lifetime of the current generation of churchgoers. *Full Pews and Empty Altars* documents the decline of U.S. priests in a random sample of 86 dioceses, forecasting a 40 percent loss in the priest population. Meanwhile the number of Catholics continues to swell. By the year 2005 there could be 2,200 parishioners for each priest in contrast with 1,100 per priest in 1966.

For most Catholics and other religious practitioners, these are astonishing figures and citing them produces an array of reactions. For some, the response is anger and denial. For others, it's grief and despair. And for still others, it's hope for a better church with more lay participation. When social scientists look at the trends they recognize an organizational crisis of immense proportions. Religious scholars see the decline as one of this century's most important changes in organized religion.

In many ways demographic data speak for themselves. Yet the numbers describing the priest shortage seem to produce a confusing babble. The first aim of the book, therefore, is to give the data a definitive voice. Precisely how bad is the decline? Will it be short-term? Are there regional differences? To answer such questions, we offer demographic statistics derived from official sources and tabulated with meticulous care, making them the most accurate data available. It will be hard to dispute the historical figures presented here, because we base them on names of priests registered in a census that was conducted under the auspices of the U.S. Catholic Conference. The population projections, too, have been tested and proved to be highly accurate.

Despite all attempts to be definitive, however, we caution readers to assess the numbers carefully and use them wisely. Population analysts do not predict the future. They merely make forecasts on the basis of past trends and reasonable assumptions. Accordingly, the study examines the past 20 years of the Catholic church in the United States, describes what the situation of the diocesan priesthood has been, and projects what can be expected at the turn of the century *if* the church doesn't do anything different. We will have achieved our first goal if all parties interested in the priest shortage have access to the same definitive data, which they may use for their own religious or political ends.

Our second aim is to contribute to the theoretical understanding of the structure of formal organizations, particularly structural change that occurs in organizations in decline. In this effort we also hope to improve the methodological tools of organizational analysis. So for social scientists the book represents a pathbreaking application of social demography to the field of organization studies.

A third aim is to alert sociologists of religion, church historians, theologians, and other religious scholars to one of the most pervasive changes in the Catholic ministry since the Reformation. The dramatic decline of the priest population raises questions about the future of the male celibate priesthood and its monopoly of control over access to the traditional Catholic means of salvation. Are the eucharistic and hierarchical traditions of the church in serious jeopardy? What is more essential to Roman Catholicism: male celibate exclusivity in the priesthood or the Mass and sacraments? These issues and many other ramifications of the priest shortage cry out for scholarly attention.

We experienced this research project as a long and arduous task. Pretests began a decade ago in 1983. The data collection campaign spread over more than three years. Processing and analyzing the data took another two years. Producing three respondent reports for the participating dioceses consumed two additional years; in 1990, the third and final volume of *The Catholic Priest in the United States: Demographic Investigations* (Schoenherr and Young 1990a) was sent to the cooperating dioceses and to all U.S. Catholic bishops. The contents of the respondent reports became the bulk of the descriptive analysis contained in this monograph.

A project of this size and scope required the efforts of many, foremost among whom were the sponsors, respondents, and research team. We are grateful to Lilly Endowment for providing extensive financial support and especially to Fred L. Hofheinz, program director for religion, and Robert W. Lynn, then vice president for religion, for the vision to recognize the practical and scholarly value of the study. The Graduate School Research Committee and the College of Letters and Science, University of Wisconsin–Madison, and the Family and Demographic Research Institute and College of Family, Home and Social Science, Brigham Young University, granted supplemental support. The U.S. Catholic Conference sponsored the project and helped maintain cordial relations with each of the cooperating dioceses, principally through the assistance of Rev. Eugene Hemrick, director of research, and Msgr. Daniel Hoye, then general secretary. We are deeply appreciative of their backing.

Scores of diocesan chancellors, vicars general, personnel directors, archivists, secretaries, and other unknown persons helped with the data collection, which in many cases required extreme dedication in understaffed chanceries. We wish to name a representative few among the countless respondents who spent many tedious hours in providing the raw data.

The chancellor of San Diego, Msgr. Brent Egan, whiled away the better part of a Friday evening on the telephone with one of us, correcting omissions in the census registry. Sister Mary Jaskel, OSF, archivist in Hartford, honed her sleuthing skills while eliminating clerical ghosts and tracing missing priests. Merton Lassonde, special assistant to the archbishop of St. Paul–Minneapolis, cut through miles of red tape with his matter-of-fact efficiency. Betty Baldwin, secretary to the chancellor of Buffalo, heroically completed the "Comprehensive Error Listing" a second time after the first one was lost in the mail.

Brother Edward Loch, archivist in San Antonio, sandwiched the priest census around the preparation for and the aftermath of Pope John Paul's visit to the archdiocese. Rev. William Coyle, CSSR, chancellor of Fargo, searched old diocesan newspapers for ordination dates over a Labor Day weekend. Ruth Cropper, secretary to the chancellor of Brooklyn, doggedly pursued clarifications of resignation data while grieving the death of her brother-in-law. To all of them and to each of their counterparts across the country, whose help was likewise invaluable and whose untold stories are equally poignant, we give our heartfelt thanks.

The faculty colleagues, professional and support staff, and many students who were associated with the long project are each gratefully listed on the following page. Research undertaken in an academic setting has special contraints, one of which is its training function. So student-trainees, at various stages of their careers, predominated on the team. Tsan-Yuang Cheng shouldered the responsibility as senior research assistant. Only he knew every detail of the massive set of computer files and programs, most of which he had designed and written. We acknowledge his extensive contributions to the project on the title page.

From among the students, we single out some of the other graduate and undergraduate research assistants at the University of Wisconsin–Madison, whom we watched juggle studies and personal lives with the demands of the project. Irene Giniat trained work-study students in coding data and in catering for CROS parties. Gerard Rodenkirch worked hard at census registries and still found time for crossword puzzles. Robert Biggert deftly handled computer tapes between baseball games. At one point Kimberly Allegretti became our mainstay in charge of computer runs, and Judith Schoenherr helped immeasurably as supervisor "in a pinch." Kathryn Kuhlow won the dual prize for most years on the project and most valuable assistant; she not only held the project together in its final stages, but also produced singlehandedly the camera-ready copy for all the tables in the book. We are very grateful to these and the other student-collaborators for sharing talent, hard work, and a segment of their lives with us.

Our first managing director, Judith Martin, helped launch the project and keep the data collection campaign humming. When she became registrar at a local college, we, alas, became self-coordinating. The reorganization worked only because of the all-encompassing secretarial skills of William Mutranowski, who later left us to study Zen in Japan. During the final phase of data collection and cleaning, our erstwhile motley crew was gently trounced into shape by Robert Patrick, newly retired air force colonel who had been weighing options for a second career. He finally left us for the seminary and was subsequently ordained. We wondered if he had gotten too personally involved in studying clergy decline.

We are very happy to acknowledge our debt to these and to everyone else named on the research team roster. Likewise, we thank Helen Rose Ebaugh, William Barnett, Fred Goldner, Gerald Marwell, Rodney Stark, James Sweet, and Karl Taeuber, who read the manuscript and offered helpful criticisms. And we remain in awesome appreciation of the indefatigable precision of Robin Whitaker, copy editor for the publisher. The collaborators have been many, but we accept final responsibility for the results of our work together.

The study intruded on family and friends for almost a decade. The senior author lavishes gratitude upon his wife, Judy, and his children, Andrew, Maria, and Joey, for not keeping too strict an account of the lost evenings, weekends, and summers that he spent counting priests. The junior author expresses appreciation for the encouragement and support of his parents and the members of the Madison Commune.

Comparative Religious Organization Studies Research Team

Director: Richard A. Schoenherr, Ph.D.

Research associates: Lawrence A. Young, Ph.D., Brigham Young
University
José Pérez Vilariño, Ph.D., University of Santiago
de Compostela

Research consultants: David Grissmer, Ph.D., Rand Corporation
Charles Halaby, Ph.D.
Eugene Hemrick, Ph.D., USCC Research Office
Tim Heaton, Ph.D., Brigham Young University
Alberto Palloni, Ph.D.

Managing directors: Judith Martin, Ph.D.
Robert Patrick, Ph.D.

Research assistants: Robert Biggert, Ph.D.
Tsan-Yuang Cheng, Ph.D.
Scott Frickel, B.A.
Xuan-Ning Fu, M.S., Brigham Young University
Irene Giniat, M.A.
Edwin Hernandez, Ph.D., University of Notre
Dame
Theron Quist, B.A., Brigham Young University
Gerard Rodenkirch, M.S.
Elizabeth Wingyee Chen, M.S., Brigham Young
University

Computer consultants: Bruno Browning, B.S.   David Weakliem, Ph.D.,
Anne Cooper, M.S.   Indiana University
William Gates, M.S   Daniel Woods, B.A.,
David Hytry   *Raleigh News and*
Jon Jones, B.S.   *Observer*
Bruce Ruzicka, B.S.   Beth Wiebusch
Pamela Stengl, B.S.

Work-study students: Kimberly Allegretti   Janette Kihm
Ana Aquino-Perez   Kathleen Patrick
Christine Belfiori   Laura Stuefen
Craig Birnbach   Nancy Stuefen
Bruce Broker   Sheryl Stumbras
Laurie Burnstein   Glenn Tanner
Michael Corbett   Susan Toellner-Krentz
Thomas Garvey   Michael Vanko
Laura Haugen   Rachel Ward

Secretarial/fiscal: Bonnie Cubalchini, B.A.
Mary Anne Klimke
Bill Mutranowski, B.A.
Norene Petersen, Brigham Young University
Virginia Rogers
Judith Schoenherr, M.P.S.

Art director: Theresa Ganshert, M.F.A.

Publications: Patricia Hobbins-Kemps, B.A.
Kathryn Kuhlow, B.A.
Robert McClory, M.A., Northwestern University
James Snight, M. Div., Archdiocese of Washington, D.C.

All at the University of Wisconsin–Madison, except as noted.

1 Overview

1   Why Count Priests?

A dynamic set of economic, political, and cultural conditions is rapidly transforming the structure of the Catholic church. Among them, this book calls attention first and foremost to the decline in sheer numbers of ordained clergy. We contend that the diminishing size of the priest population is the major driving force for social change within late 20th-century Catholicism. Our primary aim is to report the results of a six-year investigation of the changing demographics of the U.S. priesthood. We also discuss some of the most obvious consequences of decline. Details of how the priest shortage interacts with other social forces for change and where these trends are leading the Catholic church are analyzed in a companion volume (Schoenherr forthcoming).

In this chapter we provide an overview of the U.S. priest shortage by describing it as a crisis unique to Catholicism and by placing clergy growth and decline in a historical and global perspective. The problem is situated in its theoretical and research background. We narrow the focus by stating precisely which aspects of the problem will be examined, and end with an outline of the book.

Demographic Forces in Contradiction

Our major assumption is that the priest shortage, in interaction with other social preconditions for structural transformation, is modifying the internal political economy of the Catholic church. Most prominent among other conditions for organizational change are six dialectical processes closely related to the priest shortage. A second trend at work, along with changing demographics, is a decline in dogmatism and a rise in pluralism of worldviews, bringing with it an array of models of the church and a variety of plausibility structures (Dulles 1974; Berger 1980). Third, secularization trends and the end of colonialism have transformed the predominantly European or Western church into a world church, with its center of gravity shifting to the Southern Hemisphere (Bühlmann 1986).

Fourth, doctrinal changes legitimated by the Second Vatican Council represent a major transitional force, particularly those pronouncements which have weakened belief in the absolute superiority of celibacy as a way of holiness and strengthened the importance of the charism of marriage as an equal but different means of grace (Schoenherr and Greeley 1974; Schillebeeckx 1985; Seidler and Meyer 1989). Fifth, the feminist movement, especially among nuns and laywomen in church-related careers, is beginning to erode male hegemony over the church's ministry and to establish a growing sense of female equality (Gilmour 1986; Wallace 1992).

Sixth, the ordained clergy's political monopoly over the technical core of the church's ministry is being called into question by increased lay participation in ministerial roles (Leege 1986). Last and inevitably, the sacramental, in particular the eucharistic, focus of the Catholic church's "means of justification" (Troeltsch 1960) is being dimmed by the growing recognition of the "saving power" of the scriptures, because fewer priests are available for Mass and more laypersons preside at Liturgies of the Word.

We single out population dynamics as especially powerful among the social forces transforming Roman Catholicism in the United States. As described in later chapters, components of demographic change in the clergy population are creating sustained negative effects on size and growth of the priesthood. Yet, in contrast, birth rates, age structure, and immigration of the Catholic lay population are producing continuous positive effects on size and growth of church membership. So, powerful demographic forces for change seem to be operating in basic contradiction within American Catholicism. One set of social trends — priesthood decline — may be undermining the very foundation of its organizational strength, while another — growth in membership — may be impelling the U.S. Catholic church into a position of expanded influence and prominence.

Roof and McKinney (1987) document several key modifications in the contemporary religious landscape that seem to be drawing Catholicism more firmly into American mainline religion. Liberal Protestantism, which once acted as the moral conscience of the "American way of life" (Herberg 1955), has experienced decline in numbers and stature since the 1960s. At the same time, Roman Catholics and African American and conservative Protestants have witnessed growth in their membership and societal influence.

The waning vitality of liberal Protestantism creates a vacuum with respect to American religion's traditional function of producing societal cohesion and consensus. Perhaps as recently as the 1950s, the WASP elite was considered the embodiment of the moral order which made national community possible. Today, however, the moral center no longer holds. Public morality has become a contested terrain for the churches (Edwards 1979; Roof and McKinney 1987). Undoubtedly, religion's ability to act as an agent of societal consensus has been significantly reduced in recent decades. At the same time, however, religious groups that were traditionally relegated to the margins, such as Catholics and conservative Protestants, are now vying for influence over the center.

The emergence of a new religious "middle" consisting of Catholics and moderate Protestants, with continued participation from liberal Protestants and new support from African American Protestants, is a distinct possibility. As evidence of growing influence on public affairs, for example, witness the unique role of Catholic bishops as a major voice of Christian morality in the United States. The Catholic hierarchy issues pronouncements on war and peace, economics and abortion, and Americans take them seriously.

New respect for the Catholic church's national influence in recent years is reinforced by the steady growth of the Catholic population in the United States. According to the Official Catholic Directory, between 1925 and 1980 the absolute number of American Catholics has grown from fewer than 20 million to more than 50 million. Catholicism's share of the religious market has also increased from less than 20 percent to more than 25 percent during the same period (Roof and McKinney 1987; Smith 1984). And the proportion is still expanding. National polls indicate that high fertility and the influx of Hispanic and Asian immigrants are generating continuous growth in the U.S. Catholic population. These demographic forces will push the absolute number of those whose religious preference is Roman Catholic well above 60 million and the proportion of Catholics in the United States toward 30 percent by the early 1990s (American Institute of Public Opinion 1987). Furthermore, the force of the trends suggests that the Catholic population will continue its historic pattern of growth beyond the turn of the century.

Of course, not all who claim Catholicism as their religious preference are considered active members of the church. But if we examine statistics on church members or those who publicly practice their religion at least minimally, the dominance of the Catholic church in the United States is even more striking. Currently, Catholic church membership represents 42 percent of all church-goers in the country (Quinn et al. 1982).

The vitality of organized religion is not just a function of size and growth of church membership. A church's well-being also depends on the strength of its internal organization. Human capital is the most critical resource in a service organization's internal political economy. In stark contrast with the burgeoning laity, the Catholic church faces a crisis in recruiting and retaining professional human resources. As in other human service organizations, the ability to provide religion is directly affected by supply and demand. Thus the ratio of laity to clergy is the more appropriate indicator of organizational well-being within religious groups. By itself, the absolute number of neither laity nor clergy provides an adequate measure of organizational health.

Recently, Hoge, Carroll, and Scheets (1988) studied parish leadership in Catholicism and three comparable Protestant denominations and found significant Catholic-Protestant differences in the ratio of clergy to church members. The contrasts they document epitomize one of the fundamental demographic contradictions within American religion today. Catholicism, on the one hand, is experiencing growth in membership but a shrinking priesthood. Major denominations within mainline Protestantism, on the other hand, are characterized by declining church membership but a surplus of clergy. Ironically, the Catholic church faces a major crisis because, despite a flourishing laity, it cannot recruit and retain a sufficient number of priests. What is more, the current clergy shortage is a distinctively Catholic crisis. This makes it all the more unusual.

Priesthood Population Change in Historical Context

Population shifts are nothing new either in the broad sweep of human history or in the annals of ancient organizations like the Catholic church. Unusual and persistent population change, however, is cause for concern, because it may be a harbinger of more pervasive social change. Thus, poring over census data to discover peaks and valleys in population trends has been a serious activity for eons. The task of counting heads has a sense of urgency for some people most of the time, but for most people only some of the time. For example, from time immemorial kings, queens, presidents, and dictators have always counted their soldiers and taxpayers with hopeful anticipation and, occasionally, all their people with fearful suspicion that some were shirking their military or internal revenue responsibilities (Alterman 1969).

The analysis of population change as a serious business for most of us, at least some of the time, awaited publication of *An Essay on the Principle of Population,* written in 1834 by Thomas Malthus, theologian, philosopher, and founding member of the Royal Statistical Society. Before Malthus, most people-counting was done with hope. Since his time, because the world's population has increased "at a rate higher than ever before in history, in many parts of the world the counting of people is done with fear" (Alterman 1969, p. 13).[1] Creating and analyzing population statistics is serious business, because demographic data seem to have a voice of their own. Everyone, not just experts, can understand the numbers.

Malthusian doom is still the subject of much debate, but using scientific techniques to understand complex population dynamics is not. American Catholic bishops, for example, have sponsored the systematic counting of their priests with the hope of understanding social forces affecting the clergy population and wider church.[2] Mapping the contours of demographic transitions in organizations is a first step toward explaining the causes and consequences of historical events that may be transforming the structures of an organization unbeknownst to its members. To understand the thrust of population change and separate it from other social trends, we need to begin by examining fluctuations in growth and decline from a historical perspective. How else can we know if the trends are unusual or persistent?

Clergy Growth

The evolution and growth of the priesthood have followed the fortunes and misfortunes of Christianity while the new religious movement has emerged and spread across entire continents (Troeltsch 1960; Schillebeeckx 1985).[3] New religions succeed in the long run only if they experience almost phenomenal growth during their launching stage, and Christianity is a primary example of this demographic rule (Stark and Roberts 1982). Two centuries of steady expansion were capped by the conversion of Constantine's troops in A.D. 312. This was followed by the establishment of the Holy Roman Empire, an enormous increase in the Christian population and, thus, further growth in the size of the clergy. Migrations of the Vandals, Goths, and Visigoths during the so-called Dark Ages likewise re-

---

1. Malthus tried to demonstrate that a "population tends to increase at a faster rate than its means of subsistence and that unless it is checked by moral restraint or by disease, famine, war or other disaster widespread poverty and degradation inevitably result" (*Webster's Seventh New Collegiate Dictionary,* 1972 ed., s.v. "Malthusian").

2. In keeping with the applied nature of our research, this book is addressed not only to research scholars but also to ecclesiastical policymakers and other church leaders. As such, it is another respondent report prepared in gratitude to the U.S. Catholic Conference for sponsoring the project and the 86 dioceses for providing the data.

3. Troeltsch presents the classic analysis of the critical importance of priesthood in the evolution of Christianity from its primitive form to Early Catholicism with its highly centralized church-form. Schillebeeckx, a contemporary theologian, provides an insightful and carefully documented analysis of the emergence, sociological development, and transformation of the priesthood from biblical to modern times.

sulted in swelling the ranks of Christian believers and augmenting the size of the presbyterates to serve them.

The colonization of the New World in the 16th and 17th centuries brought the Christian faith and its priest-missionaries to North and South America. Roman Catholicism was on its way to becoming a world religion. Waves of Catholic immigrants swarmed to Latin America and the United States during the 18th and 19th centuries. They brought their own clergy initially, but they also generated large families with many sons who soon established a vibrant and large native Catholic priesthood, at least in the United States (Ellis 1971).

Clergy Decline

The history of the Catholic clergy is marked by relatively steady but not unmitigated growth in numbers. Epochal events also visited misfortune on the priest population, sometimes merely as a subgroup of the general population, but other times with singular precision. During the 14th century, for example, the Black Death all but decimated the general population along with the monasteries and secular presbyterates of western Europe. Two centuries later the Protestant Reformation witnessed thousands of Catholic clergy forsaking celibacy to become married pastors of the Reformed churches (Troeltsch 1960; Ozment 1972). Additionally, during the late 16th century the political compromise of Roman Catholic and Protestant rulers in Germany, summarized by the principle *cuius regio, ejus religio,*[4] resulted in loss to the Catholic priesthood of countless clerical positions. A few centuries later, during the potato famine of the 1840s over 2 million Irish inhabitants, including a proportionate number of priests, died. Thousands of Catholic priests were assassinated during the French Revolution (Gargan and Hanneman 1978) and thousands more during the Spanish civil war (Payne 1984).

Factors Contributing to Growth and Decline

The briefest of historical sketches reveals that a variety of political, economic, environmental, and organizational conditions has affected the demography of the Catholic priesthood over the centuries. Certain ecological conditions such as disease, famine, and migration patterns have inevitable and universal demographic consequences, sparing no population subgroups including the clergy. Some environmental factors, involv-

---

4. The phrase is translated literally, "whose region, his or her religion" and means the inhabitants of a region had to follow the religion of its sovereign regardless of their individual preferences.

ing the interaction of organized religion with other institutions in society, however, may focus more specifically on religious leaders. Thus during revolutions and wars tied to religious disputes, hostile forces have intentionally singled out the clergy for assassination.[5]

Politico-legal action can likewise reduce and swell the ranks of the clergy. Perhaps no other decree did so as dramatically as *cuius regio, ejus religio,* although the alliance with Constantine may have been the single most effective political move in the Catholic church's history for inducing long-range clergy growth. Organizational processes internal to the church, such as reformation and counterreformation movements, are also highly visible forces that have altered the size and structure of the priesthood.

The overall history of the demography of the Roman Catholic clergy is one of growth interrupted by major and minor periods of decline. Certain historical events such as the French Revolution, Irish potato famine, and Spanish civil war affected only the national clergy. In France, Ireland, and Spain the churches and priesthood at the diocesan level were not very different after these events from what they were before them, and the demographic and sociological consequences were mitigated with time. Other events, such as the Protestant Reformation, however, had universal and lasting effects on the organization demography and social structure of Christianity and its priestly ministry. The Christian churches and clergy before and after the religious upheavals of the 16th century were vastly different organizational populations and sociological forms.

A mere glance at the long history of the Catholic priesthood reveals that overall growth in the Catholic clergy has been the rule, but unusual decline has persisted for varying lengths of time. Some persistent losses, such as those sustained during the Protestant Reformation, have had serious and permanent consequences. The panoramic view of history, however, raises more questions than answers. Is the priest decline in the United States a national phenomenon like those that occurred in Ireland, France, and Spain? Or is it part of a worldwide trend? Is it caused by external environmental factors, the demographic and sociological effects of which may be relatively minor and brief? Or is it caused by internal organizational factors, and if so, are they pervasive with far-reaching structural consequences? The latter questions are better addressed after we present our empirical analysis, but the first issue deserves attention at the start.

---

5. The recent deaths of Archbishop Oscar Romero, two nuns, two laywomen catechists, six Jesuit priests and their housekeeper and her daughter, along with an unknown number of other missing priests in El Salvador — not to mention other similarly affected countries in Central and South America — are a current example of a hostile political environment having violent demographic consequences for a clergy population (see Windsor 1990).

A Worldwide Trend?

The Central Office of Church Statistics in the Vatican Secretariat of State recently reported a rise in the priest populations in some countries of Europe, Africa, Asia, and Latin America but continued decline throughout North America.[6] Recent growth in the absolute numbers of priests might indicate that, even if the clergy shortage is not over, at least in some parts of the world the church may be seeing light at the end of the tunnel.

In understanding complex population trends, however, absolute numbers are often deceiving. For example, although the priest population is growing noticeably in some areas, the lay population may be growing even faster. Thus in terms of the availability of priestly services, higher numbers of priests could be hiding a steady or even growing shortage because of increased demand. Therefore, as we argued earlier, the more accurate index of availability of priestly service must be the priest-to-layperson ratio.

Figure 1.1 presents the number of priests per 10,000 Catholics by continent from the end of the Second Vatican Council to the present. Table 1.1 displays the same data in more detail and includes the percentage of change from 1965 to 1986.[7] The graph shows that, without exception, the priest-to-layperson ratio has declined steadily over the entire 20-year period. In addition, it dramatizes the huge difference between the Catholic church in Africa and South America, on the one hand, and the church in Europe, North America, and India, on the other. As of the mid-1980s, the European, North American, and Indian churches had almost five times more priestly resources than the African churches and about eight times more than the South American churches.

Examining the statistics in table 1.1, we discover that Poland represents an anomalous situation. It alone, among all the selected Western countries listed, has been experiencing improvement in its priest-to-layperson ratio during these two decades. All other major countries in Europe and North America have suffered notable decline. The overall trend ranges from a 6 percent loss in West Germany to a 40 percent loss in the Netherlands between 1965 and 1986. The average decline in the number of priests per 10,000 laypersons for the European and North American countries listed is 23 percent. Note that the decline in the United States falls below the average.

6. The Catholic press reported the increases soon after the data were released (Castelli 1989; Windsor 1989; Cleary 1989).
7. The data stop in 1986, because they are published after a three-year lag. The graph covers a 20-year and the table a 21-year period.

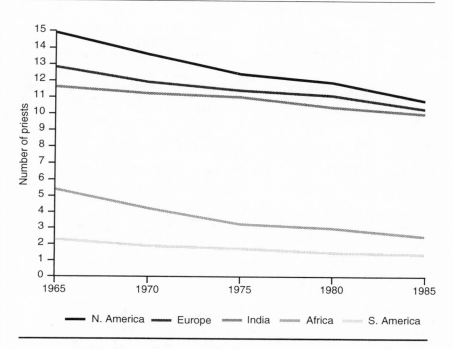

Figure 1.1. Number of diocesan and religious priests per 10,000 Catholics, 1965–85, by year and continent

Source: table 1.1.
Note: Data plotted for North America are averages for Canada and the United States given in table 1.1; the data points for Europe are averages for the 10 European countries listed in table 1.1.

Examining trends in individual countries reveals that, apart from Poland, the downward curve has been remarkably steady with minimal fluctuations; some few countries saw growth or stability for brief periods. Belgium experienced a temporary upswing between 1970 and 1975, and Austria witnessed the same between 1975 and 1980; in addition, some areas such as West Germany and Italy recorded stable ratios for a period before the numbers fell. Overall, however, the decline has been relentless up to and including 1986, the last year for which data are available. A few areas, namely, Austria, Belgium, India, and South America, show stability for the last two data points, 1985 and 1986. Whether this means the decline is bottoming out in those areas is impossible to tell, because those data represent only a one-year trend.

In ecclesiastical circles much has been made of the recent rise in voca-

Table 1.1. Number of diocesan and religious priests per 10,000 Catholics and
percentage of change, 1965–86, by year, nation, and continent

| | Year | | | | | | % change |
	1965	1970	1975	1980	1985	1986	1965–86
Western nations							
Austria	11.1	9.3	9.0	9.3	8.8	8.8	-20.8
Belgium	17.2	15.0	15.4	14.3	12.8	12.8	-25.8
Canada	16.9	15.1	13.1	12.2	10.7	10.4	-38.7
France	12.3	9.9	9.3	8.5	7.7	7.5	-39.1
Great Britain	20.4	16.4	15.9	15.3	15.0	14.9	-26.8
Ireland	19.6	17.6	17.4	16.4	14.8	13.6	-30.8
Italy	12.3	12.4	11.5	11.5	10.9	10.8	-11.9
Netherlands	17.5	14.2	11.8	12.3	10.8	10.4	-40.4
Poland	5.6	5.8	5.8	5.9	5.9	6.0	6.7
Spain	11.0	10.7	9.6	8.9	8.4	8.1	-25.9
United States	12.9	12.1	11.7	11.6	10.7	10.5	-18.7
West Germany	—[a]	8.2	8.2	8.2	7.8	7.7	-6.1
Southern continents							
Africa	5.4	4.3	3.3	3.0	2.5	2.4	-54.7
India	11.6	11.2	11.0	10.4	10.0	10.0	-13.5
South America	2.3	1.9	1.7	1.5	1.4	1.4	-37.6

Sources: for 1965–80, Hoge 1987; for 1985 and 1986, Statistical Yearbook of the
Church for those years. The original source for Hoge's 1965 data is the National Catholic
Almanac; his 1970–80 data are from the Statistical Yearbook of the Church.
[a]Separate data for West Germany were not available before 1970.

tions in parts of Africa, Latin America, and Poland (Castelli 1989; Windsor 1989; Cleary 1989). The positive attention is justifiable, given the centrality of priesthood in the ministry of the Catholic church. Note, however, these are precisely the areas with the worst priest-to-layperson ratios recorded by the data. Poland is noticeably below France and West Germany, which together are the three with the lowest number of priests per Catholics among the European countries listed.

Similarly, the data show that the churches of Africa and Latin America face tremendous constraints, given their low priest-to-layperson ratios and the eucharistic traditions of Catholicism. The celebration of the Mass is a rare occasion for many Catholics who live on these populous continents, where only 2.4 and 1.4 priests, respectively, are available for every 10,000 lay members of the church. Given the global statistics, any increase in priestly vocations is a cause for joy among church administrators. But in view of the abysmally low and steadily shrinking availability of eucharistic and other priestly services in the Southern Hemisphere, the absolute size of the increase may actually be a cause for grave concern. Africa and Latin America both have a tough game of catch-up ball to play in recruiting and retaining a sufficient number of priests to man their burgeoning churches.

We may conclude from the available evidence that the priest shortage in the United States, though not the worst in the Catholic church, is part of a steadily worsening worldwide phenomenon. Furthermore, at least among Christians in this country, the paucity of pastors in contrast with the steady growth in church membership is a crisis unique to Roman Catholicism. As such the problem deserves serious attention.

Demography and Organization Science

As social analysts we address the unusual Catholic dilemma of full pews and empty altars principally from the angle of organization demography. Organization research is paying systematic attention to social demography as more and more studies show that demographic trends are a driving force for social change. For example, in a recent study of internal labor markets in churches, public school systems, and police agencies, Stewman (1986, p. 212) notes: "The importance of demography for organizations is becoming increasingly recognized as the organizations in national labor markets deal with baby booms, baby busts, the aging of workers and their retirement decisions."

In his short but influential paper on the practical implications of organization demography, Pfeffer (1983) lays out some provocative theoretical issues concerning the impact of demography on organization behavior. The hypotheses generated from his review of the literature illustrate the broad potential of demography to organization analysts and managers alike. Researchers in both organization science and sociology of religion are turning to social demography and population studies for explanations of social change.

Organizations in General

The application of demographic concepts and techniques to organizational analysis has been a growing development since Keyfitz (1973) introduced the topic. In commenting on Keyfitz's seminal article, Matras (1975) distinguishes between the demographic analysis of populations of organizations and the analysis of the individual organization as a population. Clearly, the area of greatest research interest has been the demographic analysis of organizational survival in populations of organizations (Hannan and Freeman 1977; Brittain and Freeman 1980; Freeman 1982; Carroll and Delacroix 1982; Freeman and Hannan 1983; Freeman et al. 1983; Singh et al. 1986; Hannan and Freeman 1989; Singh 1990).

Our empirical focus, however, is on the individual organization as a population of its professional members. This type of organization demography is most frequently represented by studies of the effects of changing cohort size (Gusfield 1957; Ryder 1965; Reed 1978) or the impact of an organization's demography on career mobility and turnover in internal labor markets (Stewman and Konda 1983; McCain et al. 1983; Wagner et al. 1984; Stewman 1986). We take a somewhat different approach by focusing on the phenomenon of population change itself as it relates to a key cadre of organizational members, in this case, Catholic priests. The study of population change within organizations provides a foundation for other types of demographic analysis in that a sustained population change affects cohort size, career mobility, turnover, and other internal labor market dynamics.

Religious Organizations

In the area of sociology of religion, Roof and McKinney (1987) also rely heavily on demographic variables in their excellent study of the changing shape and future of American mainline religion. But no two social scientists have attacked the social demography of organized religion with more zest, ingenuity, and productivity than Stark and Finke (1988, forthcoming; Finke and Stark 1988, 1989, 1992; Finke 1989; see also Stark and Bainbridge 1985). They methodically apply the tools of demography in their efforts to correct widespread misconceptions about the health, growth, and decline of American churches and sects from the colonial period to the present.

The fact that the Catholic church in the United States is an organization in decline — that is, with regard to its technical human resources — has been partly documented elsewhere.[8] Several years ago Schoenherr and Sørensen (1982) proposed a preliminary model of the demographic transition of the Catholic priesthood. They also recorded clergy losses from 1966 to 1973 and presented projections of the U.S. priesthood population to 2000 based on their limited time-series and cross-sectional data. Recently, we and another colleague tested a more precise hypothetical model of the priestly demographic transition in one U.S. and one Spanish diocese as an exploratory analysis of some of the data to be presented here (Schoenherr et al. 1988). We also applied the same test in a further reconnaissance, using 15 U.S. dioceses (Schoenherr and Young 1990b). The research reported in this book completes and extends these earlier demographic studies of the Catholic clergy.

---

8. For clergy losses immediately following the Second Vatican Council, see NORC 1972; for steady decline in the number of nuns, brothers, and seminarians, see the annual Official Catholic Directory, especially from 1970 to the present.

Why Count Only Priests?

Sociologists count what counts, to society and to themselves. In their passionate desire to know why the rich get richer and the poor poorer, how the powerful increase their domination, why some groups achieve high status and others do not, or how conformists differ from deviants, what do social scientists do? They begin by enumerating the affluent and poverty-stricken, superiors and subordinates, professionals and workers, participants and criminals. Enumeration is the basis of measurement. And for empirical research, measurement and theoretical interest go hand in hand.

We decided to count priests because priests count prominently in organized religion. And, as Pfeffer and Salancik (1978) argue, critical organizational resources count even more in the event of their scarcity. Limiting our attention to the clergy, however, is not to say that numbers of the laity are unimportant elements in the social demography of the Catholic church. Indeed the priesthood is meaningless outside a community of believers. Undoubtedly, both groups are important for understanding social change in the church. Nevertheless, given the hierarchical structure and sacramental focus of Catholicism, we view the clergy as a more critical participant in organizational change than the laity, particularly at this moment in history.

The transformation of the Catholic church, as it approaches entry into its third millennium, will be affected most pervasively by a transformation of the structure of the ministry. From its earliest history priesthood and ministry were practically synonymous. Even today the status quo of Catholic ministry equates priesthood with responsibility for administering the primary "means of salvation." Troeltsch (1960) describes how the unique churchlike organization of Catholicism, firmly based on sacramental priesthood, emerged immediately following Pauline Christianity (see also Schillebeeckx 1985). With the development of monasticism and apostolic religious orders for the nonordained, nuns and brothers performed ancillary services for the ordained clergy. Of course, throughout the history of the church, lay volunteers handled other minor ministerial tasks. By and large, however, the scope and domain of what was considered most essential and important to organized Catholic ministry has always been circumscribed by those tasks and responsibilities performed by the ordained clergy.

This recounting of the status quo is not meant to belittle the important contributions now made by nuns and brothers, specifically in the areas of education and health care, or those made by the laity engaged in a wide variety of pastoral ministries (Doohan 1986; Dolan et al. 1989; Ray 1991). We mean to highlight the essential fact, however, that organizational activities which form the technical core of the Catholic church — providing, coordinating, and controlling access to the means of salvation — have been almost exclusively assigned to the ordained clergy.

Admittedly, social forces preceding and following the Second Vatican Council have begun to question and to alter that status quo — a topic addressed in another report (Schoenherr forthcoming). As the century wanes, nuns, brothers, and laypersons are actively participating in the questioning and restructuring of Catholic ministry at its very core. Can and should ministry continue to be the predominant, let alone exclusive, responsibility of the clergy? This is the burning issue in post–Second Vatican Council Catholicism.

Deacons as Clergy

Catholic usage limits the term "clergy" to those who receive the Sacrament of Holy Orders. The reestablishment of the permanent diaconate after the Second Vatican Council has expanded the ordained clergy population in many dioceses. Strictly speaking the diocesan clergy now includes not just priests but growing numbers of permanent deacons. Deacons, however, work as part-time volunteers, and their ministry is limited by canon law and custom. They may not preside at the celebration of Mass or the Sacrament of Reconciliation (formerly the Sacrament of Penance or Confession). Nevertheless, deacons perform some ministerial tasks once reserved to priests and so augment clerical manpower.

We contend that priestly dominance in Catholicism continues in spite of developments in lay and deaconal ministries. Hence, the priesthood deserves careful analysis in and of itself. A full investigation of the priest shortage has theoretical and practical priority, precisely because it is the driving force for change in the structure of Catholic ministry.

Laypersons as Members and as Part of the Ecological Niche

Drawing organizational boundaries is both a theoretical and an operational problem. In the empirical models of the diocesan church that we present, laypersons are considered part of the organization's environment or ecological niche. As we explained, however, in a wider theoretical model laywomen and laymen — including religious sisters and brothers among them[9] — are considered important actors within the organization.

It is not theoretically contradictory to consider organizational members, such as those of the Catholic laity, within the boundaries of the organization in one model and as part of its environment in another. The selection of a particular organizational model is an integral part of a research de-

---

9. According to canon law, nuns and brothers are technically considered laypersons.

sign. The proper choice is primarily a function of which aspects of reality need to be highlighted given the task at hand. Consequently, the issue of where organizational boundaries ought to be drawn is essentially heuristic in nature, with the correct placement growing out of the research agenda (Salaman 1981; Hannan and Freeman 1989).

We adopt the perspective that individuals in a society form the ecological niche from which religious organizations draw their members in a competitive religious market. As Berger (1967, p. 138) explains: "The pluralistic situation is above all a *market situation*. In it, the religious institutions become marketing agencies and the religious traditions become consumer commodities. And at any rate a good deal of religious activity in this situation comes to be dominated by the logic of market economies." Thus, not even religious organizations, as Marx and Weber strongly reminded us, are exempt from economic forces.

Berger's theoretical work has been applied to religious organizations in several empirical studies. Westhues (1971), basing his framework on Berger as well as Thompson's pioneering model of rational activity of organizations in their environments, analyzed the effects of environmental competition and hostility on the education activities of Catholic dioceses. In their extensive studies of organized religion, Stark and Bainbridge (1980, 1985) have developed a systematic cost-benefit theory for investigating the religious economy of societies; Stark and McCann (1989) apply aspects of the model in a study of market forces and Catholic commitment in U.S. dioceses.

In the same conceptual vein, Iannaccone (1990) is developing a rational choice approach to understanding organized religion. He (p. 297) employs an economic model of "nonmarket" activities to explain "observed patterns in denominational mobility, religious intermarriage, conversion ages, the relationships between church attendance and contributions, and the influence of upbringing and interfaith marriage on levels of religious participation." Greeley (1989a) has also used rational choice concepts to analyze intergenerational stability of religious choice.

In the various frameworks that conceptualize religious groups as rational organizations in a competitive marketplace, each individual in society is considered a potential resource, either a possible "provider" or "consumer" of services. That is, society's members face a wide array of organizations and must decide to participate in certain ones either as providers or as consumers of goods and services. Thus, through a process in which organizations compete for resources in their ecological niches, professors and students are attracted to work in or attend certain colleges and universities; doctors and patients, certain hospitals; lawyers and clients, certain law firms; ministers and parishioners, certain churches; and so forth. For purposes of our analysis, the boundary of the focal organization (the diocese) is drawn around the full-time, part-time, and volunteer workers who compose the technical core and participate in its coordination and control. Future service providers along with active and potential clients are outside the organization thus conceived and form part of its environment and ecological niche.

Hence a population of religious organizations, such as U.S. Catholic dioceses, must compete for active professional participants and loyal lay members in their ecological niche. As such, members of the laity—including future priests among them—are part of the environment of the diocesan organization. Those who become priestly officeholders and so participate in the diocese's core technology have to move from the environment into the organization; their passage is through seminary training. The choice of a church career is made in competition with job opportunities available in all other organizations in the environment. Likewise, the decision to join or remain in the Catholic church is a choice made in competition with membership opportunities available in all other denominations and sects in the environment.

From this theoretical viewpoint, priests are service providers and laypersons are service consumers. Our model, which defines priests as part of the diocesan organization and the laity as part of the environment, is constructed for heuristic purposes, as are all empirical research models. Let it be noted that, although our model provides only a partial view of reality, it provides, we contend, at least one important view of reality.

Religion as a societal institution is another matter. In its broader conceptualization, religion is a social institution circumscribed by communities of believers with widely varying creeds, codes, and cults, some highly organized and others hardly organized at all. The clergy-laity dichotomy is prominent in some organization forms and hardly distinguishable in others. The understanding of the essence or core of religion and of the relationship between religion as an institution and its concrete organization forms, which undergirds our work, is treated elsewhere (see Schoenherr 1987a, forthcoming).

Focus of the Research

Our research problem is social change, more precisely, change in organized religion. We narrowed this vast topic to change in the late 20th-century Catholic church, more exactly, change in the structural form of ministry. From among its many manifestations we restricted our focus further to structural transformation of the priesthood population, more accurately, decline in size and some of its consequences.

A major question confronted in narrowing our interests springs from the dilemma of so-called pure versus applied research. McKelvey and Aldrich's (1983) recent plea for more applied research echoes Argyris' (1972) earlier critique of the inapplicability of organizational sociology (see also Lawler et al. 1985). We hear these as welcome cries in the wilderness of apractical research agendas. We agree that it's time to bring policymakers back into the picture. Thus our design, which evolved during two decades of prior research on the Catholic church, aims for a balance between emphasizing practical application and advancing sociological knowledge.

The strategy adopted to achieve our practical and substantive goals is threefold. We decided to analyze demographic trends for a 19-year period following the Second Vatican Council, project these trends into the next century, and explain differences in the trends across dioceses. The *first* goal, analyzing historical trends, is realized by isolating the structural process that is generating decline in the priest population. For this we use Hernes' (1976) model of process structure, parameter structure, and output structure, as was done in a preliminary investigation of clergy decline (Schoenherr and Sørensen 1982). We adopt his conceptual framework because it has several useful qualities. As Hernes (1976, p. 513) explains, "Models of structural change should be able to explain constancy as well as change, must combine micro- and macrolevel analysis, and must encompass endogenous sources of change." Our analysis of population change adopts all three of his goals.

For the population projections, the *second* part of our research strategy, we use straightforward demographic techniques. Stable population theory allows us to construct multiple increment and decrement life tables and project changes in the priesthood population at the national, regional, and diocesan levels. We use the component method for the projections and create a high, middle, and low series based on assumptions gleaned from our analysis of historical trends (see Shryock, Siegel, and Associates 1971).

In making the projections we conduct a "what-if" experiment by asking: *What* would happen to the priest population over the next 20 years *if* certain assumptions held true? The projections are based on three key assumptions: (1) Past variation, selection, and retention mechanisms determining the size of the priest population will prevail in the future. (2) The same process structure generating growth and decline in the priest population during the previous two decades will continue unchanged for at least two more decades. (3) The parameter structure of the process is allowed to vary so as to produce high, medium, and low projections. These assumptions are clarified in chapter 2.

In the *third* step of the research design we use descriptive analysis to

examine differences in size and age composition of the changing priesthood population, comparing the high, medium, and low projection series
at the national, regional, and diocesan levels. We then account for variations across dioceses. With the help of multiple regression analysis we examine the impact of environmental and organizational variables on growth
and decline at the local level.

Constructing a Data Set

Collecting, storing, and retrieving the data needed to accomplish our
research goals tested the skills and patience of all involved, including contact persons in cooperating dioceses. Repeatedly we were asked, "Why
bother creating a population register of Catholic priests?" The question
is not trivial, because constructing the census registries consumed extensive resources. The answer, though, is simple: No data set at the organizational level of analysis existed that met our needs. The Official Catholic
Directory lists extensive information on all U.S. dioceses and Catholic priests
but proved to be only partly useful. The annual does not include data on
priests' ages or resignations, for example, and began to list the number
of newly ordained only as recently as 1987. We can state categorically that
no data suitable for comparative trend analysis and projections of the U.S.
priesthood population are available, except those provided by our census
project.

In effect, we created a "vital statistics registration system" for the U.S.
Catholic clergy covering 1966 through 1984. The purpose of such a system,
according to Shryock, Siegel, and Associates (1971, p. 389), is the "registration, statistical recording and reporting of the occurrence of vital events,
and the collection, compilation, analysis, presentation, and distribution
of vital statistics." This type of census uses the registration method of collecting data on relevant vital events, which for priests in a diocesan organizational setting include not only birth and death but also resignation,
sick leave, migration, and retirement. We describe the population register
in an expanded version of appendix A, noting the special problems facing
organization demographers who collect original data.[10] For example, we
frequently encountered poor records, unstandardized definitions, and lack
of skill in accurate counting on the part of those responsible for diocesan
record keeping.

In the course of the project we also have been asked why the census
register begins in 1966. This question has been posed by church leaders

---

10. Appendix A was shortened for inclusion in this book; the full version is available
at the address noted in the appendix.

who consider the study's results discouraging or embarrassing. Fixing the time period was basically a theoretical decision. Most important, 1966 began the aftermath of the Second Vatican Council (1962–65), an event recognized as a major catalyst for organizational change in the church (O'Dea 1968; Greeley 1977; Kim 1980; Seidler and Meyer 1989; Ebaugh 1991; Hegy 1993). Further, the late 1960s in the United States and the early 1970s in Spain marked the cusp of a sustained growth curve for the priest populations in those countries and probably in many others as well (Schoenherr et al. 1988). Accordingly, we believe ours and any further cross-national studies of the demographic transition of Catholic clergy would need to begin at least in the mid-1960s. And as we shall report in chapter 6, the demographic transition in the United States was in its launching stage in the 1960s, so beginning the census then permitted us to capture all its phases.

Plan of the Book

Part Two is dedicated mainly to descriptive analysis. In it we delineate the extent, speed, timing, duration, and variation of the demographic transition of the clergy in U.S. dioceses. Chapter 2 provides national statistics delineating the change process, chapter 3 contrasts regional variations in the transition, and chapter 4 compares differences in growth and decline at the local diocesan level. Chapter 4 also extends the comparative investigation in earnest, when we turn to the diocese itself as unit of analysis. Chapter 5 unfolds a pattern underlying the decline process by mapping out stages of the demographic transition. In chapter 6 we begin to explain the variance in the demographic transition across dioceses using multiple regression analysis.

Part Three combines descriptive and causal analysis, continues to focus on the diocese as unit of analysis, but concentrates on individual components of population change, namely, entrance and exit events themselves. Hence, chapter 7 addresses ordination as the major entrance into the population. We consider the problem of recruitment by analyzing number and rate of ordinations, rising age at ordination, and organizational and environmental conditions that explain variation in diocesan ordination rates. In chapter 8 we deal with two types of migration events affecting the priest population: permanent migration through incardination and excardination and temporary migration through extended leave and return from leave. Here we also raise the issue of whether net gains from the surplus of incardinations (in-migration) over excardinations (out-migration) may actually mask the true extent of clergy decline locally and nationally.

The problem of retention, the other side of the recruitment coin, is treated in chapter 9. Voluntary resignation is a significant exit event affecting the size of the priest population, so we study number and rate of resignation, age at resignation, and conditions in the organization and environmental niche that account for variation in resignation rates across dioceses. We also discuss evidence for assuming that current levels of resignation will continue in the decades ahead. In chapters 10 and 11 we handle two biologically linked decrements to the population, retirement and mortality. Chapter 10 focuses on retirement and preretirement mortality as interrelated exit events. Chapter 11 describes priest mortality rates nationally and regionally and also compares their favorability and unfavorability with relevant subgroups in the general population.

In Part Four we address the consequences of demographic change. Chapter 12 presents data on the replacement rate, or ratio of gains to losses in the diocesan priest work force, as a gauge of severity of decline. The story is told in terms of an impending priest deficit at the turn of the century, given rapid growth of the Hispanic Catholic population and a minimally acceptable priest-to-layperson ratio. Chapters 13 to 15 place the results of the study in the context of relevant literature on organization science. With equal emphasis we also highlight practical contributions of the study. For example, we discuss policy applications in terms of reliance on nonnative clergy, postponing retirement, effectiveness in priestly recruitment, and problems of organizational drift and myopia. Chapter 15 concludes by accenting one of the most visible and volatile issues raised by the priest shortage: the relationships between celibacy, sacrament, and patriarchal control in the Catholic church.

2 The Demographic Transition in Catholic Dioceses

2   National Trends

The raw numbers produced by a 19-year census of U.S. diocesan priests were introduced in "Respondent Report I" (Schoenherr 1987b) sent to the 86 dioceses cooperating in the study. Like the skin of a pomegranate, however, the census numbers by themselves are dense and uninteresting, though they contain the full data base for the investigation. The purpose of the present chapter is to peel back the first layer of data and examine the main trends at work.

Highlights

1. The data indicate a probable decline of 40 percent in the number of diocesan priests over a 40-year period. The number of active diocesan priests, which stood at 35,000 in 1966, will fall to approximately 21,000 by the year 2005. Priests will be older, with almost half 55 or above and only an eighth 34 or younger by 2005.

2. The decrease in priestly ordinations is the most significant factor in the overall clergy decline — far more significant than resignations, retirements, or other factors. But analysis shows that if priestly ordinations were to be increased by 25 percent (other conditions remaining the same), the moderate decline in the number of U.S. diocesan priests between 1966 and 2005 would still stand at about 34 percent.

3. The empirical data cover only the first 19 years (1966 through 1984) of this 40-year period. Projections were employed for the subsequent years. We devised three separate projections for clergy size: an optimistic, a pessimistic, and a moderate projection. The moderate projection presumes that a certain leveling off of trends, as experienced in the years 1980–84, will continue into the next century. We believe the moderate projection is the most realistic. To test these assumptions, trends in 12 dioceses were studied in detail for the years 1985–89, a four-year period beyond that

25

covered by the full national study. The moderate projections are closest to the actual experience in those dioceses. When several other variables are considered as well, it seems likely that the trends currently are falling somewhere between the moderate and pessimistic projections.

Making Population Projections

Admittedly, the plausibility of population projections decreases with each additional year, but forecasts over two decades are by no means useless. They shed light on the consequences of the what-if models contained in our projection assumptions. Stable population theory, which is used in this analysis, posits the simple question: *What* would happen to population size and composition over time *if* entrances and exits continued at assumed constant levels?

Population analysts increase the plausibility of their projections by hedging their bets. Instead of making one projection we usually make three on the basis of optimistic, pessimistic, and moderate assumptions. We prefer to describe each set of assumptions and let the reader make the final judgment about which is most plausible.

Thus, as it turns out, population projections are both an art and a science. Scientific method guarantees the data are as accurate and the techniques as appropriate as possible. Art enters the picture with the choice of assumptions. The optimistic, pessimistic, and moderate assumptions should make sense in light of the history, tradition, and other social forces governing change in the given population. And they should be useful — neither too wild nor too tame.

One basic premise governs all the projections to be presented. We presume that the principal variation, selection, and retention mechanisms that have determined the size and shape of the Catholic priest population for the past 20 years will continue unchanged for the next 20 years. The key mechanisms are well-known. Variation among potential candidates in the church's ecological niche is limited to healthy Catholic males who are willing to be life-long celibates. With almost negligible exceptions all Roman Catholic dioceses select this variety of priestly minister by church law.[1] As for retention, the male celibate form of priesthood has been retained uniformly since the Second Lateran Council of 1139, when celibacy became the universal law of the Roman rite; before that time mandatory

---

1. Fichter (1989) lists the most recent exceptions to this selection strategy in his analysis of married Roman Catholic priests who began their ministerial careers as Episcopalian priests or Lutheran pastors; he estimates that by the end of the 1980s 42 of the former and about 15 of the latter had been ordained in the Roman rite.

celibacy was sporadically enforced in the Western church (Lynch 1972; Coriden 1972; Schillebeeckx 1985; Sipe 1990).

Of course, expanded dimensions of variation, selection, and retention mechanisms are found in other Christian churches. Dioceses belonging to the Eastern Catholic church, for example, have continued to select married men for priestly ordination.[2] Protestant churches have allowed both married and celibate men to become pastors since their inception in the 16th century. Furthermore, various Protestant sects and denominations have selected women for ordination since the late 19th century, but many only since the mid- to late 20th century (Lehman 1985; Clouse and Clouse 1989; Fichter 1989).

For all our projections, however, we assume that variation in the candidacy pool will be limited to Catholic male celibates, all dioceses will select only this variety of recruit, and the selection mechanism will be retained uniformly for the entire projection period. Following this fixed assumption, we constructed three different projection series. In brief, our optimistic assumptions are based on the best possible interpretation of the historical data, the pessimistic on the worst possible past scenario, and the moderate on the current trends being experienced in the sampled dioceses. The moderate assumptions are designed to produce a projection curve which falls approximately midway between the optimistic and pessimistic models.

The *optimistic projection* assumes that the relatively high ordinations and net migrations, on the one hand, and low resignations and retirements, on the other, experienced during certain specific years between 1966 and 1985 will dominate in the future. Furthermore, if any of these events showed consistent trends toward even more optimistic levels in the future than were experienced in the past, estimates of their 1990–94 levels are used.

The *pessimistic projection* assumes the opposite, namely, the relatively low ordinations and net migrations and relatively high resignations and retirements that occurred during certain other past years are likely to con-

---

2. The structure of ministry in the Eastern churches, which allows ordination of married men, occasionally attracts the attention of churches in the Latin rite. For example, Hastings (1972, p. 154) reports that as a result of mandatory celibacy "the vast majority of Catholic Africans are being deprived of any sort of regular Eucharist." One solution posed in 1890 by Cardinal Lavigerie, "the greatest Catholic missionary thinker of the nineteenth century," and repeated by the hierarchy of Zambia in 1968 was for the African church to "model its ministry in part upon that of the Eastern Churches," still remain Catholic but allow ordination of married men (Hastings 1972, p. 152). Hastings notes that in reply Rome insisted that Cardinal Lavigerie conform to Western discipline and told the Zambian bishops not to discuss the matter further.

tinue in the years ahead. Similarly, if any of these events showed consistent movement toward more pessimistic levels, estimates of their 1990–94 levels are used.[3]

The *moderate projection,* or middle-of-the-road model, results from assuming that the level of ordinations, net migrations, resignations, and retirements occurring in 1980–84 will continue more or less unchanged from 1985 until the turn of the century.

The assumptions about future death rates are based on life tables for U.S. white males produced from national census data.[4] We use the same mortality assumptions for the optimistic, moderate, and pessimistic models.

On the basis of our reading of the data and understanding of the American Catholic church, we make a few other reasonable adjustments to these general assumptions. The modifications are described in appendix B, which also contains a detailed and more technical discussion of the assumptions used in each of the projection models.

An important caveat: Our population projections do not predict the future. They are merely forecasts based on past trends and reasonable assumptions. The forecasts in this book should be assessed carefully and used wisely.

Change in Population Size, 1966–2005

Table 2.1 and figure 2.1 show the size of the active diocesan priest population for the United States from 1966 through 1984 and projections to the year 2005. In one sweep, the graph reports the changes in the number of priests during the first 19 years after the close of the Second Vatican Council and the most likely changes for the next two decades. Nationally, the long-term loss is apparent from the steeply descending curve. The same is true on the local scene for the vast majority of dioceses, as the data in chapter 4 will demonstrate.

According to the top curve on the right-hand side of the figure, even under optimistic assumptions, the U.S. priest population would show a

3. Actually the pessimistic projections are not based on the worst-case scenario. Instead, they are based on the most pessimistic trends that we deem realistic. Thus, we do not allow resignations to rise above the level experienced in 1980–84. We think capping the rates at the level experienced toward the end of the census period more accurately captures the long-range trends. In chapter 9 we present data showing that resignations peaked during the "mass exodus" years (1968–73), leveled off during the mid-1970s, and remained stable throughout the 1980s. Although the rates experienced during the mass exodus years are the most pessimistic, using them would be unrealistic, because we see them as a high point that is unlikely to recur in the foreseeable future.

4. In chapter 10 we assess the suitability of using these mortality rates, concluding that the choice was appropriate.

Table 2.1. Size of U.S. diocesan priest population, 1966–2005

Year	Weighted census count	Projection series		
		Optimistic	Moderate	Pessimistic
1966	35,070			
1970	33,523			
1975	30,785			
1980	29,633			
1985		28,141	28,077	27,721
1986		27,783	27,645	26,962
1987		27,444	27,236	26,247
1988		27,109	26,834	25,562
1989		26,779	26,442	24,909
1990		26,454	26,062	24,288
1995		25,017	24,230	21,421
2000		23,983	22,511	18,852
2005		23,040	21,030	16,653

Note: Formulas for the projection models are:

$$X_{ij} = [X_{i-1,j-1} + (A_{j-1}/2)](S_{j-1}) + (A_{j-1}/2)$$

where X_{ij} is the age-specific population at the beginning of the year for age group j in year i;

A_{j-1} is the additions to age group j-1;

S_{j-1} is the survival probability for age group j-1; and

$$A_{j-1} = N_{j-1} + O_{j-1} + I_{j-1}$$

where N_{j-1} is the number of returns from leave of absence for age group j-1;

O_{j-1} is the number of ordinations for age group j-1;

I_{j-1} is the number of incardinations for age group j-1; and

$$S_{j-1} = (R_{j-1})(E_{j-1})(T_{j-1})(D_{j-1})(L_{j-1})$$

where R_{j-1} is the probability of surviving the risk of resignation for age group j-1;

E_{j-1} is the probability of surviving the risk of excardination for age group j-1;

T_{j-1} is the probability of surviving the risk of retirement for age group j-1;

D_{j-1} is the probability of surviving the risk of death for age group j-1; and

L_{j-1} is the probability of surviving the risk of leave of absence for age group j-1.

substantial loss in the four-decade period under study. The number of active priests in 2005 will be about 23,000, over 34 percent fewer than the 35,000 recorded for 1966. The bottom curve shows that if the pessimistic assumptions were to hold true, the average loss across the country would cut the population by more than half, reaching close to a 53 percent decline between 1966 and 2005, with numbers of about 16,700.

The moderate assumptions are calculated to fall approximately midway

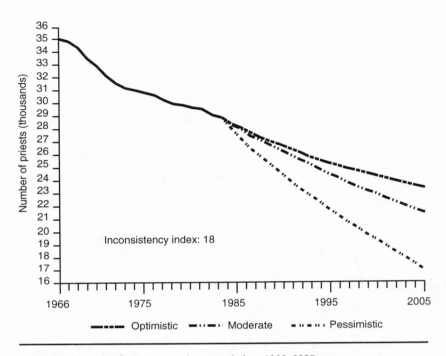

Figure 2.1. Size of U.S. diocesan priest population, 1966–2005

Source: table 2.1.
Note: See appendix E for interpretation of the inconsistency index.

between the optimistic and pessimistic extremes, which means, as figure 2.1 shows, a drop of about 40 percent in the national population as a whole and thus in the average diocese. If the trends of the early to mid-1980s continue — from which the moderate assumptions are taken — the number of active diocesan priests in 2005 will be slightly over 21,000.

Change in Age Composition, 1966–2005

One of the most important and immediate concomitants of sustained decline in size is transformation of a population's age composition. Figure 2.2 illustrates the changing age distribution of active diocesan priests at 10-year intervals (the first is a 9-year period, since our historical data begin in 1966). The projected ages, which begin with 1985, are based on the moderate entrance and attrition assumptions described in appendix B. The moderate assumptions posit that declining ordinations will level off in 1985. As a consequence, the data for age composition presented in the figure

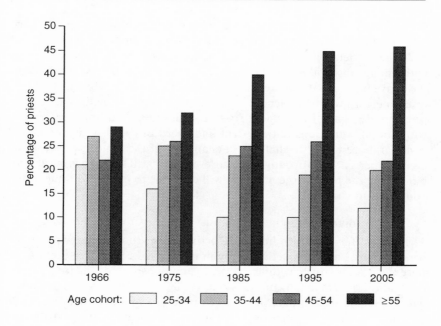

Figure 2.2. Age distribution of U.S. diocesan priest population, 1966–2005

Age cohort	Year				
	1966	1975	1985	1995	2005
25–34	21	16	10	10	12
35–44	27	25	23	19	20
45–54	22	26	25	26	22
55–64	18	21	26	26	28
65–74	8	10	13	17	16
≥ 75	3	1	1	2	2
Total[a]	99	99	98	100	100

Sources: weighted census counts for 1966 and 1975; moderate projection series for 1985–2005.
[a]Not 100 because of rounding.

may be somewhat optimistic if the drop in ordinations has not yet bottomed out.

As the first bar graph in figure 2.2 and column 1 in the accompanying chart show, U.S. dioceses, on the average, enjoyed a fairly well-balanced age distribution in 1966, with 21 percent of the active priests below age 35 and 29 percent age 55 or older. By 1985, the end of the census period, the average clergy population had aged notably with only about 10 percent in the youngest and 41 percent in the most senior age group.

If the moderate assumptions hold true to 2005, the imbalance in the national age distribution will have increased considerably. Nearly half of the active priests in the United States will be 55 or older, while just a little over an eighth will be under 35. The dominant trend in the U.S. diocesan priesthood is one of movement from a young to an old population, but with notable variations in the extent and speed of the change among individual dioceses, as we shall see in chapter 4. If the trends persist, however, the percentage of younger priests eventually will begin to grow again, but during the process the numbers will continue to decline, a topic to be addressed in chapter 5.

Total Priesthood Population

The data so far have been limited to active priests, but the growing numbers of retired and semiactive clergy in the United States (see table A.1) raise the question of how different the age composition of the total priest population is from that of the active clergy. Table 2.2 summarizes the same data presented in figure 2.2 for active priests, includes comparable data for the total priest population, but uses mean and median age distributions instead of the full age distribution.

Examining average age at the beginning, middle, and end of the period reveals the amount of change that has already occurred and is likely to occur. First of all, differences between the mean age (arithmetic average) and median age (half the population is above and half below) reflect changes in the shape of the age pyramid as a population gets older. Thus, in 1966 the median is lower than the mean age, indicating a young population with

Table 2.2. Mean and median ages of active and all U.S. diocesan priests, 1966–2005

	Year								
	1966	1970	1975	1980	1985	1990	1995	2000	2005
Mean									
Active	46.8	47.0	48.2	49.3	50.7	51.5	52.0	52.1	51.9
All	47.6	48.6	50.7	52.4	53.6	54.4	55.1	55.4	55.6
Median									
Active	45	45	47	49	51	52	53	53	53
All	46	47	50	52	54	55	56	56	57

Sources: weighted census counts for 1966–80 and moderate projection series for 1985–2005.

a triangle-shaped pyramid. By 1985, the mean and median are practically identical, showing that the pyramid is beehive-shaped because the population is aging.[5] In 2005, the median is higher than the mean, indicating an old population with an inverted triangle shape.

Obviously, the active population is always younger than the total population. The gap, however, has been widening since the end of the Second Vatican Council. In 1966, the difference between the active and total population for both mean and median age was only one year, and by 1985 it had grown to three years. In 2005, the mean and median age for the total population will be four years older than for the active priest population.

The age difference between active and total population is widening, because the proportion of retired, sick, and absent priests has been growing. In 1966, only 3.4 percent of U.S. priests were categorized as retired, sick, or absent; by 1985 the proportion had increased almost fivefold, reaching 15.7 percent. In 2005, the retired, sick, and absent category will account for 20.1 percent of the total priest population in the country.

Citing the median age is a more accurate indication of the age distribution when a population is very young or very old. Currently (in 1990), the median age of active U.S. priests is 52, and of all priests it is 55. By 2005, we project the median age of active priests will be 53, and that of the total priest population, 57. Thus, between the beginning and end of the study period, the median age of active priests will have gone up eight years, and that of the total priesthood population, 11 years.[6]

Major Components of Growth and Decline

The demographic transition of the Roman Catholic priesthood is progressing according to a process structure, which must be examined in its constitutive parts. As Hernes (1976, p. 521) says, "Stability and change are both process outcomes generated by the dynamic interrelations of the component parts of the system." Thus we focus in this section on the structural components of change and how they are affecting the demographic transition of the clergy.

We have identified five entrance and six exit events that together determine the size and age composition of the priesthood population. A priest enters or reenters the active population by ordination, incardination, or return to active duty after a period of resignation, sick leave, or awaiting

5. Demographers conventionally use the term "pyramid" to describe the shape of a population distribution, even when the shape is one of a beehive.

6. Our estimates of mean and median age for 1985 to 2005 are low, because the projection procedures arbitrarily truncate the population at age 80; the differences between our projected estimates and the "true" means and medians will be slight.

assignment. Each of these transition events represents an increment to the clergy population. A priest may exit from the active population by excardination, resignation, sick leave, awaiting assignment, retirement or, finally, death, all of which are considered decrements to the population. The data displayed in table 2.3 present the annual entrance, exit, and net growth rates for the country over the census period. The rates give the average annual number of entrances or exits per 100 active priests and so can be read as percentages of the active population.

Entrance Rates

Examining row 1 of table 2.3, we see that annual ordination rates dropped sharply from 2.8 percent in the late 1960s to around 1.8 percent in the early 1980s. The results shown in the last column indicate that, over the 19 years, the country as a whole experienced ordinations yielding almost a 39 percent overall gross increase in the active priest population.

The imbalance of incardinations over excardinations, or net migration, also played an important demographic role in altering the U.S. clergy population. The surplus of incardinands over excardinands comes from either religious orders or foreign dioceses, because in the U.S. presbyterate each loss through excardination in one diocese is matched by a gain through incardination in another.

If we subtract excardination from incardination rates, as they appear in the table, we discover that the diocesan priest population experienced a gross increase, since the cumulative difference is positive: 4.2 percent during roughly two decades. This accounted for over one-fifth of the overall population change that occurred.

If there had been no surplus incardinations, the overall decline in the national population between 1966 and 1984 would have been 24 percent rather than 20 percent. Thus, gains through incardinations are dampening the average clergy decline in the United States as a whole. But chapters 3 and 8 will document that migration is producing a notable gross increase in only certain regions and dioceses.

In addition, leaves of absence and returns to active duty are important. Subtracting leave rates (labeled Other Exit in the table) from return rates (Other Entrance) produces a net decline, since all the differences are negative. The negative difference between the cumulative gain from returns and the cumulative loss from leaves, given in the last cell of rows 3 and 8, respectively, is 2.0. Because the overall loss between 1966 and 1984 from all entrance and exit events was just under 20 percent, this 2 percent loss accounted for about one-tenth of the decline. Thus, as the statistics reveal, the effect of both types of movement — net immigration and

Table 2.3. Growth and decline rates of U.S. diocesan priest population and percentage of gross change, 1966–84, by year and transition event (number of entrances or exits per 100 active priests)

Event	Average annual rate				% gross change 1966–84[a]
	1966–69	1970–74	1975–79	1980–84	
Entrance					
Ordination	2.82	2.32	2.21	1.77	38.77
Incardination	0.22	0.41	0.60	0.67	8.18
Other entrance[b]	0.10	0.15	0.20	0.23	2.89
Exit					
Resignation	1.32	1.71	0.85	0.65	19.50
Excardination	0.08	0.18	0.30	0.37	3.97
Retirement	1.40	1.49	1.56	1.59	25.77
Death	1.19	0.94	0.77	0.77	15.58
Other exit[c]	0.27	0.28	0.30	0.29	4.86
Net decline	-1.13	-1.71	-0.77	-0.99	-19.84

Source: weighted census counts.
Notes: Formulas for the rates in order of appearance are as follows:

$$(O/P)k \qquad (I/P)k \qquad (N/P)k \qquad (R/P)k$$
$$(E/P)k \qquad (T/P)k \qquad (D/P)k \qquad (L/P)k$$
$$[(O + I + N - R - E - T - D - L)/P]k$$

where O is the number of ordinations;
    I is the number of incardinations;
    N is the number of returns from leave;
    R is the number of resignations;
    E is the number of excardinations;
    T is the number of retirements;
    D is the number of deaths;
    L is the number of leaves of absence during the calendar year;
    P is the total population of active incardinated priests at the beginning of the calendar year; and
    k is 100.
Number of priests registered in the 19-year national census: 36,370.
[a]Using 1966 base figures and the cumulative numbers of entrance and exit events for numerators.
[b]Returns from sick leave, awaiting assignment, and resignation.
[c]Sick leave and awaiting assignment.

net leave — on population change in the average United States diocese has been noteworthy.

Exit Rates

The period under study began with notably high attrition through resignations, as the data in the fourth row of table 2.3 indicate. The exodus of American priests peaked at an annual crude rate of 1.7 percent during the early 1970s and then dropped in the early 1980s to a level only half as high as at the beginning of the census. The figure in row 4, column 5, reports that the resignation drain averaged a gross national loss of almost 20 percent in 19 years.

Recruitment and retention both changed significantly during the period under observation. Ordinations dropped by about two-fifths, and resignations were cut in half. The overall picture is affected heavily not only by recruitment and retention but also by retirement and death. Table 2.3 reveals that retirement and death rates among the U.S. active clergy showed opposite tendencies since the mid-1960s. The number of retirements per 100 active priests rose steadily between 1966 and 1984, while deaths per 100 active priests declined notably.

Two explanations help account for these differences. First, retirement was a relatively new avenue of exit for U.S. priests after the Second Vatican Council, which closed in 1965. Although many dioceses had a large pool of priests who qualified for retirement at that time, formal programs had to be developed before those who were ready could retire. As a result, during the late 1960s most deaths occurred while the elderly priests were still categorized as active, thereby inflating preretirement mortality rates and deflating retirement rates.

Second, over the last two decades the life expectancy of U.S. white males has been increasing. So by the end of the census, fewer priests were dying before the age of retirement than at the beginning of the period. During the early years of the census, the combination of both situations artificially raised death rates among the active clergy and set retirement rates lower than expected.

Comparing the statistics in rows 6 and 7 of the table shows that, throughout the entire census period, exits from the active clergy through retirement were higher than those through death. The final column confirms that the decline for 1966–84 attributable to retirements was 25.8 percent, while the loss through preretirement deaths was only 15.6 percent.

Overall Decline

The net gain or loss from all transition events is displayed in the bottom row of table 2.3. The clergy population in the United States sustained a mean cumulative net decline of just under 20 percent during the 19 years following the end of the Second Vatican Council. Each five-year period showed net loss, with the average annual rate peaking at 1.7 percent in the early 1970s. The rate was notably less severe in the late 1970s but began to rise again in the first half of the 1980s.

High resignations accounted substantially for the early period of decline, whereas low ordinations, sustained resignations, and rising retirements can be blamed for the more recent period of loss. The decline may have been dampened, at least temporarily, by more favorable death rates experienced among white males in the United States. Further analysis presented in chapter 11, however, tests the hypothesis that mortality of priests is negatively affected by stress produced in a dwindling and aging work force.

From a Theoretical Perspective

To begin the empirical investigation of social change in religious organizations, we have closely followed Hernes' (1976) insight that the process of changing size has a structure of its own, which must be understood in each of its component parts. On the basis of the national analysis thus far, we may specify in detail the process that is generating change in size of the diocesan priest population.

We have assumed that the change process deals with structures at three interrelated levels, namely, process structure, parameter structure, and output structure. Each structural level of the process is illustrated in the data presented. Thus, the data in table 2.1 and the graph depicted in figure 2.1 record changes in the *output structure* that defines the size of the population. Output structure, which is the most visible level of structural change, is interrelated with other levels of the change-generating process, because "the structure at one level is the output of a process which itself has a structure" (Hernes 1976, p. 519).

The equations given in the footnotes of table 2.3 formally depict the *process structure* that is generating the decline. As Hernes (1976, p. 519) observes, "The simplest and most compact way of expressing a process structure is by a mathematical model or formulas which give its functional form." So the process structure of the priest decline is determined by the relationships among the entrance and attrition rates as specified by these formulas.

The statistics in the main body of table 2.3 define the *parameter structure* of the national population at five-year intervals. That is to say, the scores of the transition rates given in the table are the parameters governing the decline process, which "take on definite values in certain situations, and their configuration may have a certain constancy" (Hernes 1976, p. 519).

Similarly, the same data and equations that defined change in organizational size were used to produce figure 2.2, so they also define the parameter and process structure of the aging process. In addition, the changing shapes of the population pyramids in the figure reflect changes in the output structure of the age transition process at 10-year intervals.

In developing his model, Hernes points out that the process may be stable or changing at any or all of the three levels. Thus the concepts of output, process, and parameter structures enable us to define four types of organizational change: (1) simple reproduction, (2) extended reproduction, (3) transition, and (4) transformation. The four types of change can be arranged on a Guttman scale, with no change in any of the three structures defining simple reproduction and change in all of them defining transformation.

Following Hernes' model, our data document an organizational transition in that both parameter and output structures of organizational size and age composition have been modified noticeably, repeatedly, and over relatively short periods of time. Note, according to the definition of an organizational transition, the process structure, or functional form of the change process, does not change during the period under investigation. In our analysis, the process structure remains constant because, by assumption, the variation, selection, and retention mechanisms governing recruitment and retention at the point of interaction between the population of organizations and its ecological niche have not and will not change. Thus no new exit or entrance events, other than those experienced by male celibates, have altered or will alter the mathematical formulas which determine the process structure of our change model.

Altering the Change Process

Organizations have limited options in the face of declining recruitment and retention. In his recent book *Future of Catholic Leadership: Responses to the Priest Shortage,* Hoge (1987) lists them as threefold: Church leaders could reduce the need for priests, get more priests, or expand lay ministry. Our empirical models permit us to explore only the second option, increasing the number of active priests. Let us examine each element of the change process and ask which ones are the most powerful forces.

Entrance and exit rates define the change process. Would increasing ordinations or net migrations slow down the decline more than reducing the number of resignations or retirements? To answer this question we designed a what-if experiment based on alternative scenarios of raising entrances and lowering exits by 25 percent. The base period for the experiment was 1980–84, since these years represent the "current" trends which have been incorporated in the moderate projections.

In a series of experimental models we compare what would happen if trends were to continue at the 1980–84 levels with what would happen if all but one of the transition events were to continue at those levels. In each scenario only one transition event is assumed to go up or down, while all others follow the assumptions of the original moderate series presented in table 2.1 and figure 2.1.

Table 2.4 displays the size of the population when projected under the

Table 2.4. Size of U.S. diocesan priest population based on original and altered projection assumptions, percentage of change, and percentage of difference, 1995–2015, by year and transition event

Event	Year		
	1995	2005	2015
	Size		
Original	24,230	21,030	19,050
Altered			
Ordination (+25%)	25,497	23,195	21,917
Net migration (+25%)	24,446	21,395	19,500
Resignation (-25%)	24,614	21,607	19,713
Retirement (-25%)	24,822	21,660	19,592
	% change[a]		
Original	-14.2	-25.5	-32.5
Altered			
Ordination (+25%)	-9.7	-17.9	-22.4
Net migration (+25%)	-13.4	-24.2	-30.9
Resignation (-25%)	-12.8	-23.5	-30.2
Retirement (-25%)	-12.1	-23.3	-30.6
	% difference[b]		
Altered			
Ordination (+25%)	31.7	29.8	31.1
Net migration (+25%)	5.6	5.1	4.9
Resignation (-25%)	9.9	7.8	7.1
Retirement (-25%)	14.8	8.6	5.8

Source: moderate projection series.

[a]Size of active priest population on January 1, 1985: 28,240; thus, the percentage of change between 1985 and 1995 based on original assumptions is [1 - (24,230/28,240)]100 = 14.2.

[b]Scores are the difference between the percentage of change based on original assumptions given in row 1, panel 2, and the percentage of change based on altered assumptions given in the other rows of panel 2.

original and the altered assumptions, the percentage of change in size and the percentage of difference in the amount of change. The top rows of panels 1 and 2 establish a base for the comparisons.

Thus, for example, the original model based on moderate assumptions projects that the size of the diocesan clergy population in 1995 will be 24,230. If, however, ordinations were to increase by 25 percent, clergy size would be considerably higher: 25,497. Under all assumptions, population size will grow smaller with each passing decade. So in panel 2, the top row of data shows that, according to our original moderate assumptions, the 1985 national priest population would decrease about 14 percent by 1995, 26 percent by 2005, and 33 percent by 2015.

Comparing statistics in the other rows of panel 2 demonstrates that ordinations are the most powerful force in the change process. Increasing the number of ordinations by 25 percent would curb the decline between 1985 and 1995 considerably. Instead of a 14 percent loss, the size of the average diocesan clergy would decrease by less than 10 percent, as the data show in row 2 for that year. Altering assumptions for the other transition events would, nevertheless, still result in a 12 percent or 13 percent decline, according to the remaining figures in the column.

The bottom panel of the table summarizes the contrasts. The scores are the percentage of difference between the original and altered percentages of change. Thus the difference between the 1995 projected percentage of decline based on original assumptions (14.2 percent) and that based on the altered assumption of increased ordinations (9.7 percent) is 31.7 percent.[7] That is to say, if all other trends were to occur as projected but ordinations were one-fourth higher than the number used in our moderate projection model, the clergy decline between 1985 and 1995 would be about 32 percent less than originally projected. Not surprisingly, therefore, ordinations have the most powerful impact of any event tested in the experiment.

Retirements would have the next strongest impact. A similar decrease in retirements would lower the decline by almost 15 percent. Altering net migrations would have the least effect. Raising the net gain of incardinations over excardinations would retard the decline by less than 6 percent.

The bottom panel of the table also shows the effects of altering each of the entrance and exit trends over time. Raising the number of ordinations would remain the most powerful force, but the magnitude of the impact would remain constant throughout the projection period, as row 1 indicates. On the other hand, because age composition is also changing over time (as figure 2.2 has demonstrated), the cumulative impact of lowering the resignation and retirement rates would change apace. While the population is aging, reducing the rate of retirement would be more effective than reducing the rate of resignation, because the number of priests reaching retirement age is increasing, and age groups in which the risk of resignation is highest are decreasing.

Thus, comparing scores in rows 3 and 4 shows that those for retirement would be higher in 1995 and 2005 than those for resignation. By

7. $[1 - (9.7/14.2)] \times 100 = 31.7$

2005, however, the proportion of younger priests would begin to grow, according to the predictions of our models. When the population is growing younger, the comparative impact of retirements and resignations is reversed.

So by 2015, reductions in resignations, which would lower the decline by 7 percent, would do more to dampen the decline than reductions in retirements, because the latter would reduce the decline by only about 6 percent.[8] Although the differences are not large, reducing retirement would have the greater short-term impact and reducing resignations the greater long-term impact on overall decline. The consequences of increasing the gain from incardinations would remain the smallest, hovering around 5 percent for the entire period.

Without a doubt, the impact of increasing ordinations would be about three to four times greater on checking the decline by 2005 than altering the next most powerful transition events, namely, resignations and retirements. Even if recruitment were increased by 25 percent, however, the impact would be noticeable but the decline would still be large. Under the most likely scenario based on our original moderate assumptions, the American diocesan priest population will decline 40 percent between 1966 and 2005. Under a 25 percent more optimistic ordination scenario, the moderate decline would still be almost 34 percent.[9]

Plausibility of Projections

Such alarming statistics raise questions about how realistic the assumptions are and whether one set is more trustworthy than the others. The historical data used in this study are highly accurate, because they were provided by reliable informants and subjected to meticulous verification and correction procedures. These data establish that the U.S. diocesan priest population declined almost 20 percent between 1966 and 1985.

Projections, however, are based on assumptions that are more or less reasonable and must be evaluated carefully. The single most important component of the model in determining future trends is the ordination assumption. Bear in mind that two decades of sustained seminarian decline have reduced the number of priest candidates enrolled in U.S. theologates by 58 percent. Between 1965 and 1989 the number of seminarians in theology schools dropped from 8,885 to 3,698, and it appears the decline is yet to bottom out (Catholic News Service 1990). So we see little probability that

8. Models extending the projections beyond 2015 are presented in chapter 5.

9. Increasing ordinations by 25 percent while retaining all other moderate assumptions would reduce the decline between 1966 and 2005 to 33.9 percent.

the population size of the national clergy will rise above the curve projected in figure 2.1 by the moderate assumptions.

If ordinations were to stabilize at the 1980–84 level, the most likely outcome would approach the trend projected by the moderate assumptions. If, on the other hand, recruitments were to continue to decline in the fashion predicted by the statistical models used in setting the assumptions (and the trend toward declining recruitment is very strong and statistically significant in the national data) then the most likely outcome would lie somewhere within the projection band set by the moderate and pessimistic assumptions.

Test of Competing Assumptions

In our design, the historical period ends December 31, 1984, and projections begin January 1, 1985. Thus, as we neared the final stage of the U.S. Catholic Conference research project, dioceses already had experienced an additional four years of population change against which to check the plausibility of the competing assumptions. So we subsampled 12 dioceses, contacting our liaison persons and asking them to provide additional data covering January 1, 1985, to January 1, 1989. All 12 agreed to cooperate.[10]

The subsample of 12 was drawn from a set of 48 dioceses in the original sample where data fluctuation during the census period was not excessive.[11] The size of their combined active priest population in 1966 was 3,737, which, when weighted to estimate national parameters, represented 6,793, or 19 percent, of the diocesan priests active in the United States that year (see table 2.1).

As table 2.5 demonstrates, however, the subsample overrepresents large dioceses in the Northeast, ignores small dioceses altogether, and underrepresents dioceses in the West. The subsample is representative, however, of those dioceses where data fluctuation was low to moderate during the census period. During the analysis we discovered that both the old small dioceses and the newly established small dioceses had experienced irregular growth or decline over the historical period. As a result, their projections were also wildly inconsistent.[12] We therefore decided they would not provide an appropriate test of plausibility of the projection models, and

10. We gratefully acknowledge the generous cooperation of the following dioceses: Burlington, Cincinnati, Covington, Fall River, Indianapolis, Little Rock, Milwaukee, Oakland, Ogdensburg, Pittsburgh, Portland, Maine, and Rockville Centre.

11. They had inconsistency scores of 35 or lower; see appendix E for a definition and discussion of inconsistency scores.

12. See appendix E for a discussion of our attempts to control for wild data fluctuation in small dioceses when projecting their populations into the future.

Table 2.5. Comparison of full sample and
subsample of dioceses, by size and region
(percentages)

	Full sample[a]	Sub-sample[b]
Size		
Small (1–100)	30	0
Medium (101–200)	26	33
Large (201–500)	27	50
Extra large (>500)	17	17
Total	100	100
Region		
New England	9	25
Middle Atlantic	16	25
East Northcentral	17	25
West Northcentral	17	0
Mountain	7	0
Pacific	12	8
East South[c]	7	8
West Southcentral	16	8
Total[d]	101	99

Note: Our sample design replicates the
sample design used in the NORC 1972 study
(see appendix F). Thus, the data in this table
reflect diocesan size and region as of 1968 and
the range of numbers in the size categories
indicates the total number of priests per diocese.
[a]$n = 89$.
[b]$n = 12$.
[c]Combines the South Atlantic region and one
diocese from the East Southcentral region.
[d]Not 100 because of rounding.

designed the subsample accordingly. The regional imbalance in the subsample simply reflects the fact that dioceses in the Northeast quadrant of the country experienced less extreme fluctuations in their data than those in the other divisions. We believe the subsample provides an appropriate data set to test our competing projection models.

Numbers

The projection results for the 12 dioceses are summarized in table 2.6. Column 1 gives census counts of the active priests at five-year intervals until 1985 and at one-year intervals through 1989. The next three columns give

Table 2.6. Size of diocesan priest population in subsample of 12 dioceses, 1966–2005

Year	Weighted census count	Projection series		
		Optimistic	Moderate	Pessimistic
1966	6,793			
1970	6,505			
1975	5,869			
1980	5,736			
1985	5,373	5,489	5,366	5,289
1986	5,289	5,509	5,269	5,123
1987	5,233	5,534	5,185	4,967
1988	5,166	5,549	5,100	4,820
1989	5,133	5,561	5,019	4,679
1990		5,561	4,935	4,541
1995		5,310	4,547	3,913
2000		4,729	4,174	3,375
2005		4,496	3,865	2,939

the projected numbers under optimistic, moderate, and pessimistic assumptions, beginning with one-year intervals through 1990 (to allow comparison with the new data) and then continuing with five-year intervals until 2005. Focusing on the data for 1989, we discover in column 1 that the updated census recorded 5,133 priests in the 12-diocese subsample; our moderate projection for the same 12 dioceses, shown in column 3, forecasted 5,019. Thus the true curve falls between the moderate and optimistic projections but very close to the moderate. The population size recorded in the updated census numbers is only 2.2 percent higher than the moderate projection, so we conclude that our projection models are reasonably accurate.

Rates
The level of the true curve is determined by the dynamic structure depicted by changing transition rates for the subsampled dioceses. Comparing the annual ordination rate for 1980–84, shown in row 1 of table 2.7, with that for 1985–88 indicates that ordinations continued to decline as expected. During 1980–84, there were 1.7 ordinations per 100 active priests per year, and during 1985–88 there were only 1.5. Likewise, annual immigration dropped considerably in the dioceses of the subsample during the 1980s, from 0.25 during the first half of the decade to only 0.14 net migrations per 100 active priests during the last half. Because ordinations declined notably (about 10 percent from the early to the late 1980s) and immigra-

Table 2.7. Growth and decline rates in subsample of 12 dioceses and percentage of gross change, 1966–89, by year and transition event (number of entrances or exits per 100 active priests)

Event	Average annual rates					% gross change[a]	
	1966 –69	1970 –74	1975 –79	1980 –84	1985 –88	1966 –84	1966 –89
Entrance							
Ordination[b]	2.85	2.39	2.31	1.69	1.51	39.10	—
Immigration[c]	0.15	0.27	0.26	0.25	0.14	3.99	—
Exit							
Resignation[b]	1.28	1.89	0.69	0.68	0.66	19.49	—
Retirement[b]	1.57	1.74	1.62	1.68	1.51	28.09	—
Death[b]	1.11	0.98	0.66	0.74	0.50	14.72	—
Net leave[d]	0.17	0.10	0.10	0.16	0.09	2.22	—
Net decline	-1.11	-2.05	-0.50	-1.32	-1.11	-21.43	-24.4

Source: weighted census counts.

[a]Using 1966 figures for denominators and the cumulative numbers of entrance and exit events for 1966–84 and 1966–89 for numerators.

[b]See footnote [a], table 2.3, for formula.

[c]Incardination rate minus excardination rate; see footnote [a], table 2.3, for formulas of these rates.

[d]Leave rate minus return rate; see footnote [a], table 2.3, for formulas of these rates.

tions dropped as well (about 44 percent during the same period), one would expect the actual decline curve to have fallen below the moderate projection curve instead of above it. Obviously, therefore, the lower entrance rates have been matched by lower exit rates, as the remaining transition statistics in the same two columns reveal.

Although resignations in the subsample remained practically constant throughout the 1980s, retirements dropped by 10 percent during the decade, deaths among active priests by almost 33 percent, and leaves by 44 percent, as a comparison of figures in columns 4 and 5 demonstrates. The impact of this offsets the entrance figures, thus creating a population size slightly above that forecasted by our moderate projection model. Note, however, the seeming advantage is short-term, because, as we learned from table 2.2 and figure 2.2, the priest population throughout most of the United States continues to age rapidly. Hence, rising retirement rates in future years are inevitable. Even if the retirement age is postponed, rising death rates in an aging population are certain. Dioceses can put a damper on extended leaves, but that produces relatively small gains in the active work force.

The final row and column of the table present the results of entrances and exits during the roughly three decades studied. The annual net loss in the 12 dioceses peaked at 2 priests per 100 during the early 1970s, declined during the late 1970s to an average of 0.5 per 100, then rose again to well over 1 priest per 100 throughout the 1980s. Thus, the assumed decline, which we incorporated into our moderate projection assumptions, continued to occur for the four years covered by our additional data. In the average subsampled diocese, the active priest population at the beginning of 1989 was only about three-fourths its size in 1966, as the final statistic in the table demonstrates. The fact that net decline continued as we assumed it would lends credence to the projection models.

Caveat

A caution is in order when relating these findings in a complete way to the full sample. Because, as we said, the subsample is not entirely representative (see table 2.5), we can expect that the change process in the full sample will differ slightly from that of the subsample. The degree of difference cannot be measured, since data for 1985–88 are not available for the full sample. It is most probable, however, that the combined retirement and death rates in the full sample are going up in both the short and long run, not down as they are in the short run for the subsample, simply because of the rapid aging trend.

It is also probable that the declining trend in ordinations documented in the subsample is being experienced in the average diocese of the full sample—though, perhaps, not to the same degree—because the dioceses overrepresented by the subsample contain a much higher proportion of the clergy than the dioceses that are underrepresented.[13] Thus, it is also likely that the true curve for the 1989 national priest population would be very close to that for our moderate projection series but might even fall between the moderate and the pessimistic projection curves.

The plausibility test has proven that the techniques used in the projection models for the 12 dioceses are accurate and reasonable. There is little doubt that the methods used in the projection models for the full national sample are equally accurate and reasonable, at least for the first four years of the projection period. Of course, new empirical data on ordinations, net migrations, and resignations of priests become available with each passing year. So analysts will be able to reassess the accuracy of our assumptions periodically. The degree of population decline already revealed by

13. The subsample overrepresents dioceses in the Northeast division, where just under 42 percent of the American clergy were located in 1966, and underrepresents those in the West division, where less than 10 percent of the national priest population resided that same year (see tables 2.4 and 3.2).

the historical data, however, is a stark reality and a harbinger of extensive structural change in the Catholic church.

Updating the demographic data to 1989 in 12 dioceses has proven useful not only for testing the plausibility of our projections but also for introducing the question of regional differences in the process. The subsample overrepresents one part of the country and underrepresents another, and it raises issues about different ordination, retirement, and death rates across regions and how these differences might affect national trends. Our next chapter examines these regional differences.

3 Regional Differences

As a whole, the Roman Catholic priesthood in the United States is undergoing steady decline in numbers along with rapid aging. The purpose of this chapter is to survey variations in the changing diocesan priesthood population seen from one region of the country to another. Stark and Bainbridge (1985) summarize a great deal of the information known about religious regionalism in the United States. As their data show, the country has a pronounced religious geography, some aspects of which are well-known while others are generally misunderstood.

It is common knowledge, for example, that Catholics are heavily concentrated in New England and West Southcentral states, Protestants dominate rural areas, and Jews favor large metropolitan cities. But Stark and Bainbridge (1985, p. 69) also point out that "the most marked feature of American religion has gone virtually unnoticed. A very prominent 'Unchurched Belt' runs along the shores of the Pacific, from the Mexican border through Canada. . . ." Contrary to popular belief, they report no evidence for the existence of a "Bible Belt" that is supposed to stretch across the American Protestant South.

Our data add to the story of Catholic regionalism in the United States by providing an account of geographic differences in the demographic transition of the clergy. For example, it is not known whether priest decline is more or less extensive in the Northeast and West Southcentral states, the traditional areas of Catholic strength, or whether the shortage is unusually severe on the Pacific Coast, thus adding another notch to the Unchurched Belt in that region. To make the analysis comparable to other relevant research, we utilize the same divisions and regions used by the U.S. Bureau of the Census (see figure 3.1).

48

Figure 3.1. Census divisions and regions of the United States

Highlights

1. Dioceses in New England will decline the most, suffering an average loss of 52 percent of their active diocesan priest population between 1966 and 2005. Those in the East South region[1] of the country will decline the least, losing only 12 percent of their active clergy, on the average, during the same period.

2. At the beginning of the 21st century, the youngest of the aging presbyterates will be found in the Mountain states. The average age distribution there will probably show 39 percent in the 55 or over category. The oldest active priests in the country will be in the New England region, where 54 percent of the clergy will be age 55 or older.

1. The name East South is not used by the U.S. Bureau of the Census; in this volume East South combines the South Atlantic region and one diocese in the East Southcentral region.

Notes on Method

Assumptions of Future Trends

The assumptions used in the regional projections are the same as those for the national and diocesan models. The diocese is the basic unit of analysis in the study, so diocesan-level data sets have been concatenated to create sample estimates of regional priest populations. Making projection assumptions to be used for comparisons on the basis of trends that vary widely across dioceses is an inherent difficulty in our design. As Blau (1965) points out, the comparative approach always sacrifices specificity for the sake of generalizability. Hence, in devising assumptions that best incorporate trends in the sample of 86 dioceses, we may risk some distortion in the projections for a specific diocese or census region. The distortion may enter because projections for a particular diocese or region might be more appropriate if only the historical trends unique to it had governed the strategy used.

More precise projections, however, could not be compared with one another, because each one would be based on different strategies. So specific distortions can be minimized only at the expense of generalizability. And generalizability is the *sine qua non* of comparative analysis. The trick in a comparative design, of course, is to accomplish both goals, and that is what we attempt to do: capture the general trends in the national population by incorporating into one set of assumptions, as closely as possible, the unique historical experience of each diocesan and regional population in the study. Thus our comparative design dictates that we employ one generalizable set of assumptions to be used uniformly in the projection models for every diocese and region.

Consistent and Inconsistent Trends

In dioceses where the census data fluctuate, the projections will also be erratic, following the principle that population projections only project the past. To the extent that dioceses in a regional area have experienced inconsistent trends over the past two decades, the projection models for the region will have a broad fan-shaped tail, as shown in figure 3.2. Where the historical trends have been consistently downward, on the other hand, the tail or band made up of the three projection curves will be narrow, as in figure 3.3 and will show further decline under all three assumptions. In general, the narrower the band the more consistent the past trends and the more reliable the projections.

The inconsistency index, described in appendix E, measures the amount of fluctuation in the demographic trends. Lower scores indicate more con-

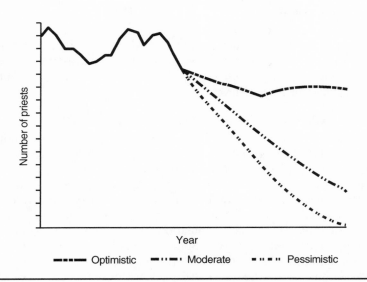

Figure 3.2. Illustration of projections based on inconsistent trends

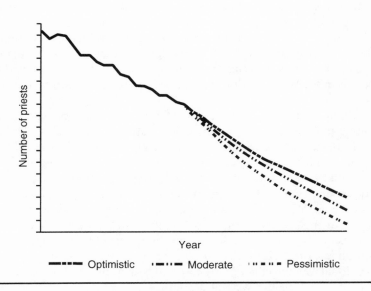

Figure 3.3. Illustration of projections based on consistent trends

51

sistent trends and more useful projection models. Low scores are in the
20–30 range. Scores approaching and exceeding 60 signify less consistent
trends and weaker but useful projection models. Inconsistency scores for
the regional projection models range from 18 to 37, so all are within the
more reliable consistency levels.

Change in Regional Population Size, 1966–2005

Figures 3.4 through 3.7 show the size of the active diocesan priest populations from 1966 through 1984 and projections to 2005 for the regions that
compose the four census divisions of the United States. Figures 3.4 and
3.5, for dioceses in the Northeast and Northcentral divisions of the country, show consistent decline over the historical and projected periods. The
other two figures for dioceses in the West and South, however, record decline until about 1975, when population size began to grow again in the
Mountain, East South, and West Southcentral dioceses and to level off in
dioceses along the Pacific Coast. In the three growth areas, the upward
trend continued until the early 1980s, when it began to dip down again.
The stable trend in the average Pacific Coast diocese continued for the entire 10-year period from 1975 to 1985.

Limiting the focus to the moderate projections, all the graphs forecast
steady decline from 1985 to 2005. However, in the West and South, the
two divisions of the country where dioceses experienced historical periods
of decline followed by periods of growth or stability, the moderate curve
is surrounded by broad fan-shaped bands — a sign of inconsistent trends —
making the projections difficult to interpret and less useful for planning
purposes. The analysis in chapter 6, though, clarifies the direction and force
of trends in the West and South divisions, by taking environmental conditions into consideration.

The figures provide a graphic view of population change, whereas table
3.1 gives part of the same information but in raw numbers. The table
presents the size of the regional populations for 1966, 1985, and 2005 — the
beginning, middle, and end points of the overall period under study —
along with the percentage of decline under optimistic, moderate, and pessimistic assumptions. Arithmetic means for the United States as a whole
facilitate comparisons. The statistics highlight the striking cleavage between
dioceses in the Northeast and Northcentral divisions, on the one hand,
and those in the West and South, on the other. Under all three sets of
assumptions, the percentage of decline in numbers of priests is well above
the national average in the Northeast and Northcentral divisions and well
below the mean in the West and South.

We continue to concentrate on the moderate projections, since the

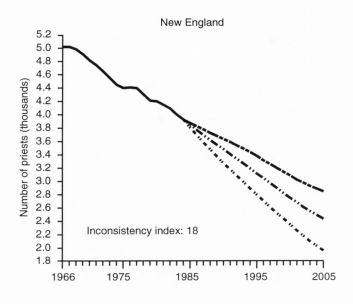

New England

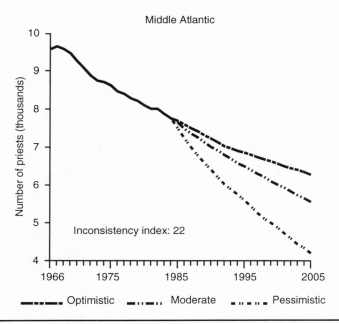

Middle Atlantic

Optimistic   Moderate   Pessimistic

Figure 3.4. Size of U.S. diocesan priest population: Northeast, 1966–2005

Sources: weighted census counts for 1966–1984; projections based on optimistic, moderate, and pessimistic series for 1985–2005.
Note: See appendix E for interpretation of the inconsistency index.

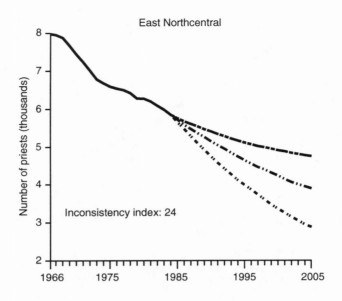

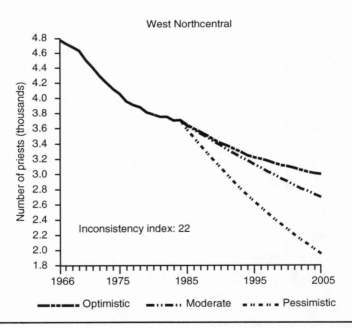

Figure 3.5. Size of U.S. diocesan priest population: Northcentral, 1966–2005

Sources: weighted census counts for 1966–1984; projections based on optimistic, moderate, and pessimistic series for 1985–2005.
Note: See appendix E for interpretation of the inconsistency index.

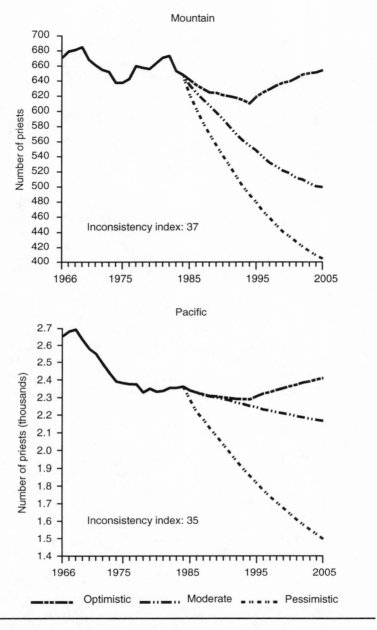

Figure 3.6. Size of U.S. diocesan priest population: West, 1966–2005

Sources: weighted census counts for 1966–1984; projections based on optimistic, moderate, and pessimistic series for 1985–2005.
Note: See appendix E for interpretation of the inconsistency index.

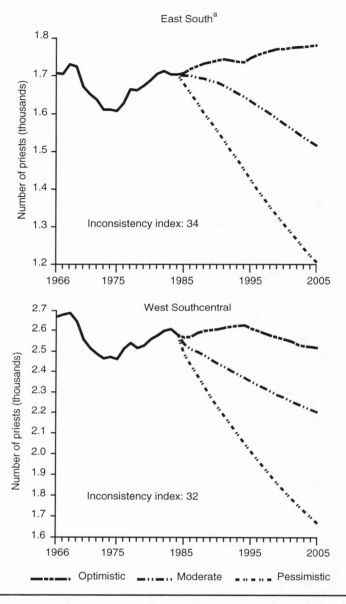

Figure 3.7. Size of U.S. diocesan priest population: South, 1966–2005

Sources: weighted census counts for 1966–1984; projections based on optimistic, moderate, and pessimistic series for 1985–2005.
Note: See appendix E for interpretation of the inconsistency index.
[a]Combines the South Atlantic region and one diocese from the East Southcentral region.

Table 3.1. Size of U.S. diocesan priest population and percentage of change, 1966–2005, by year, nation, division, and region

	1966	1985	2005 Projection series			% change 1966–2005 Projection series			In-consis-tency index[a]
			Opt.	Mod.	Pes.	Opt.	Mod.	Pes.	
United States	35,070	28,240	23,040	21,030	16,653	-34	-40	-53	18
Divisions and regions									
Northeast	14,604	11,518	9,148	7,996	6,163	-37	-45	-58	20
New England	5,025	3,879	2,849	2,431	1,964	-43	-52	-61	18
Middle Atlantic	9,579	7,639	6,299	5,565	4,199	-34	-42	-56	22
Northcentral	12,769	9,418	7,756	6,591	4,831	-39	-48	-62	23
East Northcentral	7,989	5,748	4,760	3,892	2,874	-40	-51	-64	24
West Northcentral	4,780	3,670	2,996	2,699	1,957	-37	-44	-59	22
West	3,319	2,997	3,064	2,666	1,899	-8	-20	-43	35
Mountain	672	639	655	500	404	-3	-26	-40	37
Pacific	2,647	2,358	2,409	2,166	1,495	-9	-18	-44	35
South	4,373	4,305	4,309	3,720	2,872	-1	-15	-34	33
East South[b]	1,706	1,721	1,781	1,516	1,205	4	-11	-29	34
West Southcentral	2,667	2,584	2,528	2,204	1,667	-5	-17	-37	32

Sources: weighted census counts for 1966 and 1985 and projections for 2005; data for 1985 are as of January 1 on the assumption that no changes in population size occurred between December 31, 1984 and January 1, 1985.
[a]See appendix E for a definition and discussion of how to interpret the inconsistency index.
[b]Combines the South Atlantic region and one diocese from the East Southcentral region.

evidence so far indicates they are the most plausible. Thus percentages in column 7 show, at the high end of the range, that New England and East Northcentral dioceses will suffer an average loss of over 50 percent of their active clergy between 1966 and 2005. Dioceses in both regions of the South will experience the smallest losses in the country, with an average 15 percent decline over the four decades. Under both optimistic and pessimistic assumptions, the picture remains exactly the same. New England and East Northcentral dioceses are again at the high extremes, showing losses of 40 percent in an optimistic forecast and losses of over 60 percent in a pessimistic scenario. Similarly, dioceses in the South are at the low extremes; they would lose as few as 1 percent of their 1966 number of clergy if optimistic assumptions hold true or as much as one-third if they approach their pessimistic projections in 2005.

Differences of this size indicate that a major shift in the regional distribution of the U.S. Catholic clergy population is occurring. Table 3.2 compares how Catholic priests were distributed nationally in 1966 with how they will most probably be distributed at the beginning of the 21st century.

The data in column 1 indicate that almost 80 percent of the nation's priest supply was concentrated in the Northeast and Northcentral divisions of the country in 1966, and those in column 3 show that the proportion will probably drop to about 70 percent by the turn of the century. Dioceses in the South division of the United States will increase their share of the priest population by almost 42 percent between 1966 and 2005. During the same period, the hardest hit areas, namely, the New England and East Northcentral regions, will witness a loss of almost 19 percent in the proportion of the priestly work force. Close by, however, in the Middle Atlantic and West Northcentral dioceses, the proportional losses will be minimal, only about 3 percent in the former and 6 percent in the latter.

Thus, social forces for change are creating shifts in the priesthood population. They seem to be draining the Northeast and Northcentral divisions

Table 3.2. Percentage distribution of U.S. diocesan priest population, 1966 and 2005, and percentage of change, 1966–2005, by division and region

Division and region	Year				% change 1966–2005	
	1966		2005			
	Division	Region	Division	Region	Division	Region
Northeast	41.6		38.0		-8.7	
New England		14.3		11.6		-18.9
Middle Atlantic		27.3		26.5		-2.9
Northcentral	36.4		31.3		-14.0	
East Northcentral		22.8		18.5		-18.9
West Northcentral		13.6		12.8		-5.9
West	9.5		12.7		33.7	
Mountain		1.9		2.4		26.3
Pacific		7.5		10.3		37.3
South	12.5		17.7		41.6	
East South[a]		4.9		7.2		46.9
West Southcentral		7.6		10.5		38.2
Total	100.0	99.9	99.7	99.8		

Sources: weighted census counts for 1966 and moderate projection series for 2005.
[a]Combines the South Atlantic region and one diocese from the East Southcentral region.

of the country of a significant part of its priest supply while proportionately swelling the ranks of the clergy in the West and South. In chapter 6 we use multiple regression analysis to explain how the trends are affected by organizational and environmental conditions.

A Closer Look at Historical Change

The period covered by our models of population change spans four decades, two of which rely on projections of past trends. Thus, it is important to underscore events that have already happened if only to distinguish them from those we project will occur.

Table 3.3 presents the historical net growth or decline rates for each of the regions for 1966–84, along with the comparable national net decline rates. These rates show the number lost (or, in some instances, gained) per 100 active priests in the average diocese in the country as a whole and in each region. The statistics readily show that, during the observation period, it was in the Northeast and Northcentral dioceses — because they included 80 percent of the national priest supply at the time — that the demographic forces shaping the decline process dominated. The cumulative national decline between 1966 and 1984, shown in the last column of the table, was just under 20 percent, and the average decline in Northeast and Northcentral dioceses ranged from about 21 percent to 28 percent.

Examining the rates over time, we discover that the national decline reached its peak during 1970–74, then dipped during 1975–79 and began to go up again during 1980–84. The same pattern is recorded in the average diocese throughout the Northeast and Northcentral divisions with one minor exception. The rate of decline did not increase during 1980–84 for dioceses in the West Northcentral region as it did in the other three regions in that half of the country.

In the West and South divisions, on the other hand, where only 20–30 percent of American diocesan priests resided, the regional trends differed extremely from the national trends. In contrast with the steady decline throughout Northeast and Northcentral states, clergy populations in all four West and South regions recorded growth for at least one five-year period. Furthermore, in both South regions the growth extended over the last 10 years of the historical period. In addition, compared with the national average loss of almost 20 percent, the cumulative change in West and South states ranged from a 1 percent growth in the average East South diocese to about a 12 percent decline in dioceses along the Pacific Coast.

So separate dynamics are at work in the Catholic church in different parts of the United States. The consistencies and inconsistencies of past trends in different regions account for the very different projection graphs

Table 3.3. Net growth or decline rates of U.S. diocesan priest population
and percentage of gross change, 1966–84, by year, nation, and region
(number of gains or losses per 100 active priests)

	Average annual rate				% gross change 1966–84[a]
	1966–69	1970–74	1975–79	1980–84	
United States	-1.13	-1.71	-0.77	-0.99	-19.84
Regions					
New England	-1.00	-1.85	-0.91	-1.64	-23.15
Middle Atlantic	-0.90	-1.39	-1.23	-1.25	-20.67
East Northcentral	-1.75	-2.44	-1.03	-1.74	-28.44
West Northcentral	-1.40	-2.14	-1.42	-0.62	-23.43
Mountain	-0.12	-0.95	0.80	-0.88	-5.61
Pacific	-0.65	-1.58	-0.44	0.10	-11.56
East South[b]	-0.50	-0.78	1.00	0.35	0.89
West Southcentral	-1.02	-0.78	0.77	0.17	-3.30

Source: weighted census counts.
Note: Formula for the rate is:
$$[(O + I + N - R - E - T - D - L)/P]k$$
where O is the number of ordinations;
       I is the number of incardinations;
       N is the number of returns from leave;
       R is the number of resignations;
       E is the number of excardinations;
       T is the number of retirements;
       D is the number of deaths;
       L is the number of leaves of absence during the calendar year;
       P is the total population of active incardinated priests at the
          beginning of the calendar year; and
       k is 100.
[a]Using the 1966 active population for the denominator and the cumulative
number of entrances and exits for the numerator.
[b]Combines the South Atlantic region and one diocese from the East
Southcentral region.

presented in figures 3.4 through 3.7. The national trend toward further
decline in numbers of priests is a balance of two extremes in the historical
data. Steep losses in the Northeast and Northcentral divisions govern the
average trend in the country, but they are in contrast with a combination
of some growth and moderate decline in the West and South.

Regional Change in Age Composition, 1966–2005

A redistribution of priests is one consequence of regional differences in
the demographic transition of the clergy; a variety of shades in the graying

of the priesthood is another. The bar graphs in figures 3.8 through 3.11 depict changing age distributions of priests from 1966 to 2005 across geographic regions. In their general outlines, each set of graphs resembles the changing national age distributions shown in figure 2.2; the differences are more ones of shading than of basic shape.

Thus, the most prominent feature of every graph is that the bar representing the oldest age category, namely, those 55 and older, gets taller with each passing decade. For most pyramids, the proportion of aging clergy grows closer and closer to 50 percent of the total active population as the demographic transition progresses.

In every region, the average diocese enjoyed its youngest age distribution just after the close of the Second Vatican Council, as the bar graphs for 1966 demonstrate in comparison with those for other years. The most advantageous distribution in terms of youthfulness is displayed in figure 3.11 for East South dioceses, where the average 1966 population pyramid showed that just under 60 percent of priests were below age 45. The advantage will be cut almost in half by the end of the projection period, however, when the average 2005 distribution in the East South region will record only 34 percent under 45.

At the other end of the range, according to figure 3.8, the average New England diocese began the census period with 33 percent of its priests age 55 and over, for the oldest regional age pyramid in the nation. New England priests in the oldest category will become the majority among their confreres by 1995, and, by 2005 they will reach an apex of 54 percent, the highest in the country.

Whereas the majority of age pyramids for regional priest populations will not reach their oldest phase until 2005, dioceses in the Mountain states arrived at the zenith of their age transition earlier than all the others and then began the process toward younger ages. As figure 3.10 shows, the proportional size of the oldest category of Mountain-region priests peaked in 1985 at about 43 percent and will descend gradually to about 38 percent by 2005. The bottom graph in figure 3.9 reveals that the oldest age group in the West Northcentral dioceses will also peak earlier than 2005, but at 49 percent in 1995; then the process toward younger ages will begin. A similar pattern will occur in the West Southcentral region, where the oldest age category will reach almost 46 percent by 1995 but then continue unchanged to 2005, as the data in the bottom graph of figure 3.11 demonstrate.

Table 3.4 summarizes the same data but with a different type of statistic, namely, mean and median ages. For the most part, differences between the means and medians at the regional level tell the same story as those for the national data. Regional population pyramids in 1966 were young

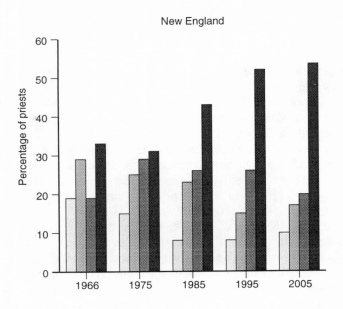

New England

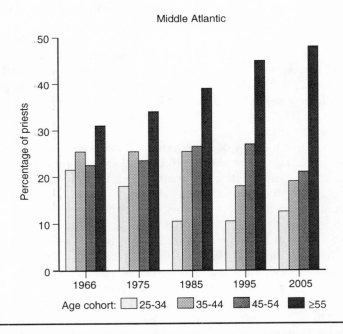

Middle Atlantic

Age cohort: ☐ 25-34 ▨ 35-44 ▧ 45-54 ■ ≥55

Figure 3.8. Age distribution of U.S. diocesan priest population: Northeast, 1966–2005

Sources: weighted census counts for 1966 and 1975; moderate projection series for 1985–2005.

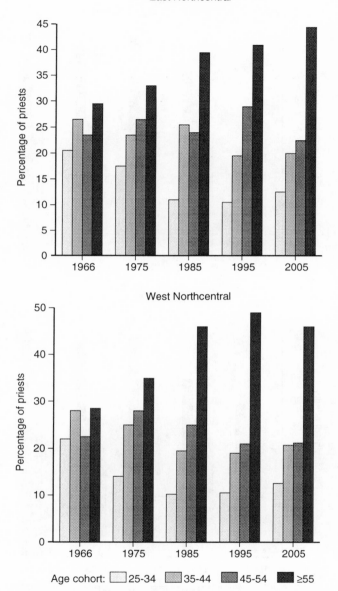

Figure 3.9. Age distribution of U.S. diocesan priest population: Northcentral, 1966–2005

Sources: weighted census counts for 1966 and 1975; moderate projection series for 1985–2005.

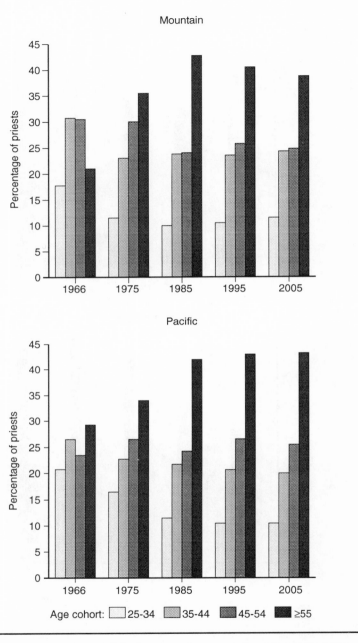

Figure 3.10. Age distribution of U.S. diocesan priest population: West, 1966–2005

Sources: weighted census counts for 1966 and 1975; moderate projection series for 1985–2005.

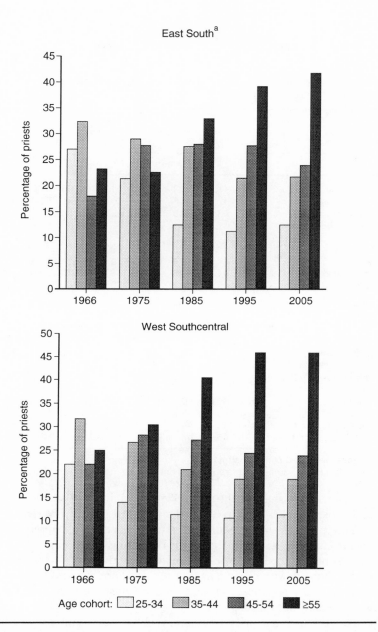

Figure 3.11. Age distribution of U.S. diocesan priest population: South, 1966–2005

Sources: weighted census counts for 1966 and 1975; moderate projection series for 1985–2005.
[a]Combines the South Atlantic region and one diocese from the East Southcentral region.

Table 3.4. Mean and median ages of active U.S. diocesan priests, 1966–2005, by year and region

Region	Year								
	1966	1970	1975	1980	1985	1990	1995	2000	2005
Mean									
New England	47.6	47.4	48.3	49.4	51.3	52.9	54.0	54.2	53.7
Middle Atlantic	47.3	47.4	48.1	49.1	50.5	51.4	52.0	52.3	52.2
East Northcentral	47.0	46.6	48.0	48.7	49.9	50.8	51.1	51.2	50.9
West Northcentral	46.7	47.2	49.1	50.8	52.0	52.7	52.9	52.7	52.1
Mountain	46.0	46.6	49.3	49.9	50.8	51.1	50.9	50.4	50.1
Pacific	46.7	47.3	48.4	50.2	50.8	51.2	51.5	51.6	51.6
East South[a]	44.5	44.4	45.6	46.5	48.5	49.8	50.4	50.6	50.6
West Southcentral	45.4	46.8	48.3	49.4	50.9	51.7	52.2	52.4	52.2
Median									
New England	45	46	47	50	52	54	55	56	56
Middle Atlantic	46	46	47	49	50	52	52	53	54
East Northcentral	46	46	48	49	50	51	51	52	53
West Northcentral	45	46	48	51	53	54	54	53	53
Mountain	45	45	50	50	52	51	51	50	50
Pacific	46	46	48	50	51	51	52	52	52
East South[a]	42	42	44	46	49	50	51	51	52
West Southcentral	43	45	47	49	52	52	53	53	54

Source: weighted census counts.
[a]Combines the South Atlantic region and one diocese from the East Southcentral region.

and so triangle-shaped, those in 1985 were aging and so beehive-shaped, and those in 2005 will be old and so shaped like an inverted triangle.

The variations in regional age distributions are most apparent by comparing changes in median age at the beginning, midpoint, and end of the 40-year period. In 1966, priest populations in the South were the youngest in the country, with median ages at about 42 and 43, and those in Middle Atlantic, East Northcentral, and Pacific Coast dioceses were the oldest, with median ages at 46.

By 1985, diocesan priest populations in the East South states had reached a median age of 49 but were still the youngest, while those in West Northcentral states had climbed to a median age of 53, the oldest in the country.

At the turn of the century, regional variations in median age will reflect a pattern altogether different from prior decades. In 2005, the oldest median age will be found in New England dioceses, where half the active priests will be older and half younger than 56. The youngest age pyramids will be recorded in Mountain dioceses, where the age dividing the active population in equal halves will be 50.

The median age of active priests in the average New England diocese will increase by 11 years between 1966 and 2005, and that in Mountain dioceses will increase by only 5 years. Although the median age of priests in the South was lowest in 1966, it will increase by 10–11 years over the four decades, bringing age pyramids for dioceses of the South in 2005 on a par with most other regions.

Conclusion

Our regional data on Catholic priests document notable geographic differences and lend some support to the findings of Stark and Bainbridge (1985) on American religious regionalism. Their data show that certain aspects of organized religion in the United States are heavily affected by regional conditions, others are affected hardly at all, and the actual similarities and contrasts often dispel popular misconceptions. Thus, they discovered definite geographic patterns in rates of church membership and church attendance, on the one hand, but minimal regional differences in conventional religious belief, prayer, and religious experience, on the other. They conclude that their results dispel the myths of the southern Bible Belt, where people are no more fervently religious than elsewhere, and the secularism of the Pacific Coast, where people are unchurched but not comparatively irreligious.

Our data provide similar evidence of American religious regionalism by documenting geographic differences in the patterns of growth and decline of the Catholic priest population. In terms of numbers lost, severe decline is limited to the Northeast and Northcentral divisions of the country, where the size of the active clergy will be cut by more than half during the final decades of the century. In contrast, during the same period the East South region will probably experience slight growth in the number of priests, while the West Southcentral and Pacific Coast regions will suffer only moderate loss.

Regional differences and changes in the age distribution of the clergy follow closely those governing alterations in the size of the population. Thus, the youngest and oldest age pyramids have been found and will continue to be found in the East South and New England. Most priest populations in the South and West, however, are expected to experience only limited aging.

Evidence suggests that the supposed American Catholic monolith as an organizational form may be, in reality, a loosely coupled system (Glassman 1973; Hernes 1976; Weick 1976). In chapter 5 we will examine regional variation further, by viewing the change process as a demographic transition that follows predictable stages. Is loose coupling in the Catholic church reflected by regional differences in the speed and staging of the demographic transition?

In chapter 6 and subsequent ones we expand the question. Are differences in the timing and development of the demographic transition rooted in a tangle of organizational and environmental conditions? Before analyzing the stages, causes, and consequences of population change, however, we need to sharpen the focus of our comparative descriptive analysis. Hence we turn in the next chapter to local differences in the changing priesthood population.

4 Describing Local Variation

With the national data, we described the extent of decline in the U.S. priesthood population; in the regional analysis, we described how fast it was progressing in different parts of the country. After peeling a pomegranate and separating its sections, one is ready to enjoy the granules of fruit inside. Just so, in this chapter we turn to the individual diocese, the primary unit of analysis.

The social dynamics driving the priest shortage are played out at the local diocesan level, where priests are ordained and incardinated and where they resign, retire, and die. Policy-oriented, or applied, research assumes that results must be available to real planners and decision makers in concrete organizations. Basic, or "pure," research in organization demography, likewise, can proceed only if scholars can build and share a data base that contains information on identifiable organizations. The purpose of this chapter, therefore, is to present some descriptive detail that brings the examination of population decline and aging trends of the American priesthood to the local level. Additionally, the tables provide raw data by diocese, making them readily available for further analysis.

Highlights

1. The number of active priests in Dubuque, Iowa, may show a decline of 73 percent between 1966 and 2005, the greatest projected loss of any diocese in the sample. At the other end of the range, Atlanta is projected to continue growing for an increase of 122 percent during the same period.

2. Aging trends in individual dioceses, especially when projected to the turn of the century, exhibit wide variation. The speed of the aging process varies significantly from one place to another. In most areas the percentage of priests 55 and older is notably larger in 1985 than in 1966 and is expected to be larger yet in 2005.

3. In 1980, the highest layperson-to-priest ratio was recorded in Los Angeles, where there were almost 4,000 Catholics per active diocesan priest. At the lowest extreme, there were only about 600 Catholics per active diocesan priest in Little Rock.

Assumptions about Future Main Trends

When describing and analyzing demographic processes that occurred during the historical period, we use a single set of data, the most reliable and accurate available. When the analysis focuses on the projection period, however, we use three sets of data and consider one, that based on moderate assumptions, more plausible than those based on either optimistic or pessimistic assumptions.

The rest of the analysis in the book focuses primarily on the historical data and the projections based on moderate assumptions. We believe the moderate assumptions produce the most plausible projections of future trends. Simply put, moderate assumptions are considered most reasonable precisely because they fall midway between the best and worst historical scenarios. It is worth repeating that our population projections do not predict the future. They merely forecast past trends. Historical trends themselves, however, represent powerful social forces, and the longer the period of observation, the more accurately one taps the deeply rooted processes that are embodied in the demographic trends under investigation.

Generally, current trends are the most reasonable base from which to forecast the immediate future, because conditions describing current trends are carriers of social forces coming from the recent and distant past (Shryock, Siegel, and Associates 1971). When social trends are fluctuating willy-nilly, however, current experience is less useful for forecasting future trends. If, on the other hand, past trends have been steady in one direction — as is the case with priest decline in the United States for the past two decades — then current trends become the most accurate ones available for establishing moderate projection assumptions.

The demographic process producing numeric decline and aging of the clergy is not a set of unknown "social forces." To the contrary, the analysis so far has carefully delineated the structure of the change process by identifying: its functional form, namely, the interrelationships among the entrance and exit events that generate change in the priest population; its parameter structure, namely, the values of the ordination, net migration, resignation, retirement, death, and net leave rates across time; and its output structure, namely, the historical and projected sizes and shapes of the priest population in the United States from 1966 to 2005 (see Hernes 1976).

So the issue of why moderate assumptions are the most reasonable may be approached with some precision. Precisely why are "current" levels of ordination, resignation, and retirement (i.e., those experienced during 1980–84) the most reasonable ones for forecasting future trends in the recruitment and retention of priests? Or, why, on the other hand, would it be unreasonable to expect that ordinations will go up in the foreseeable future and that resignations and retirements will go down, thus making the moderate projections implausible? Both sides of the issue deserve discussion. Before addressing them directly, however, we shall provide further analysis of each transition event in Part Three. Then, in its own context, we will consider arguments for and against plausibility of the moderate assumptions for each individual transition event.

Specifying the pros and cons supports the likelihood that each of the current trends will continue into the future, as we shall see in later chapters. At this point, though, the evidence from our 12-diocese plausibility test, available empirical data from ours and other relevant studies, and our understanding of historical conditions affecting the Catholic church strongly suggest that the projection models based on moderate assumptions are reasonably accurate. They also appear to be the most plausible of the three competing models. Therefore, we continue the analysis focusing exclusively on the historical data and the results of population projections based on moderate assumptions.

Local Variation in Changing Size of Priest Populations, 1966–2005

Table 4.1 reveals the wide range of local variation within geographic areas, grouping dioceses by census region.[1] The table displays changes in population size and the percentage of difference, and rank orders the data within region by percentage of change in the priest population.

The data presented in column 4 of the first subsection in the Northeast panel of the table show that the majority of New England dioceses will lose from one-half to about three-fifths of their active diocesan clergy between 1966 and 2005. The next subsection in the Northeast panel reveals that Middle Atlantic dioceses at the high end of the range will lose almost three-fifths and those at the low end about one-fifth of their active priest populations between 1966 and 2005.

The statistics for East Northcentral states disclose that by 2005 one dio-

---

1. Listing extremes in the range of expected outcomes considers only sampled dioceses. Occasionally, dioceses not included in the sample may fall outside the specified ranges; see the next subsection in the text, "Cautionary Notes for Policymakers."

Table 4.1. Size of U.S. diocesan priest population and percentage of difference, 1966–2005, by year and diocese (rank order within region by percentage of difference)

Region and diocese	Year			% difference 1966–2005
	1966	1985	2005	
Northeast				
New England				
Burlington VT	181	131	68	-62
Fall River MA	236	174	101	-57
Hartford CT	564	450	245	-57
Boston MA	1,330	961	569	-57
Portland ME	250	178	124	-50
Worcester MA	308	279	190	-38
Norwich CT	138	121	101	-27
Providence RI[a]	—	—	—	—
Middle Atlantic				
Brooklyn NY	1,039	701	428	-59
Albany NY	463	306	196	-58
Rochester NY	396	259	166	-58
New York NY	1,221	831	560	-54
Buffalo NY	629	497	318	-49
Philadelphia PA	1,042	815	590	-43
Newark NJ	876	710	528	-40
Scranton PA	467	372	285	-39
Camden NJ	356	345	222	-38
Ogdensburg NY	187	166	122	-35
Pittsburgh PA	566	537	432	-24
Altoona–Johnstown PA	159	165	123	-23
Rockville Centre NY	449	418	358	-20
Allentown PA	286	258	238	-17
Northcentral				
East Northcentral				
La Crosse WI	318	193	101	-68
Indianapolis IN	264	164	97	-63
Marquette MI	147	100	57	-61
Milwaukee WI	665	478	268	-60
Rockford IL	178	142	73	-59
Detroit MI	734[b]	462	310	-58
Grand Rapids MI	172[b]	114	81	-53
Chicago IL	1,340	925	657	-51
Youngstown OH	256	193	126	-51
Belleville IL	180	139	95	-47
Columbus OH	237	185	136	-43
Cincinnati OH	458	368	266	-42
Gaylord MI	66[c]	55	41	-38
Cleveland OH	618	530	460	-26
Saginaw MI	135[b]	114	108	-20

(continued on following page)

Table 4.1. Size of U.S. diocesan priest population and percentage of difference, 1966–2005, by year and diocese (continued)

Region and diocese	Year			% difference 1966–2005
	1966	1985	2005	
Northcentral (continued)				
West Northcentral				
Dubuque IA	427	286	117	-73
New Ulm MN	128	88	56	-56
Fargo ND	154	106	69	-55
Salina KS	86	64	43	-50
Sioux City IA	209	174	107	-49
St. Cloud MN	174	140	94	-46
Des Moines IA	131	100	73	-44
Wichita KS	165	121	97	-41
Rapid City SD	77	40	49	-36
St. Paul–Minneapolis MN	430	333	280	-35
Kansas City–St. Jos. MO	173	136	115	-34
Dodge City KS	65	54	43	-34
St Louis MO	555	508	390	-30
Springfield–C. Girard. MO[d]	72	68	76	6
Lincoln NE[a]	—	—	—	—
West				
Mountain				
Las Cruces NM	27[c]	26	15	-44
Pueblo CO	85	76	56	-34
Santa Fe NM	141[b]	116	98	-30
Cheyenne WY	59	45	45	-24
Boise ID	77	81	60	-22
Gallup NM	15[b]	53	53	253
Pacific				
Stockton CA	48	37	24	-50
San Diego CA	208[b]	177	140	-33
Monterey CA	69[e]	66	50	-28
Baker OR	45	39	33	-27
San Jose CA	110[c]	89	82	-25
San Bernardino CA	135[c]	110	113	-16
San Francisco CA	244[b]	198	206	-16
Los Angeles CA	572[b]	528	495	-13
Oakland CA	147	135	129	-12
Orange CA	102[c]	125	161	58
Fresno CA[a]	—	—	—	—
South				
East South[f]				
Baltimore MD	332	286	189	-43
Covington KY	210	164	130	-38

(continued on following page)

Table 4.1. Size of U.S. diocesan priest population and percentage of
difference, 1966–2005, by year and diocese (continued)

Region and diocese	Year			% difference 1966–2005
	1966	1985	2005	
South (continued)				
East South[f] (continued)				
Wilmington DE	112	110	104	-7
Orlando FL	72[g]	95	90	25
St. Petersburg FL	83[g]	94	152	83
Atlanta GA	49	93	109	122
West Southcentral				
Alexandria–Shreveport LA	134	92	42	-69
Little Rock AK	128	91	59	-54
Victoria TX	47[c]	48	34	-28
Austin TX	91	91	70	-23
Galveston–Houston TX	154[b]	157	127	-18
Lafayette LA	141[b]	138	117	-17
San Antonio TX	149[b]	154	126	-15
Baton Rouge LA	72	79	64	-11
Fort Worth TX	49[h]	59	46	-6
Beaumont TX	44	49	43	-2
Corpus Christi TX	68[b]	70	67	-1
El Paso TX	53[b]	58	56	6
Dallas TX	98[h]	104	128	31
Lake Charles LA	33[c]	41	53	61

Sources: census counts for 1966 and 1985, and moderate projection series for 2005.

[a]Refused to participate.

[b]Divided during the census period; the figure given is the 1966 active population minus the number of active priests transferred in the year of the split. Adding the number of active priests transferred to the figure shown produces the actual size of the 1966 population. (Appendix D gives the year of the split and the numbers transferred.)

[c]Established during the census period by being divided from others in the sample; see appendix D for year of establishment and parent diocese(s).

[d]"C. Girard." abbreviates "Cape Girardeau" in each table that it appears, throughout the volume.

[e]Divided in 1967. The figure given is the size of the active population as identifiable in 1966 (see appendix D).

[f]Combines the South Atlantic region and one diocese from the East Southcentral region.

[g]Established in 1968. The figure given is the size of the 1968 active population (see appendix D).

[h]Divided in 1969. The figure given is the size of the active population as identifiable in 1966 (see appendix D).

cese will suffer a loss of over two-thirds of its 1966 number of clergy. Of the 15 dioceses sampled in the region, only 3 will see their priest supply drop less than the national average.[2] The majority of West Northcentral dioceses will likewise exceed the national average, losing more than 40 percent of their active clergy populations between 1966 and 2005. At the other extreme, one diocese in the region is projected to grow 6 percent during the period.

The picture changes considerably for dioceses in the West division of the United States. Only one diocese in the Mountain region and one along the Pacific Coast are projected to lose more than the average for the nation. Projected losses in all other dioceses of the West are well below 40 percent. Two priest populations in West dioceses should grow in size between 1966 and 2005.[3]

Turning to the last two subsections of the table we see that, similar to dioceses in the West, the demographic transition of the clergy in the South is progressing much more slowly than in the Northeast and Northcentral divisions of the country. Of the entire 20 dioceses sampled in the South census division, the population decline in only 3 is above the 40 percent national average. At the opposite extreme, 6 dioceses in the South will most likely witness growth in their active priest populations between 1966 and 2005.[4]

Cautionary Note for Policymakers

Dividing old dioceses and creating new ones are major organizational events that affect priest population trends; they must be borne in mind in interpreting local variation (see appendix D). Other caveats are also necessary for understanding the distribution of differences among dioceses,

2. Demographic events in dioceses such as Gaylord and Saginaw were affected by organizational divisions and boundary changes during the period under study; Gaylord was created in 1971 from several Michigan dioceses, including Saginaw. Appendix D identifies the new and divided dioceses in the sample, notes how many priests were affected by the divisions, and describes the techniques we use to standardize the data in order to maintain comparability over the entire period.

3. Gallup, New Mexico, may increase by as much as 253 percent. This situation, however, is highly unusual; the diocese lost 13 of 29 active diocesan priests in 1969, when the Diocese of Phoenix was created. Those 13 have already been subtracted from the 1966 population as a standardization technique. Thus, an increase from the 15 remaining priests in 1966 to 53 active clergy members by 2005 reflects some heavy catch-up activity as well as genuine growth.

4. In West Southcentral states, Lake Charles, Louisiana, is projected to expand the most, possibly reaching a 61 percent increase. But it is a newly established diocese, so the change from 33 priests in 1966 to 53 by 2005 is proportionately large but not unusual.

especially for grasping the extremes. The nature of statistical analysis and the rules of random sampling, for example, bear on the interpretation of technical results of projection models based on historical trends. According to the "law of large numbers," a strong trend becomes evident only after observing larger and larger numbers of relevant events. Deeply rooted social forces or underlying trends are not manifest from only a few observations. Thus, recording thousands upon thousands of transition events in many dioceses over many years has revealed the national trends in the demographic transition of the clergy. So the evidence is strong that, if the 1980–84 trends continue unchanged over the following two decades, the *average* diocese will probably decline 40 percent during the period under investigation.

The average diocese, however, does not exist. There are only unique dioceses — and many with very small priest populations — undergoing unique change processes. The national trend, therefore, is the arithmetic mean of the local trends, some of which show high decline, others medium, others low, and still others slow growth. Thus, for example, Dubuque and Atlanta are at the high and low ends of the range, ignoring the unique circumstances of growth in Gallup. These dioceses, though, represent relatively small populations in terms of the law of large numbers. So given the unique fluctation in the relatively small number of entrance and exit events in that diocese, Dubuque will *probably* come close to losing 73 percent of its 1966 population size by 2005. Another sampled diocese, however (or indeed one not included in the sample but with similar historical trends), may reach or even exceed that figure. When 2005 arrives, Dubuque's loss may be noticeably lower than 73 percent, falling somewhere between its moderate and optimistic projection, because certain events may intervene to change the projected trends. Following the same reasoning, Atlanta may be surpassed in growth by some other diocese.

The actual extremes of decline and growth between 1966 and 2005 will most likely be close to those projected for these two dioceses. Likewise, those dioceses whose decline scores in table 4.1 lie close to the national mean are most likely to lose around 40 percent during the period. In every case, the numbers given in the table are the best possible ballpark estimate of the true figures, since they are based on the moderate assumptions. The true figures will most likely fall close to these moderate projections, but some will be between the moderate and optimistic bands of their projection models, and others will fall between the moderate and pessimistic bands. The projected size of each diocese in the sample, for all three projection series, is given in appendix E.

Parishioner-to-Priest Ratio[5]

Raw numbers can be deceiving in understanding decline. Interpreting the extent of the priest shortage, especially at the local diocesan level, depends not only on the changing size of the clergy population but also on the size and growth of church membership in that area. Therefore, when measuring the availability of priestly ministers it is important to examine the parishioner-to-priest ratio.

Hoge raises this issue in his attempt to put the clergy population decline in a practical light. He asks, How many priests are "needed to maintain satisfactory access of the laity to the sacraments?" (Hoge 1987, p. 34). He concludes that a practical measure of severity of decline would be change in the parishioner-to-priest ratio and how it may affect the availability of the Mass and sacraments, the central focus of Catholic piety.

A National Standard

When analyzing change over time, it is necessary to establish a standard, or point of comparison. In most demographic studies, the choice of a standard population or time period may be a totally arbitrary matter, because the comparative statistics based on the standard "have no other use than to make the desired comparisons" (Pressat 1972, p. 102). In organization demography, however, it helps if the comparative standard makes some sense in terms of real administrative issues. Rev. Robert Sherry, former director of the National Conference of Catholic Bishops Office of Vocations and Priestly Formation, thinks the present concern about availability of the Mass and sacraments may not antedate 1975. So he proposes the 1975 parishioner-to-priest ratio as a minimum standard for assessing the severity of the priest shortage (Sherry 1985). His proposal provides a criterion of comparison that is not totally arbitrary, so we incorporated it in the analysis.

Part of the information needed for constructing a 1975 standardized index of parishioners to priests was available from the Glenmary Research Center, where national statistics on the number of Catholic parishioners per county are gathered and aggregated by diocese (Quinn et al. 1982).[6]

---

5. Ratios based on all who claim preference for Catholicism are labeled layperson-to-priest ratios, whereas those based on the number of Catholics in the diocese who participate in the parish, no matter how minimally, are more accurately called parishioner-to-priest ratios.

6. The Glenmary figures rely on diocesan contacts, who estimate the number of active parishioners in the diocese. Estimates from Gallup polls and other national surveys show that figures provided by dioceses notably underestimate the number of Americans who claim

These data were combined with our priest population figures and yielded the following national parameters: In 1975, according to the Glenmary census, there were an estimated 43,674,174 Roman Catholic participants in the United States and, according to our data, 29,629 active diocesan priests. Hence the 1975 ratio in the average American diocese was 1,474 Catholic parishioners per active diocesan priest. (These figures are weighted estimates which have been calculated on the basis of sampling probabilities.[7] A description of our sampling methods and the weighting factors for each diocese in the sample are given in appendix F.)

The ratio we derived as a standard is considerably higher than the one Sherry reached in his calculations for 1975, which was 791 Catholic parishioners per priest. Sherry's figure appropriately includes religious order priests and probably inactive ones as well, whereas ours refers exclusively to active diocesan priests. His ratio may be more suitable for determining the minimum size of the *overall* priestly staff needed to promote the sacramental mission of the church. In the context of the present analysis, however, our estimated parishioner-to-priest ratio is appropriate, because all the variables for the study have been constructed to measure only the characteristics of active diocesan clergy.[8]

Table 4.2 displays the 1970 and 1980 parishioner–to–active diocesan priest ratios in each sampled diocese, a percentage score that standarizes the local ratio by the 1975 national average, and the percentage of difference between the 1970 and 1980 statistics. This gives an earlier and later point of comparison with the 1975 standard. The data in the table are ranked in order within region by the 1980 ratios, because they reflect the most re-

---

a preference for the Roman Catholic religion (see Hoge 1987). In chapter 12, where we discuss consequences of the priest decline, we use the layperson-to-priest ratio based on the higher Gallup estimates. In this chapter we use the parishioner-to-priest ratio, because estimates of the number who claim a preference for Catholicism based on survey data are not available by diocese.

7. The estimate of the national Catholic population is the sum of the sampled diocesan estimates, which were derived by weighting aggregated county-level data. The estimate for the national priest population is the sum of the weighted 1974–76 mean number of active diocesan priests in the sampled dioceses (see appendix F).

8. Limiting our systematic comparisons to active diocesan priests eliminates multiple sources of error that contaminate other measures. We believe the most comparable measure of availability of priestly ministers, across all dioceses and over time, is size of active diocesan clergy. But when applying results from the following analysis, diocesan planners and other policy-oriented readers must take into consideration the size of the religious order clergy available for pastoral ministry and also estimate the amount of time retired priests might spend administering the sacraments.

cent situation for which data were available. Summary statistics for the census regions as a whole are also included.

The standardized index was constructed so a score of 100 indicates that the parishioner-to-priest ratio was exactly at the national standard, that is to say, 1,474 Catholic parishioners per active diocesan priest. Subtracting a low standardized index from 100 or, vice versa, subtracting 100 from a high index, reveals the percentage by which the parishioner-to-priest ratio in that particular region or diocese is lower or higher than the 1975 national standard.

Regional Contrasts

Looking down column 2 of table 4.2 reveals the range of regional parishioner-to-priest ratios in 1980, and inspecting column 4 discloses the extent to which they were higher or lower than the 1975 standard. Thus, the 1980 regional parishioner-to-priest ratio ranges from a low of 909 Catholics, on the average, in West Northcentral dioceses to a high of 2,291 Catholics per active diocesan priest in Pacific Coast dioceses. The former is 38 percent below and the latter is 55 percent above the standardized index.

We also discover that in 1980 the number of Catholic parishioners per active diocesan priest was just about at the national standard in half the country. The parishioner-to-priest ratio did not deviate from the standardized index by more than 6 percentage points in the average New England, Middle Atlantic, East Northcentral, and East South diocese. The 1980 ratio for the average diocese in three other regions, however, was significantly above the standard, indicating less availability of priestly ministers in those regions. In Mountain dioceses the number of Catholic parishioners per diocesan priest was 20 percent higher, in West Southcentral dioceses 37 percent higher, and in Pacific Coast dioceses 55 percent higher than the arbitrary 1975 standard.

Ratios were significantly below the standardized index in only one region. In West Northcentral states, where the average index was 62, the number of Catholic parishioners per diocesan priest was 38 percent lower than the minimum standard. Thus in terms of the Sherry Index, average West Northcentral dioceses may be the only ones in the country where there are significantly more priests than might be needed to serve adequately the sacramental needs of Catholic parishioners.

Matching the Standard

The highest score in columns 2 and 4 is found in the Archdiocese of Los Angeles and the lowest in the Diocese of Little Rock. In Los Angeles there

Table 4.2. Number of parishioners per active diocesan priest and standardized index, 1970 and 1980, and percentage of difference, 1970–80, by nation, region, and diocese (rank order within region by 1980 standardized index)

Region and diocese	Parishioners/priest		Standardized index		% difference 1970–80
	1970	1980	1970	1980	
United States	1,328	1,570	90	107	19
Northeast					
New England	1,266	1,535	86	104	21
Boston MA	1,486	1,929	101	131	30
Hartford CT	1,459	1,773	99	120	21
Fall River MA	1,373	1,770	93	120	29
Norwich CT	1,394	1,673	95	113	20
Portland ME	1,194	1,462	81	99	22
Worcester MA	1,155	1,073	78	73	-6
Burlington VT	802	1,063	54	72	33
Providence RI[a]	—	—	—	—	—
Middle Atlantic	1,268	1,455	86	99	15
Rockville Centre NY	2,125	2,512	144	170	18
New York NY	1,609	1,941	109	132	21
Newark NJ	1,556	1,926	106	131	24
Pittsburgh PA	1,792	1,774	122	120	-2
Brooklyn NY	1,587	1,711	108	116	7
Philadelphia PA	1,345	1,509	91	102	12
Buffalo NY	1,145	1,356	78	92	18
Rochester NY	1,007	1,274	68	86	26
Albany NY	957	1,259	65	85	31
Allentown PA	961	1,132	65	77	18
Altoona–Johnstown PA	1,077	1,021	73	69	-5
Scranton PA	862	1,014	58	69	19
Ogdensburg NY	888	976	60	66	10
Camden NJ	837	966	57	66	16
Northcentral					
East Northcentral	1,174	1,424	80	97	21
Detroit MI	2,268[b]	2,425	154	165	7
Chicago IL	2,068	2,333	140	158	13
Cleveland OH	1,506	1,885	102	128	25
Saginaw MI	1,335[b]	1,564	91	106	16
Gaylord MI	1,185[c]	1,554	80	105	31
Youngstown OH	1,147	1,553	78	105	35
Rockford IL	1,236	1,383	84	94	12
Cincinnati OH	1,214	1,271	82	86	5
Milwaukee WI	1,070	1,268	73	86	18
Grand Rapids MI	957[b]	1,251	65	85	31
Columbus	738	1,075	50	73	46
Indianapolis IN	830	1,055	56	72	29
La Crosse WI	659	1,030	45	70	56

(continued on following page)

Table 4.2. Number of parishioners per active diocesan priest and standardized index, 1970 and 1980, and percentage of difference, 1970–80, by nation, region, and diocese (continued)

Region and diocese	Parishioners/priest		Standardized index		% difference
	1970	1980	1970	1980	1970–80
Northcentral (continued)					
East Northcentral (continued)					
Marquette MI	696	898	47	61	30
Belleville IL	702	811	48	55	15
West Northcentral	700	909	47	62	32
St. Paul–Minneapolis MN	1,318	1,703	89	116	30
Rapid City SD	614	1,069	42	73	74
Kansas City–St. Jos. MO	832	1,055	56	72	29
St. Louis MO	918	1,027	62	70	13
St. Cloud MN	840	1,011	57	69	21
Salina KS	694	851	47	58	23
Fargo ND	684	834	46	57	24
Springfield–C. Girard. MO	505	818	34	55	62
Wichita KS	574	814	39	55	41
Des Moines IA	641	761	43	52	21
New Ulm MN	571	741	39	50	28
Dubuque IA	570	726	39	49	26
Dodge City KS	507	688	34	47	38
Sioux City IA	535	632	36	43	19
Lincoln NE[a]	—	—	—	—	—
West					
Mountain	1,385[d]	1,775	94	120	28
Las Cruces NM	2,397[c]	2,992	163	203	25
Santa Fe NM	2,025[b]	2,654	137	180	31
Cheyenne WY	733	1,298	50	88	76
Pueblo CO	1,025	1,121	70	76	9
Boise ID	748	810	51	55	8
Gallup NM[d]	—	—	—	—	—
Pacific	1,826	2,291	124	155	25
Los Angeles CA	2,557[b]	3,958	173	269	55
Orange CA	2,676[c]	3,465	182	235	29
Oakland CA	2,439	2,955	165	200	21
Stockton CA	1,868	2,466	127	167	31
San Jose CA	2,187[c]	2,378	148	161	9
San Bernardino CA	1,655[c]	2,097	112	142	27
San Diego CA	1,559[b]	1,867	106	127	20
San Francisco CA	1,611[b]	1,665	109	113	4
Monterey CA	1,218	1,407	83	95	14
Baker OR	486	656	33	45	36
Fresno CA[a]	—	—	—	—	—

(continued on following page)

Table 4.2. Number of parishioners per active diocesan priest and standardized index, 1970 and 1980, and percentage of difference, 1970–80, by nation, region, and diocese (continued)

Region and diocese	Parishioners/priest		Standardized index		% difference 1970–80
	1970	1980	1970	1980	
South					
East South[e]	1,238	1,381	84	94	12
St. Petersburg FL	1,806	2,470	123	168	37
Orlando FL	1,369	1,544	93	105	13
Baltimore MD	1,545	1,359	105	92	-12
Atlanta GA	1,128	1,149	77	78	1
Wilmington DE	1,068	1,132	72	77	7
Covington KY	514	632	35	43	23
West Southcentral	1,875	2,017	127	137	8
San Antonio TX	3,274[b]	3,411	222	231	4
Corpus Christi TX	2,817[b]	2,917	191	198	4
Galveston–Houston TX	2,033[b]	2,741	138	186	35
El Paso TX	2,758[b]	2,585	187	175	-6
Lafayette LA	2,137[b]	2,267	145	154	6
Baton Rouge LA	2,390	2,192	162	149	-8
Lake Charles LA	2,284[c]	2,140	155	145	-6
Victoria TX	1,487[c]	1,885	101	128	27
Dallas TX	1,349	1,786	92	121	32
Austin TX	1,577	1,690	107	115	7
Beaumont TX	1,515	1,675	103	114	11
Fort Worth TX	1,445	1,559	98	106	8
Alexandria–Shreveport LA	684	790	46	54	17
Little Rock AK	502	599	34	41	21

Sources: for parishioners, Quinn et al. 1982; for priests, census counts.

[a]Refused to participate.

[b]Divided during the census period; the ratios given are for numbers of Catholics and active priests standardized as if the split had occurred by 1970. (Appendix D gives the year of the split and describes the standardization techniques.)

[c]Established during the census period by being divided from others in the sample. The number of Catholics is based on the size of the population in those counties that composed their new jurisdiction.

The number of priests is the size of the active clergy population estimated from the number(s) transferred from the parent diocese(s), weighted when necessary, and standardized as if establishment had occurred by 1970. (See appendix D for year of establishment, parent diocese[s], and procedures for estimating and standardizing clergy size.)

[d]Data for Gallup are not included in the Mountain region averages because of extreme fluctuations there when the Diocese of Phoenix was created in 1969, which our adjustment procedures could not smooth out; the statistics for Gallup, following the same order as the table columns, are: 2,950; 1,056; 200; 72; -64.

[e]Combines the South Atlantic region and one diocese from the East Southcentral region.

were 3,958 Catholic parishioners per active diocesan priest in 1980, 169 percent higher than the standard. In Little Rock the ratio was only 599 church members per priest, 59 percent lower than the arbitrary 1975 standard.

We can look at these numbers another way, focusing on the size of the active priest population, but conclusions should be drawn from such an exercise with extreme caution. For example, instead of the 522 priests recorded in the census counts for 1980, Los Angeles would have had to have 1,409 active diocesan priests that year to match the national standard of 1,474 Catholic parishioners per priest. In Little Rock, instead of 96 active priests in 1980, the diocese could have achieved the standard parishioner-to-priest ratio with only 39 active diocesan priests.[9]

Such comparisons are useful to highlight extreme differences in standardized ratios of Catholic parishioners to active *diocesan* clergy. Providing the Mass and sacraments, however, does not depend solely on the diocesan clergy. Many dioceses — Los Angeles is a good example — rely heavily on religious order priests and permanent deacons for meeting sacramental ministry needs.

Los Angeles is well above the national average on both the religious priest–to–diocesan priest ratio and the permanent deacon–to–diocesan priest ratio. Others, like Little Rock, which is just above the average on these two variables, have relatively fewer religious priests and deacons working in the diocese.[10] In addition, urban dioceses can be more efficient, because the Catholic population is more concentrated, whereas rural dioceses need relatively more priests to serve the far-flung membership. For example, in Los Angeles, Catholic parishioners are concentrated at 240 per square mile, but in Little Rock there is only 1 Catholic parishioner per square mile.

Nevertheless, even controlling for size of religious priest population, size of the permanent deaconate, and urban concentration, many of these large differences in the standardized ratios of Catholic parishioners to diocesan priests would undoubtedly remain. Furthermore, the contrasts have a direct bearing on determining how adequately different dioceses are meeting the needs of the laity, especially once we know whether dioceses are operating with comparable resources and under similar environmental conditions. Thus, for example, during the decade under examination, the parishioner-

9. There were an estimated 2,076,589 Catholic parishioners in Los Angeles in 1980; thus, 2,076,589/1,474 = 1408.8. The same figures for Little Rock are 56,911/1,474 = 38.6.

10. The religious priest–to–diocesan priest ratio for Los Angeles is at the 89th percentile and the permanent deacon–to–diocesan priest ratio is at the 75th percentile of the national distributions; in Little Rock, the scores are at the 60th and 59th percentiles, respectively.

to-priest ratio in Rockville Centre was the highest of all the New York dioceses in the sample, yet the size of its active priest population was declining the least.

One could conclude from table 4.1 that Rockville Centre is the most fortunate diocese in the state, because its active priest population is declining least. The opposite is true, however, as table 4.2 demonstrates. Rockville Centre's 1980 parishioner-to-priest ratio is 70 percent higher than the national standard, whereas, close by, New York City's and Brooklyn's are only 32 percent and 16 percent higher, respectively. Furthermore, relative to the size of the diocesan clergy, the Archdiocese of New York has five times as many and Brooklyn almost half again as many religious order priests as Rockville Centre.[11] The Diocese of Rockville Centre may be trying to compensate for the obvious imbalance in the distribution of clergy by increasing the size of its permanent diaconate. Its ratio of permanent deacons to diocesan priests is at the 75th percentile of the national distribution, whereas that of New York is at the 67th percentile and Brooklyn's is at the 47th percentile.

The predicament of Rockville Centre's clergy vis-à-vis the large number of parishioners is mitigated somewhat because its Catholic population is heavily concentrated, although it is not as dense as in Brooklyn. In round numbers, the Diocese of Brooklyn has 7,500 Catholic parishioners per square mile, the highest density in the country, while Rockville Centre is at the 95th percentile of the national distribution, with 850, and New York is at the 92nd percentile, with 375 Catholic parishioners per square mile.[12]

In terms of availability of priestly ministers, the data suggest that true disparities exist among dioceses in the United States, disparities which probably would not disappear if relevant comparable conditions were taken into consideration. The few comparisons made in this descriptive analysis are merely suggestive, however.

The parishioner-to-priest ratio may be systematically affected by the religious priest–to–diocesan priest ratio, by the permanent deacon–to–diocesan priest ratio, by urbanization, and by a host of other variables. These variables, too, may affect one another. Before any solid conclusions about differences in the availability of priestly service can be drawn, the data must

11. The religious priest–to–diocesan priest ratios for New York City, Brooklyn, and Rockville Center are 174, 50, and 35, religious priests per 100 active diocesan priests, respectively.

12. The Archdiocese of New York includes three boroughs of New York City and seven outstate counties, so its population is more scattered than the other two. Brooklyn is limited to Kings and Queens counties in the one borough and Rockville Centre to Nassau and Suffolk counties, which compose Long Island.

be subjected to an appropriate analysis. Accordingly, correlates of the parishioner-to-priest ratio and similar issues are addressed in chapter 6.

More Parishioners per Priest

The last column in table 4.2 shows the percentage of difference between the 1970 and 1980 statistics. The data show that the ratio of Catholic parishioners to active diocesan priests increased from 1970 to 1980 in every part of the country.[13]

The average increase is significantly lower in three regions compared with the rest of the country. The lows in the distribution occurred in West Southcentral dioceses, where the parishioner-to-priest ratio grew only 8 percent, in East South dioceses, where Catholic parishioners per priest expanded 12 percent, and in Middle Atlantic states, where dioceses experienced a 15 percent increase during the decade. In all other regions, the increase was higher. In a period of only 10 years, growth in the ratios ranged anywhere from 21 percent to 30 percent. Although the most advantageous parishioner-to-priest ratio in the country is found in West Northcentral states, the average diocese in the region saw a 32 percent increase in the number of Catholic parishioners per priest between 1970 and 1980, for the highest regional growth in the country.

Variations in the degree of change among individual dioceses ranged from a high of 76 percent in Cheyenne, where the ratio increased from 733 in 1970 to 1,298 Catholic parishioners per active diocesan priest in 1980, to a low of −12 percent in Baltimore, where the numbers dropped from 1,545 to 1,359 during the same 10 years.

Local Variation in Changing Age Distribution of Priest Populations, 1966–2005

Trends in the national data indicate that the U.S. clergy population is not only declining in size but also aging rapidly. The regional-level analysis reveals major differences in the aging process across census regions. With the diocese as the unit of analysis we can also examine local variation.

We begin with an overview which attempts to simplify the presentation. Instead of providing the full age pyramid for each diocese, table 4.3 displays only the percentages of active priests age 55 and older in 1966, 1985,

---

13. The difference scores are the same whether calculated for the 1970 and 1980 number of Catholic parishioners per priest, given in columns 1 and 2, or for the 1970 and 1980 index of the national standard, given in columns 3 and 4; rounding errors account for any different results.

Table 4.3. Percentage distribution of U.S. diocesan priests age 55 and older and percentage of difference, 1966–2005, by year and diocese (rank order within region by percentage of difference)

Region and diocese	Year 1966	Year 1985	Year 2005	% difference 1966–2005
Northeast				
New England				
Burlington VT	23	49	56	143
Hartford CT	27	51	61	126
Boston MA	30	44	55	83
Norwich CT	30	50	54	80
Portland ME	38	45	52	37
Worcester MA	37	39	50	35
Fall River MA	38	36	50	32
Providence RI[a]	—	—	—	—
Middle Atlantic				
Camden NJ	12	32	61	408
Newark NJ	23	38	54	135
Buffalo NY	29	41	54	86
Rochester NY	28	39	49	75
Ogdensburg NY	28	40	45	61
Brooklyn NY	29	39	47	62
Pittsburgh PA	32	37	50	56
Albany NY	34	39	52	53
Altoona–Johnstown PA	32	42	48	50
New York NY	37	51	51	38
Rockville Centre NY	29	39	38	31
Philadelphia PA	36	40	45	25
Scranton PA	37	42	45	22
Allentown PA	47	24	36	-23
Northcentral				
East Northcentral				
Milwaukee WI	25	42	51	104
Belleville IL	25	39	49	96
Marquette MI	25	52	48	92
Rockford IL	29	39	55	90
Saginaw MI	27[b]	35	49	81
Indianapolis IN	29	34	51	76
Gaylord MI	31[c]	53	53	71
Columbus OH	27	39	42	56
Youngstown OH	28	37	42	50
La Crosse WI	24	55	36	50
Detroit MI	30[b]	42	45	50
Grand Rapids MI	32[b]	34	47	47
Cincinnati OH	31	38	43	39
Chicago IL	32	37	43	34
Cleveland OH	36	32	36	0

(continued on following page)

Table 4.3. Percentage distribution of U.S. diocesan priests age 55 and older and percentage of difference, 1966–2005, by year and diocese (continued)

Region and diocese	Year			% difference 1966–2005
	1966	1985	2005	
Northcentral (continued)				
West Northcentral				
Dodge City KS	23	53	55	139
Dubuque IA	32	59	66	106
St. Louis MO	23	37	43	87
Salina KS	29	40	54	86
New Ulm MN	28	45	51	82
Kansas City–St. Jos. MO	22	45	40	82
Sioux City IA	29	42	52	79
Des Moines IA	29	31	51	76
Fargo ND	29	58	49	69
Springfield–C. Girard. MO	28	36	40	43
St. Paul–Minneapolis MN	30	39	41	37
St. Cloud MN	27	55	37	37
Wichita KS	26	55	35	35
Rapid City SD	47	55	40	-15
Lincoln NE[a]	—	—	—	—
West				
Mountain				
Gallup NM	15[b]	29	58	287
Boise ID	23	45	53	130
Pueblo CO	19	43	37	95
Santa Fe NM	17[b]	42	33	94
Las Cruces NM	26[c]	45	49	88
Cheyenne WY	29	44	31	7
Pacific				
Baker OR	11	49	47	327
San Jose CA	31[c]	43	63	103
San Bernardino CA	23[c]	49	42	83
San Diego CA	23[b]	42	40	74
Stockton CA	29	35	50	72
Los Angeles CA	27[b]	38	40	48
Orange CA	27[c]	32	38	41
Oakland CA	37	41	48	30
San Francisco CA	31[b]	43	40	29
Monterey CA	35[d]	55	43	23
Fresno CA[a]	—	—	—	—
South				
East South[e]				
Atlanta GA	14	17	37	164
Orlando FL	18[f]	27	47	161

(continued on following page)

Table 4.3. Percentage distribution of U.S. diocesan priests age 55 and older and percentage of difference, 1966–2005, by year and diocese (continued)

Region and diocese	Year			% difference 1966–2005
	1966	1985	2005	
South (continued)				
East South[e] (continued)				
St. Petersburg FL	16[f]	35	34	113
Baltimore MD	27	36	53	96
Wilmington DE	26	55	35	35
Covington KY	23	43	31	35
West Southcentral				
Victoria TX	19[c]	58	69	263
Beaumont TX	18	30	59	228
San Antonio TX	20[b]	38	57	185
Austin TX	23	42	65	183
Galveston–Houston TX	18[b]	38	47	161
Alexandria–Shreveport LA	21	54	43	105
Lake Charles LA	29[c]	33	51	76
Baton Rouge LA	24	32	37	54
Lafayette LA	29[b]	38	42	45
Corpus Christi TX	23[b]	43	31	35
Little Rock AK	30	59	36	20
El Paso TX	27[b]	25	28	4
Dallas TX	36[g]	33	34	-6
Fort Worth TX	31[g]	28	29	-6

Sources: census counts for 1966 and moderate projection series for 1985 and 2005.

[a]Refused to participate.

[b]Divided during the census period; the percentage given is for the age distribution of the 1966 intact active population, ignoring the split. (Appendix D gives the year of the split and the numbers transferred.)

[c]Established during the census period by being divided from others in the sample; the age distribution for 1966 is that of the parent diocese(s), weighted when necessary. (See appendix D for year of establishment and parent diocese[s].)

[d]Divided in 1967. The percentage given is for the distribution of the active population as identifiable in 1966 (see appendix D).

[e]Combines the South Atlantic region and one diocese from the East Southcentral region.

[f]Established in 1968. The percentage given is for the age distribution of that year.

[g]Divided in 1969. The percentage given is for the distribution of the active population as identifiable in 1966 (see appendix D).

and 2005, along with the percentage of difference in the proportional size of that age group between 1966 and 2005. This furnishes sufficient detail to identify some major characteristics of the changing age structure. The difference scores may be interpreted as a rough indicator of speed of the aging process. The bigger the difference in the proportional size of the oldest age category over the four decades, the faster the population as a whole is shifting toward an unbalanced older age pyramid.

The aging trends in individual dioceses, when projected to the turn of the century, exhibit wide variations. A few comparisons will show the diversity. In the Middle Atlantic states, for example, the shape of Camden's age pyramid is projected to change by 408 percent, which is the biggest change in the country. The oldest age group in Camden will increase from just 12 percent of the total population of active priests in 1966 to 61 percent in 2005. At the other end of the range in that geographic region, and likewise of the national distribution, Allentown, with a difference score of −23 percent, may see its proportion of younger priests begin to grow; the proportion of oldest priests is projected to decrease from 47 percent in 1966 (the highest in the nation) to only 36 percent in 2005.

The contrasts between these two dioceses illustrate how phases of the demographic transition flow from one another and are dependent on modifications in the component parts of the process. Camden began the period with a large young-priest population, but soon diocesan ordination rates started to fall.[14] The relatively large young cohort will move through the decades and thus up through the age pyramid and, as it ages, will be replaced by relatively small younger cohorts because of falling recruitment rates. On the other hand, Allentown began the period with a relatively large old cohort of priests, which soon moved out of the age pyramid through retirement and preretirement mortality. This older cohort has been replaced by younger ones. Hence a "younging" phase has begun in Allentown and, as the data show, will be maintained throughout the period under investigation.

Conclusion

The statistics in tables 4.1 and 4.3 greatly oversimplify the intricate dynamics of aging populations during periods of sustained decline. In the following chapter we will examine how closely population pyramids at the regional and local levels follow predictable stages during the decline and aging process. The analysis is designed to provide sufficient detail on variations in the priest shortage to make the results useful, not only for further basic

14. See table 7.4.

research in organization science, but also for organizational planning.

Geographic differences in the decline and aging of the priesthood population are affected by organizational and environmental conditions. One's understanding of the differences is changed notably once these conditions are considered. Beginning with chapter 6, we attempt to disentangle them through multivariate regression analysis. When examined from this perspective a great deal of the regional and local variation evens out. Note, however, the priest shortage is better understood but not changed by this further analysis.

5 Mapping the Demographic Transition of Organizations in Decline

Population change refers to differences in population size and composition at different times (Shryock, Siegel, and Associates 1971). Unidirectional population change — either growth or decline — is inherently a transitory state with a beginning and an end. When either growth or decline is sustained over a long period, however, the population undergoes a transition or transformation (Barclay 1958; Matras 1975; see also Hernes 1976). Population transitions have important consequences to the extent that they produce major changes in size and composition.[1]

Highlights

1. The decline in the priesthood population is not a random process. It is progressing according to a definite pattern. The analysis discovers that a large, young, and growing population of diocesan priests is moving through theoretically predictable phases of transformation. The phases include, midway, an extreme stage of an old declining population and, eventually, a final stage with a pyramid reflecting a small, young, and stable population.

2. If recruitment and attrition trends of the 1980s continue unaltered, we can expect three-fourths of the dioceses in this country to reach the oldest stage of the aging process at the turn of the century. Almost two-thirds are projected to continue the demographic transition into the new century's early decades.

3. Progress of the demographic transition varies by region. The average East Northcentral, West Northcentral, and Middle Atlantic diocese should move through all five stages and New England dioceses through four stages

---

1. The analysis in this chapter draws on Schoenherr et al. 1988 and Schoenherr and Young 1990b.

of the transition. Most dioceses in the South and West should not progress beyond the first or second stage.

Theoretical Background

The most widely studied sequence of population changes, known as the demographic transition, began in the 17th century in western Europe. It resulted in population growth and eventual stability in some regions of the world but continuous and often unwelcomed growth in others. Population "explosion" became one of the overriding concerns of the modern era, prompting, for example, Malthus' celebrated essay on the topic. Matras (1975, pp. 304–5) summarizes the history of this well-known population transition as a sequence of changes marked by:

1. high mortality and high fertility ("high balance" in a relatively small population);
2. declining mortality and high fertility;
3. declining mortality and declining fertility;
4. low mortality and declining fertility;
5. low mortality and low fertility ("low balance" in a relatively large population).

The theory of the worldwide demographic transition focuses on the transition as *explanandum*. As a theory it deciphers the structure of the demographic process (see Hernes 1976) whereby a relatively small and stable societal population with high mortality and fertility is transformed into a relatively large and, eventually, stable population with low mortality and fertility. Our interest is in adapting the theory to nonbiologically reproducing organizations where fertility is replaced by recruitment and mortality by multiple decrements of resignation, sick leave, retirement, and death.

We assume the priest shortage — which, according to our data, is well underway during the second half of the 20th century — is the driving force for pervasive structural change in the Roman Catholic church. It is expedient, therefore, to understand the change process in detail. In the argot of social science model-building, if the demographic transition is to be an independent variable explaining structural change, we must examine carefully the dynamics behind it and describe precisely how it unfolds in concrete dioceses.

Thus, in previous chapters we identified and described three interrelated structural levels of a change process that is generating decline in the priesthood population. We saw that the changing parameter and output structures of priest population pyramids, along with an unchanging process structure, describe a decline process of notable force and magnitude.

We now wish to complete the descriptive analysis of the process by examining whether it progresses according to predictable stages in organizations similar to phases of the societywide demographic transition. We are also interested in how an organizational demographic transition develops under different environmental conditions. Hence, the descriptive analysis is deepened to examine other possible structural regularities and widened to gain a comparative perspective.

As a first step toward formulating a theory of the demographic transition in organizational settings, we shall examine a series of historical and projected changes in U.S. priest populations as they unfold during the period 1966–2045. Projecting an organization's professional population more than a decade or two ahead may seem a foolhardy venture, because future events are bound to intervene and change the dynamics at work. However, such a criticism overlooks the nature of analytic modeling, which is to be a what-if or how-if device. Theories always oversimplify for the sake of gaining precision. Our question, based on stable population theory embodied in life-table analysis, asks: *How* would the demographic transition of the clergy develop over several decades *if* nothing intervenes to change the dynamics currently at work?

A distinction must be made between efforts to "forecast" and those merely to "project" diocesan priest populations (Shryock, Siegel, and Associates 1971). Up to this point, and for the most part throughout our analysis, we attempt to forecast the overall size, age distribution, and individual components of diocesan clergy populations. In doing so we have designated the current (1980–84) or moderate projections as "most probable" or as a "best judgment" series. We argue that our moderate-series forecasts are the most reasonable estimates available of the extent and speed of future population change. Because of the magnitude of the decline, projections beyond the turn of the century cease to be reasonable forecasts but nevertheless continue to be useful analytic tools.

For example, the U.S. Social Security Administration finds projections made nearly a century ahead useful for long-range cost estimates of the Social Security system. Similarly, organization theorists interested in applied research must begin to understand how population projection techniques can test their what-if models when time-series data are available. The first phase of the undertaking, therefore, is to tame the independent variable after it has been corralled. Now that we have verified that the beast of population decline exists and have described its process, parameter, and output structures, we shall examine how it behaves under careful scrutiny.

Demographic Transition of Organizations in Decline

Because diocesan organizations are experiencing mostly decline, our model of the demographic transition includes a sequence of population changes different from that which characterizes the societal demographic transition. The hypothetical stages of population change in our model may be illustrated by the typical male-female pyramids used by demographers and displayed in figure 5.1. The series represents overall decline geometrically, in that the area covered by each successive pyramid is smaller than that of the previous one. The changing pattern in the length of the age-bars that are stacked on top of one another depicts the changing age structure of the population.

The triangular shape delineating the first stage of low attrition and high recruitment reflects a large, young population that is either growing slowly or is in a state of stationary stability. At this stage, recruitment must be at least as high as attrition in order for the population to maintain its characteristically young shape. Whether the youngest or the second youngest age-bar is the longest one in the pyramid depends on the average age at recruitment. To reflect these different possibilities, the two youngest age-bars are set at equal lengths in the theoretical model.

The smaller pyramid for Stage 2 assumes increasing attrition and declining recruitment. With attrition higher than recruitment, growth stops and decline begins; the smaller pyramid takes on a beehive shape, indicating an aging and declining population. Note the longest age-bar may be positioned above or below the midpoint of the pyramid depending on the exact phase the aging process has reached.

Stage 3 of the demographic transition is pictured by an inverted triangle that has shrunk further in size. The third phase of high attrition and declining recruitment produces an old and further declining population. Stage 4, which incorporates declining attrition and low recruitment assumptions, reverts to the beehive shape; it is likewise smaller, and the longest age-bar has moved downward over time and is positioned lower in the pyramid than in Stage 3. These changes show that the population is both declining and "younging." If the vital rates stabilize at an advanced stage of the young-

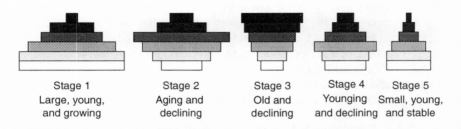

Figure 5.1. Stages of the demographic transition

ing process and remain constant over an indefinite period, the population will have entered the fifth stage of the transition.

Once the period of balance between relatively low attrition and low recruitment is sustained over time, the population will have become young again. The shape of the pyramid also returns to a normal triangle if the average age at recruitment is relatively young during the period. If, however, the average age at recruitment settles at a relatively older level, the youngest age-bar will be shorter than the one above it. Still, the position of the longest age-bar must be relatively low in a young population; the lower the longest age-bar, the younger the population.

At this end stage, the population could remain stable with regard to age composition, as long as the relationship between the vital rates remains constant. If, however, the constant crude recruitment rate were to settle at a higher level than the constant crude attrition rate, the population would start to grow and perhaps return to its former size. It would also retain its triangular shape throughout the growth period.

In the following sections, we analyze the component processes of this transformation as it would unfold over 80 years and document its consequences for changing the size and age distribution of the clergy. Analyzing the priesthood populations in eight U.S. census regions provides an overview. This is followed by analysis of the changing clergy population in each diocese in our sample.

As the historical data have shown, by the end of the census period the average diocesan presbyterate in the country had been transformed from a moderate-sized, relatively age-balanced population into a notably smaller and older population. And, as we saw in chapter 4, in the case of some dioceses, the transformation resulted in extremely smaller and older populations. According to our projections, the declining and aging trends will continue unabated into the 21st century. The model tracks the progress of the demographic transition over the last four decades of the current century and the first four decades of the next.

Stages of the Demographic Transition in U.S. Regions, 1966–2045

Although the unit of analysis is the diocese, we begin by presenting results by region for several reasons. First, regional comparisons highlight major trends in the data and serve as an overview. Second, using larger units of analysis avoids some of the noise created by data fluctuation in small diocesan priest populations. Third, explaining the findings and techniques, which are complicated by visual comparisons, is simplified by focusing on fewer cases. Furthermore, during the analysis we examined the results in all 86 cases and determined that the variation across dioceses could be reduced to five major categories, four of which are represented by differences in regional priest populations. Thus, regional analysis facilitates the explanation of a complicated serial change process and lays the foundation for the comparative exploration of local-level variations presented later.

The graphs in figures 5.2 to 5.5 permit us to examine our hypothetical model of the incidence, stages, speed, and extent of the demographic transition of the clergy. *Mutatis mutandis,* the bar graphs may be interpreted as a series of population pyramids similar to those shown in figure 5.1. Because the Roman Catholic priesthood is exclusively male, only the left side of the typical population pyramid can be constructed. To simplify graphing techniques, we present the age-bars vertically as a bar chart rather than horizontally, which is the traditional manner. The geometric forms in the figure, therefore, are male pyramids with ascending age-bars arranged vertically from left to right instead of piled horizontally from bottom to top.

The data for the 10-year age-bars that form the pyramids were aggregated from distributions based on 1-year cohorts. As a summary statistic that would conveniently and accurately describe the shape of the pyramids, we calculated the skewness of the distributions of the one-year cohorts. Skewness is an index measuring the degree to which high values of a variable are bunched either below or above the mean, rendering the distribution asymmetrical. A positively skewed distribution of age indicates that high numbers of the population are bunched in the younger and a negatively skewed distribution that they are bunched in the older age categories.

Thus a high positive value of the skewness statistic depicts a young population with a typical triangle-shaped pyramid, a high negative value depicts an old population with an inverted triangle-shaped pyramid, and low or zero values depict an aging or younging population with a diamond- or beehive-shaped pyramid. The properties of the skewness statistic make it a most useful and accurate index of the shape of the pyramid and allow us to examine our hypotheses about the demographic transition of the clergy (see Schoenherr 1967).

Careful study of the historical and projected populations in the series of pyramids displayed in figures 5.2 to 5.5 and the skewness indices of the age distributions shown in table 5.1 reveals that the demographic transition is well underway for the U.S. clergy as a whole but only in half the census regions. Dominant trends are following the process as hypothesized. In addition, similarities and differences among the eight sets of age distributions show that, although the same social forces are at work in the sample of organizations, the pattern, speed, and extent of the population

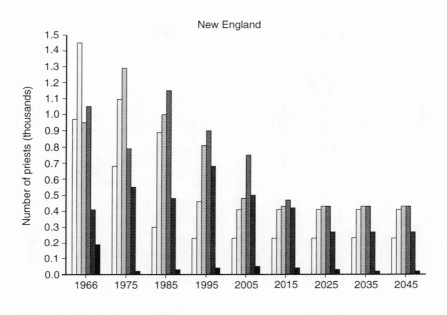

New England

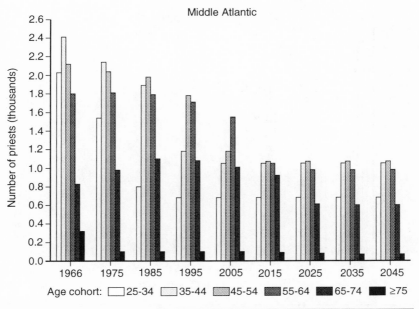

Middle Atlantic

Age cohort: ☐25-34 ☐35-44 ▨45-54 ▨55-64 ■65-74 ■≥75

Figure 5.2. Population pyramids of U.S. diocesan priests: Northeast, 1966–2045

Sources: weighted census counts for 1966 and 1975; moderate projection series for 1985–2005.

East Northcentral

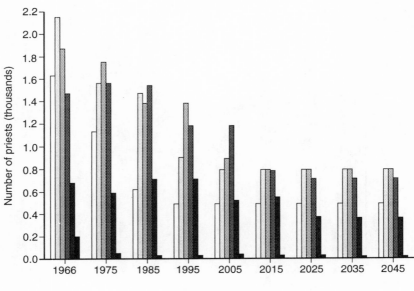

West Northcentral

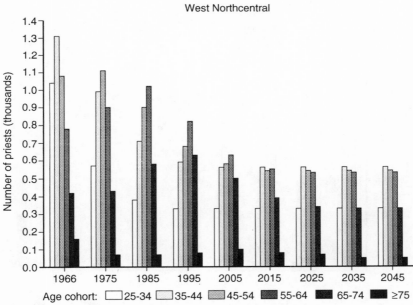

Age cohort: □ 25-34 ▨ 35-44 ▨ 45-54 ▨ 55-64 ■ 65-74 ■ ≥75

Figure 5.3. Population pyramids of U.S. diocesan priests: Northcentral, 1966–2045

Sources: weighted census counts for 1966 and 1975; moderate projection series for 1985–2005.

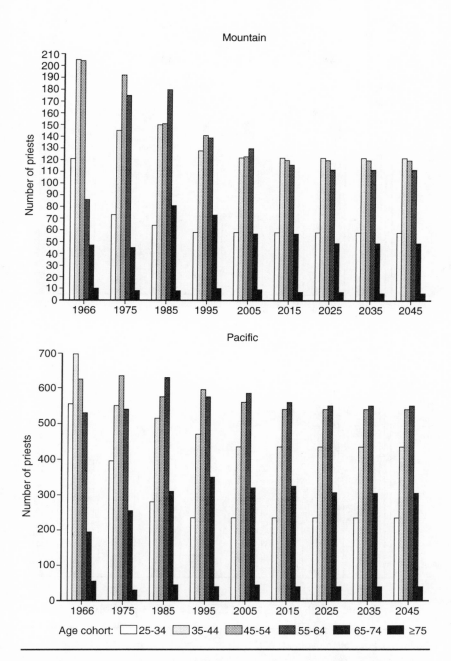

Figure 5.4. Population pyramids of U.S. diocesan priests: West, 1966–2045

Sources: weighted census counts for 1966 and 1975; moderate projection series for 1985–2005.

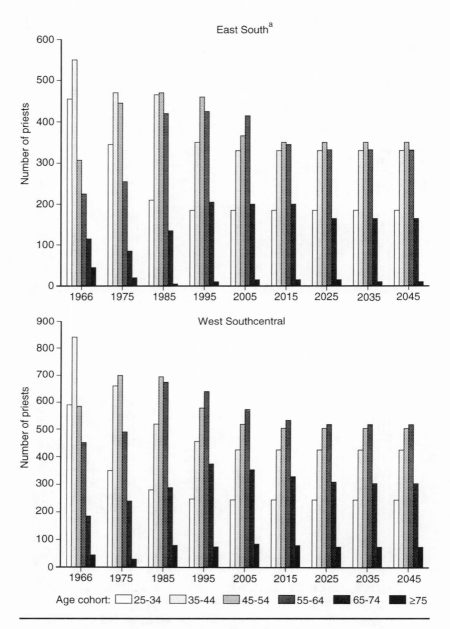

Figure 5.5. Population pyramids of U.S. diocesan priests: South, 1966–2045

Sources: weighted census counts for 1966 and 1975; moderate projection series for 1985–2005.
[a]Combines the South Atlantic region and one diocese from the East Southcentral region.

Table 5.1. Skewness and shape of population pyramids for U.S. diocesan priests, 1966–2045, by year, nation, and region

Region/nation	Year								
	1966	1975	1985	1995	2005	2015	2025	2035	2045
Skewness (in rank order for 1966)									
East South[a]	.730	.445	.088	-.046	-.053	.028	.083	.071	.072
West Northcentral	.517	.194	-.074	-.154	-.014	.088	.131	.128	.128
West Southcentral	.516	.227	.078	-.049	-.021	.005	.032	.031	.031
United States	.481	.183	.025	-.133	-.116	.002	.081	.068	.068
New England	.450	.231	-.039	-.324	-.289	-.097	.048	.030	.030
East Northcentral	.430	.082	.014	-.114	-.168	-.005	.130	.112	.112
Mountain	.427	.215	-.054	.064	.103	.124	.166	.157	.158
Middle Atlantic	.427	.215	.105	-.131	-.152	.011	.138	.127	.127
Pacific	.362	.126	.034	-.046	-.077	-.055	-.031	-.035	-.034
Shape									
Class A									
East Northcentral	+2	0	0	-1	-1	0	+1	+1	+1
West Northcentral	+2	+1	0	-1	0	0	+1	+1	+1
Middle Atlantic	+2	+1	+1	-1	-1	0	+1	+1	+1
Class B									
New England	+2	+1	0	-1	-1	0	0	0	0
United States	+2	+1	0	-1	-1	0	0	0	0
Class C (none)									
Class D									
Pacific	+2	+1	0	0	0	0	0	0	0
West Southcentral	+2	+1	0	0	0	0	0	0	0
East South[a]	+2	+2	0	0	0	0	0	0	0
Class E									
Mountain	+2	+1	0	0	+1	+1	+1	+1	+1

Sources: weighted census counts for 1966 and 1975 and moderate projection series for 1985–2045.
[a]Combines the South Atlantic region and one diocese from the East Southcentral region.

transformation is notably different in almost every region of the country.

Recall, the skewness indices in the table are based on age distributions of 1-year cohorts, although the graphs present aggregated data in 10-year age groups. Furthermore, the graphs displayed here are different from those in figures 3.8 through 3.11, in that the earlier ones reflect percentages. These give the distributions in absolute numbers to demonstrate geometrically the declining size of the population.

The 1966 bar chart for the pooled dioceses in the East South states, displayed in figure 5.5, has the highest skewness score (.730) in the entire set of 81 age distributions represented in table 5.1 and is a close example of a Stage 1 pyramid. It shows a large, young population with a characteristic triangle-shaped pyramid, except that the second age-bar is longest instead of the first. Similarly, at the beginning of the census period all the other regional populations had age distributions that were positively skewed. Although the second age-bar was longest in all of them, the configurations of age-bars — with the exception, perhaps, of the New England population shown in figure 5.2 — are close to a triangle-shaped pyramid.

Comparing values of the skewness index for each of the years reported in table 5.1, however, shows that every regional priest population registered its youngest age distribution in 1966. Thus, although some clergy populations were younger than others, all appear to have been in the launching stage of a demographic transition.

Following the changes at 10-year intervals reveals that the longest bars begin to move across each chart and thus up the age pyramid. According to the data, before the turn of the century the bar charts for each region will take on the beehive shape of the Stage 2 pyramid illustrated in figure 5.1. This is clearly indicated by the declining values of the skewness statistic. When the value of skewness approaches zero it indicates a symmetrical age distribution, which, when aggregated by 10-year age groups as in our graphs, becomes a symmetrical beehive-shaped population pyramid.

Stage 3, the oldest phase of the aging process, is evident when the pyramid takes on the shape of an inverted triangle. As figures 5.2 and 5.3 show, the inverted form appears in Northeast and Northcentral priest populations by 1995 and persists till 2005. The similarity between the contours of distributions for those years and the Stage 3 pyramid in figure 5.1 is not exact but is close enough to provide evidence for our hypothetical model.

Once again the ambiguity of the visual comparisons is removed by examining the changes in the skewness measures. For each of the four regions in the Northeast and Northcentral half of the country and for the United States as a whole, the most negatively skewed distribution appears for either the 1995 or 2005 population. Focusing on each of these locales in turn and the more negative of its two scores for these years, we see that the most negatively skewed scores in this distribution range from $-.324$ to $-.133$. These scores indicate that the longest bars or largest age cohorts are bunched toward the top of the pyramid.

The distribution for the New England region, with a skewness score of

−.324 in 1995, comes closest to resembling an inverted triangle-shaped pyramid, even though the oldest age-bar is smaller than the second oldest one. Only an extremely old population will take on the exact shape of an inverted pyramid. The New England approximation is close, and the population is the oldest one displayed in the figures.[2]

We conclude that most aged populations in organizations will only approach the inverted triangle shape, even when aging trends continue for a long time. When the aging process is both rapid and sustained, however, the extreme of Stage 3 will occur during the demographic transition. As we shall see, the pyramid in one American diocese, with a score of −.663 in 2005, closely resembles the hypothetical inverted pyramid of Stage 3.[3]

Certain regional populations reflect much less variation over time than others. For example, the data for Mountain dioceses remain positively skewed except for one short period, whereas those for Pacific dioceses are negative from 1995 to the end of the projection period. Some priest populations, however, continue to follow the phases of the transition as outlined in the model. The priest population in the Middle Atlantic states provides the clearest example of the full demographic transition. The Stage 3 inverted triangle, which is approximated by the distributions in figure 5.2 for 1995 and 2005, is transformed into a Stage 4 quasi-beehive shape when the younging process begins in 2015. The Middle Atlantic priest population continues younging, and by 2025 the pyramid begins to take on the appearance of a normal triangle shape again, signifying Stage 5. The size of the pyramid is also much smaller in successive decades in comparison to previous ones, until stability is reached about 2035, when decline stops.

The overview provided by visual comparisons of the graphs and systematic examination of skewness scores demonstrates that priest population change in different parts of the country is progressing in a variety of distinct patterns. The data presented in the bottom panel of table 5.1 simplify interpretation by sorting out the patterns of changing skewness scores. Because skewness describes the shape of the age distribution, the scores have been recoded to indicate more clearly the five hypothetical stages of the demographic transition.

Recall that differences in skewness scores are an index of changing shape only, whereas the diminishing area covered by age distributions in succes-

2. In the visual comparison we ignore the small cap (75 and over) at the top or right of the pyramid. Adding it to the 65–74 age groups would yield an even closer fit to our hypothetical model.

3. In a comparative study of Spanish dioceses, skewness scores would reach −1.27 in 1995 for several dioceses; their population pyramids perfectly match the postulated Stage 3 shape (see Schoenherr et al. 1990).

sive years reflects declining population size. So the analysis must consider both the changing size of the pyramids, by visually inspecting the distributions in the figures, and the changing shape, by examining the skewness scores in the table.

Recoded positive skewness scores of +1 represent relatively young pyramids, and those of +2, still younger ones; they reflect the shape of either Stage 1 or Stage 5, which are both triangular pyramids at the beginning and end of the population transformation. Scores of 0 indicate that pyramids are beehive-shaped and symmetrical; they exhibit either Stage 2 or Stage 4, depending on whether population size is growing or declining. Negative scores (−1 and −2) manifest old pyramids represented by the inverted triangle of Stage 3.[4]

Hypothetically, patterns of change can fall into five classes, one for each stage of the demographic transition. As the table demonstrates, pyramids in Class A pass through all five phases. Those in Class B cover four stages; Class D, two stages; Class E, only one stage of the transition. Class C is not represented, because no regional population is projected to cover only three stages during the transition period; but, as we shall see, certain diocesan populations fall into Class C.

Class A Transitions

Thus, according to the recoded skewness measures, in Class A transitions an approximately symmetrical Stage 2 pyramid (code 0) appears among the changing distributions for the East Northcentral region by 1975 and lasts for at least a decade. So the demographic transition was occurring faster in that region than anywhere else in the country, as comparison of the data in column 2 for all three classes proves. Stage 2 appears in West Northcentral dioceses by 1985. The pyramid for Middle Atlantic states passes through Stage 2 sometime between 1985 and 1995, but the year is not captured by our analysis.[5]

After reaching the symmetry of Stage 2, the populations begin aging toward Stage 3. The smaller inverted triangle shape (code −1), begins to appear in all three regions by 1995 and, except for the West Northcentral region, continues to manifest the inverted triangle shape into the 21st century.

4. The following coding scheme was used: $-2 =$ skewness LT $-.35$; $-1 =$ skewness GE $-.35$ and LT $-.10$; $0 =$ skewness GE $-.10$ and LT $.10$; $+1 =$ skewness GE $.10$ and LT $.35$; $+2 =$ skewness GE $.35$. Similar coding was used by Schoenherr (1967) for organization hierarchies.

5. We computed skewness for distributions at 10-year intervals; if we had done so for 1-year intervals, the exact year would have been recorded.

The younging process begins during the next 10 years and, by 2015, beehive-shaped pyramids (code 0), which are close replicas of the Stage 4 pyramid in figure 5.1, once again characterize all the Class A distributions. The younging process changes the population back to a symmetrical distribution, which continues for a decade, except in the West Northcentral area, where the beehive shape begins earlier and lasts longer.

All age distributions displayed from 1985 onward are the result of a constant set of attrition and recruitment assumptions, which we incorporated to test the implications of stable population theory. The data show that Class A pyramids reach stability six decades after the demographic transition begins: the skewness measures are constantly changing during the period from 1966 to 2015 but then remain fixed at the same code from 2025 to 2045. The skewness index for the 2045 populations — the end point of the transition — ranges from .112 to .128 (code +1). These scores indicate that the transition process stops short before returning to as young a pyramid in Stage 5 as existed in Stage 1, when the 1966 scores ranged from .427 to .517 (code +2).

An observable triangle-shaped pyramid, characterizing a young Stage 5 population (code +2), does not appear in any regional pyramid under moderate assumptions by 2045. This is partly because the average recruitment age in the later decades of the model would be relatively high owing to a rising average age at ordination and the influx of incardinations at older ages.[6] The final size and age composition of the diocesan priest populations continues without alteration so long as the attrition and recruitment assumptions remain unchanged.

Class B Transitions
Class B distributions contain the central tendencies captured by the national average. Population pyramids for the New England region and the nation as a whole begin the process as predicted (with code +2 in 1966) but do not change beyond Stage 4 (code 0). The fourth phase represents the younging process, which starts in 2015 after Stage 3 runs its course. The age pyramid of the national and New England priest populations continues unchanged, remaining in Stage 4 during the last four decades of the transition period.

Class C Transitions
No regional priest population stops in Stage 3 of its demographic transition.

6. We would observe Stage 5 pyramids if the distributions were based on tenure or number of years in the organization rather than on biological age.

Class D Transitions

For priest populations in the Pacific and in both regions of the South the aging process begins with young pyramids in 1966 (code +2). Population change along the West Coast and in the South reaches Stage 2 of the transition in 1985, as it does in most other areas of the country. Unlike the change process elsewhere, however, the transition in these regions is arrested in Stage 2. Hence, the distributions become somewhat older but, given whatever unique conditions affect them, priest populations in those areas do not continue aging.

Class E Transitions

The priest population in Mountain states likewise starts as a young triangle-shaped pyramid, moves to Stage 2 by 1985, but then reverts to a Stage 1 population by 2005. The aging process in Mountain dioceses is transformed to a younging process without passing through Stage 3, the phase of advanced aging characterized by an inverted triangle shape (code −1 or −2). Hence, according to the data, the Mountain population returns to Stage 1 and continues relatively unchanged through 2045. Except for a slight aging trend lasting about one decade, aging dynamics in the Mountain region remain relatively stable over the entire period. In effect, the age pyramid hardly leaves the launching phase of the demographic transition.[7]

Discussion

How young they are at the beginning of the transition does not explain why age pyramids in West and South regions hardly age at all in comparison to other regional priest populations. Pyramids at opposite ends of the range of the skewness variable both belong to Class D transitions. Scores in the top section of the table, which are in rank order for 1966, show that the age distribution in the East South priest population was skewed most (.730) and the pyramid in the Pacific Coast population least (.362). This indicates the former was the youngest and the latter the oldest regional age pyramid in the country at the time. Nevertheless, neither of them advance beyond Stage 2 of the demographic transition. These regions are not experiencing notable aging because they are not undergoing rapid decline, as chapter 3 has shown.

Differences in the speed and extent of the demographic transition across regions are highlighted by sharp contrasts between Class A and B transi-

---

7. Strictly speaking, this population moves to Stage 2, which we consider a minor phase in the overall transition. But because this stage is both minor and brief, we prefer to emphasize that, for the most part, Class E populations reside in only one stage of the transition.

tions prevalent in the Northeast and Northcentral divisions and Class D and E transitions dominant in the South and West. Undoubtedly, wide variation among classes of transitions at the regional level is related to contrasting recruitment and/or retention experiences in different dioceses, which are described and analyzed in later chapters.

Stages of the Demographic Transition in Local Priest Populations, 1966–2045

Because of the intricacy of the change process and relatively large number of cases in our sample, exploring the variety of species in the jungle of demographic transitions presents a daunting challenge. Fortunately, use of the analytic techniques devised for the regional analysis greatly reduces the complexity.

In our analysis, we attempt to provide sufficient information concerning the demographic transition in order to advance basic research in organizational science and also to facilitate organizational planning. Adapting to change is hard under any circumstances, but planning for the organizational consequences of rapid decline and aging of key personnel is exceptionally difficult.

Our aim, therefore, is to specify the pattern the demographic transition has taken or will most likely take in each of the sampled dioceses. The hypothetical model summarized in figure 5.1 and the coding scheme introduced in table 5.1 enable us to categorize diocesan demographic transitions into five classes, albeit with a few subclasses. The full transition follows five predictable phases. During periods of sustained decline, a population pyramid moves in stages from one that is large, young, and growing, to aging and declining, to old and declining, to younging and declining, and finally to one that is small, young, and stable. Codes ranging from $+2$ to -2 identify the stages of the transition.

Table 5.2 presents results of coding the changing shape of the age pyramid for each diocese while it progresses through hypothetical stages from 1966 to 2045. Recall that only the changes during the first two decades are based on historical data, and those for the remainder of the period are grounded in our moderate projection series. Once again, the projected changes result from our what-if experiment: *What* would the demographic transition look like *if* the priest population in each diocese actually were to change as forecasted? The transition will occur as described only if trends continue as assumed by our projection model.

Table 5.2 introduces subclasses within classes. These are used to reflect roughly the speed and consistency with which the population moves across stages. Thus, the dioceses in Subclass A-1 follow the stages of the transi-

Table 5.2. Stages of the demographic transition, 1966–2045, by year, class, and diocese (recoded skewness scores; rank order within subclass by speed and consistency of movement through stages)

Subclass and diocese	Year								
	1966	1975	1985	1995	2005	2015	2025	2035	2045
Class A									
A-1									
Wichita KS	+2	0	-2	0	+2	+1	+1	+1	+1
La Crosse WI	+2	0	-2	-1	+1	+1	+1	+1	+1
Alexandria–Shreveport LA	+2	+1	-1	-2	0	+1	+1	+1	+1
Dubuque IA	+2	+1	-1	-2	-2	-1	+1	+1	+1
Rockford IL	+2	+2	0	-2	-1	+1	+1	+1	+1
Fall River MA	+2	+1	0	-2	-1	0	+1	+1	+1
Sioux City IA	+2	+1	0	-2	-1	0	+1	+1	+1
A-2									
Marquette MI	+2	-1	-1	0	0	+1	+1	+1	+1
Santa Fe NM	+2[a]	+1	-1	+1	+1	+1	+1	+1	+1
St. Cloud MN	+2	+1	-1	-1	+1	+1	+1	+1	+1
Kansas City–St. Jos. MO	+2	+1	-1	0	+1	+1	+1	+1	+1
Rochester NY	+2	0	0	-1	-1	0	+1	+1	+1
Indianapolis IN	+2	0	0	-1	-1	0	+1	+1	+1
Milwaukee WI	+2	+1	0	-1	-1	0	+1	+1	+1
Buffalo NY	+2	+1	0	-1	-1	0	+1	+1	+1
Brooklyn NY	+2	+1	0	-1	-1	0	+1	+1	+1
Albany NY	+2	+2	+1	-1	-1	0	+1	+1	+1
Baltimore MD	+2	+1	+1	-1	-1	-1	+1	+1	+1
Belleville IL	+2	+1	+1	0	-1	0	+1	+1	+1
Grand Rapids MI	+1[a]	+1	+2	0	-1	0	+1	+1	+1
Cincinnati OH	+2	0	+1	0	-1	0	+1	+1	+1
A-3									
Little Rock AK	+1	-1	-1	0	+2	+1	+1	+1	+1
Fargo ND	+1	-1	-1	-1	0	+1	+1	+1	+1
Cheyenne WY	+1	0	-1	+1	+2	+1	+1	+1	+1
New Ulm MN	+1	0	0	-1	0	+2	+1	+1	+1
Chicago IL	+1	0	+1	0	-1	0	+1	+1	+1
Class B									
B-1									
Baker OR	+2	-1	-2	-1	0	0	0	+2	0
Burlington VT	+2	+1	-1	-2	-2	0	0	0	0
Hartford CT	+2	+1	-1	-2	-2	-1	0	0	0
Boston MA	+2	+1	0	-2	-1	0	+1	0	0
Des Moines IA	+2	+2	+1	-2	-2	-1	0	0	0
Camden NJ	+2	+2	+1	-2	-2	-1	0	0	0
Stockton CA	+1	+1	+2	0	-2	0	0	0	0

(continued on following page)

Table 5.2. Stages of the demographic transition, 1966–2045, by year, class, and diocese (continued)

Subclass and diocese	Year								
	1966	1975	1985	1995	2005	2015	2025	2035	2045
Class B (continued)									
B-2									
Pueblo CO	+2	-1	-1	0	-1	-1	0	0	0
San Diego CA	+2[a]	0	-1	-1	-1	0	0	0	0
Youngstown OH	+2	+1	-1	-1	-1	0	0	0	0
Covington KY	+2	+2	-1	0	+1	0	0	0	0
Columbus OH	+2	0	0	-1	-1	0	0	0	0
Detroit MI	+2[a]	0	0	-1	-1	0	0	0	0
Boise ID	+2	0	0	-1	-1	0	0	0	0
Salina KS	+2	+1	0	-1	-1	-1	0	0	0
Worcester MA	+2	+1	+1	-1	-1	0	0	0	0
Orlando FL	+2[d]	+2	+1	-1	-1	0	0	0	0
Saginaw MI	+2[a]	+1	0	0	-1	-1	0	0	0
Las Cruces NM	+2[b]	+1	0	+1	-1	0	0	0	0
San Antonio TX	+2[a]	+1	+2	0	-1	0	0	0	0
Beaumont TX	+2	+1	+2	0	-1	-1	0	0	0
B-3									
Rapid City SD	+1	-1	-1	0	+1	0	0	0	0
New York NY	+1	0	-1	-1	-1	0	0	0	0
Gaylord MI	+1[b]	+1	-1	-1	0	0	0	0	0
Portland ME	+1	+1	-1	-1	-1	-1	0	0	0
Pittsburgh PA	+1	+1	+1	0	-1	-1	0	0	0
Oakland CA	0	0	+1	0	-1	-1	0	0	0
Class C									
C-1									
Monterey CA	+2[c]	-1	-1	0	-1	-1	0	0	-2
Corpus Christi TX	+2[a]	+1	-1	-2	-1	-1	-1	-1	-1
Victoria TX	+2[b]	+1	-1	-2	-2	-2	-1	-1	-1
Newark NJ	+2	+1	0	-2	-2	-1	-1	-1	-1
Austin TX	+2	+2	0	-2	-2	-1	-1	-1	-1
San Jose CA	+2[b]	+1	0	-1	-2	-2	-2	-2	-2
C-2									
San Bernardino CA	+2[b]	0	-1	-1	0	-1	-1	-1	-1
Galveston–Houston TX	+2[a]	+1	0	-1	-1	-1	-1	-1	-1
St. Petersburg FL	+2[d]	+1	0	0	0	0	-1	-1	-1
C-3									
Dodge City KS	+1	0	-1	-1	-1	-1	-1	-1	-1
Norwich CT	+1	+1	-1	-1	-1	-1	-1	-1	-1

(continued on following page)

Table 5.2. Stages of the demographic transition, 1966–2045, by year, class, and diocese (continued)

Subclass and diocese	Year								
	1966	1975	1985	1995	2005	2015	2025	2035	2045

Class D									
D-1									
San Francisco CA	+2[a]	+1	0	0	0	0	0	0	0
Rockville Centre NY	+2	+1	0	0	0	0	0	0	0
St. Paul–Mineapolis MN	+2	+2	0	0	0	0	0	0	0
Lake Charles LA	+1[b]	+1	+2	0	0	0	0	0	0
Orange CA	+2[b]	+1	+1	+1	0	0	0	0	0
Dallas TX	+1[e]	+1	+2	+1	+1	0	0	0	0
D-2									
Scranton PA	+1	0	0	0	0	0	+1	+1	+1
Philadelphia PA	+1	0	+1	0	0	0	+1	+1	+1
Springfield–C. Girard. MO	+1	0	+1	+1	0	0	+1	0	0
D-3									
Lafayette LA	+1[a]	+1	0	0	0	+1	+1	+1	+1
Los Angeles CA	+2[a]	+1	0	0	0	+1	+1	+1	+1
Altoona–Johnstown PA	+2	+1	+1	0	0	0	+1	+1	+1
St. Louis MO	+2	+2	+1	0	0	0	+1	+1	+1

Class E									
E-1									
Atlanta GA	+2	+2	+2	+1	+1	+1	+2	+1	+1
E-2									
Allentown PA	0	+1	+2	+1	+1	+1	+1	+1	+1
Fort Worth TX	+2[e]	0	+1	+1	+2	+2	+2	+2	+2
El Paso TX	+2[a]	+1	+1	0	+1	+1	+1	+1	+1
E-3									
Baton Rouge LA	+1	+2	+1	0	0	+1	+1	+1	+1
Ogdensburg NY	+2	+1	+1	0	0	+1	+1	+1	+1
Cleveland OH	+2	+1	+1	+1	0	0	+1	+1	+1
Wilmington DE	+2	+1	+1	+1	0	0	+1	+1	+1

Sources: census counts for 1966 and 1975 and moderate projection series for 1985–2045.

[a]Divided during the census period; the code given is for the age distribution of the 1966 intact active population, ignoring the split. (Appendix D gives the year of the split and the numbers transferred.)

[b]Established during the census period by being divided from others in the sample; the population pyramid for 1966 is that of the parent diocese(s), weighted when necessary. (See appendix D for year of establishment and parent diocese[s].)

[c]Divided in 1967; the code given is for the distribution of the active population as identifiable in 1966 (see appendix D).

[d]Established in 1968; the code given is for the population distribution of that year.

[e]Divided in 1969; the code given is for the distribution of the active population as identifiable in 1966 (see appendix D).

tion as hypothesized more consistently than those in Subclass A-2 and the latter more consistently than those in Subclass A-3. The same ordering of consistency is followed in the subclasses of Classes B through E.

The dioceses are also ordered within subclasses according to the speed with which they move from one *major* stage to the next. The first, third, and fifth stages are considered major and the second and fourth are considered minor. Movement from one stage to the next occurs most quickly in those dioceses at the top of each subclass and most slowly in those listed at the bottom.[8]

Class A Transitions

The top section of the table reveals that about three-tenths of the dioceses would pass through all five stages if moderate trends were to continue to 2045. Those in Subclasses A-1 and A-2 begin with notably young age pyramids in 1966 (code +2), whereas those in A-3 start their transitions with somewhat older populations (code +1). Additionally, dioceses in Subclass A-1 are transformed into notably old populations when they reach Stage 3 (code −2), whereas those in Subclasses A-2 and A-3 are not quite as old in their third stage (code −1).

Marquette, Little Rock, and Fargo plunge into the transition immediately and, by 1975, are among the first in the sample to register a Stage 3 pyramid, which is old and declining. Note, their priest populations pass through Stage 2 sometime between 1966 and 1975. But since we did not calculate annual scores, the actual years are not captured by the data presented.

A Stage 2 aging and declining population (code 0) appears in Wichita and La Crosse by 1975, in Alexandria–Shreveport and Dubuque sometime between 1975 and 1985, and in the remaining Subclass A-1 dioceses by 1985. A similar pattern is followed in Subclass A-2 dioceses, except the last three in the group — Belleville, Grand Rapids, and Cincinnati — do not reach Stage 2 until 1995. In Subclass A-3 transitions, two of the five dioceses shift into

---

8. When the criteria conflict, the diocese is listed according to rank order of the speed of its transition. Thus, Monterey, for example, appears at the top of Subclass C-1 because it is first in that group to move from Stage 1 to Stage 3. On the basis of consistency, however, it would be listed last, because it fluctuates in and out of Stages 2 and 3, which is a pattern inconsistent with the hypothetical model. In general, the small diocesan populations, of which Monterey is an example, are more inconsistent in following the hypothesized phases of the transition than the large ones. Recall, the same is true with regard to projection models. Trends in small populations tend to fluctuate a great deal, so their projection results are inconsistent. That is to say, the spread between the optimistic and pessimistic curves is extremely wide (see our discussion of correcting for wild fluctuations in appendix E).

Stage 2 sometime between 1966 and 1975 and the other three by 1975.

As they move beyond the symmetry of Stage 2, the populations continue the aging trend. The vast majority of dioceses in Class A transitions reach Stage 3 before the turn of the century. Only Belleville, Grand Rapids, Cincinnati, and Chicago are delayed until 2005 in entering the middle phase of the transition.

Santa Fe and Cheyenne are first to move into Stage 4, which begins the younging process after the populations have passed through the oldest phase of the transition. At some point between 1985 and 1995 the populations in these dioceses are once again characterized by beehive-shaped pyramids (code 0), but they are smaller in size than during previous phases. Wichita, Marquette, Kansas City–St. Joseph, and Little Rock reach Stage 4 by 1995. And La Crosse, St. Cloud, Fargo, and New Ulm are in the Stage 4 younging process by 2005. The remaining dioceses in Class A do not reach Stage 4 until 2015, except for Dubuque and Baltimore, where it occurs a little later; these last two dioceses are characterized by younging and declining populations sometime between 2015 and 2025.

An observable triangle-shaped pyramid characterizing a young Stage 5 population is coded +2. A full Stage 5, therefore, does not appear in the vast majority of the dioceses. As the data show, even for the Class A dioceses, the demographic transition ends in a mitigated Stage 5 (code +1). Thus, in all the priest populations except for Wichita, Little Rock, Cheyenne, and New Ulm (along with Baker in the Class B transitions) the transition process stops short before returning to as young a pyramid in Stage 5 as existed in Stage 1. Note, too, in the last five dioceses mentioned the very young population (code +2) is not stable, but appears briefly and then becomes somewhat older (code +1) before it stabilizes.[9]

In two dioceses, Santa Fe and Cheyenne, the mitigated Stage 5 is reached as early as 1995, or only three decades after the demographic transition begins. For the largest number of dioceses in Class A, however, the fifth and final phase of a small, young, and stable population is entered by 2025, which is six decades after the transition begins.

9. Nine of 10 Spanish priest populations, which we compared with 10 matched U.S. dioceses in a cross-national analysis, fall into the category of Class A demographic transitions (Schoenherr et al. 1990). One of the Spanish dioceses, however, completes the full five stages of its transition as hypothesized. The priest population there begins Stage 1 with a skewness of .59 in 1975 (it is still growing and younging between 1966 and 1975) and ends the transition by entering Stage 5 with a score of .58 in 2025, but begins aging slightly before stabilizing at a score of .48 in 2035. This is the most complete and one of the fastest organizational demographic transitions recorded by our cross-national data. If this Spanish priest population were to continue aging at the rate observed from 1975 to 1985, it would pass through all five hypothesized stages of its demographic transition in only half a century.

Despite variations in speed and slight inconsistencies resulting mainly from erratic fluctuations in small dioceses, 31 percent of the populations probably complete all five stages of the transition. They move from relatively large, young, and growing populations of priests through theoretically predictable phases of transition, which midway include a stage depicting an old declining population, and eventually reach a final stage with a pyramid reflecting a relatively small, young, and stable population.

Class B Transitions

The second panel of table 5.2 shows that an additional three-tenths of the dioceses would pass through four stages if the moderate forecast were to hold true until 2045. Similar to dioceses undergoing Class A transitions, those in Subclasses B-1 and B-2 all begin with notably young age pyramids in 1966, whereas those in B-3 start their transitions with slightly older populations.[10] Likewise, when they reach Stage 3 (code -2) dioceses in Subclass B-1 are transformed into older populations than those in Subclasses B-2 and B-3 (code -1).

Baker, Pueblo, and Rapid City are aging fastest among the dioceses in Class B transitions. They pass through Stage 2 sometime after 1966. By 1975 they enter Stage 3, the oldest phase of the transition. The other dioceses in Class B likewise follow the pattern, and in successive decades from 1985 to 2015 all enter Stage 3. The priest populations start younging after the turn of the century. By 2015 all of them enter Stage 4. Except for an inconsistency in Baker and another in Boston, all the transitions stabilize by 2025. They remain fixed in Stage 4 without returning to as young a population at the end as at the beginning of the period.

Class C Transitions

In the next panel of table 5.2 we find that a small group of dioceses, about 13 percent, experience only the first three stages of the demographic transition. Just like dioceses that undergo four or five stages, however, those in Subclasses C-1 and C-2 all begin with notably young-age pyramids in 1966, whereas the two dioceses in C-3 start their transitions with somewhat older populations. In keeping with the rank ordering used for Class A and B transitions, dioceses in Subclass C-1 are likewise transformed into noticeably older populations when they reach Stage 3 than those in Subclasses C-2 and C-3.

Of all Class C transitions, the Diocese of Monterey begins the aging process most quickly. It passes through Stage 2 soon after the end of the

---

10. Stockton is an exception but is included in Subclass B-1 because code $+2$ appears in 1985.

Second Vatican Council and enters Stage 3 by 1975. Monterey's is a very small priest population, so the age distribution fluctuates in and out of Stages 2 and 3 for the remainder of the projection period. The rest of the dioceses in Class C, except for St. Petersburg, shift into the oldest phase by 1995; St. Petersburg experiences a much slower aging process and arrives at Stage 3 as late as 2025. Once the populations age to the level of Stage 3, the change process halts and the pyramids remain stable in size and shape for as long as the trends underlying our moderate projection series continue unaltered.

Class D Transitions

The populations in Class D, which represent 15 percent of the sample, experience only two phases of the transition. The dioceses in Subclass D-1 follow the first two phases but then remain in Stage 2 permanently. No further change occurs, because the populations have stabilized. Those in Subclasses D-2 and D-3 are less consistent. After aging to the Stage 2 level, the populations start younging and move back to Stage 1, remaining in it for one or more decades. What distinguishes Subclass D-2 from D-3 is that populations in D-2 remain in Stage 2 longer overall than those in D-3. Indeed, the shorter the time in Stage 2, the more questionable it is whether any notable measure of aging has actually occurred — at least any that would have noticeable organizational consequences.

Class E Transitions

Only 9 percent of the dioceses witness no change or very minimal change in their priest population pyramids while the moderate projection series runs its course. The bottom panel of the table reveals that Atlanta's age distribution changes least, fluctuating only twice from a very young to a moderately young population. The three dioceses in Subclass E-2 record some fleeting aging of their priest populations. The pyramids in that subclass take on the characteristic symmetry of Stage 2, but the transition phase lasts for the shortest observable period possible. Likewise, those in Subclass E-3 move out of the youngest phase only briefly and then revert back to it, though the beehive shape of Stage 2 appears for a period twice as long as in E-2. By and large, however, dioceses in Class E are spared the aging trends intrinsic to the demographic transition of the clergy.

Different Projection Models

After analyzing the effect of the moderate assumptions on changing population size and age structure in individual dioceses, we also checked the impact of our optimistic and pessimistic assumptions (although we do not show the optimistic and pessimistic models here). We discovered that dioceses would undergo a demographic transition similar to the process revealed under the moderate assumptions. Obviously, however, under optimistic assumptions the populations are larger in size and under pessimistic assumptions they are smaller than under moderate assumptions.

We also observed that when using either optimistic or pessimistic assumptions changes are accentuated. Thus, in some dioceses the populations projected under pessimistic assumptions more strongly resemble an inverted triangle-shaped pyramid when they reach their oldest distributions in Stage 3 and a truer normal triangle shape when they return to a young distribution in Stage 5 than those we project under the moderate assumptions.

In the pessimistic model, the demographic transition in American dioceses behaves in a fashion similar to the decline and aging process in Spanish dioceses when the latter populations are projected under moderate assumptions. In 10 Spanish dioceses, priest populations decline in size more rapidly and so age much more quickly than those in a matched set of 10 United States dioceses (Schoenherr et al. 1990). We may conclude, therefore, that our demographic transition model is robust, since it holds true not only under different projection assumptions but also across national boundaries.

Conclusion

We now have a working knowledge of the speed, stages, and duration of a complex population transition underway in the U.S. Catholic priesthood.[11] The empirical models exhibit a full range of the extent to which local clergy populations will undergo a demographic transition. Dioceses can be classified in descending order from Class A transitions, all of which are expected to run the gamut of decline and aging in priest populations, to Class E, most of which are expected to decline in size but remain practically unchanged in age composition.

If recruitment and attrition trends of the early 1980s continue unaltered for just two decades, we can expect three-fourths of the dioceses in this country to reach the most extreme stage of the aging process by the turn of the century.[12] Each phase has its problems, but Stage 3 is probably the most critical, because it represents the most top-heavy, or oldest, pyramid.

11. Our analysis is preliminary and has focused primarily on the development of a formal theory of the demographic transition in organizational populations experiencing decline in membership. The next step in the analysis, which lies beyond the scope of this book, is the further testing and development of the theory through the application of more rigorous statistical tools.

12. This proportion includes 31 percent of the populations in Class A, 32 percent in Class B, and an additional 13 percent in Class C transitions.

Dioceses in Class C, therefore, may face unusual difficulties. Class C priest populations are projected to stabilize in Stage 3 by the turn of the century and remain old for as long as the moderate projection trends are operative.

In addition to clarifying how much change to expect, the analysis also provides a rough estimate of how fast the stages of the demographic transition will unfold and how long they will last. Thus, dioceses are rank ordered within Classes A, B, and C by the speed with which their priest populations pass from Stage 1 to Stage 3.

With the help of table 5.2, personnel planners in each diocese can identify the approximate years when the transition process will change the population from a young, to an aging, and then to an old pyramid. This knowledge is valuable for policy and planning. For example, various assignments and promotions in an organization are tied to career stages. Career stages, in turn, are linked to age and seniority, such that the age distribution of the work force inevitably constrains the promotion and replacement process. Foreknowledge of how fast the age distribution is changing and how long each stage will last should help planners meet the demographic constraints when they occur.

The speed and staging of population change varies across regions and within regions from one diocese to another. Differences in the timing and development of the demographic transition are rooted in a tangle of organizational and environmental conditions. In chapter 6 and subsequent chapters we try to untangle some of the major causes of these variations.

6   Explaining Local Variation

The descriptive analysis of change in the U.S. priesthood has provided a picture of the demographic transition in rough brush strokes. The clergy population is steadily decreasing and aging, more rapidly in one half of the country than the other. Diocesan presbyterates in the Northeast and Northcentral divisions are declining by almost 50 percent compared with only a 15–20 percent decline for those in the South and West. The number of parishioners per priest is relentlessly growing, much more swiftly in the West than elsewhere.

Why such large differences in a supposedly homogeneous population of organizations? Are South and West dioceses becoming a subspecies of American Catholicism, recruiting and retaining priests through mechanisms that are substantially different from those operating elsewhere?

Although "species" can be applied to groups of organizations only after adjusting for obvious differences between them and biological organisms (Young 1988), it is nevertheless a useful concept for organizational analysis (McKelvey and Aldrich 1983; Perrow 1986). The gradual transformation of groups of dioceses into distinct subspecies may reflect a trend toward loose coupling in the Roman Catholic monolith. To the extent the Catholic church is a loosely coupled system, a perturbation — as cataclysmic as losing half of its professional work force — in one of its component parts will not reverberate throughout the entire system (Weick 1976). Thus, part of U.S. Catholicism, such as dioceses in the South and West, could remain locally stable while others in the Northeast and Northcentral divisions are undergoing demographic change and structural transformation.

In this chapter we analyze local variations in clergy decline by examining the causal influence of a number of environmental and organizational conditions. We develop two models to explain variation in the supply of priests and the demand for priestly services. First, we present a time-series

117

model assessing conditions that account for variation in the growth and decline of diocesan priest populations between 1970 and 1980. Second, in a cross-sectional model of supply and demand, we explain local variation in the ratio of parishioners to priests in 1980. Throughout the analysis we are interested in whether the impact of geographic location, ecological niche, and organizational structure provide evidence of subspecies development or loose coupling within the American Catholic church.

Highlights

1. The results of the first causal model show that clergy decline in the West is not so different from that on the East Coast once rapid growth in church membership in the West and slow growth on the East Coast are taken into account.[1]

2. In the second explanatory model we find that parishioners living along the Pacific Coast and in the West Southcentral states are probably the most disadvantaged in the country because of the priest shortage, both before and after taking environmental conditions into account. Those residing in the Northeast and West Northcentral states tend to be the most advantaged, especially after considering environmental constraints.

3. The active clergy population is growing in some dioceses because the Catholic population is relatively large and growing, or the parishioner-to-priest ratio is expanding in others because the Hispanic population is relatively large. When the impact of environmental conditions is removed through statistical techniques, however, dioceses are seen to vary little from one another with regard to the laity's access to priests. The exception: East Coast dioceses enjoy some advantage over all others.

A Model Explaining Clergy Growth and Decline

Our first model focuses on the internal economy of diocesan organizations, specifically, change in the supply of priests between 1970 and 1980. To focus the issue we limit the data set to a few key longitudinal measures: geographic region, Catholic population size and priest population size in 1970, and Catholic population growth and priest population growth between 1970 and 1980.[2] The number of explanatory elements we include in the model

1. The term "East Coast" refers mainly to dioceses in the Middle Atlantic and South Atlantic regions and, to a lesser extent because it is represented by only one diocese in the sample, the East Southcentral region.
2. In chapters 6–11 we use the terms "Catholics" and "Catholic population" to refer to active church members or parishioners rather than to those who profess a preference for Roman Catholicism. In chapter 12 we focus on all those who claim Catholicism as their religious preference.

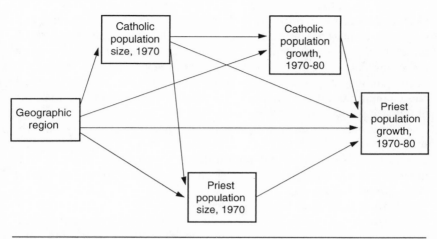

Figure 6.1. Model of demographic change, 1970–80

depend not only on substantive relevance but also on availability of data for two points in time.[3]

The simple model addresses an obvious yet crucial question: What effects do changes in the environmental resource pool have on growth or decline of the work force in an organization? That is to say, how does the absolute and changing size of the Catholic population, the major resource pool of dioceses, impact growth or decline of the priest population? Further, are these effects influenced by geographic location? Does the evidence show that regional churches are loosely coupled with one another?

Time-Series Regression Model

Because the model that addresses these questions includes a time factor, it is an appropriate test of the effects of change. Figure 6.1 presents the model graphically. As the arrows indicate, we posit no causal relationship between priest population size in 1970 and Catholic population growth from 1970 to 1980; otherwise each variable is assumed to have a possible direct and indirect causal relationship with each variable to its right.

Geographic region is the predetermined physical and social context in which all human interaction occurs, thus, it logically precedes all causal

3. Creating the dependent variable, change in the number of priests, is costly, as we explain in an expanded version of appendix A. Likewise, procedures for obtaining census data for other longitudinal variables and aggregating them by diocese are very labor intensive, so we had to rely on readily available data sources.

processes affecting organizations like Catholic dioceses. For a couple reasons we assume that Catholic population size has a direct effect on priest population size and an indirect effect, through priest population size, on priest population growth. First, recruitment of new priests depends on the size of the seminary candidate pool, which is determined by the absolute and changing number of males in the Catholic population. Second, the initial size of the Catholic population has a direct impact on how much it would grow or decline during the 1970s, since we are dealing with absolute numbers in both variables.[4] We also assume that part of the influence of the 1970 Catholic population size on priest population growth is mediated by Catholic population growth, as its indirect path through the latter variable indicates.

Likewise, the size of the priest population in 1970 largely governs the magnitude of change in its size between 1970 and 1980, because the measures are in absolute numbers; hence, it is entered between region and priest population growth. We assume the size of the priest population in 1970 has little if any effect, however, on growth of the Catholic population during the decade. The dynamics of population growth for biologically reproducing groups depend directly on fertility, migration, and mortality rates. To be sure, fertility may be influenced by religious beliefs and values. We assume, though, that the degree to which religious beliefs and values about fertility are operative among Catholics does not depend on the absolute size of the local clergy population.

To test the model we examine relationships among the variables in 85 dioceses.[5] The time period covers 1970–80 rather than 1966–84 (the period covered by our clergy census), because comparable data from the Glenmary Research Center are available only for those years.[6] (The measures are defined and their data sources identified in appendix C.)

Descriptive Overview

Table 6.1 shows how dioceses differ across regions in the conditions represented in the model.[7] In 1970, the largest Catholic populations, on the

4. For example, an increase of 10 in a population of 100 is equivalent to an increase of 100 in a population of 1,000.

5. One case, Gallup, is omitted here and in all subsequent analytic models, because scores on dependent variables and several independent variables are so deviant; the percentage of growth in clergy population from 1970 to 1980 in Gallup, for example, is 7.8 standard deviations from the mean.

6. At the time of writing, data from the 1970 U.S. census, which would allow us to test more complicated models of priest population growth, were not incorporated into our data set; aggregating county-level data for diocesan-level analysis is a very time-consuming task.

7. Although we use regional means to illustrate variations in diocesan conditions, the unit of analysis is the diocese itself. The results reported are estimates of conditions reflecting

Table 6.1. Selected conditions of U.S. Catholic laity and clergy, 1970–80, by region (weighted means)

Region	Catholic pop. size, 1970[a]	Priest pop. size, 1970	Catholic pop. growth 1970–80[a]	Priest pop. growth 1970–80	Number of cases
New England	905	690	37.2	-91.0	7
Middle Atlantic	877	662	6.1	-81.5	14
East Northcentral	643	494	3.0	-78.3	15
West Northcentral	236	323	11.1	-52.9	14
Mountain	188	145	35.0	-11.5	5
Pacific	516	258	87.6	-26.5	10
East South[b]	311	280	33.2	1.9	6
West Southcentral	332	181	38.5	-1.2	14
Grand mean	520	395	27.5	-47.3	85
Standard deviation	477	273	91.1	56.4	85

Sources: for laity, Glenmary Research Center (see appendix C); for clergy, weighted census counts.
[a]In thousands.
[b]Combines the South Atlantic region and one diocese from the East Southcentral region.

average, were found in Northeast and East Northcentral dioceses and the smallest in Mountain and West Northcentral dioceses. Average size of the 1970 priest population was also largest in those areas and, likewise, smallest in Mountain dioceses. Surprisingly, given the small church membership in West Northcentral states, size of the clergy population there was not far below the national mean, while in West Southcentral states average numbers of both laity and clergy were among the smallest in the country.

Catholic church membership was growing most along the Pacific Coast; the average increase during the 1970s was huge, over 87,000 additional Catholics per diocese. The smallest growth was recorded in East Northcentral and Middle Atlantic dioceses, where church membership grew by only 3,000 and 6,000, respectively.

---

the regional populations of sampled dioceses; they are subject to margins of error based on probability theory. The variables, too, though constructed with care, are subject to measurement error. So our figures may vary slightly from those published elsewhere; they also vary from the estimates presented in chapters 2 and 3, because there we use priest as the unit of analysis and here diocese. On the basis of evidence from a companion study, we assume sampling bias is minimal (see NORC 1972, appendix A). We do not assess measurement error but likewise assume it is negligible. These comments also apply to regional statistics presented in the following tables: 6.4, 7.5, 8.7, 9.5, and 10.7. Note: means given in table 6.1 are weighted, whereas those in the last-named tables are not.

As for priest population growth — the dependent variable — we saw in prior chapters that numbers of active diocesan priests were falling precipitously in the Northeast and Northcentral states, declining, but less dramatically, in the West and most areas of the South, and actually growing in the East South region. Thus table 6.1 shows that, while dioceses in Middle Atlantic states lost about 81 active priests during the 1970s, diocesan churches in East South states actually gained about 2 priests on the average. The "typical" U.S. diocese lost about 47 priests between 1970 and 1980. This is the national average; some dioceses dropped a couple hundred from their active priest roster, some declined by fewer than a dozen, while others grew by several dozen priests during the decade.

Findings

The results of testing our causal model are displayed in table 6.2.[8] The statistics show that region, clergy size in 1970, and Catholic population growth during the decade each have powerful independent effects, all other things being equal. Together these independent variables explain almost 70 percent of the variance in clergy population growth and decline. This is a powerful model by traditional social science standards.[9]

Priest Population Size

The results show, not surprisingly, that dioceses with a larger clergy roster in 1970 lost more priests during the decade than those with smaller initial numbers of active priests. In addition to confirming the obvious, the sta-

8. Here and in the discussion of subsequent regression models, we present unstandardized coefficients, because they have a straightforward substantive interpretation. As we shall see, the coefficients tell us how much a one-unit increase in an antecedent variable will affect the dependent variable in the model. Additionally, unstandardized coefficients are suitable for calculating adjusted means, which facilitate understanding regional differences.

The F-ratio for the equation, which indicates the overall statistical power of the model, is given at the bottom of the table. Adjusted t-ratios, which reflect the statistical power of each term in the equation, are also provided, and their statistical significance is coded with the asterisks in the table.

We use adjusted t-ratios, since finite population theory shows that the standard error of b will be too large and the t-ratio too small when a large proportion of the total population is included in the sample (Mendenhall et al. 1971). We adjust for this with a finite population correction factor: the square root of $1 - (n/N)$. In our sample, $n = 85$ and $N = 169$; hence, the standard error of b is multiplied by 0.705. These calculations yield the adjusted t-ratios presented in the following tables: 6.2, 6.5, 7.6, 8.8, 9.6, 10.8 and 10.9. The reported significance levels are based on two-tailed tests.

9. The equation in table 6.2 tests the net influence of each of the antecedent conditions while holding the others constant. So statements modified with the phrase "all other conditions tested being equal" mean just that.

Table 6.2. Effects of environmental and organizational conditions on priest population growth, 1970–80, in U.S. Catholic dioceses (unstandardized regression coefficients)

Independent variable	b	Adjusted t-ratio[a]
New England	-7.2	-0.698
East Northcentral	-25.7	-3.032**
West Northcentral	-27.7	-2.973**
Mountain	-22.8	-1.693
Pacific	-25.6	-2.245*
East South[b]	15.4	1.298
West Southcentral	-8.2	-0.748
Catholic population size, 1970	0.000017	1.428
Priest population size, 1970	-0.197	-8.030***
Catholic population growth, 1970–80	0.000088	3.172**
n of dioceses	85	
Constant	33.6	3.144**
F-ratio	19.9***	
R^2	.729	
Adjusted R^2	.692	

Note: The omitted category for region is Middle Atlantic.

[a]Adjustment is based on a finite population correction factor of 0.705 or the square root of 1 - (n/N) applied to the standard error of b; see Mendenhall et al. 1971.

[b]Combines the South Atlantic region and one diocese from the East Southcentral region.

*p ≤ .05.
**p ≤ .01.
***p ≤ .001.

tistics also estimate the precise impact of initial clergy size. Thus for example, if Diocese A began the decade with 100 more priests than Diocese B, the model shows that Diocese A probably lost 20 more priests during the 1970s than Diocese B, all other conditions tested being equal.

Catholic Population Growth

As expected, growth in the lay population produced growth in the clergy population, net of other conditions tested. Thus, dioceses with rapidly growing Catholic populations are more likely to experience growth — or relatively less decline — in the number of priests than dioceses experiencing slow growth or decline in Catholic church membership. The regression coefficient shows that if church membership in the average diocese had grown by an additional 10,000 between 1970 and 1980, the clergy population would have grown (or not declined) by almost one more priest (precisely an average of 0.88 priest). This is a powerful impact both statistically and substantively.

Generally, however, the actual result of church membership growth was not to increase the clergy population but only to slow its decline. For as we discovered in chapter 4, the vast majority of American dioceses experienced clergy losses during the 1970s despite growth in the recruitment candidacy pool represented by Catholic laity.

Region of the Country[10]
Table 6.3 is particularly appropriate for explaining the effects of geographic region on priest population growth and decline.[11] The unadjusted means in column 1, taken from table 6.1, reflect historical decline or growth between 1970 and 1980. The adjusted means in column 2 result from another type of what-if experiment. This test asks: *What* kinds of regional differences would have existed *if* all dioceses had begun the decade with an equal number of priests and parishioners and had experienced the same amount of growth in the number of parishioners.[12]

For example, table 6.3 shows the extent to which low declines in West dioceses, given in column 1, can be explained by environmental and organizational conditions. Mountain and Pacific Coast dioceses began the decade with relatively small priest populations and experienced rapid growth in church membership during the 1970s. Column 2 shows that if these conditions had been the same there as elsewhere, West dioceses would have been among the hardest hit in the nation.

Likewise, in actuality the average New England and Middle Atlantic diocese experienced the greatest number of clergy losses in the United States during the 1970s. The analysis demonstrates, though, that the magnitude of the decline was due to large clergy populations in 1970 and, for Middle Atlantic dioceses, small increases in church membership during the decade. Again, if New England and Middle Atlantic dioceses had been at the na-

10. The technique of using a variable such as region (referred to as dummy variable analysis) necessitates omitting one category from the regression equations. In this case the omitted dioceses are in the Middle Atlantic region; we chose them because they fall at the mean of some key variables, which facilitates interpretation. Middle Atlantic dioceses are not removed from the analysis; they are the reference group against which other dioceses are compared. Thus, table 6.2 shows that priest population decline in the Middle Atlantic region differs significantly from growth and decline in all others except the New England, East South, Mountain, and West Southcentral regions.

11. For a clear explanation of the techniques used to calculate adjusted means see Agresti and Finlay 1986, especially chapter 13 and the treatment of analysis of covariance models without interaction terms.

12. The technique equalizes all independent variables at the national average.

Table 6.3. Unadjusted and adjusted means on U.S.
diocesan priest population growth, 1970–80, by region

Region	Unadjusted[a]	Adjusted[b]
New England	-91.0	-40.2
Middle Atlantic	-81.5	-33.0
East Northcentral	-78.3	-58.7
West Northcentral	-52.9	-60.7
Mountain	-11.5	-55.7
Pacific	-26.5	-58.6
East South[c]	1.9	-17.6
West Southcentral	-1.2	-41.1
Range	92.9	43.1

[a]Source: table 6.1.
[b]Adjusted means are calculated from regression
statistics in table 6.2.
[c]Combines the South Atlantic region and one diocese
from the East Southcentral region.

tional average in terms of initial clergy size and lay population growth,
they would have been among those suffering the lowest losses.

Hence, holding causal conditions constant produces a very different pattern of demographic outcomes from what actually occurred between 1970
and 1980. Another surprise is the magnitude of the differences between
unadjusted and adjusted means. Comparing the statistics in the bottom
row shows that the range of clergy decline across regions is much narrower
once environmental factors other than geographic location are taken into
account. The unadjusted means in column 1 have a regional range of 92.9
priests. After eliminating the known impact of prior conditions, the range
in the growth or decline variable in column 2 is cut almost in half to 43.1
clergymen.

Thus, the big winners and losers in terms of priest population growth
and decline are apparent only after conditions that influence the change
process have been equalized. Taking environmental factors into account,
we find that dioceses of the South and West do not constitute a subspecies
of organizations distinct from dioceses in the Northeast and Northcentral
divisions. At least regarding the conditions tested, we have not discovered
evidence of loose coupling between the two halves of the U.S. Catholic
church.

Our results, however, raise the same question anew, only now it is directed to other regional cleavages. Table 6.3 reveals that Middle Atlantic
and East South dioceses may be distinctively different from those in the
rest of the country, since in terms of standardized numbers they are the

ones least affected by clergy losses. So, perhaps an East Coast "establish-ment" — comprising Middle Atlantic and East South dioceses — constitutes a subspecies or subsystem loosely coupled from the rest of the church.[13] Given the limitations of our first causal model, this part of the analysis must stop here, leaving some unanswered questions. Further discussion of the "East Coast church" hypothesis is postponed until we consider additional evidence provided by our second causal model.[14]

A Model Explaining Supply and Demand in Catholic Dioceses

Catholic priests are ordained to serve a community of believers. Among their myriad priestly tasks is the unique responsibility of presiding at Mass and celebrating the other sacraments. According to recent research, lay Catholics are welcoming new opportunities to share in the ministry, an emphasis in parish life encouraged by the Second Vatican Council (Leege 1986; Wallace 1992). Nevertheless, when it comes to the Mass and those sacraments attached to important rites of passage — principally, birth, marriage, and death — the vast majority of Catholics want a priest present, not another type of minister (Leege 1986; Hoge 1987; Hoge, Carroll, and Scheets 1988).

Concern over the priest shortage takes on poignancy for most Catholics because it threatens access to the traditional "means of justification" (Troeltsch 1960; Schoenherr forthcoming). Undoubtedly, the severity of the priest decline should rightly be assessed in terms of the widening

13. The statistical evidence for the existence of an East Coast church distinct from the rest of the country is more complex than our summary statement implies. The dummy variable analysis reported in table 6.2 shows that East Northcentral, West Northcentral, and Pacific dioceses are all significantly different from Middle Atlantic dioceses, which is the omitted category. Dioceses in the remaining regions — New England, East South, Mountain, and West Southcentral — however, are not significantly different from those in the Middle Atlantic states.

Adjusted means provided in table 6.3 reveal, additionally, that even though New England, Mountain, and West Southcentral dioceses are not significantly different from Middle Atlantic dioceses by statistical tests, nevertheless standardized losses in these three regions are notably higher than standardized losses in both Middle Atlantic and East South dioceses. Taken together, these findings suggest that the combination of Middle Atlantic and East South dioceses may form one homogeneous grouping distinct from dioceses in the remaining regions of the country. As we shall see, the second causal model lends additional support for the suggestion.

14. Other environmental and organizational conditions undoubtedly have an impact on clergy decline. Further controls could not be included in the analysis, however, since appropriate measures were not available given limits of time and resources. Consequently, the regression model dealing with priest population decline — as powerful as it is — should be viewed as a first step toward explaining demographic change in U.S. dioceses.

parishioner-to-priest ratio, not just the drop in numbers of priests. As growth in Catholic church membership continues unabated, many feel the clergy population should be keeping pace and certainly not declining.[15] Therefore, the next step of the analysis considers those conditions that explain why certain dioceses are plagued by astronomical parishioner-to-priest ratios while others enjoy favorable ones.

Our second empirical model, though limited to one point in time, considers a more complex set of issues than the first. We address the situation of full pews and empty altars, a uniquely Catholic problem created by the shrinking supply of priests and the growing demand for sacramental services coming from an expanding church membership. In addition, we examine the impact of a wider set of environmental conditions and organizational traits than merely church membership. We integrated the variables created for this project with excellent 1980 data prepared by the Glenmary Research Center. The Glenmary data describe the ecological niche of diocesan organizations in terms of racial-ethnic groups, age distribution, marital status, education, health, housing, occupation, family income, and religion of the general population living there.[16]

Cross-Sectional Regression Model

Figure 6.2 summarizes the model proposed for explaining local variation in parishioner-to-priest ratios. Similar to the previous causal diagram, the arrows demonstrate that geographic region is assumed to have a possible causal influence: on Catholic population growth; on the degree to which the general population in the diocese is urban, Hispanic, Catholic, and affluent; on two internal characteristics of the diocese, namely, the religious priest–to–diocesan priest ratio and the ineffectiveness of recruiting young men to the priesthood; and, ultimately, on the number of parishioners per active diocesan priest.[17] The influence may be direct or indirect, flowing through any variable that intervenes between geographic region and a later condition.

In like manner, any variable in the drawing may have a direct influence

---

15. In a front-page *New York Times* headline, July 9, 1989, Peter Steinfels claims "Shortage of Qualified New Clergy Causing Alarm for U.S. Religions." In the accompanying article he writes, "For Catholics, the nation's largest religious denomination, the situation assumes crisis proportions."

16. We gratefully acknowledge the help of Clifford A. Grammich, Jr., and Rev. Lou McNeil in acquiring the data from the Glenmary Research Center.

17. The use of ratios as dependent variables when either their numerators or denominators are used as control variables has been disputed methodologically. Fuguitt and Liebersen (1974), however, have laid the debate to rest, demonstrating that ratios are appropriate as dependent variables. If theoretical reasons dictate their use, there are no fatal methodological constraints.

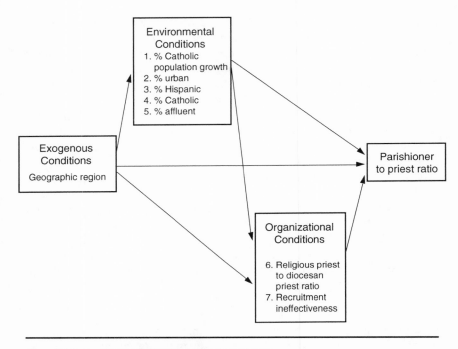

Figure 6.2. Model of availability of priestly ministers

on the parishioner-to-priest ratio as well as on all other subsequent, higher-numbered variables. Further, each variable is hypothetically capable of indirectly influencing the number of parishioners per priest through any of the conditions that intervene between it and the ultimate dependent variable.[18]

Descriptive Overview

Table 6.4 presents a picture of the average diocese in each census region in terms of the variables defining our empirical model.[19] According to sample estimates, the highest growth in Catholic population during the 1970s occurred in East South dioceses: 23 percent. The lowest growth took place in Middle Atlantic states: only 2 percent. We also discover that Pacific Ocean dioceses, on the average, were the most urban (86 percent), most affluent

18. Further discussion of the assumed causal precedence among the variables and the definitions and data sources for the variables are provided in appendix C.

19. Because the averages are estimates based on a probability sample, they may differ slightly from regional and national figures published elsewhere; see footnote 7 in this chapter.

Table 6.4. Selected environmental and organizational conditions of U.S. Catholic dioceses, 1980, by region (means)

Region	% Cathlc. growth 1970–80	% urban	% Hispn.	% Cathlc.	% aflunt.	Rel./dio. priest ratio[a]	Recruit. ineffctv.[b]	Parishnr./ priest ratio
New England	3.8	79.8	1.9	42.3	33.5	70	10,507	1,535
Middle Atlantic	2.4	82.3	4.4	36.8	34.9	57	7,223	1,455
East Northcentral	4.9	72.2	1.9	24.1	36.0	57	7,972	1,424
West Northcentral	7.6	49.1	1.4	19.8	30.4	60	4,903	909
Mountain	19.5	56.6	21.4	21.1	29.9	66	7,303	1,775
Pacific	11.2	85.8	15.6	17.3	41.3	110	14,325	2,291
East South[c]	23.0	70.6	1.8	9.8	31.0	84	6,721	1,381
West Southcentral	12.1	69.6	17.0	21.9	31.6	87	10,371	2,017
Mean	8.9	70.8	7.5	24.6	33.9	72	8,567	1,571
Standard deviation	14.6	23.4	12.2	13.3	8.4	49	6,512	731

Sources: see appendix C.
[a]Number of religious order priests per 100 active diocesan priests.
[b]Number of young Catholic males required per newly ordained priest.
[c]Combines the South Atlantic region and one diocese from the East Southcentral region.

(41 percent), had the highest ratio of religious priests to diocesan priests (110:100), and were the least effective in attracting young men to the priesthood (requiring 14,325 young Catholic males per newly ordained priest).

In 1980, Mountain dioceses had the highest average percentage of Hispanics (21 percent) and West Northcentral dioceses the lowest (1 percent). West Northcentral and Mountain dioceses were similar, however, in being the least urban (49 percent and 57 percent, respectively) and least affluent in the United States (30 percent each). The highest proportion of Catholics relative to the general population resided in New England (42 percent) and the lowest in East South dioceses (10 percent). Middle Atlantic and East Northcentral dioceses were alike in having the lowest ratio of religious to diocesan priests (57:100). Dioceses in West Northcentral states were the most effective in their recruitment efforts; in 1980, on the average, one priest was ordained for every 4,903 Catholic males of ages 25–34 residing in the diocese.

A description of the final dependent variable completes the portrait of regional ranges in the variables. Clergy in the average Pacific Coast diocese labored under the highest number of parishioners per active diocesan priest: 2,291. Those in West Northcentral dioceses were the most fortunate, working with only 909 parishioners per priest. Nationally, the "typical" diocese faced a ratio of 1,571 parishioners per active diocesan priest. This figure is an average of some wide extremes. In Los Angeles each ac-

tive priest was matched by almost 4,000 church members, the highest recorded in our sample. The most advantageous ratio was found in Little
Rock, 500:1.

Besides the set of variables that composes the final version of our model,
we also examine the impact of other key environmental characteristics. We
find no important effects on the availability of priestly ministers from age
distribution of the general population, percentage of African Americans,
percentage of American Indians, divorce rates, average family size, education, availability of health care, substandard housing, or occupation.[20]
Systematic examination of the interrelations among the expanded set of
variables based on our causal assumptions yields the model summarized
in figure 6.2. Thus, of all the possible subsets examined, this system of
variables best describes and explains the sequence of social forces that leads
to the availability of priestly ministers in the local diocesan church.[21]

We have examined the existence and strength of causal relationships
among all eight independent variables in the model. The presentation is
limited, however, to equations explaining the variance of the last two variables, because they are most relevant to our practical and theoretical
concerns.[22]

Explaining Local Variation in Parishioner-to-Priest Ratio

Column 3 of table 6.5 presents the regression model explaining why the
balance of supply and demand in some dioceses is so divergent from the
national average. Once again, the model is powerful, explaining more than
three-fourths of the variation in parishioner-to-priest ratios. As the coefficients reveal, the net effect of all the independent variables is positive.
That is, all the environmental and organizational conditions tested act as
constraints on the availability of priestly ministers by raising the number of
parishioners per active diocesan priest. Which conditions have the *strongest*

20. Some of these variables are correlated with the parishioner-to-priest ratio, but the
correlations do not persist when these variables are added to our fully developed model.

21. We test for interaction effects between all the independent variables except region
and the religious priest–to–diocesan priest ratio and discover none. Region is omitted in
the test because, in addition to the other six independent variables and their 15 interaction
terms already included, it would require another 42 interaction terms with n = 85. The re-
ligious/diocesan ratio was added later in the analysis after the test for interactions had been
performed; on the basis of the other negative tests, we assumed no interaction with this
variable.

22. The full set of structural equations for each variable in the path model, the correlation matrix, and summary statistics are available upon request from the authors; the same
information is available for all subsequent models presented.

Table 6.5. Effects of environmental and organizational conditions on recruitment ineffectiveness and parishioner-to-priest ratio in U.S. Catholic dioceses, 1980 (unstandardized regression coefficients)

Independent variable	Recruitment ineffectiveness		Parishnr./priest ratio	
	b	Adjusted t-ratio[a]	b	Adjusted t-ratio[a]
New England	2,780	1.495	-42	-0.367
East Northcentral	2,363	1.454	254	2.514*
West Northcentral	-776	-0.409	11	0.094
Mountain	-3,731	-1.407	201	1.218
Pacific	5,513	2.428*	527	3.683***
East South[b]	1,342	0.570	240	1.651
West Southcentral	849	0.436	447	3.717***
% Catholic growth, 1970–80	83	2.513*	15	7.277***
% urban	-33	-0.930	5	2.206*
% Hispanic	220	4.054***	20	5.657***
% Catholic	132	2.723**	20	6.437***
% affluent	50	0.554	14	2.601*
Rel./diocesan priest ratio	14	1.335	3	4.267***
Recruit. ineffectiveness			0.010	2.030*
n of dioceses	85		85	
Constant	1,378	0.523	-536	3.295**
F-ratio	3.462***		22.399***	
R^2	.388		.818	
Adjusted R^2	.276		.781	

Note: The omitted category for region is the Middle Atlantic.

[a]Adjustment is based on a finite population correction factor of 0.705 or the square root of 1 - (n/N) applied to the standard error of b; see Mendenhall et al. 1971.

[b]Combines the South Atlantic region and one diocese from the East Southcentral region.

*$p \leq .05$.
**$p \leq .01$.
***$p \leq .001$.

impact? We discover the heaviest influence from three environmental conditions: percentage of Catholics, percentage of Hispanics, and percentage of growth in the Catholic population.

Percentage of Catholics

The results indicate that the larger the proportion of Catholics to the total population in the diocese, the higher the parishioner-to-priest ratio, all other conditions being equal. The data demonstrate that if the proportion of Catholics in Diocese A were 10 percent higher than in Diocese B, the number of parishioners per priest would be 200 higher in A than in B.

Percentage of Hispanics

The higher the proportion of Hispanics in the general population, the higher the parishioner-to-priest ratio in the diocese. Two dioceses that are identical on all other conditions tested but differ by 10 percent in the proportion of the total population that is Hispanic would differ by 200 in their parishioner-to-priest ratio. In other words, the laity in dioceses with relatively large Hispanic populations may be systematically underserved because of relatively high numbers of parishioners per priest. This effect from the percentage of Hispanics cannot be explained by other variables in the model, because they have been controlled by statistical techniques.

Catholic Population Growth

Dioceses that experience a relatively high increase in church membership are likely to have a higher parishioner-to-priest ratio than dioceses with little membership growth. More precisely, a diocese that records a 10 percent growth in its Catholic population in comparison to one where there has been no growth would experience an increase of 150 more Catholics in its parishioner-to-priest ratio than the static diocese, if all other causal influences were equal. The data show that the demand for priestly services is outstripping the supply of priests in dioceses with rapidly growing church membership.

Two other variables in the model have *moderate* effects on the number of parishioners per priest, namely, the number of religious order priests who reside in the diocese relative to the number of active diocesan priests, and the geographic region.

Religious Priest–to–Diocesan Priest Ratio

Dioceses with larger numbers of religious order priests relative to the size of the diocesan clergy face a higher parishioner-to-priest ratio than dioceses with smaller concentrations of religious priests. Remember, however, the dependent variable is measured by the number of active diocesan clergy only. So the data show that where diocesan clergy face larger numbers of parishioners, religious clergy are present in larger numbers to assist with priestly ministry. In actuality, therefore, raising the religious priest–to–diocesan priest ratio increases the laity's access to priestly ministers.

Accordingly, our model is designed to control for the greater contribution made by religious order priests in some dioceses than in others. Hence, other causal relationships discovered in the analysis, such as the impact of proportionately large Hispanic populations on the parishioner-to-priest ratio, are independent of diocesan reliance on religious order priests to help meet the needs of the faithful. As the coefficient indicates, all other conditions being equal, an increase in the religious priest–to–diocesan priest ratio of 1 additional religious priest per 100 diocesan priests would increase the number of parishioners per active diocesan priest by almost 300.[23]

Although some religious priests work exclusively in parish ministry, many others commonly have specialized jobs unique to the traditions of their order or congregation. So, in comparison to active diocesan priests, whose primary duties are parish based, the average religious order priest is at most a part-time parish minister.[24] One might conclude, therefore, that all relevant conditions being equal, in 1980 the average religious priest in the diocese provided priestly services for about 300 Catholic parishioners.[25]

Region[26]

Notable regional differences in the parishioner-to-priest ratio are found in the data, which persist even after controlling for differences in relative size and growth of the Catholic population, Hispanic ethnicity, urbanization, affluence, the presence of religious order priests, and recruitment ineffectiveness. Because Middle Atlantic dioceses are the omitted category, table 6.5 shows that, all other things being equal, ratios in Middle Atlantic dioceses differ significantly from those in East South, West Southcentral, and Pacific Coast dioceses but not from those in the other regions.

Table 6.6 simplifies the complex statistics describing the effects of geographic location. It reveals how many parishioners per priest there would be in each region if every diocese in the sample were to face equal environmental and organizational conditions, that is, equal to the national average. As the adjusted means in column 2 indicate, once the influence of the other tested conditions has been taken into account, dioceses fall into three regional groupings.[27] Those along the Pacific Coast and in West

23. Using the unrounded coefficient, precisely: $2.84 \times 100 = 284$.

24. Since some religious order priests actually work full time in local parishes, our comments stress the influence of conditions *on the average*.

25. This number has probably gone up as observers report that religious order superiors are now reassigning their dwindling numbers of priests away from parish work and into the more specialized ministries that distinguish their orders from the diocesan clergy (Eifert 1990).

26. Middle Atlantic dioceses are the omitted category; see footnote 10 in this chapter.

27. Strictly speaking, given the tests for statistical significance presented in table 6.5, only two regional categories appear in the model: one group that differs significantly from Middle Atlantic dioceses and another that does not. The data in table 6.6, however, suggest a more detailed grouping of dioceses by region: one above the mean, a second at the mean, and a third below the mean. Dioceses in only two regions are subject to ambiguity. The adjusted regional means for Mountain and East South states are close to the mean, but some dioceses in the Mountain region may fall closer to the below-the-mean group while some in the East South may fall closer to the above-the-mean group.

Table 6.6. Unadjusted and adjusted means on
parishioner-to-priest ratio in U.S. Catholic
dioceses, 1980, by region

Region	Unadjusted[a]	Adjusted[b]
New England	1,535	1,321
Middle Atlantic	1,455	1,363
East Northcentral	1,424	1,617
West Northcentral	909	1,374
Mountain	1,775	1,564
Pacific	2,291	1,890
East South[c]	1,381	1,603
West Southcentral	2,017	1,810
Range	1,382	569

[a]Source: table 6.4.
[b]Adjusted means are calculated from regression
statistics in table 6.5.
[c]Combines the South Atlantic region and one
diocese from the East Southcentral region.

Southcentral states would form the most disadvantaged group in terms
of availability of priestly ministers. In the hypothetical situation of equal
environmental and organizational conditions, the number of parishioners
per active diocesan priest in the average West Southcentral diocese would
be about 1,800 to 1, 16 percent above the national mean. In the average
Pacific Coast diocese it would be almost 1,900 to 1, 21 percent above the
national mean.

Local diocesan churches in East Northcentral, Mountain, and East South
states form a second group. The number of parishioners per priest in each
diocese in this cluster would be close to the national mean (1,571:1), ranging from about 1 percent to 3 percent above it. Dioceses in New England,
Middle Atlantic, and West Northcentral states can be grouped together
in a third set, with their ratios falling notably below the average. If dioceses in this set were to face the same environmental conditions, the number of parishioners per priest would range from just over 1,300:1 to just
under 1,400:1, or 16–13 percent below the national mean.

Because it is a powerful explanatory model, the range of the parishioner-
to-priest ratio across geographic regions was reduced by over half through
the tested control variables alone, as a comparison of the entries in the
last row of data reveals. The unadjusted regional means in column 1 range
from 909 to 2,291 parishioners per priest, for a difference between extremes
of 1,382. Those standardized for causal conditions, given in column 2, range
from 1,321 to 1,890 parishioners per priest, for a difference of only 569.

Finally, the other three variables in the regression equation have a statistically weaker but nonetheless important impact on how many Catholic parishioners reside within diocesan boundaries per active diocesan priest available to serve them. The findings reveal that dioceses with higher proportions of *affluent* families also have a higher parishioner-to-priest ratio than dioceses with less affluence. Local churches with higher percentages of their populations living in *urban* counties likewise have higher numbers of parishioners per priest. And dioceses that tend to be more *ineffective in recruiting* new priests, not surprisingly, also tend to have a higher parishioner-to-priest ratio.

Balancing Supply and Demand

The model reveals that the wide variation in parishioner-to-priest ratios is heavily influenced by constraints in the environment which vary in different parts of the country. Without the evidence, one might presume that something internal to diocesan organizations creates such large differences in the relationship between supply and demand of priestly services. The regression equation demonstrates, however, that a great deal of variance in parishioner-to-priest ratios is explained by natural selection processes, whereby dioceses adjust and adapt to their environments in a fashion that is probably beyond the conscious awareness of organization members.

This is not to say that internal conditions and the purposive behavior of people in dioceses have no effect whatsoever on decline or growth of the priesthood population. On the contrary, the data also show that staffing patterns and recruitment effectiveness, which are subject to manipulation by organization actors, likewise influence the parishioner-to-priest ratio. We call attention to the environmental effects, however, not only because they are easily overlooked but also because they are so strong.

The data demonstrate that U.S. Catholics do not have equal access to priests mainly because of environmental constraints. Parishes are most likely to be underserved in dioceses with large proportions of Hispanics and relatively large church memberships that are growing rapidly. The same tendency toward sparse priestly service is prevalent in dioceses with relatively high concentrations of affluent and urban populations or that are ineffective in recruiting new priests. The negative impact of these conditions is cumulative, such that dioceses characterized by high scores on all the variables would tend to have a very light supply of priestly ministers in the face of the very heavy demand. Additionally, parishioners living along the Pacific Coast and in the West Southcentral region are probably the most disadvantaged in the country, both before and after taking environmental conditions into account, while those residing in Northeast and West

Northcentral states tend to be the most advantaged, especially after considering environmental constraints.

Further Evidence of Loose Coupling
After controlling for conditions that affect the dwindling of priestly resources, differences in clergy decline across dioceses are notably reduced but not entirely eliminated. Thus both regression models revealed persistent and heretofore unknown regional contrasts in the demographic transition. We drew two conclusions from the time-series analysis. First, once environmental conditions are accounted for, the extent of the clergy decline in the Northeast and Northcentral division is not so different from that in the South and West. Second, a more substantial cleavage may exist between East Coast dioceses—again, roughly those included in the Middle Atlantic, South Atlantic, and East Southcentral regions—and all other dioceses in the country.

The data in tables 6.5 and 6.6 provide additional evidence supporting the second conclusion from the longitudinal model. The tables show that West Southcentral and Pacific Coast dioceses have parishioner-to-priest ratios that not only are significantly different from those in Middle Atlantic states but also are by far the largest in the country, both before and after they have been standardized. Thus, combining the results from both causal models, the evidence seems to indicate that Middle Atlantic and East South dioceses constitute one fairly homogeneous and "advantaged" subsystem, and those in the rest of the country another fairly homogeneous but "disadvantaged" subsystem within the American Catholic church.

Until further research provides more definitive results, we may conclude that East Coast dioceses form a distinctive subdivision of the Catholic church. Further, our findings suggest that East Coast dioceses, which under standardized conditions enjoy the advantage of low clergy losses and low to average parishioner-to-priest ratios, may be only loosely coupled to the rest of the wider system. The remainder of the country is suffering notably greater clergy losses and more burdensome parishioner-to-priest ratios under standardized conditions.[28]

28. Further research would have to examine the issue more closely, using more variables and, perhaps, oversampling from the South Atlantic and East Southcentral regions. Two hypotheses need to be tested. The first, which flows from the results shown in table 6.2, should focus on whether the Northeast and South divisions in their entirety constitute a homogeneous group of dioceses distinctively different from and so only loosely coupled to the rest of the church. The second, which is raised by the model presented in table 6.5, should test whether the Texas and California dioceses and, to a lesser extent, those in the Northcentral division form a subsystem distinct from the other dioceses in the country. Our summary of

Explaining Local Variation in Recruitment Ineffectiveness

Although the recruitment ineffectiveness variable has a relatively weak impact on the number of parishioners per active diocesan priest, nevertheless the effectiveness with which dioceses recruit young men to the priesthood has a direct bearing on the local priest shortage. We measure the effectiveness of recruitment efforts by considering the number of young Catholic males of ages 25–34 that it takes to produce one ordained priest. We construct the variable by dividing the total Catholic male population in that age bracket in 1980 by the average number of priests ordained from 1978 to 1982.[29] A high score indicates that the size of the candidacy pool required for one ordination is large, so we label the variable recruitment ineffectiveness.

As the first column of statistics in table 6.5 shows, recruitment ineffectiveness is strongly influenced by three environmental conditions. Together with the other variables in the model, they explain over one-fourth of the variance in this dependent variable. The proportion of Hispanics and, to a lesser degree, the proportion of Catholics in the general population and Catholic church membership growth have the positive net effect of increasing the size of the candidacy pool it takes to recruit one ordained priest.[30]

Percentage of Hispanics

After controlling for the influence of geographic region and other relevant conditions, raising the proportion of Hispanics in the diocesan population by 1 percentage point would increase by 220 the number of young Catholic males required to provide one newly ordained priest. In a related study, Hemrick and Hoge (1986) reported that Hispanics are greatly underrepresented in U.S. seminaries. Therefore, our findings support their results and further specify that the effect of Hispanic ethnicity is operative, even controlling for several other environmental conditions. In addition,

---

the results, which suggests the existence of an "East Coast church," combines the strongest evidence from the two models presented here.

29. Mean ordinations for a five-year period around 1980 is used as the denominator in order to smooth out erratic fluctuations in the number of ordinations in small dioceses.

30. The antecedent variables in the model summarized in figure 6.2 have been selected on the basis of their ability to explain the ultimate dependent variable, parishioner-to-priest ratio. The focus of the model is not to identify the variables that best explain recruitment ineffectiveness, which is an intervening variable in the causal chain. Consequently, our analysis of conditions affecting recruitment ineffectiveness is preliminary. Further conclusions about the sequence of social forces leading to recruitment ineffectiveness await systematic analysis of a more complete set of variables. Nevertheless, though caution is needed in interpreting our findings, the preliminary analysis provides important insights for theory and policy.

our regression model specifies the magnitude of the negative impact of Hispanic ethnicity on recruitment to the priesthood.

The evidence does not suggest that Hispanics cause ineffectiveness in the recruitment of priests; rather, it indicates that the pressures of proportionately larger Hispanic populations result in poorer recruitment results. This effect could be due to a tradition of how Hispanics relate to the priesthood, as Hemrick and Hoge's (1986) finding of relatively few Hispanics in seminaries would suggest. Or the impact may flow from the way the church relates to Hispanics, perhaps by not aggressively recruiting or retaining Hispanic seminarians or, more generally, by failing to adapt adequately to the special needs of this bicultural population.

Percentage of Catholics and Percentage of Catholic Population Growth

A relatively high proportion of Catholics in the general population also makes diocesan recruitment efforts more ineffective. An increase of 1 percent in the proportion of Catholics in the population would raise by 132 the number of young men needed in the candidacy pool for each ordination. Likewise, if the number of Catholics grows just 1 percent, it requires an additional 83 young Catholic males for each newly ordained priest in the diocese.

Curiously, the more the Catholic church is in a minority situation and is growing slowly, the more effective it is in recruiting priests. Westhues (1971) discovered, similarly, that in states where the percentage of Catholics was low relative to the general population and thus the Catholic church was in a minority position, dioceses had greater involvement in education. He reasoned that "the more any distinctive group finds itself in a minority, the more it will feel threatened by its environment" (Westhues 1971, p. 282), and the more effective the group needs to be in its efforts to survive in that environment. The combined evidence shows that a local diocese seems to be more effective to the degree it is a minority church, not only in strengthening its parochial education system, but also in recruiting priests.

On the other hand, dioceses in which the Catholic population tends to be a majority may be performing like the "lazy monopoly" described by Hirschman (1970) and Seidler (1979; Seidler and Meyer 1989). According to their findings and those of others who have tested the theory (Stevens 1974; Birch 1975), when an organization is a virtual monopoly, executives are slow to improve the quality of its services, policies, or, as in the case of monopoly diocesan churches, its procedures for recruiting key professional personnel. The recent work of Stark and McCann (1989) on market forces and Catholic commitment and of Iannaccone (1990) on the rational choice approach to religion provides further theoretical and empirical evidence for the weakness of monopoly churches.

Region

The size of the candidacy pool needed for one ordination differs widely by region both before and after controlling for conditions that account for its variation across local dioceses. Column 1 of table 6.5 indicates that only Pacific Coast dioceses are significantly different in recruitment results from dioceses in other regions. The difference is easier to examine in a comparison of adjusted and unadjusted regional means provided by the data in table 6.7; as in table 6.6, the adjusted means are the result of statistically equalizing environmental conditions in all dioceses.

The only notable contrast in either column of data in table 6.7 is between Pacific Coast dioceses, which are at the high end of the range, and dioceses in the other regions at the low end. The data show that even net of all social forces in the model, dioceses in other regions of the country are all more effective in recruiting for the priesthood than dioceses along the Pacific Coast, where the standardized number of potential candidates required for one ordination is 12,900. Before adjusting for environmental conditions, West Northcentral dioceses appeared to be the most effective of all, recruiting one priest for every 4,900 young Catholic males living within diocesan jurisdictions. But once environmental constraints are taken into account—notably the effects of the percentage of Hispanics, the percentage of Catholics, and the percentage of growth in the Catholic population—Mountain dioceses enjoy the distinction of being the most effective recruiters in the country, with an adjusted average ratio of only 3,700 candidates per newly ordained priest.

Table 6.7. Unadjusted and adjusted means on recruitment ineffectiveness in U.S. Catholic dioceses, 1980, by region (in thousands)

Region	Unadjusted[a]	Adjusted[b]
New England	10.5	10.2
Middle Atlantic	7.2	7.4
East Northcentral	8.0	9.7
West Northcentral	4.9	6.6
Mountain	7.3	3.7
Pacific	14.3	12.9
East South[c]	6.7	8.7
West Southcentral	10.4	8.2
Range	9.4	9.2

[a]Source: table 6.4.
[b]Adjusted means are calculated from regression statistics in table 6.5.
[c]Combines the South Atlantic region and one diocese from the East Southcentral region.

Several of the findings seem to highlight the competitive nature of the natural selection processes at work in ecological communities in various parts of the country. We suggested that the traditional Catholic religious affiliation of Hispanics may be shifting as a result of competition from Protestant evangelical, Pentecostal, and other churches. Gallup polls (American Institute of Public Opinion 1987) show that 70 percent of Hispanic respondents claimed Roman Catholicism as their religious preference. Church officials at the U.S. Catholic Conference, however, dispute the figure and estimate from studies available to them that currently about 85 percent of Hispanics are affiliated with the Catholic church.[31]

Many other divergent estimates of how many Hispanics are Catholic could be cited, all of which indicate that the Hispanic population in the United States is fluid, not only because it is growing rapidly, but also because of religious switching.[32] Because competition in the religious marketplace seems to draw Hispanics away from the Catholic church, we find that recruiting new ordinands to the male celibate priesthood is less effective when the Hispanic population is relatively large in a diocese.

Competition and Monopoly

Exactly how religious competition, size of the Hispanic population, and recruitment of priests in Catholic dioceses influence one another is an issue that is raised by our findings but cannot be solved with the data at hand. Obviously, however, because Hispanics are underrepresented in Catholic seminaries, large proportions of Hispanics living within a diocese will inevitably lower the effectiveness of recruitment efforts that are measured by the ratio of young Catholic males to newly ordained priests. Given that relatively few Hispanics become priests, large proportions of Hispanics in a diocese's environment raise the numerator of the ratio and at the same time lower the denominator. The combined effect is automatically to raise the diocese's score on recruitment ineffectiveness.

Our findings, though, reflect more than a statistical artifact. A multi-

---

31. Personal communication with Pablo Sedillo of the U.S. Catholic Conference, fall 1989.

32. Sullivan and colleagues (1983, p. 118), citing the General Social Surveys of 1971–77, report that "93.6% of Mexican Americans were reared as Catholics and another 1.2% converted to Catholicism . . . the General Social Surveys show that 5.8% of Mexican Americans report that although they were reared Catholics, they now prefer no religion. Moreover, many Hispanics do not regularly attend church." In her study of Guatemalan immigrants in Houston, Hagan (1990) reports that 61 percent of her snowball sample identify themselves as Protestants. Of the minority who say they are Catholic, only 28 percent actually participate in the church, whereas 55 percent of those who say they are Protestant participate in their churches.

level, complex set of social forces affect recruitment to the priesthood. At the level of purposive social action, for example, individuals of Hispanic origins are making choices about religious preference. As more of them become Protestants the pool of candidates for the Protestant ministry expands and the pool for the Catholic priesthood contracts. At the same time, Catholic dioceses and Protestant churches are adapting to the changing resource pools and, through natural selection, are evolving organizational forms that either attract or repel religious seekers and potential ministerial candidates among them.

The natural selection process that affects recruitment to the priesthood is influenced not only by competitive forces tugging at the growing Hispanic population but also by competition—at least in latent forms—between Catholic and non-Catholic churches. Thus we discovered that when the Catholic church is in a minority position the diocese shows more effective results in recruiting priests than when the church is in a majority position. Again, other variables are needed to complete the explanation of why minority churches compete more successfully for priestly recruits than majority churches. Our findings thus far, however, point out the need to examine the forces of competition as an important aspect of organizational evolution. For it is a principle of the natural selection process that successful organizational forms—such as effective recruitment mechanisms—evolve, persist, and decline as a result of the competitive struggle among organizations.

Discussion and Conclusion

Several conclusions may be drawn from the results of testing our two causal models. Explaining clergy loss in terms of absolute numbers and of the corresponding increase in the number of parishioners per priest reveals some otherwise hidden implications of the forces driving demographic decline in the U.S. Catholic priesthood.

First of all, the advantage that some dioceses enjoy—because they may actually be growing or at least declining less rapidly than the majority, and/or because they have a significantly lower parishioner-to-priest ratio—is somewhat deceptive. In both cases, causal conditions account for more than three-fourths of the advantage. On the basis of the evidence, we can conclude that, if the ecological conditions identified in the models were suddenly equalized across the country, clergy growth in "advantaged" dioceses would turn into decline, trickling losses would become a steady stream, and low parishioner-to-priest ratios would climb to nearly the same heights as elsewhere. In "disadvantaged" dioceses the opposite would occur.

When we examine the adjusted average losses in Northeast and East

Northcentral states, for example, the decline in numbers is lower after being standardized for the effects of prior causal conditions. In the West and South, however, the true extent of the decline is masked when we inspect only the unadjusted averages.

The powerful impact from causal conditions, which dampen actual losses in the West and South, could affect the ability of church leaders there to be fully aware of the force of the demographic transition underway in the U.S. clergy. On the other hand, large dioceses with relatively little church membership growth, which predominate in the Northeast and Northcentral half of the country, suffer greater absolute decline. So church leaders in these areas may be more aware of the demographic forces of decline than their colleagues to the West and South.

It is relatively easy to "remove the effects" of environmental conditions with statistical experiments. To do so in reality is another story. Nevertheless, the unalterable fact behind diverse environmental conditions in Catholic dioceses is that, once these conditions are equalized, a common and pervasive organizational crisis rooted in dramatic loss of professional personnel is apparent. Furthermore, the sobering message for dioceses affected by sustained personnel losses and high parishioner-to-priest ratios is that the social forces producing higher decline and greater reductions in the availability of priestly ministers are largely environmental conditions outside the control of church leaders.

The descriptive analysis raises the question of why the South and West remained relatively stable with only minimal clergy losses while the priest decline was precipitous in the other half of the nation. The regression analysis in this chapter shows that the priest shortage in the West and South is not substantially different from clergy decline in the rest of the country, once environmental conditions are considered. The findings reveal, further, that if any subgroup of dioceses is distinctive in terms of availability of priestly resources it is that comprising the Middle Atlantic and East South dioceses. We discovered that after controlling for environmental forces dioceses in these areas would enjoy the lowest decline in standardized losses and low to average standardized parishioner-to-priest ratios.

Our question of whether some subsystem of the American church might be spared the repercussions and ramifications of the priest shortage because it is only loosely coupled to the wider system can now be directed to the East rather than the West and South. Is the East Coast church substantially different — perhaps with distinctive recruitment and retention mechanisms that minimize priest decline net of environmental influences — because it is only loosely coupled with diocesan churches in the rest of the nation? Our findings suggest this may be the case but offer no further evidence.

More research is needed to determine whether these are qualitative, not merely quantitative, differences. That is to say, are contrasts between the availability of priests in the East and elsewhere so strong that East Coast churches can isolate themselves from the driving force of the demographic transition? Or are the differences only quantitative? May we conclude that, although the eastern dioceses are at the low end of the distribution, they are, nevertheless, part of the same decline process affecting the entire Catholic church in the United States?

The analysis also raises several issues relevant for future studies of recruitment success. Investigators need to examine why minority churches compete more effectively for priestly recruits than majority churches. Additionally, the impact of Hispanic culture and tradition, rapid growth in the Hispanic population, and competition among the churches for Hispanic religious allegiance must all be given systematic attention. Given the critical nature of recruitment mechanisms for a population of organizations facing sustained decline in human resources, research in this area should be given high priority.

Finally, we are convinced that social forces other than those captured by our test variables could account for some of the remaining variance in diocesan clergy decline and parishioner-to-priest ratios. It is crucial, however, to bear in mind that explaining the variance in clergy decline does not change historical reality. The average diocese in the United States has already lost well over 20 percent of its active priests since the close of the Second Vatican Council. No endogenous empirical models can explain away that fact. Furthermore, the projection results demonstrate that historic trends have demographic consequences. During the final decades of the 20th century, the Catholic church in this country is facing an overall 40 percent decline in priestly manpower along with a rapid aging of its remaining active clergy. In Part Three we examine this decline process in its component parts, with emphasis on recruitment and retention rates, the forces that dominate priest population change.

3   Components of Population Change

7 Ordination

Our study of the Catholic church concerns social change linked to demographic processes. Hence, in Part Two we described the demographic transition of U.S. dioceses in terms of changing size and aging of the priesthood population. We also explained some of the environmental and organizational conditions that account for variations in population change at the local diocesan level.

To explore the process driving the demographic transition we followed Hernes (1976), who provides conceptual tools to distinguish social change at three levels, namely, the output, process, and parameter structures of change. He explains that an organizational transition occurs when both the parameter and the output structures of change are altered while the process structure remains the same.

Thus, in chapters 2 to 5 we provided evidence showing that the process generating change in the diocesan clergy has resulted in altered output structures, namely, smaller priest populations with older age pyramids. Further, the parameters or values of the entrance and exit rates affecting the transition have likewise changed considerably. For example, ordination rates decreased, resignation rates peaked and declined, and retirement rates increased during the period under investigation.

In contrast, the functional form of the change process (i.e., the mathematical formula governing relationships among the various entrance and exit events) has remained constant. Thus, entrances into the clergy population remain the sum of ordinations and net migrations; exits, the sum of resignations, net leaves, retirements, and deaths; and the difference between the two determines decline or growth in the population.

In Part Three, we analyze the changing parameter values of entrance and exit rates, those dynamic forces that make up the generating process of the demographic transition. Chief among the components of structural change are ordination events. So in this chapter we consider the problem of recruiting male celibates to the priesthood by analyzing number and rate of ordinations, rising age at ordination, and organizational and environmental conditions that explain variation in diocesan ordination rates.

Highlights

1. Ordinations to the U.S. diocesan priesthood continue to fall, with 47 percent fewer men ordained during 1980–84 than during 1966–69. By the mid-1990s, the decline for the period could plunge to 69 percent, averaging a 23 percent drop per decade.

2. Regionally, the highest ordination rates were recorded in the East South region of the country, where between 1966 and 1984 ordinations in the average diocese equaled 55 percent of the 1966 number of priests. The lowest rates were experienced in West Northcentral dioceses: 30 percent.

3. The average age at ordination rose from 27.2 in 1966 to 31.5 in 1984. Thus, assuming retirement by age 71, the average career span has been reduced from 42.8 to 38.5 years of priestly service.

4. Causal analysis indicates that ordination rates tend to be lowest in relatively affluent rural dioceses where concentrations of Hispanics are highest. In addition, newer dioceses have higher ordination rates than older ones, all other things being equal.

Descriptive Analysis

Because of their critical impact on the size and shape of the priest population in the United States, the trend in ordinations bears particularly close examination. In chapter 2, we asked what would happen if entrances in the priest population were to go up 25 percent or if exits were to go down 25 percent. The results showed that an increase in the number of ordinations would have two to four times greater impact than altering any other transition event affecting clergy decline.

Numbers

We begin the analysis with a look at the numbers. Table 7.1 presents historical data for ordinations in standardized and unstandardized numbers for the country as a whole. The standardization, as explained more fully in appendix C, takes into account fewer man-years gained for the diocese by the older ordinands of recent years. Declining figures in column 1 reveal a startling drop in the number of ordinations to the U.S. diocesan priesthood over the census period. If we smooth out the year-to-year fluctuations by using four- and five-year averages, the data show that there were 47 percent fewer men receiving priestly orders annually during 1980–

Table 7.1. U.S. diocesan ordinations and
percentage of difference between standardized
and unstandardized numbers, 1966–84, by year

Year	Number		
	Unstan-dardized	Stan-dardized[a]	% difference[b]
1966	994	945	5.2
1967	1,062	1,008	5.4
1968	1,034	972	6.4
1969	847	803	5.5
1970	842	791	6.4
1971	692	651	6.3
1972	647	612	5.7
1973	831	779	6.7
1974	732	691	5.9
1975	768	713	7.7
1976	700	644	8.7
1977	667	613	8.8
1978	574	518	10.8
1979	647	576	12.3
1980	544	488	11.5
1981	544	476	14.3
1982	511	456	12.1
1983	530	452	17.3
1984	465	395	17.7
Total	13,631	12,583	8.3

Source: weighted census counts.
[a]Standardized by constant man-years gained,
assuming an average career span of 45 years.
[b][(Col. 1/Col. 2) - 1]100.

84 than during 1966–69.[1] The actual numbers were 519 annual ordinations in the United States during 1980–84 in contrast with 984 during
1966–69.

Standardized for age at ordination, the decline is somewhat higher. The
annual number of ordinations in terms of years of service would have been
932 at the beginning of the census period and only 453 per year at the
end, a 51 percent drop instead of the 47 percent decrease in unstandardized numbers. The last column shows that the percentage of difference in

1. When smoothing data, we consistently use a 4-year period at the beginning and 5-year
periods for the remainder of the 19-year time span.

the unstandardized and standardized numbers has been increasing steadily over the entire period.

The standardization assumes that the career span of the average priest is 45 years, beginning with ordination at age 26 and ending with retirement by age 71.[2] Thus, table 7.1 shows that the potential years of service gained by the diocese from newly ordained priests during 1966–69 was about 6 percent less than expected, because some priests were ordained after age 26. By 1980–84, however, the average U.S. diocese was gaining about 15 percent fewer years of service than expected from its newly ordained priests, because men were being ordained at ages significantly older than 26.

Figure 7.1 plots the percentage of difference in standardized and unstandardized ordinations for the country as a whole and the four major census divisions. During 1966–69, men were being ordained at a slightly older age in the West and South than in the Northeast and Northcentral divisions. By the early 1980s, not only had the age at ordination increased significantly, but also the difference between the West and South dioceses, on the one hand, and the Northeast and Northcentral dioceses, on the other, had been maintained over the two decades. Thus age at ordination is significantly above the national average in the West and South, whereas it is consistently lower in the Northeast and Northcentral divisions. Accordingly, West and South dioceses invariably gain fewer years of service from their ordinations than dioceses in the other half of the country.

From an organizational viewpoint, human resources should be assessed in terms of some constant metric, just as economic resources are calculated in terms of constant values of the dollar. Therefore, one useful forecast of ordination trends focuses on standardized number of ordinations, which takes account of years of service gained. Figure 7.2 plots the standardized number of ordinations at the census-division level for the historical period (1966–84) and continues from 1985 to 1994 with projections derived from a regression model.[3]

The statistical force of the trend embodied in the historical data suggests that the decline could continue well into the current decade. As the data below the graph show, the standardized number of ordinations is pro-

2. The assumption is not entirely arbitrary, because, as data presented later will show, the average age at ordination in 1966 was 27.2, and the average age at retirement was 70.4.

3. The number of ordinations between 1985 and 1994 are projected on the basis of regressing ordinations on time for the historical period and then extending the predicted regression curve to 1994. This procedure results in a more pessimistic forecast than the one we actually use in our pessimistic projection model. Although the regression-based technique is appropriate and produces a statistically reasonable forecast, for reasons discussed in the following section we consider the results too pessimistic to be used for the projections.

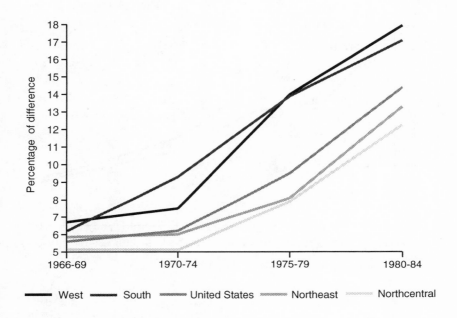

| | West | South | United States | Northeast | Northcentral |

	Year			
	1966–69	1970–74	1975–79	1980–84
United States	5.6	6.2	9.5	14.4
Divisions and regions				
Northeast	5.8	6.0	8.1	13.3
New England	7.0	8.7	8.7	17.6
Middle Atlantic	5.3	4.9	7.9	11.7
Northcentral	5.1	5.1	7.9	12.2
East Northcentral	5.0	5.0	8.2	11.2
West Northcentral	5.2	5.2	6.9	13.8
West	6.7	7.6	14.0	17.9
Mountain	8.0	17.0	18.4	22.4
Pacific	6.3	5.8	12.3	16.7
South	6.2	9.3	13.9	17.1
East South[a]	4.5	7.9	9.5	13.8
West Southcentral	7.6	10.6	16.9	19.6

Figure 7.1. Percentage of difference in standardized and unstandardized average annual number of U.S. diocesan ordinations, 1966–84, by year, nation, and division

Source: weighted census counts.
[a]Combines the South Atlantic region and one diocese from the East Southcentral region.

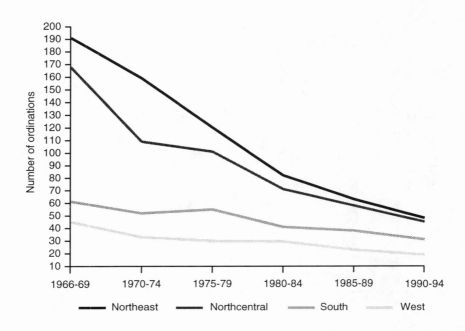

	Year						% diff. between
	1966 –69	1970 –74	1975 –79	1980 –84	1985 –89	1990 –94	1966–69 and 1990–94[a]
United States	932	705	613	453	365	289	69.0
Divisions and regions							
Northeast	192	158	121	82	63	47	75.5
New England	122	97	83	47	37	27	77.9
Middle Atlantic	262	218	158	118	90	67	74.4
Northcentral	167	109	102	72	57	45	73.1
East Northcentral	224	152	146	84	69	51	77.2
West Northcentral	111	65	58	59	45	38	65.8
West	45	33	30	30	22	18	60.0
Mountain	22	11	17	13	11	9	59.1
Pacific	68	56	42	47	34	26	61.2
South	62	53	54	42	37	32	48.4
East South[b]	55	48	44	36	31	27	50.1
West Southcentral	69	57	64	48	43	36	47.8

Figure 7.2. Standardized average annual number of U.S. diocesan ordinations, 1966–94, by year and division

Sources: weighted census counts for 1966–84; regression-based projections for 1985–94.
[a][1 - (Col. 6/Col. 1)]100.
[b]Combines the South Atlantic region and one diocese from the East Southcentral region.

jected to be only 289 per year during 1990–94. Thus, the overall decline would produce 69 percent fewer ordinations in the mid-1990s than were recorded three decades earlier when the standardized number was 932 per year.

The differences by geographic region, captured by the graph and accompanying statistics in figure 7.2, present an overview of local variation. Regional trends in ordination decline mirror the geographic differences we discovered in the diminishing size of the overall population.

The drop in standardized numbers of ordinations is notably steeper in the Northeast and Northcentral divisions than in the South and West. Generally, if trends continue, dioceses in the Northeast and Northcentral half of the nation will be ordaining about 75 percent fewer priests in the early 1990s than they did during the late 1960s. Over the same period, however, the forecasted decline for South and West dioceses will be less drastic; recruitment efforts will produce about 50 percent fewer standardized numbers of ordinations in the South and 60 percent fewer in the West.[4]

Remember, these are conditional forecasts. The extremes of decline in standardized ordinations, which we have projected to 1994, are highly *probable* but not inevitable. The forecasts are likely *if* the rate of decline experienced during 1966–84 continues until 1994. This likelihood is reinforced, though, by the continuous decline in the number of seminarians and the rising age at ordination. We explore this issue more fully when we consider the plausibility of the ordination assumptions utilized in our projection model.

Plausibility of Ordination Assumptions
Ordinations are tied to seminary recruitment, which has been cut in half during the two decades following the Second Vatican Council. Hoge and colleagues (1984) reviewed the literature on studies that investigated how to recruit priesthood candidates for best results. They found that one of the most extensive surveys was undertaken by Fee and colleagues (1981). Another recent investigation was conducted by Potvin (1985), who compared his new findings with 1966 data on seminarians (Potvin and Suziedelis 1969) and 1970 data on young priests (NORC 1972). Hemrick and

4. Regional differences reveal sharp contrasts in recruitment decline, but local diocesan extremes exhibit an even greater range of variation. Forecasts of standardized ordinations for individual dioceses in the sample are not presented; however, figures for each diocese were included in "Respondent Report II" (Schoenherr 1988). A full set of private respondent reports are stored at the U.S. Catholic Conference and another at the University of Wisconsin–Madison; standardized ordination figures for individual cases are available only by writing to the dioceses.

Hoge (1986) also replicated parts of Fee and colleagues' survey in their national profile of seminarians in theology. In brief, the consistent evidence over time shows that "the two principal determinants of interest in vocations remain the 'big two' emphasized by Fee and her associates — the encouragement factor and the deterrence of celibacy" (Hoge 1987, p. 132).

Reflecting on his comprehensive review, the updated surveys and his own recent contributions to the literature, Hoge (1987, p. 119) concludes: "Most important: the shortage of vocations is not a temporary thing which is self-correcting or a short-term low point in a cyclical pattern. It is a long-term situation with no end in sight. No large increases in the number of seminarians can be expected, even if recruitment efforts are expanded and improved." While these conclusions are not infallible, as Hoge openly admits, they are based on the best empirical evidence available. This evidence comes from one of the largest series of studies on recruitment of professionals that exists in the social sciences.

Given the long-term decline in the number of seminarians, the prognosis that the bottom of the descending curve is not in sight, and the complex nature of the two main deterrents to priestly vocations (low encouragement and celibacy), it is reasonable to suppose that the number of new recruits to the male celibate priesthood will not be greater than and, indeed, may be less than the number of ordinations experienced during 1980–84. Simply stated, there is little evidence that ordinations in the United States will go up noticeably in the foreseeable future. So we conclude that the moderate projection model, based on the number of ordinations between 1980 and 1984, is the most plausible of the three.

Figure 7.3 displays the historical trends just described and the number of ordinations projected under optimistic, moderate, and pessimistic assumptions. The graph shows that the moderate projection, which continues the 1980–84 ordination trends, is closer to the optimistic than to the pessimistic model. As Shyrock, Siegel, and Associates (1971, p. 775) observe in their treatment of population projection techniques, "the distribution of the high and low series about the medium series does not have to be symmetrical." Symmetry in establishing projection bands may be unreasonable given the social forces affecting population change. Thus, if we had relied mechanically on past historical trends in establishing our projection models, the forecasted numbers of optimistic and pessimistic ordinations would have been different.

Instead of projecting the highest number of ordinations recorded during the historical period, we lower the optimistic projections because they would be unreasonably high. We assume that the extremely high ordinations of the late 1960s were the apex of a trend that would not be repeated

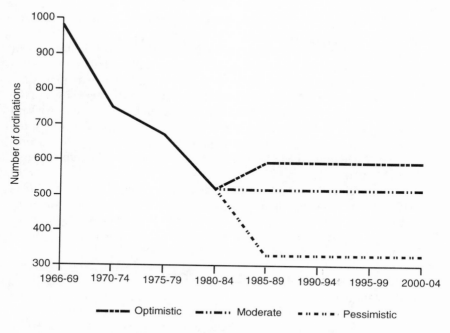

Figure 7.3. Average annual number of U.S. diocesan ordinations, 1966–2004

in the foreseeable future, given the dramatic structural changes in the Catholic church following the Second Vatican Council.[5] Note, the steadily declining numbers of ordinations projected in figure 7.2 would be lower than the pessimistic figures given in figure 7.3, because the projections in figure 7.2 are based on standardized numbers which take into account the rising

5. Social forces affecting the decline in ordinations are discussed in more detail in chapter 9.

age at ordination. The forecasts given in figure 7.3 are not standardized for the rising age of ordinands.

Note also, because a complex set of factors determined the number of past ordinations, factors which we only partly understand, we project a constant number in each of the three projections rather than an increasing or decreasing function. The direction of the curve, once it is known in the year 2005, will be upward if the actual numbers are higher and downward if they turn out to be lower than the moderate projection. Obviously, the curve could fluctuate around the straight line formed by our moderate projections. We assume the latter possibility is more probable than either of the other two.

More specifically, there is some evidence to expect the curve for 1985–2005 to be slightly lower than the moderate projection. So the unstandardized number of ordinations at the turn of the century would most likely be 400–500 per year. The standardized number, as noted in figure 7.2, would be considerably lower, falling below 300 per year.

Age at Ordination: Man-Years Gained

As the data demonstrate, men are seeking ordination at increasingly old ages. This rising age at ordination has repercussions on the internal labor pool of Catholic dioceses, because the average number of years of service gained per ordination is declining. Table 7.2 presents the mean age at ordination from 1966 to 1984, showing the extent of the additional loss in priestly manpower that results from the aging trends.

The data show that the average age of newly ordained priests increased from 27.2 to 31.5 during the 19-year period. Assuming retirement by 71, the career span of the average priest has been reduced from 42.8 years to 38.5 years. Hence the aging trend represents a 10 percent further loss in manpower beyond that resulting from the decline in sheer numbers of ordinations. Furthermore, the rise in age was notably faster at the end of

Table 7.2. Mean ages at ordination of U.S. diocesan priests, 1966–84

Year	Age
1966	27.2
1970	27.5
1975	28.3
1980	29.8
1984	31.5

Source: weighted census counts.

the period; the mean age increased by only 1.1 years between 1966 and 1975, but it increased by 3.2 years, or three times as fast, between 1975 and 1984. If trends continue, the losses from fewer man-years of service are likely to grow at increasingly faster rates, at least until the aging trend approaches an upper limit, after which ordinations become highly improbable.

Regional and Diocesan Rates

Another way to standardize the number of ordinations so that comparisons may be made across dioceses regardless of their size is to calculate the ratio or rate of ordinations per 100 active priests. Table 7.3 displays ordination trends on this basis by census region, with averages for the United States as a whole in the first row.

Ordinations in three regions followed the same pattern over time as the national trends. That is to say, for the average diocese in New England, Middle Atlantic, and East South states, the rates were highest in the beginning of the historical period, declined steadily throughout, and were lowest during 1980–84. Ordination trends deviated slightly from the national pattern in East Northcentral dioceses by showing modest growth during 1975–79 before dropping sharply again during 1980–84. Rates in the West

Table 7.3. Ordination rates of U.S. diocesan priests and percentage of gross change, 1966–84, by year, nation, and region (number of ordinations per 100 active priests)

	Average annual rate				% gross change 1966–84[a]
	1966–69	1970–74	1975–79	1980–84	
United States	2.82	2.32	2.21	1.77	38.77
Regions					
New England	2.61	2.25	2.07	1.32	35.12
Middle Atlantic	2.87	2.55	2.02	1.66	39.17
East Northcentral	2.97	2.27	2.43	1.54	37.37
West Northcentral	2.48	1.58	1.57	1.80	30.44
Mountain	3.44	1.89	3.17	2.50	50.83
Pacific	2.68	2.35	2.01	2.34	41.18
East South[b]	3.38	3.17	2.95	2.42	55.13
West Southcentral	2.80	2.48	2.97	2.22	47.61

Source: weighted census counts.
[a]Using the 1966 active population for the denominator and the cumulative number of ordinations for the numerator.
[b]Combines the South Atlantic region and one diocese from the East Southcentral region.

Southcentral region are another exception: ordinations were fairly steady for the first 15 years and then declined only during 1980–84. Ordinations in the West Northcentral and Pacific regions fell steadily during the first three time brackets but then began to increase during 1980–84. And ordination rates in the Mountain states are a final exception to the national trend of steady decline; dioceses there experienced two periods of high growth, each followed by decline.

The last column provides the cumulative increase from ordinations during 1966–84 as a percentage of the presbyterate's size in 1966. Not surprisingly, because the number of ordinations is the single most important factor of decline, and because decline was most severe in Northeast and Northcentral states, this cumulative percentage was below the national average in the Northeast and Northcentral half of the country in all but the Middle Atlantic states, where it was just above the national mean. The increase was notably above average in the West and South half of the nation. The high end of the distribution, therefore, is found in the East South, where ordinations equaled just over 55 percent of the 1966 presbyterate's size. At the low end, ordination rates were poorest in the average West Northcentral diocese, where ordinations equaled slightly more than 30 percent of the 1966 number of priests.

The fourth column of the table contains data for 1980–84, the period that governs our moderate assumptions. An examination of the rates in column 4 shows that regional differences for the last 5-year period were essentially the same as for the entire 19 years. Therefore, we can expect that ordinations during the final decades of the century will be below average in Northeast and Northcentral dioceses and above average in West and South dioceses.[6]

The data in table 7.4 reflect local ordination rates and reveal the wide variation in recruitment trends across dioceses. Noting the range of the distribution for the full sample by major geographic divisions and pointing out certain anomalies at the local level will complete the descriptive analysis.

Northeast

Two dioceses in Pennsylvania recorded the highest ordination rates in the Northeast division of the country. As column 5 shows, Allentown, with

---

6. Trends in West Northcentral dioceses are somewhat anomalous, because ordination rates in 1980–84 were higher than during the previous 10 years; furthermore, the 1980–84 rates were above the national mean. Note, however, cumulative ordinations in this region were by far the lowest in the country during the 19 years. So the recent rise in ordination rates was part of a catch-up process, which our moderate series model captures and projects into the future.

Table 7.4. Ordination rates of U.S. diocesan priests and percentage of gross change, 1966–84, by year and diocese (number of ordinations per 100 active priests; alphabetical order within region by state then diocese)

Region and diocese	Average annual rate				% gross change
	1966 –69	1970 –74	1975 –79	1980 –84	1966 –84[a]
Northeast					
New England					
Hartford CT	2.67	1.91	1.37	0.99	29.82
Norwich CT	3.01	1.37	1.98	2.51	38.27
Portland ME	1.96	1.97	2.26	1.51	30.34
Boston MA	2.60	1.99	1.20	1.18	28.69
Fall River MA	2.83	2.07	2.42	1.23	35.70
Worcester MA	2.77	3.41	3.57	1.34	50.96
Providence RI[b]	—	—	—	—	—
Burlington VT	2.92	3.09	1.03	1.28	36.11
Middle Atlantic					
Camden NJ	4.23	2.70	1.41	1.19	44.42
Newark NJ	3.12	2.52	1.70	1.47	37.02
Albany NY	2.66	2.53	1.56	1.44	32.08
Brooklyn NY	2.62	2.28	1.95	1.35	33.16
Buffalo NY	3.39	2.52	1.41	1.30	37.28
New York NY	2.19	1.45	1.28	1.54	25.40
Ogdensburg NY	3.39	3.19	2.43	1.85	48.42
Rochester NY	2.75	1.70	1.83	1.72	31.33
Rockville Centre NY	3.43	2.47	2.44	2.21	47.45
Allentown PA	2.99	3.80	3.11	2.75	58.85
Altoona–Johnstown PA	2.26	3.39	3.77	1.63	55.41
Philadelphia PA	2.54	2.96	1.89	1.63	38.26
Pittsburgh PA	3.38	3.56	2.52	1.90	51.71
Scranton PA	2.15	2.08	2.81	1.58	36.15
Northcentral					
East Northcentral					
Belleville IL	2.72	3.20	1.82	1.48	38.55
Chicago IL	3.27	2.74	3.01	1.50	41.72
Rockford IL	3.15	2.06	2.51	0.93	37.08
Indianapolis IN	3.52	2.52	2.37	1.23	37.81
Detroit MI	3.00[c]	1.64	2.20	1.83	31.78
Gaylord MI	2.39[d]	1.91	1.80	1.50	31.60
Grand Rapids MI	1.65[c]	1.21	3.64	1.50	29.44
Marquette MI	2.94	1.65	1.38	1.14	28.67
Saginaw MI	4.45[c]	2.22	2.26	1.93	45.36
Cincinnati OH	2.39	3.20	2.86	1.61	43.39
Cleveland OH	3.65	2.79	3.20	2.35	51.50
Columbus OH	3.31	2.69	1.84	2.01	41.70
Youngstown OH	2.95	2.54	3.51	1.41	41.18
La Crosse WI	1.62	1.22	0.76	1.35	18.93
Milwaukee WI	3.46	1.93	1.81	1.11	34.97

(continued on following page)

159

Table 7.4. Ordination rates of U.S. diocesan priests and percentage of gross change, 1966–84, by year and diocese (continued)

Region and diocese	Average annual rate				% gross change
	1966 –69	1970 –74	1975 –79	1980 –84	1966 –84[a]
Northcentral (continued)					
West Northcentral					
Des Moines IA	2.90	1.99	2.62	1.36	36.64
Dubuque IA	2.09	1.04	0.87	0.51	18.46
Sioux City IA	2.43	1.35	1.29	1.13	26.63
Dodge City KS	2.33	0.99	1.08	1.81	26.36
Salina KS	2.91	1.72	1.36	1.16	30.23
Wichita KS	1.32	1.29	0.81	2.82	24.30
New Ulm MN	2.39	1.71	0.56	1.33	24.41
St. Cloud MN	2.29	0.65	1.37	1.70	24.50
St. Paul–Minneapolis MN	3.31	1.73	2.51	2.37	39.44
Kansas City–St. Jos. MO	4.48	1.73	0.87	2.54	38.73
St. Louis MO	2.77	2.33	3.08	1.79	45.00
Springfield–C. Girard. MO	1.75	3.69	1.92	3.09	47.55
Lincoln NE[b]	—	—	—	—	—
Fargo ND	1.65	1.35	1.00	1.97	23.45
Rapid City SD	1.22	1.45	2.35	6.29	28.57
West					
Mountain					
Pueblo CO	5.62	2.50	2.34	2.19	57.50
Boise ID	4.77	2.30	3.44	2.12	61.04
Gallup NM	1.72[c]	7.87	12.22	4.03	255.44
Las Cruces NM	3.78[d]	1.65	3.72	1.16	50.58
Santa Fe NM	1.95[c]	2.03	2.10	2.17	34.57
Cheyenne WY	2.89	0.00	1.60	3.04	30.51
Pacific					
Fresno CA[b]	—	—	—	—	—
Los Angeles CA	3.28[c]	2.33	1.80	2.71	44.94
Monterey CA	1.39[e]	3.04	1.78	1.78	38.85
Oakland CA	3.10	2.32	2.62	2.27	43.77
Orange CA	3.29[d]	2.33	3.04	3.93	57.42
San Bernardino CA	2.15[d]	1.82	0.80	2.78	31.45
San Diego CA	2.15[c]	1.82	1.46	1.96	31.97
San Francisco CA	2.20[c]	2.53	2.33	2.35	38.47
San Jose CA	2.20[d]	2.53	2.33	1.44	34.64
Stockton CA	3.58	4.16	1.70	1.88	52.63
Baker OR	3.23	1.28	2.56	1.52	38.20
South					
East South[f]					
Wilmington DE	3.54	3.62	3.42	2.36	58.15
Orlando FL	7.10[g]	2.91	1.99	2.60	72.89

(continued on following page)

Table 7.4. Ordination rates of U.S. diocesan priests and percentage of gross change, 1966–84, by year and diocese (continued)

Region and diocese	Average annual rate				% gross change 1966 –84[a]
	1966 –69	1970 –74	1975 –79	1980 –84	
South (continued)					
East South[f] (continued)					
St. Petersburg Fl	3.59[g]	2.13	3.10	3.24	64.13
Atlanta GA	9.22	4.82	4.42	4.38	142.85
Covington KY	2.06	1.63	2.09	2.31	33.09
Baltimore MD	2.89	4.46	3.23	1.42	52.5
West Southcentral					
Little Rock AK	1.65	0.80	2.09	1.75	23.26
Alexandria–Shreveport LA	1.57	1.65	1.48	1.00	23.48
Baton Rouge LA	2.15	5.52	2.93	3.32	73.61
Lafayette LA	3.56[c]	1.84	3.55	2.35	51.86
Lake Charles LA	3.56[d]	1.84	3.55	3.66	59.83
Austin TX	3.38	3.20	2.93	1.33	50.56
Beaumont TX	3.67	3.42	4.12	2.02	69.67
Corpus Christi TX	2.93[c]	2.79	2.95	1.77	48.23
Dallas TX	3.30[h]	3.26	4.38	4.22	67.01
El Paso TX	3.88[c]	1.63	3.84	3.02	62.39
Fort Worth TX	1.98[h]	1.64	5.81	4.62	74.00
Galveston–Houston TX	3.29[c]	3.31	2.84	2.43	54.76
San Antonio TX	2.97[c]	2.66	2.12	1.19	40.92
Victoria TX	3.00[d]	2.72	2.20	0.83	39.34

Source: census counts.

[a]Using the 1966 active population for the denominator and the cumulative number of ordinations for the numerator.

[b]Refused to participate.

[c]Divided during the census period. The division does not affect the rate, because it is standardized.

[d]Established during the census period by being divided from others in the sample. The annual rates prior to the year of the split are those of the parent diocese(s), weighted when necessary. See appendix D for year of establishment and parent diocese(s).

[e]Divided in 1967. The rate for 1966 is based on size of the active population as identifiable in 1966 (see appendix D).

[f]Combines the South Atlantic region and one diocese from the East Southcentral region.

[g]Established in 1968. The figure given for 1966–69 is the average of the 1968 and 1969 rates (see appendix D).

[h]Divided in 1969. The average given for 1966–69 is based on size of the active population as identifiable in years prior to and in the year of the split (see appendix D).

ordinations equaling 59 percent of its 1966 priest roster, and Altoona–Johnstown, with a similar increase of 55 percent, stand out at the high end of the range. The smallest number of ordinations during the period, in proportion to the size of its presbyterate in 1966, was recorded by the Archdiocese of New York: 25 percent.

Northcentral

According to statistics in the second panel of the table, the cumulative result of recruitment efforts in Cleveland was 52 percent of the number of active priests in 1966, for the highest growth through ordinations in the Northcentral states. The lowest gains from ordination in the Northcentral division as well as in the entire country were registered in Dubuque and La Crosse. It is not surprising that these two dioceses experienced the lowest ordination rates, because, as we reported in chapter 4, they are suffering the highest overall priest decline in the sample. During the entire census period, cumulative ordinations amounted to only 18.5 percent of the 1966 clergy population in Dubuque and 18.9 percent of the 1966 clergy population in La Crosse.

West and South

The high end of the range in dioceses of the West is represented by a 61 percent cumulative growth through ordinations in Boise, and the low end is established by ordinations equaling 31 percent of the 1966 presbyterate in San Bernardino and Cheyenne.[7] The data in the bottom panel of the table reveal the exceptionally favorable ordination rates in Atlanta, which set the high for dioceses of the South as well as for the entire United States. Atlanta increased its active clergy almost one and one-half times, augmenting the size of the 1966 priest population by 143 percent through ordinations during the 19-year period. The low end of the range in the South is anchored by Little Rock and Alexandria–Shreveport: 23 percent.

Local Anomalies

In keeping with the national trends already presented, the pattern in ordination rates for the vast majority of dioceses shows that recruitment was notably lower toward the end of the period than at the beginning. If we compare ordination rates for the first half, that is, those for 1966–74, with rates for the second half of the period under investigation, namely, those for 1975–84, the national trend showing steady decline also emerges at the

---

7. Table 7.4 shows Gallup at 255 percent. But as noted in chapter 6, Gallup is a highly unusual case, so is omitted in all statistical descriptions and analytic models.

local level, with few exceptions. Only 6 out of 50 dioceses, or 12 percent, in the Northeast and Northcentral half of the country experienced higher ordination rates during 1975–84 than during 1966–74. In the South and West half of the country, however, 12 dioceses out of 35, or 34 percent, recorded more ordinations per 100 active priests during the second 10 years than during the first 9.

Dioceses where ordinations were growing rather than declining, and specifically those where ordination rates during 1980–84 were the highest of the entire period, deserve a closer look. In West Northcentral states, the dioceses of Wichita, Fargo, and Rapid City all recorded their highest ordination rates of the period during 1980–84. But the cumulative gain from ordinations during the 19 years ranges from 23 percent to 29 percent of the 1966 presbyterates in these three dioceses, while the average nationally was 39 percent. Thus it appears that the abnormally high growth at the end of the period was part of a catch-up process, which, however, still has a long way to go before catching up with the national average.

In West and South states, the dioceses of Santa Fe, Cheyenne, Orange, San Bernardino, Covington, and Lake Charles showed the strongest ordination trends of the period during 1980–84. Dallas and Fort Worth began their strongest ordination growth in 1975–79, and the trend continued through 1980–84. Various factors appear to have affected the growth spurt in these dioceses. First, ordination trends in half of the anomalous dioceses were below the national mean. In Santa Fe, Cheyenne, Covington, and San Bernardino ordinations during the census period ranged from 31 percent to 35 percent of the 1966 priest roster. So, once again, unusually high growth during the latter five years only made up for unusually low increases during earlier years; furthermore, the process fell short of catching up with the national average.

In the remainder of the South and West dioceses with distinctive growth trends, the cumulative increase from ordinations was notably above the 39 percent national average. Ordinations between 1966 and 1984 ranged from 57 percent to 74 percent of the 1966 priest roster in the dioceses of Orange, Lake Charles, Dallas, and Fort Worth. Lake Charles was created in 1980, so whether high growth from ordinations during the first five years of its existence was a short-range surge or the beginning of a trend is impossible to say. The dioceses of Orange, Dallas, and Fort Worth are situated in areas where the Catholic population is growing rapidly. As the analysis in chapter 6 demonstrated, church membership growth has a strong positive impact on growth in the priest population.

Observations that high ordination rates balance earlier low rates, that new dioceses may have unusually high ordination trends, and that environmental conditions such as church membership growth affect ordination rates are not the result of systematic analysis. They flow from a descriptive reconnaissance of the data, through which one gains familiarity with the distribution and range of scores on the variables of interest and generates hypotheses that can be incorporated in a controlled causal analysis. In the next section of the chapter we present a model that tests these and other hypotheses regarding the causes of high or low ordination rates.

Causal Analysis

At one level of abstraction we attempt to explain organizational change through natural selection theory, and so focus heavily on environmental and organizational conditions in our explanatory models. We construct our models, however, with a view to questions that interest policymakers, who must consider possible intervention strategies which they hope will improve organizational survival. One of the fundamentals of good policy is empirical knowledge, for example, knowledge about the complex social forces that affect the evolution, persistence, or decline of organizational forms such as the male celibate priesthood. How to insure a sufficient supply of recruits to the priesthood in Catholic dioceses is the practical question, and how to explain the ongoing generation, persistence, or decline of the male celibate priesthood, which is the current organizational form of the Catholic priestly ministry, is the theoretical question underlying the analysis in this section.

Explaining variation in components of the change process is part of an attempt to construct a theory of the demographic transition of the clergy. Organizational change from a population perspective occurs at three interrelated structural levels, as Hernes (1976) and Aldrich (1979) explain. The model presented in this chapter explicates differences in the parameter structure of the decline and aging process, more specifically, variations in the ordination rate, which is the most important component in the change process.

A Causal Model of Ordination Rate

Like the cross-sectional model in chapter 6, the variables used to explain variance in the 1980 ordination rates were all measured at the same point in time. In the exploratory stages of the analysis we examined the entire set of environmental measures from the Glenmary data as well as all the organizational variables constructed from our data set and other available sources. Among the many models tested, figure 7.4 depicts the final model which best explains diocesan variations in ordination rates.

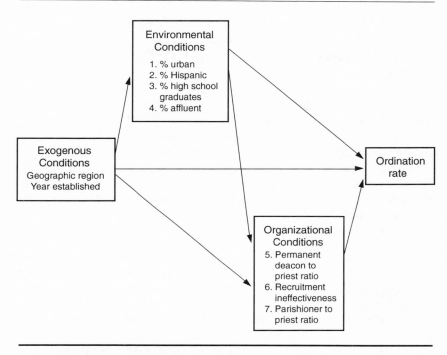

Figure 7.4. Model of priestly recruitment

The arrows in the figure indicate that two exogenous conditions, geographic region and the year the diocese was established, are assumed to have had possible causal effects on the following 1980 conditions: environmental conditions, such as the extent to which the general population was urban, Hispanic, educated, and affluent; three organizational traits of the dioceses, namely, the ratio of permanent deacons to active diocesan priests, recruitment ineffectiveness, and the ratio of parishioners to active diocesan priests; and the ultimate dependent variable, the ordination rate. The influence may have been direct or it may have flowed through any variable that intervenes between geographic region or year of establishment and a later variable; we assume no causal precedence between region and year of establishment.

Similarly, any variable in the diagram may have had a direct influence on the ordination rate as well as on all other subsequent, higher-numbered variables. Moreover, each variable was theoretically capable of indirectly influencing the number of ordinations per 100 active priests through any of the conditions that intervene between it and the ultimate dependent variable. The definitions and data sources for the variables are provided in appendix C.

Descriptive Overview

Table 7.5 adds to the portrait of the average diocese in each census region, which we began in chapter 6; the new data describe those variables that influence ordination rates but were not included in previous models.[8] Scanning the first column of the table reveals that the establishment of Catholic dioceses generally follows the historic patterns of settlement and migration in the United States. The oldest dioceses are concentrated in the Northeast and Northcentral divisions, where the average year of establishment ranges from 1873 in Middle Atlantic states to 1894 in West Northcentral dioceses. The most recently established dioceses are found in the South and West, where the average year of creation ranges from 1900 in East South dioceses to 1936 for those along the Pacific Coast. As noted in chapter 6, growth of the Catholic population has been astronomical in California; the increase in church membership resulted in the creation of several new dioceses in recent decades and hence a set of relatively young diocesan churches overall.

The restoration of the permanent diaconate in the Catholic church was one of the reforms following the Second Vatican Council.[9] The church in the United States welcomed the innovation and adopted the reform in 1971. Deacons are sacramentally ordained for a ministry of service in the church and occupy a level in the hierarchy of holy orders just below priests. Deacons may be married but must be male. Along with many diverse responsibilities included in a ministry of service, the church confers upon deacons the right to preach, baptize, and witness sacramental marriage. Thus permanent deacons, for the most part, are married men who perform several ministerial tasks which, until recently, were reserved exclusively to priests.

Table 7.5 shows that education among the general populace living within

---

8. Because the averages presented are estimates based on a probability sample, they may differ slightly from regional and national figures published elsewhere; see footnote 7, chapter 6.

9. The diaconate is traced to biblical times. It was abandoned as a life-long ministerial function after several centuries and became a step on the way to full ordination to the priesthood. Today there is a distinction between "transitional" deacons—those who will soon be ordained priests—and "permanent" deacons—those who have no plans to be ordained to priestly orders but will remain deacons throughout their ministerial careers (see Suenens 1964; Ziade 1964).

Table 7.5. Selected conditions affecting ordination rates in U.S. Catholic dioceses, 1980, by region (means)

Region	Year established	% high school grads.	Perm. deacon to priest ratio[a]	Ordination rate[b]
New England	1881	21.6	11	1.34
Middle Atlantic	1873	22.6	9	1.93
East Northcentral	1876	22.5	13	1.99
West Northcentral	1894	22.4	10	1.83
Mountain	1911	20.0	27	2.18
Pacific	1936	19.2	16	2.33
East South[c]	1900	19.9	11	2.78
West Southcentral	1916	16.2	35	2.97
Grand mean	1896	20.7	16	2.17
Standard deviation	53	3.1	19	1.27

Sources: see appendix C for columns 1 and 2 and for numerator in column 3; weighted census counts for denominator in column 3 and for column 4.
[a]Number of permanent deacons per 100 active diocesan priests.
[b]Number of ordinations per 100 active diocesan priests.
[c]Combines the South Atlantic region and one diocese from the East Southcentral region.

diocesan jurisdictions is highest in the Northeast and Northcentral divisions, where regional averages of the percentage of high school graduates are around two points above the national mean. Dioceses in the West and South are situated in ecological niches characterized by notably lower levels of education. In this half of the country all the regional means are below average, as much as 4 percentage points lower in West Southcentral states.

The third column reveals that the permanent diaconate is flourishing most in dioceses where the priest shortage is greatest, at least as the shortage is reflected by high parishioner-to-priest ratios. Hence, the distribution of permanent deacons reinforces the pattern of Catholic regionalism discovered in previous chapters. The number of permanent deacons per 100 active diocesan priests is below the national average in the Northeast and Northcentral divisions of the country, where standardized parishioner-to-priest ratios are lowest, and above average in the South and West divisions, where the ratios are highest. There is one exception to the pattern. East South dioceses have a high standardized number of parishioners per active diocesan priest like other dioceses in the South but, nevertheless, have one of the lowest deacon-to-priest ratios in the country.

Not surprisingly, regional differences in the dependent variable, number of ordinations per 100 active priests, fall along the same line of demarcation created by local variations in the other major variables. Dioceses in the Northeast and Northcentral divisions are characterized by below average ordination rates and those in the South and West by above average rates. The extremes reach from 1.3 ordinations per 100 active priests in New England to a ratio of nearly 3.0 per 100 in the West Southcentral states.

Besides these and the other variables that compose the final model, we examined the influence of other environmental and organizational conditions on ordination rates and found no significant effects. Of all possible combinations examined, given the order of assumed precedence among the variables, the system of variables summarized in figure 7.4 best describes the sequence of social forces that explain variation in diocesan ordination rates.

Explaining Local Variation in Diocesan Ordination Rates

In 1980, the bishop in the "typical" diocese in our sample ordained 2.2 young men per 100 active diocesan priests.[10] However, as table 7.4 shows, ordination rates vary greatly across dioceses, ranging from a high in 1980–84 of 6.3 in Rapid City to a low of 0.5 in Dubuque. Table 7.6 contains the regression equation that explains why this variation in ordination rates exists.[11] The adjusted R^2 statistic indicates that the impact of one exogenous and seven environmental and organizational factors accounts for over 57 percent of interdiocesan variation in ordination rates. The adjusted t-ratios reveal that all the variables in the model exert strong, statistically significant effects on priestly recruitment; we will discuss them in their assumed order of precedence.

Exogenous Conditions[12]

Examining the possible effects of *region* produced an important negative finding. Geographic location of the diocese had no influence on ordination rates, once other variables were accounted for. The result was unexpected, because ordination rates vary notably by region. Additionally, causal

10. The dependent variable is the mean ordination rate for 1979–81.

11. Following the same procedures established in chapter 6, although we examined the existence and strength of relationships among all variables in the model, we present only the equation explaining the variance of the final dependent variable, ordination rate.

12. Variables are considered exogenous when their causes are external to the causal chain that affects a dependent variable, such as ordination rate. Exogenous variables include the givens of any situation, such as region. We also treat the year the diocese was established as a given within which the process leading to high or low diocesan ordination rates in 1980 occurs.

Although three dioceses in the sample were created after 1980, we were able to adjust the population registers in both the new and parent dioceses so that we could assume the former already existed in 1980. See appendix D for details of the data adjustments.

Table 7.6. Effects of environmental and organizational conditions on ordination rates in U.S. Catholic dioceses, 1980 (unstandardized regression coefficients)

Independent variable	b	Adjusted t-ratio[a]
Year established	.0087	6.705**
% urban	.0158	3.464**
% Hispanic	-.0363	-4.316**
% high school graduates	-.0991	-3.803**
% affluent	-.0378	-3.161*
Perm. deacon/priest ratio	.0186	4.332**
Recruit. ineffectiveness	-.00011	-9.149**
Parishioner/priest ratio	.00072	4.343**
n of dioceses	85	
Constant	-12.3268	-4.757**
F-ratio	15.050**	
R^2	.613	
Adjusted R^2	.572	

[a]Adjustment is based on a finite population correction factor of 0.705 or the square root of 1 - (n/N) applied to the standard error of b; see Mendenhall et al. 1971.
*$p \leq .01$.
**$p \leq .001$.

models in chapter 6—used to explain variation in overall decline and parishioner-to-priest ratios—revealed that the geographic location of dioceses continues to affect the availability of priests even after controlling for the influence of environmental and organizational conditions.

When we decompose the decline process and focus on one of its major components, however, we discover that it is not geographic region in and of itself but the impact of certain environmental and organizational conditions that explains why some dioceses are able to recruit more priests than others. The new evidence calls into question whether any regional subgroup of dioceses, such as those referred to as the East Coast church, has successfully isolated itself from the brunt of declining recruitment and so is loosely coupled with other parts of the church. At least with regard to ordination rates, dioceses appear to be homogeneous in their relationships to their ecological niche, once relevant environmental and organizational conditions are accounted for.

Although geographic region exerts no exogenous influence on ordinations in dioceses, the *year of establishment* does. Newer dioceses are likely to have higher ordination rates than older ones. If two dioceses were similar in other conditions tested, but one was established in 1975 and the other in 1875, the younger diocese experienced almost 1 more ordination (precisely 0.87) per 100 active priests in 1980 than the older one.

Stinchcombe (1965) has pointed out that new organizations behave very differently from those that have been established longer. In many cases newness is more a liability than an asset; several studies have documented empirically that organizational failure rates decline with age (Freeman et al. 1983). In Catholic dioceses, however, where organizational failure, even through merger, is a rare event, newness appears to be an asset for raising recruitment rates. Hannan and Freeman (1984, 1989) note that structural inertia is weaker in younger organizations. Hence, newer dioceses can adapt to changing conditions faster than older ones, perhaps by experimenting and comparing different results of novel recruitment efforts.

Environmental Conditions
We examined the possible influence of environmental conditions other than those listed in figure 7.4, but found no important effects on ordination rates from age distribution of the general population, percentage of African Americans, percentage of American Indians, divorce rates, average family size, availability of health care, occurrence of substandard housing, or occupation.[13] The extent to which the diocese is urban or rural, its ethnic profile, education profile, and income differences, however, all exert a strong influence on priestly recruitment.

Urban dioceses experience higher ordination rates than rural ones, other conditions being equal. If the concentration of urban dwellers were 20 percentage points higher in one diocese than another, the more urban diocese would experience about 1 additional ordination per 100 priests over a three-year period than the less urban diocese.[14] The greater recruitment success of urban dioceses may result from advantages such as population density, more elaborate communication systems, better transportation, and similar characteristics.

A higher proportion of *Hispanics* in the total population is negatively related to diocesan ordination rates. For example, if two dioceses were alike on other variables in the model but the segment of the population with Hispanic origins were 10 percentage points higher in Diocese A than in Diocese B, over a three-year period the bishop in Diocese A would ordain about 1 fewer priest per 100 active priests than the bishop in Diocese B.[15]

---

13. Some of these variables are correlated with the ordination rate, but the relationships do not persist when these variables are added to the fully developed model.

14. Precisely: $0.0158 \times 20 \times 3 = 0.948$.

15. Precisely: $-0.0363 \times 10 \times 3 = -1.089$.

This is not surprising given the underrepresentation of Hispanics in U.S. seminaries documented by Hemrick and Hoge (1986). Possible explanations of the lack of vocations among Hispanics are widely discussed by church leaders.

Furthermore, as noted in chapter 6, Catholics residing in dioceses with a large Hispanic component are more likely to encounter an inadequate supply of priestly services. These findings corroborate one another. A relatively large Hispanic population increases the parishioner-to-priest ratio, thus reducing the availability of priestly services. Less contact with priests appears to reduce the level of ordinations to the priesthood. Lower ordinations, in turn, increases the parishioner-to-priest ratio.

Higher levels of *education* in the general population tend to lower diocesan ordination rates, controlling for other conditions in the model. Specifically, if the proportion of the population educated at the high school level or beyond were 10 percentage points higher in one diocese than in another, each year the first diocese would record almost 1 fewer ordination per 100 active priests than the second.[16]

Similarly, higher *income* in the general population has the effect of dampening ordination rates. Assuming all other conditions are equal, dioceses with a larger proportion of families at annual incomes over $25,000 have lower ordination rates than less affluent dioceses. For example, when the proportion of affluent families is 10 percentage points higher in Diocese A than in Diocese B, every three years Diocese A will have about 1 fewer ordination per 100 active priests than Diocese B.[17]

These results from testing the impact of education and income do not provide evidence that ordinands come from relatively less educated or poorer families. They reflect an environmental constraint that is more structural in nature. That is to say, ordination recruitment efforts are less successful generally in an environment where large proportions of the population are well-educated and affluent.

Organizational Conditions

We identified three organizational variables as important predictors of ordination rates in the multiple regression model, namely, the ratio of permanent deacons to priests, recruitment ineffectiveness, and the ratio of parishioners to priests. As a group, the organizational conditions have a larger direct impact than the environmental variables in causing variation in diocesan ordination rates.

16. Precisely: $-0.0991 \times 10 = -0.991$.
17. Precisely: $-0.0378 \times 10 \times 3 = -1.134$.

Permanent Deacon–to–Priest Ratio
Dioceses with proportionately more permanent deacons also have higher priestly ordination rates. If two dioceses have identical values for the other variables in the model but Diocese A has 20 more permanent deacons per 100 active diocesan priests than Diocese B, every three years Diocese A will have approximately 1 more priestly ordination per 100 active priests than Diocese B.[18] Perhaps whatever diocesan conditions account for a flourishing permanent deacon program also promote more successful recruitment to the diocesan priesthood.

Recruitment Ineffectiveness
All other conditions held constant, dioceses that require larger pools of young Catholic males per ordination tend to have lower ordination rates. This obvious relationship emerges as the single most powerful predictor of ordination rates. The importance of including this variable in the model is that other conditions tested still explain variance in ordination rates even when we account for diocesan differences in recruitment ineffectiveness.

Parishioner-to-Priest Ratio
Dioceses with a high ratio of church members per diocesan priest are likely to have higher ordination rates, all conditions tested being equal. For example, if the number of Catholics per priest is 1,000 higher in Diocese A than in Diocese B, every three years Diocese A would have about 2 more ordinations per 100 active priests than Diocese B.[19] This finding does not mean that Diocese A is in a more advantageous situation than Diocese B because it has a higher ordination rate. Rather, it shows that Diocese A is responding to a relatively poor parishioner-to-priest ratio by ordaining proportionately more priests than Diocese B.[20]

18. Precisely: $0.0186 \times 20 \times 3 = 1.118$.
19. Precisely: $0.00072 \times 1,000 \times 3 = 2.16$.
20. Preliminary analysis revealed a strong effect on recruitment from age distribution of the priest population: the higher the proportion of priests under 35, the higher the ordination rate. This finding would have interesting theoretical and practical implications in view of the dramatic drop in ordinations and the aging process underway in most dioceses. If a young age pyramid raises ordinations, rapid aging can only exacerbate an already severe recruitment problem. We reasoned further, however, that the presence of a relatively large group of young priests may merely reflect successful recruitment in recent years, because large ordination classes increase the size of young age cohorts. A regression model testing these hypotheses, however, is affected by collinearity, because the percentage of young priests in 1980 and the mean ordination rate for 1969–78 are correlated at 0.702. Adding both variables to the model presented in table 7.6 shows that the percentage of young priests continues to have a strong positive effect on the 1980 ordination rate when controlling for the mean or-

Discussion and Conclusion

The national picture is one of plummeting ordinations to the priesthood. The numbers have been declining at well over 20 percent per decade since the end of the Second Vatican Council. The U.S. Catholic church can expect about two-thirds fewer ordinations in the mid-1990s than in the mid-1960s. At the same time, the age at ordination is rising. So the number of years of service gained by each ordination is also decreasing. Trends indicate that the downward trajectory has not yet bottomed out. Hence, further decline in recruitment is likely.

Poor recruitment is endemic in the U.S. Catholic church, but some dioceses are more successful in attracting young men to the priesthood than others. Our causal analysis paints a portrait of the typical diocese with relatively high ordination rates. Ordinations are higher in those dioceses that are newly established in urban areas where the general population is relatively poor and uneducated. Few Hispanics live in the area, and the diocese has a thriving permanent deacon program that perhaps tries to compensate for a low supply of priestly services.

In contrast, therefore, ordinations are lower in old, rural dioceses where the population is relatively affluent and well-educated. Many Hispanics live in the area. The diocese has few permanent deacons relative to priests, perhaps because the ratio of parishioners to priests is low, so lack of priestly services is not yet a critical problem.

In addition, we discovered negative evidence for the hypothesis that the U.S. Catholic church is a loosely coupled system. Geographic region in and of itself has no net impact on ordination rates. The environmental and organizational conditions that we identified in our model explain variation in recruitment success regardless of where the diocese is situated geographically. Thus the reverberations of sustained poor recruitment are being felt throughout the system. With ordinations in disarray, dioceses may be turning to incardinations as another avenue of recruitment, the main topic of the next chapter.

---

dination rate for the prior 10 years. But the collinearity problem makes it impossible to interpret the results unambiguously.

8 Migration

Two sets of minor transition events play a significant role in the demographic transition of the Catholic clergy in some regions and dioceses of the United States. An excess of incardinations over excardinations has a notable impact in stabilizing the change process in certain dioceses. Furthermore, the incardination phenomenon may actually mask the true extent of the clergy decline nationwide. Likewise, the imbalance of extended leaves for illness and other serious reasons and returns from leave adds to the difficulties of organizations faced with recruitment, retention, and retirement problems.

In this chapter we turn our attention to two types of net migration. In Catholic dioceses, permanent "net immigration" produces a gain in clergy size through an excess of incardinations over excardinations. After priests incardinate, they rarely migrate again, so the increments in population size are permanent. Temporary "net emigration," on the other hand, usually creates a loss for diocesan clergy populations when the numbers of priests beginning extended leaves exceed those returning from leave on an annual basis. When priests take a leave because of illness or some other incapacitating problem, they often depart from the diocese and return later; the migration is temporary. Whether or not they continue to reside in the diocese, they are gone from the active labor pool for a year or more.

To simplify terminology, we shall refer to permanent net immigration as simply *net immigration* and temporary net emigration as *net leave*. We examine both types of organizational migration with data describing regional and local variation and use a causal model to explain why differences in net immigration rates exist. We will also reassess our projection models in light of zero net migration, that is, under the experimental assumption that incardinations and excardinations occur at equal rates.

174

Highlights

1. Without the gain created by excess incardinations, the number of active native clergy in the average U.S. diocese would drop about 45 percent between 1966 and 2005. This is a 13 percent greater loss than the 40 percent decline projected under the assumptions that the gains of net immigration would continue until the turn of the century.

2. Causal analysis demonstrates that dioceses with higher numbers of parishioners per priest and those with lower ordination rates have higher net immigrations. Thus priestly immigration in U.S. Catholic dioceses works basically on rational principles of supply and demand.

3. Extended leaves of absence for serious illness or other incapacitating problems have created a net loss of about 1 percent of the active diocesan clergy per decade. If leaves and returns to active duty had been in balance, the cumulative net decline in priestly manpower between 1966 and 1984 would have been reduced by 10 percent.

Net Immigration

Numbers

The number of priests who were incardinated and excardinated in the United States between 1966 and 1984 are recorded in table 8.1. Incardinations averaged 152 per year and excardinations 79 per year for a net gain of almost 74 priests annually during the 19-year period. The net gain from permanent immigrations ranged from a low of 34 in 1966 to a high of 99 in 1983; no year registered a net loss. The data show that the typical pattern in this country has been to allow almost twice as many incardinations as excardinations, at least during the two decades following the Second Vatican Council.

An examination of the first two columns of data reveals unusually high migrations during 1971, 1976, 1978, and 1980–82. These are the years new dioceses were created from older ones in the sample, so in each case the extra transitions represent incardinations into the new diocese(s), which are balanced by excardinations from the parent diocese(s).[1] As the final .column shows, however, the net surplus of incardinations over excardinations for those years is not unusual, because all the figures fall within the range of gains experienced in other years when no new dioceses were established.

Projecting Migration

Figure 8.1 plots the historical trends in the surplus of incardinations over excardinations, along with the number of net gains projected under opti-

---

1. These are *ipso facto* incardinations and excardinations that occurred when the decree creating the new diocese went into effect; see appendix D for the dioceses involved.

Table 8.1. Number of incardinations, excardinations, and net gains of U.S. diocesan priests, 1966–84

Year	Incardinations	Excardinations	Net gains[a]
1966	56	22	34
1967	62	16	46
1968	95	37	58
1969	100	46	54
1970	105	23	82
1971	239	185	54
1972	111	30	81
1973	107	21	86
1974	110	35	75
1975	118	33	85
1976	201	130	71
1977	126	36	90
1978	344	248	96
1979	132	42	90
1980	159	88	71
1981	256	186	70
1982	311	230	81
1983	140	41	99
1984	123	48	75
Total	2,895	1,497	1,398

Source: weighted census counts.
[a]Col. 1 - Col. 2.

mistic, moderate, and pessimistic assumptions. The curve depicting the 1966–84 historical data shows that the upward trend peaked at an annual high of 86 net immigrations during 1975–79 and then declined to about 79 during 1980–84.

How plausible are the assumptions underlying the projected numbers of net immigrations? Nationally, the projected surplus of incardinands over excardinands must come from either religious orders or foreign dioceses, for the U.S. diocesan presbyterate forms a closed population in which each loss through excardination in one diocese is matched by a gain through incardination in another. Priest populations in religious orders, however, are declining faster than those in dioceses (Shields and Verdieck 1985). Furthermore, the decline is also affecting most European countries, the traditional foreign source of incardinations for the United States (figure 1.1). The data in figure 8.1 may indicate that these constraints have begun to take effect already, because net gains were notably lower during the early

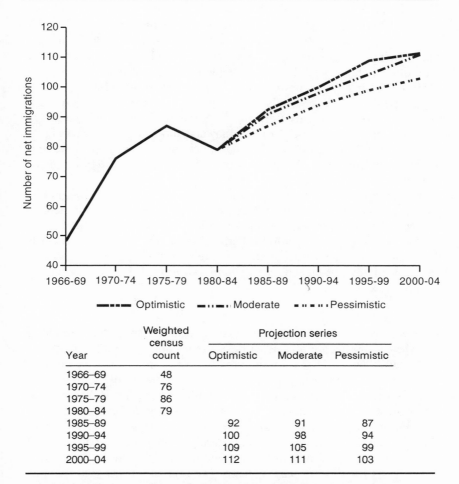

Figure 8.1. Average annual number of net immigrations of U.S. diocesan priests, 1966–2004

Year	Weighted census count	Projection series		
		Optimistic	Moderate	Pessimistic
1966–69	48			
1970–74	76			
1975–79	86			
1980–84	79			
1985–89		92	91	87
1990–94		100	98	94
1995–99		109	105	99
2000–04		112	111	103

1980s than during the previous five years. Hence, we might argue that the net immigration rate in American dioceses will not rise in the future.

Priestly net immigration trends could continue their past upward trajectory despite the recent drop in net gains, however, if U.S. dioceses begin to draw more foreign priests from Latin America and Asia.[2] For example,

2. Jim Castelli (1989, p. 1) reports growing concern in Catholic parishes over the numbers of "foreign-born priests from such nations as Poland, Korea, India, Mexico and the Philippines."

rapid growth of the Hispanic population in the United States has begun to attract more priests from Latin America and the Philippines, some of whom enter as illegal aliens, as do members of their flock. Incardination is an official channel for bishops to replenish a dwindling priest supply, but informal and illegal networks also have an unmeasured but significant impact on increasing the availability of priestly services to Hispanics, especially in the southwestern portion of the country.[3] The growing number of Korean and Vietnamese Catholics may also motivate more priests from those countries to come to the United States. Accordingly, we argue that the net imbalance of incardinations over excardinations will continue to rise in the next two decades.

Although our projection of trends results in relatively large net immigration gains at the national level, as we shall see later, gains from net immigration are not spread evenly across regions and dioceses of the United States. One of the methodological strengths of our projection model is that these differences are accounted for. Hence some regions and dioceses remain virtually untouched by net immigration both historically and in the projected future.

Age

Table 8.2 gives the average age at incardination and excardination along with the average age for all active priests in the country from 1966 to 1984. In the late 1960s, priests who migrated to and from dioceses were somewhat older than the average priest and, during the early 1970s, those who excardinated were somewhat younger. All other comparisons, however, reveal almost no age differences between migrants and nonmigrants.

From the organizational point of view, as an increment to the manpower pool an incardination represents significantly fewer years of service gained than an ordination. Assuming retirement at 70, the average incardinated priest enters the diocese past midcareer and represents only 20 years of priestly service gained by the diocese.

National and Regional Rates

Table 8.3 presents the number of excess incardinations over excardinations per 100 active priests in five-year intervals from 1966 to 1984. The average diocese experienced a cumulative net increase from surplus incardinations of just over 4 percent of its 1966 number of priests during the roughly two decades. Regional contrasts in the data, however, are large.

---

3. Personal communication with Helen Rose Ebaugh, sociologist of religion at the University of Houston.

Table 8.2. Mean ages at incardination, excardination, and
for all active U.S. diocesan priests, 1966–84

Year	Incardination	Excardination	All active priests
1966–69	48.1	48.9	46.8
1970–74	47.8	45.6	47.5
1975–79	48.8	48.4	48.5
1980–84	50.1	49.4	49.9

Source: weighted census counts.

As we discovered in the last chapter, dioceses in the West and South enjoyed relatively high ordinations compared with the rest of the country. This advantage was reinforced by net immigration rates that are two, three, and four times higher in these divisions than the national average, which is shown in the top row of the table. Similarly, the poor ordination records of the Northeast and Northcentral dioceses shown in the last chapter were matched by net immigration rates that ranged from about one-half to one-fourth the size of the national average.

Table 8.3. Net immigration rates of U.S. diocesan priests and percentage of gross change, 1966–84, by year, nation, and region (number of net migrations per 100 active priests)

	Average annual rate[a]				% gross change 1966–84[b]
	1966–69	1970–74	1975–79	1980–84	
United States	0.14	0.23	0.30	0.30	4.21
Regions					
New England	0.10	0.16	0.24	0.07	2.41
Middle Atlantic	0.12	0.14	0.18	0.16	2.54
East Northcentral	0.04	0.10	0.11	0.11	1.48
West Northcentral	-0.06	0.06	0.02	0.12	0.54
Mountain	0.17	0.55	1.03	0.15	9.03
Pacific	0.77	0.84	1.00	1.29	17.19
East South[c]	0.29	0.42	0.81	0.53	9.68
West Southcentral	0.21	0.65	0.63	0.79	10.74

Source: weighted census counts.
[a]Incardination rate minus excardination rate.
[b]Using the 1966 active population for the denominator and the cumulative number of incardinations minus excardinations for the numerator.
[c]Combines the South Atlantic region and one diocese from the East Southcentral region.

Pacific Coast dioceses are most attractive to migrating priests, where, on the average, active clergy populations were augmented by 17 percent between 1966 and 1984. The influx of migrating priests was four times greater in Pacific states than the national average of a little over 4 percent during the roughly two decades under observation. West Northcentral dioceses were least attractive, actually losing more priests through excardinations than were gained by incardinations during the late 1960s; the overall net gain was less than 1 percent for the entire period.

National Trends in Historical Perspective

Net immigration rates increased steadily throughout the United States between 1966 and 1984. The change reflects a rational response of organizations in a state of decline. Low net immigration rates of the mid-1960s reflect professional human resources in a state of growth and prosperity, since the clergy population decline did not begin until the late 1960s and early 1970s. At midcentury, diocesan organizations in the United States were at their zenith after many decades of internal equilibrium (Kim 1980; Seidler and Meyer 1989). Between 1966 and 1984, however, the average diocese had lost almost 20 percent of its active priest population. So replenishing the clergy supply from external sources became a reasonable reaction.

The history of the U.S. Catholic church is undoubtedly filled with periods of high net immigration rates among the clergy. There are no known records, though, from which to construct comparable measures of the annual number of excess incardinations over excardinations. Roman Catholicism in this country, along with many other Christian denominations, began as an immigrant church, supplied in large measure by foreign clergy. Successive waves of Irish, German, and Polish immigrants brought their own priests, some of whom may have been officially incardinated when fledgling dioceses expanded their activities and became more efficient. Expediency and informality in this regard were probably more the rule than bureaucratic efficiency, however, even into the 20th century. Note the Catholic church in the United States maintained its missionary status vis-à-vis Rome until 1918, when the Code of Canon Law was promulgated (Ellis 1971).

Preference for Native Clergy

Traditionally, and in keeping with canon law, Roman Catholic dioceses are supposed to be self-generating and self-supporting with regard to their internal economy. The diocese is a "particular church" in the full theological and canonical sense. That is, the diocesan church is "not primarily a subdivision of the universal Church but rather a community of the baptized confessing the Catholic faith" and "sharing in sacramental life" (Coriden et al. 1985, p. 316). As a fully established particular church, a diocese should be capable of providing all human and financial resources necessary to make the diocesan organization viable.

In a well-established national church where dioceses have enough native priests recruited from within their own jurisdictions and trained in approved seminaries, bishops tend to be cautious about incardinating priests from other dioceses or religious orders. The reason is that parishioners prefer pastors who "speak their own language." Additionally, though usually a reason that remains unspoken, excessive incardinations could increase the probability of having misfits and malcontents among the clergy.

Incardination and excardination procedures under conditions of abundance were always slow and cumbersome, involving endless probation periods and lengthy correspondence between officials in the diocese or religious order of origin and those in the diocese of destination. For example, during fieldwork for a comparative study in Spain, we learned of dozens of extern priests in an attractive cosmopolitan diocese with plenty of native clergy who had been petitioning for incardination for over a decade without success.[4] In one California diocese, however, where the Catholic population was growing rapidly and recruitment and retention of native priests was poor, we discovered that the process had been streamlined considerably. Extern priests became automatically eligible for incardination after a few years' residence in the diocese, probation periods were no longer than required by official guidelines, and all correspondence was handled with dispatch. We discovered that, as a result of these or similar policies, for extended periods in some U.S. dioceses there were more entrances in the local priest population from incardinations than from ordinations.

Adapting to Shortages

Case studies of organizations facing crises teach many lessons — among them, that organizations usually seek solutions to problems from among their stock of tried-and-true procedures and programs (Starbuck et al. 1978; Starbuck 1983). The studies show that organizations act unreflectively and nonadaptively most of the time. So during times of stress it is reassuring

---

4. Extern priests are those who are on leave from their diocese or religious order of origin, are currently living in the focal diocese, but are not incardinated therein. In their diocese of origin they are categorized as "active outside the diocese" (see the section "Net Leave" below).

to turn to programs and procedures that offer some relief but "require no information-bearing stimuli because they are activated through job assignments, clocks, and calendars" (Starbuck 1983, p. 93). Increasing the local priest supply through more incardinations is a ready-made, though short-term and perhaps short-sighted, solution to a long-term, pervasive recruitment and retention problem.

Nevertheless, allowing increasing incardinations in the diocese appears to be one solution to the priest shortage in several areas of the country. For the entire period under observation, the surplus of incardinations over excardinations was higher in the South and West than in other divisions. Moreover, in Pacific and West Southcentral dioceses, where rates were among the highest in the nation during 1966–69, net immigration increased by well over one and one-half times in the former region and by four times in the latter region by the 1980s. In all other regions of the country, rates grew steadily until the late 1970s and then either stabilized or began to go down again.

Hence, the dominant pattern emerging from the data demonstrates that surplus incardinations had already begun to fall all over the country by the end of the census period, except in the most attractive geographic areas. As the shortage of priests in religious orders and European dioceses of origin becomes more acute, American dioceses will have to look elsewhere — perhaps to India, Korea, Vietnam, the Philippines, and Latin America — for foreign priests to assist their dwindling and aging native clergy.

A strategy that is rational under the politics of abundance, however, could become a parasitic response to shortages under the politics of scarcity (Pettigrew 1973). Excessive incardinations during periods of pervasive clergy shortages inevitably put strain on other parts of the national or global church. Dioceses in this country will need to increase their political finesse in order to find cooperative host dioceses and religious congregations that will allow them to import notably more priests than they export.[5]

Local Rates

The numbers in table 8.4 reflect local net immigration rates and reveal wide variation. We will make a statistical tour of the nation by citing the highs and lows within each geographic region, but include only those dioceses that have been established for at least 10 years.[6]

5. According to church officials, national bishops' conferences are beginning to negotiate guidelines for balancing the flow of incardinations and excardinations across international borders.

6. Newly created dioceses often experience a flurry of incardinations for several years after establishment, which produces artificial extremes in the distribution.

Table 8.4. Net immigration rates of U.S. diocesan priests and percentage of gross change, 1966–84, by year and diocese (number of net migrations per 100 active priests; alphabetical order within region by state then diocese)

Region and diocese	Average annual rate				% gross change
	1966 −69	1970 −74	1975 −79	1980 −84	1966 −84[a]
Northeast					
New England					
Hartford CT	0.09	-0.07	0.16	0.09	1.07
Norwich CT	0.53	1.07	0.83	0.67	13.72
Portland ME	0.10	0.09	0.31	0.32	3.19
Boston MA	-0.04	0.00	0.13	0.04	0.52
Fall River MA	0.22	0.00	0.10	0.11	1.72
Worcester MA	0.08	0.48	0.39	-0.13	3.84
Providence RI[b]	—	—	—	—	—
Burlington VT	0.00	0.11	0.00	-0.43	-1.11
Middle Atlantic					
Camden NJ	0.07	0.11	-0.05	0.11	1.10
Newark NJ	0.06	0.15	0.34	0.78	5.58
Albany NY	0.00	0.41	0.46	0.00	3.44
Brooklyn NY	0.20	0.06	0.31	0.03	2.40
Buffalo NY	0.16	0.10	0.25	0.00	2.21
New York NY	0.08	0.08	0.21	0.32	2.63
Ogdensburg NY	0.26	0.00	-0.23	-0.12	-0.53
Rochester NY	0.26	0.23	0.06	0.00	2.26
Rockville Centre NY	0.27	0.55	0.73	0.47	9.31
Allentown PA	0.09	0.34	0.07	0.15	3.15
Altoona–Johnstown PA	0.16	0.00	0.24	-0.12	1.27
Philadelphia PA	0.00	-0.04	-0.09	0.02	-0.48
Pittsburgh PA	0.09	0.07	0.40	0.07	2.98
Scranton PA	0.06	0.00	-0.10	0.11	0.22
Northcentral					
East Northcentral					
Belleville IL	-0.14	0.13	0.13	0.13	1.12
Chicago IL	-0.10	0.00	-0.09	-0.04	-0.89
Rockford IL	0.14	0.00	0.25	0.13	2.25
Indianapolis IN	0.10	0.27	0.10	0.22	2.65
Detroit MI	-0.03[c]	0.39	0.51	0.29	4.18
Gaylord MI	0.38[d]	0.64	1.08	0.37	10.48
Grand Rapids MI	0.33[c]	0.12	0.33	0.00	2.94
Marquette MI	0.17	-0.15	0.00	0.00	0.00
Saginaw MI	0.51[c]	0.09	0.35	0.53	6.10
Cincinnati OH	-0.06	0.15	0.05	0.10	1.10
Cleveland OH	0.08	0.07	-0.04	0.11	0.97
Columbus OH	0.00	0.09	-0.10	0.00	0.00
Youngstown OH	0.10	0.00	0.50	0.30	3.53
La Crosse WI	0.00	0.00	0.00	0.00	0.00
Milwaukee WI	-0.04	0.06	-0.03	0.00	0.00

(continued on following page)

183

Table 8.4. Net immigration rates of U.S. diocesan priests and percentage of gross change, 1966–84, by year and diocese (continued)

Region and diocese	Average annual rate				% gross change
	1966 –69	1970 –74	1975 –79	1980 –84	1966 –84[a]
Northcentral (continued)					
West Northcentral					
Des Moines IA	0.00	0.00	-0.19	0.39	0.76
Dubuque IA	-0.12	0.00	0.00	0.06	-0.24
Sioux City IA	0.00	0.00	0.00	0.11	0.48
Dodge City KS	0.39	-0.33	0.36	0.73	4.65
Salina KS	0.00	0.00	-0.27	0.29	0.00
Wichita KS	-0.33	0.00	-0.32	-0.33	-3.74
New Ulm MN	-0.20	0.00	0.19	-0.22	-0.79
St. Cloud MN	0.00	0.39	-0.14	0.00	1.14
St. Paul–Minneapolis MN	0.18	0.10	0.18	0.24	2.79
Kansas City–St. Jos. MO	-0.29	0.13	-0.15	0.15	-0.58
St. Louis MO	-0.04	-0.04	0.12	0.04	0.36
Springfield–C. Girard. MO	-0.35	0.85	0.32	0.93	8.39
Lincoln NE[b]	–	–	–	–	–
Fargo ND	-0.17	0.00	0.00	0.18	0.00
Rapid City SD	0.41	0.00	0.00	0.00	1.36
West					
Mountain					
Pueblo CO	0.28	0.68	0.47	0.46	9.07
Boise ID	0.00	1.28	1.72	0.23	16.88
Gallup NM	1.04[c]	0.00	2.22	0.40	36.09
Las Cruces NM	1.97[d]	2.64	2.25	0.66	37.80
Santa Fe NM	0.18[c]	0.31	0.00	-0.18	1.31
Cheyenne WY	0.00	0.34	2.00	1.30	15.25
Pacific					
Fresno CA[b]	–	–	–	–	–
Los Angeles CA	-0.04[c]	0.50	0.72	0.45	7.58
Monterey CA	4.51[e]	0.55	0.59	0.89	28.78
Oakland CA	1.21	2.32	0.92	2.12	28.28
Orange CA	-0.04[d]	0.50	2.43	2.68	26.38
San Bernardino CA	1.26[d]	0.69	0.33	2.96	21.44
San Diego CA	1.26[c]	0.69	0.84	0.54	14.27
San Francisco CA	-0.07[c]	0.44	0.35	1.34	8.34
San Jose CA	-0.07[d]	0.44	0.35	2.23	11.52
Stockton CA	1.53	0.83	1.27	0.00	16.84
Baker OR	-0.54	0.00	0.51	0.51	2.25
South					
East South[f]					
Wilmington DE	0.66	0.19	0.57	0.36	7.93
Orlando FL	1.29[g]	2.24	2.99	0.37	38.82

(continued on following page)

Table 8.4. Net immigration rates of U.S. diocesan priests and percentage of gross change, 1966–84, by year and diocese (continued)

Region and diocese	Average annual rate				% gross change
	1966 –69	1970 –74	1975 –79	1980 –84	1966 –84[a]
South (continued)					
East South[f] (continued)					
St. Petersburg FL	4.79[g]	1.42	4.21	3.64	66.96
Atlanta GA	0.92	0.32	0.55	0.46	14.29
Covington KY	-0.24	0.00	0.12	0.00	-0.48
Baltimore MD	-0.08	0.27	0.20	0.07	2.13
West Southcentral					
Little Rock AK	0.00	0.00	0.84	0.00	3.10
Alexandria–Shreveport LA	0.00	0.00	0.00	-0.20	-0.76
Baton Rouge LA	0.00	1.31	0.49	0.00	9.72
Lafayette LA	0.27[c]	0.23	0.12	0.24	3.99
Lake Charles LA	0.27[d]	0.23	0.12	1.04	8.34
Austin TX	0.28	0.69	0.23	0.22	6.74
Beaumont TX	0.52	1.28	0.37	0.00	11.24
Corpus Christi TX	0.37[c]	1.55	0.59	1.69	20.07
Dallas TX	-1.10[h]	0.50	0.46	0.60	3.09
El Paso TX	2.09[c]	2.79	2.40	1.61	45.78
Fort Worth TX	0.50[h]	0.00	1.55	0.33	12.00
Galveston–Houston TX	0.21[c]	1.32	0.39	0.65	12.20
San Antonio TX	0.26[c]	0.33	0.85	0.91	11.34
Victoria TX	-0.23[d]	0.44	0.81	1.16	10.78

Source: census counts.

[a]Using the 1966 active population for the denominator and the cumulative number of incardinations minus excardinations for the numerator.

[b]Refused to participate.

[c]Divided during the census period. The division does not affect the rate, because it is standardized.

[d]Established during the census period by being divided from others in the sample. The annual rates prior to the year of the split are those of the parent diocese(s), weighted when necessary. See appendix D for year of establishment and parent diocese(s).

[e]Divided in 1967. The rate for 1966 is based on size of the active population as identifiable in 1966 (see appendix D).

[f]Combines the South Atlantic region and one diocese from the East Southcentral region.

[g]Established in 1968. The figure given for 1966–69 is the average of the 1968 and 1969 rates (see appendix D).

[h]Divided in 1969. The average given for 1966–69 is based on size of the active population as identifiable in years prior to and in the year of the split (see appendix D).

Northeast

The highest gain in New England was recorded in Norwich, where the influx between 1966 and 1984 equaled almost 14 percent of the 1966 number of active clergy. At the other extreme, Burlington experienced a net loss of just over 1 percent of its 1966 priest population size as a result of more excardinations than incardinations during the same period.

In the Middle Atlantic states, Rockville Centre recorded a gross increase from net immigration of more than 9 percent during the roughly two decades, for the high end of the range, and Ogdensburg suffered a net loss of just over 0.5 percent, at the low end. As we learned in chapter 4, Rockville Centre has the most unfavorable parishioner-to-priest ratio in the entire sample of Northeast dioceses, so encouraging priests to incardinate appears to be a rational adjustment by Rockville Centre to this relative deprivation.

Northcentral

According to statistics for East Northcentral dioceses, the cumulative result of net immigration in Gaylord amounted to over 10 percent of the 1966 number of active priests during the period, for the highest growth through immigration in the region. In Chicago, however, priestly migrations produced a loss of almost 1 percent between 1966 and 1984.

The balance between in-migration and out-migration in West Northcentral dioceses ranged from a high of over an 8 percent net increase in Springfield–Cape Girardeau to a low of almost a 4 percent net cumulative loss in Wichita during the 19-year period. Wichita experienced the least favorable priestly migration trends in our national sample.[7]

West

The high end of the range in Mountain states is represented by almost a 17 percent cumulative increase through favorable incardination trends in Boise, and the low end was established at just over 1 percent in Santa Fe — ignoring Gallup and Las Cruces as deviant cases. Boise also enjoyed the highest growth through ordinations in states of the West, a situation that merits closer examination.

Along the Pacific Coast, Monterey had the highest influx through priestly

7. Note, Gallup lost 25 percent of its active clergy through an excess of excardinations over incardinations during the period, but this is an anomalous situation, because included in the loss are 13 priests transferred to Phoenix when it was established in 1969. Similarly, Las Cruces, at a 37.8 percent increase, is one of those newly established dioceses that experience a one-time flurry of incardinations during their early years, so it, too, is excluded from this description.

immigrations in the region, equaling in 19 years almost 29 percent of its 1966 priest population size. The lowest increase, 2 percent, was registered in Baker.

South

The data for dioceses in the East South reveal the exceptionally favorable immigration rates in St. Petersburg, which set the extreme high for the region and the country as a whole. Between 1966 and 1984, St. Petersburg expanded its active clergy by more than two-thirds of its 1966 number of priests because of the surplus of incardinations over excardinations. The low end of the range among dioceses in the East South was established by Covington, where migrations resulted in a cumulative loss of almost half of 1 percent of the 1966 number during the same 19 years.

In the West Southcentral states, the highest number of excess incardinations over excardinations was recorded in El Paso, where a gross increase of almost 46 percent was experienced from immigrations during the period. The low end of the range in the West Southcentral region is anchored by Alexandria–Shreveport, where excardinations were higher than incardinations, resulting in a loss of almost 1 percent of the 1966 number of priests.

Zero Net Migration

Globally, the Catholic church is a closed system in which the number of incardinations and excardinations is in balance, although obviously some countries have higher net immigration rates than others. If the clergy decline worsens throughout the world, surplus incardinations as a response to local scarcity may become a contested accommodation to the shortage (Seidler and Meyer 1989). This consideration prompted us to reexamine our population projections, controlling for net immigration.

In a responsible global ecclesial economy, an even balance of incardinations over excardinations would be dictated by dynamics of supply and demand, at least as they are played out within separate regions of the world. One estimate of the real loss of priestly manpower within a country might focus on each autonomous diocese and its ability to recruit and retain its own native clergy. To make such an estimate, we need to remove the effects of net immigration. Two modifications in the projection procedures are necessary. First, we recalculate the size of the active priest population after removing the number of incardinations in excess of the number of excardinations for each year of the historical period. Then we estimate the three projection models, using the same assumptions as before for all other transition events except incardination and excardination. For the altered projections we assume that zero net migration would continue throughout the

Table 8.5. Adjusted size of U.S. diocesan priest population and percentage of difference, 1966–2005, by year, nation, division, and region

| | | | Size | | | % difference 1966–2005[a] | | |
| | | | | 2005 | | | | |
	1966	1985	Opt.	Mod.	Pes.	Opt.	Mod.	Pes.
United States	35,070	26,736	21,262	19,209	14,906	-39	-45	-57
Divisions and regions								
Northeast	14,604	11,152	8,654	7,629	5,819	-41	-48	-60
New England	5,025	3,733	2,662	2,344	1,879	-47	-53	-63
Middle Atlantic	9,579	7,419	5,992	5,285	3,940	-37	-45	-59
Northcentral	12,769	9,215	7,391	6,344	4,727	-42	-50	-63
East Northcentral	7,989	5,609	4,552	3,751	2,793	-43	-53	-65
West Northcentral	4,780	3,606	2,839	2,593	1,934	-41	-46	-60
West	3,319	2,533	2,456	2,095	1,556	-26	-37	-53
Mountain	672	577	561	468	377	-17	-30	-44
Pacific	2,647	1,956	1,895	1,627	1,179	-28	-39	-55
South	4,373	3,829	3,613	3,178	2,604	-17	-27	-40
East South[b]	1,706	1,543	1,535	1,331	1,076	-10	-22	-37
West Southcentral	2,667	2,286	2,078	1,847	1,528	-22	-31	-43

Sources: weighted census counts for 1966; projections for 1985 and 2005 based on assumption of zero net migration.

[a]Optimistic: [(Col. 3/Col. 1) - 1]100; moderate: [(Col. 4/Col. 1) - 1]100; pessimistic: [(Col. 5/Col. 1) - 1]100.

[b]Combines the South Atlantic region and one diocese from the East Southcentral region.

projection period, that is, that the number of incardinations would always be balanced by an equal number of excardinations.

Table 8.5 contains the results of the new projections for the United States as a whole and for each census region.[8] Remember we concluded from the examination of table 2.2 that growth from net immigration alone accounted for over one-fifth of the overall population change that occurred between 1966 and 1984. Thus, if net immigrations had been held at zero, the decline in the national diocesan priest population during the historical period would have been 24 percent rather than 20 percent.

Not surprisingly, therefore, the projections adjusted for zero net immigration show considerably greater losses in numbers of priests between 1966

8. The data are presented in the same format as in table 3.1, which contains the original projections.

and 2005 than the original projections. The adjusted moderate projection, displayed under "% difference" in the table, reveals that the national population of diocesan priests would show a drop of 45 percent between 1966 and 2005. The corresponding figure in table 3.1 for native and nonnative priests together shows a loss of 40 percent. The projected size of the native diocesan clergy in 2005, under adjusted moderate assumptions, is just over 19,200. The unadjusted model, which includes excess incardinations, forecasts a diocesan clergy population of some 21,000 as the new century dawns.

An examination of differences across regions reveals, further, that the advantage created by the imbalance of incardinations over excardinations is particularly strong in certain areas but slight in others. For easier comparison, table 8.6 presents the adjusted and unadjusted estimates of the

Table 8.6. Unadjusted and adjusted percentage of decline in the U.S. diocesan priest population and percentage of difference, 1966–2005, by nation, division, and region (based on moderate assumptions adjusted for zero net migration)

| | % decline, 1966–2005 | | |
	Unadjusted	Adjusted[a]	% difference[b]
United States	-40.0	-45.2	13.0
Divisions and regions			
Northeast	-45.3	-47.8	5.5
New England	-51.6	-53.0	3.3
Middle Atlantic	-41.9	-44.8	6.9
Northcentral	-48.4	-50.3	3.9
East Northcentral	-51.3	-53.3	3.4
West Northcentral	-43.5	-45.8	5.2
West	-19.7	-36.9	87.3
Mountain	-25.6	-30.4	18.8
Pacific	-18.2	-38.5	111.5
South	-14.9	-27.3	83.2
East South[c]	-11.6	-22.0	89.7
West Southcentral	-17.4	-30.7	76.4

Sources: weighted census counts for 1966 and moderate projection series for 2005.

[a]The adjusted assumption projects the decline in native clergy, as defined in the text.

[b][(Col. 2/Col. 1)/Col. 1]100.

[c]Combines the South Atlantic region and one diocese from the East Southcentral region.

percentage of decline from 1966 to 2005 based on the moderate assumptions. The table demonstrates that Sunbelt states absorb the vast majority of surplus incardinations in the country.

At the national level, there is a 13 percent difference between the projected decline of native clergy and that of the combined native and incardinated clergy, as the data in the first row of table 8.6 show.[9] The national average, however, balances very wide extremes. The differences in unadjusted and adjusted projections for Northeast and Northcentral dioceses range from 3 percent to 7 percent, and the differences for South and West dioceses range from 76 percent to 112 percent.

The advantage gained by excess incardinations in the Mountain region is generally more than three times higher than in the Northeast and Northcentral half of the country. Even so, Mountain dioceses do not enjoy the advantage from incardinations realized in the South and along the West Coast. In the South the advantage is more than 15 times higher and on the West Coast more than 20 times higher than in the Northeast and Northcentral divisions.

Finally, when the advantages of net immigration are included in the projection, clergy losses in the South and West are notably below the national average, as the first column shows. According to the second column, however, the Sun Belt dioceses, too, have serious problems. When gains from surplus incardinations are removed, adjusted losses between 1966 and 2005 in that half of the United States range from 22 percent fewer native clergy in East South states to 39 percent fewer native clergy along the Pacific Coast.

The ability of West and South dioceses to generate sufficient *native* clergy to serve growing numbers of Catholics appears to be in almost as serious jeopardy as that of sister dioceses east of the Rocky Mountains and north of the Mason-Dixon line. Trends and projections based on assumptions of zero net immigration indicate that the shortage of native priests does not respect geographic boundaries or favorable climatic conditions. Furthermore, evidence from the causal analysis in chapter 6 demonstrated that, after controlling for several conditions affecting the availability of priestly ministers, Pacific and West Southcentral dioceses have higher parishioner-to-priest ratios than any other area in the country, even though surplus incardinations are included in the number of active clergy.

In view of a national and indeed global church economy, the priest shortage may be defined in terms of a diocese's ability to produce its own native clergy in sufficient supply to meet the demand of resident Catholics who seek the Mass and sacraments. The analysis thus far has demonstrated that,

9. $\{[-45.2 - (-40)]/-40\}100 = 13$.

if all dioceses in the United States were held equally to this definition, regional differences in clergy decline would be greatly muted.

Causal Model of Net Immigration

In this section, we turn our attention to explaining why some dioceses gain priests through higher incardinations than excardinations, others remain in net balance, and still others lose priests in the migration process. Following the same assumptions about causal precedence used to develop regression models in earlier chapters, we have selected those variables that best explain differences in net immigration. The final model accounts for nearly half the variation in the 1980 net immigration rate.

The independent variables in the model include three environmental conditions (percentage of Catholics, percentage of African Americans, and percentage of growth in the Catholic population between 1970 and 1980) and four organizational conditions (parishioner-to-priest ratio, recruitment ineffectiveness, ordination rate, and organizational newness or year established).[10] One of them has not been included in previous causal models, so its descriptive statistics and those for the dependent variable are presented in table 8.7.

The table gives summary figures by region as an overview of variation across dioceses.[11] The highest concentration of African Americans is found in East South and West Southcentral dioceses, where the proportion ranges from 15 percent to 16 percent. The proportion of African Americans in the general population of the remaining regions ranges from 1 percent to 9 percent. As shown in table 8.4 and summarized by region here, net immigration rates vary notably at the local level. In 1980, the national average was 0.40 surplus incardinands per 100 active priests.[12] Rates were low

10. Besides the variables that compose the final model, we have examined the influence of other environmental and organizational conditions on the net immigration rate and find no significant effects (see appendix C for the full list). Of all possible combinations examined, given the order of assumed precedence among the variables, the set of relationships summarized in table 8.8 best describes the social forces that explain variation in diocesan net immigration rates. Recall that estimates of the number who claim Roman Catholicism as their religious preference based on survey data are not available by diocese (see chapter 4, footnote 6). Thus, "percentage of Catholics" and "percentage of growth in Catholic population" are based on estimated numbers of Catholic parishioners provided by the Glenmary Research Center.

11. Because the averages presented are estimates based on a probability sample, they may differ slightly from regional and national figures published elsewhere; see footnote 7, chapter 6.

12. Net immigration rate equals incardination rate minus excardination rate. The rate used in the regression model is the average of the 1979–81 rates.

Table 8.7. Percentage of African Americans and net
immigration rates in U.S. Catholic dioceses, 1980, by
region (means)

Region	% African American[a]	Net immigration rate[b]
New England	2.63	0.33
Middle Atlantic	9.33	0.12
East Northcentral	8.61	0.11
West Northcentral	3.41	0.20
Mountain	1.21	0.83
Pacific	5.74	1.01
East South[c]	14.51	0.75
West Southcentral	15.97	0.48
Grand mean	8.24	0.40
Standard deviation	8.09	0.76

[a]Source: see appendix C.
[b]Source: weighted census counts.
[c]Combines the South Atlantic region and one diocese
from the East Southcentral region.

in the Northeast and Northcentral divisions, ranging from 0.11 to 0.33, and high in the South and West, ranging from 0.48 to 1.01.

Table 8.8 summarizes the findings of the causal analysis. Given the large regional differences in net immigration, one might wonder why region does not emerge as a significant explanatory variable. The reason is that regions of the country vary systematically on some of the variables included in the model. Once the impact of these variables is accounted for, regional differences are reduced and become unimportant. Recall, geographic location in and of itself does not influence diocesan ordination rates either.

As a group, organizational variables have a larger direct role than environmental variables in explaining the variation of net immigration rates. In the following summary of effects, variables are discussed in the order of magnitude of their direct impact.

Parishioner-to-Priest Ratio
Dioceses with higher numbers of parishioners per active diocesan priest are likely to have higher immigration rates. The model suggests that dioceses suffering from a relatively high demand for priestly services turn to importing priests from other dioceses and religious orders as a means of

Table 8.8. Effects of environmental and organizational conditions on net immigration rates in U.S. Catholic dioceses, 1980 (unstandardized regression coefficients)

Independent variable	b	Adjusted t-ratio[a]
% Catholic growth	.0073	2.096*
% African American	-.0240	-4.070***
% Catholic	-.0170	-4.329***
Year established	.0026	2.748**
Recruit. ineffectiveness	-.000062	-6.105***
Parishioner/priest ratio	.00090	9.708***
Ordination rate	-.1840	-3.675***
n of dioceses	85	
Constant	-4.5439	-2.526*
F-ratio	11.270***	
R^2	.506	
Adjusted R^2	.461	

[a]Adjustment is based on a finite population correction factor of 0.705 or the square root of 1 - (n/N) applied to the standard error of b; see Mendenhall et al. 1971.

*p ≤ .05.
**p ≤ .01.
***p ≤ .001.

improving the situation. The data show that if two dioceses are similar with respect to other variables in the model but Diocese A faces 1,000 more parishioners per diocesan priest than Diocese B, each year Diocese A will welcome almost 1 more surplus incardination per 100 active priests.[13]

Recruitment Ineffectiveness
When the effects of other variables in the model are held constant, dioceses requiring larger numbers of young Catholic males to produce an ordination have lower net immigration rates. For example, if Diocese A requires 10,000 more Catholic males of ages 25–34 to produce an ordination than the number required by Diocese B, every five years Diocese A is likely to experience about 3 fewer surplus incardinations per 100 active priests than Diocese B.[14] Apparently, if priestly service in a diocese seems less attractive to potential ordinands, it also seems less attractive to potential incardinands.

13. Precisely: 0.00090 × 1000 = 0.9.
14. Precisely: −0.000062 × 10,000 × 5 = −3.1.

Ordination Rate

Dioceses with higher ordination rates tend to have lower net immigration rates, other conditions tested being equal. If Diocese A has 1 more annual ordination per 100 active priests than Diocese B, every five years it will have almost 1 fewer surplus incardination than Diocese B.[15] One might conclude that if a diocese is meeting priestly manpower needs through ordinations, church leaders are less likely to use incardination as a means of recruitment. Or, on the other hand, it may be that bishops in dioceses with relatively high ordinations are more likely to allow priests to leave through excardination.

Percentage of Catholics

When other conditions are equal, the higher the proportion of Catholic church members, the lower the priestly immigration rate. Thus, if two dioceses differ by 10 percentage points in the relative size of their Catholic populations, every six years the diocese with proportionately more Catholics will gain almost 1 fewer incardinand per 100 active priests than the other.[16] Hence, priests who want to exercise their ministry somewhere else seem to migrate to relatively non-Catholic areas.

Percentage of African Americans

The higher the proportion of the total population that is African American, the lower the net immigration rate. Thus, if two dioceses differ by 10 percentage points in the proportion of the general population that is African American, but are similar in other conditions, every four years the diocese with the proportionately larger African-American population will have about 1 fewer surplus incardination per 100 active priests than the other.[17]

Care must be given to interpreting why the percentage of African Americans is related to net immigration. Does the relationship mean that priests are less likely to immigrate to and more likely to emigrate from an area with a relatively large African-American population because of the presence of African Americans? Or is it because historic patterns of discrimina-

15. Precisely: $-0.1840 \times 5 = -0.92$.

16. Precisely: $-0.0170 \times 10 \times 6 = -1.02$.

17. Precisely: $-0.0240 \times 10 \times 4 = -0.096$. Although the impact of increasing the proportion of African Americans by 10 percentage points is larger than a similar increase in the Catholic population, the standardized regression coefficients (which are not presented) show that, in fact, the percentage of Catholics has a larger causal impact on net immigrations. Standardization takes into account the greater variance of the percentage of Catholics compared with the percentage of African Americans.

tion result in African Americans living disproportionately in areas that lack certain quality-of-life resources and that the poor living conditions deter priests from immigrating? We cannot answer the question with the data at hand.[18]

Organizational Newness
Recently established dioceses have higher net immigration rates than older dioceses, once other variables in the model are controlled for. Thus, if Diocese A had been established in 1975 and Diocese B in 1875, every four years Diocese A would gain 1 more incardinand per 100 active priests than Diocese B. Not surprisingly, new dioceses appear to have a more aggressive policy toward incardinations than older ones. As we noted in chapter 7, organization analysts who study the "liabilities of newness" report that organizations face considerable odds during the initial years after establishment (Stinchcombe 1965). Stark (1988) found that religions such as Christianity, Islam, and Mormonism were more successful than other new religious sects because of aggressive recruitment, which resulted in rapid growth very early after they were founded.

Percentage of Growth in Catholic Population, 1970–80
Finally, growth in the size of the Catholic population is positively related to immigration, but the relationship is relatively weak.

The causal analysis suggests that two conditions which strongly affect priestly immigration rates are related to rational principles of supply and demand. We discover that dioceses with higher numbers of parishioners per priest and lower ordination rates have higher net gains from incardinations. This implies that where demand for priestly services is high, a diocese increases its priest supply by expanding incardinations and/or limiting excardinations.

Further, although principles of supply and demand seem to govern priestly migration, they appear to be constrained by a lazy monopoly effect. Hence, we find that the higher the proportion of Catholic church members in the general population, the lower the net immigration rate. That is to say, as a diocese tends toward a monopoly position, it makes less effort to recruit through incardination. Finally, the relationship between inef-

18. We examined the influence of several other environmental conditions, including education, income, health care opportunities, and housing standards, but found no effects that diminish the influence of the percentage of African Americans on diocesan net immigration rates. We were unable to test the hypothesis further because other quality-of-life variables were not available in our data set.

fective recruitment of new ordinands and low net immigration rates indicates that the programs and strategies for recruiting ordinands and incardinands may be similar; when recruitment of priests is poor, so is recruitment of incardinands. Given the importance of providing adequate priestly services, further study of the decision-making process surrounding recruitment through both ordination and immigration is warranted.

Net Leave

"Net leave" is the term we apply to attrition that takes the form of larger numbers of priests beginning extended leaves than returning from leave on an annual basis. By definition, a priest on extended leave is gone from the active labor pool for a year or more, so the leave is a decrement to the priestly labor force. His return is counted as an increment. We distinguish two categories of leave and return. A priest may leave because of (1) serious illness or (2) some other incapacity. He may return to active duty after (1) a voluntary resignation or (2) a serious illness or other incapacitation.

Thus, the essential criterion defining an extended leave is some form of incapacitation. The problem motivating the leave must impair the priest to the extent that he is unable or unwilling to take an official job assignment for at least one full year. This category does not include those who are on leave of absence for study, priests serving as military chaplains, or those on loan outside the diocese. All these are considered "active outside the diocese," because they are usually expected to perform parish duties when their other responsibilities allow, especially to celebrate Mass and preach regularly in the diocese where they reside.

Numbers

Table 8.9 summarizes the movement resulting from temporary migrations among the American clergy between 1966 and 1984. These transitions were relatively infrequent but still had a noticeable impact. Sick leave was dominant, amounting to just over 1,200 absences during the census period and outnumbering other leaves more than two to one. Returns from resignation were relatively rare, totaling only 132 during the entire 19 years. Other returns, from both illness and other incapacities, reached just over 900 reentrances to the active clergy population. The net result of leaves and returns was an overall loss of almost 700 from the active diocesan priest roster.

From the data in the final column, we can calculate that nationally the number of net leaves averaged 63 vacant positions on a yearly basis during the late 1960s but only about 17 per year by the early 1980s. So attrition from temporary migrations dropped 73 percent during the census period.

Table 8.9. Number of leaves, returns, and net losses or gains of U.S. diocesan priests, 1966–84

Year	Leaves		Returns		Net loss/gain[a]
	Sick	Other	Resignation	Other	
1966	96	14	0	23	-87
1967	71	12	1	34	-48
1968	60	28	2	41	-45
1969	95	14	0	39	-70
1970	79	25	4	46	-54
1971	68	20	6	48	-34
1972	64	18	6	47	-29
1973	61	27	14	36	-38
1974	71	23	15	34	-45
1975	60	18	9	57	-12
1976	13	8	11	36	26
1977	49	65	5	26	-83
1978	89	59	8	64	-76
1979	60	38	10	76	-12
1980	52	30	4	91	13
1981	32	8	5	37	2
1982	65	52	13	53	-51
1983	64	26	7	59	-24
1984	70	36	12	67	-27
Total	1,219	521	132	914	-694

Source: weighted census counts.
[a](Col. 3 + Col. 4) - (Col. 1 + Col. 2).

Projecting Net Leaves

Figure 8.2 depicts the downward trend in the number of net leaves during the census period and the number forecasted in the optimistic, moderate, and pessimistic series of projections. The graph shows that we assume the number of net leaves will continue to decline in all three scenarios. The assumptions governing the forecasts are described fully in appendix B.

Note, however, the projected number of net leaves is smallest under pessimistic assumptions and largest under optimistic ones. At first glance, this seems counterintuitive. But the smallest number appears in the pessimistic series because a pessimistic scenario produces a small projected population. The smaller the population, the fewer the priests at risk of taking a leave. The same explanation applies, *mutatis mutandis,* to the seeming anomaly in the optimistic forecast.

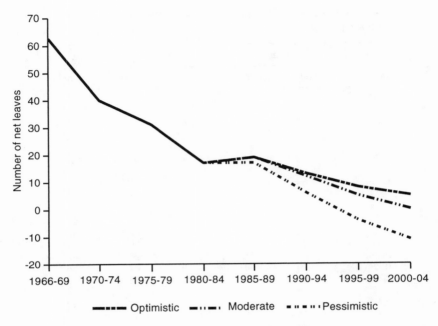

Figure 8.2. Average annual number of net leaves of U.S. diocesan priests, 1966–2004

Year	Weighted census count	Projection series		
		Optimistic	Moderate	Pessimistic
1966–69	63			
1970–74	40			
1975–79	31			
1980–84	17			
1985–89		19	19	17
1990–94		13	12	6
1995–99		8	5	-4
2000–04		5	0	-11

Age

Table 8.10 presents the mean age at the time of a leave and return, along with the mean age for the active priest population from 1966 to 1984. All leaves are combined in one category, but returns from resignation are displayed separately, because they are significantly different from other returns. As the data in the second column show, the few returns from voluntary resignation at the beginning of the census period were among priests notably younger than average, but those at the end of the period were among

Table 8.10. Mean ages at leave and return and for all active
U.S. diocesan priests, 1966–84

| Year | All leaves | Returns | | All active priests |
		Resignation	Other	
1966–69	50.0	37.5	50.0	46.8
1970–74	48.2	39.5	45.9	47.5
1975–79	48.6	44.1	47.6	48.5
1980–84	47.7	50.7	47.7	49.9

Source: weighted census counts.

those about the same age as the active population. The rising age of those
who changed their mind about resignation and return is, at least in part,
a reflection of the increasingly older age at resignation, as we shall see in
the following chapter.

In contrast with priests who returned from resignation, those who left
and returned for reasons of health and other problems were younger at
the end than at the beginning of the census period. The average priest leaving and returning to active duty was 50 years old during 1966–69 but was
just under 48 during 1980–84. In addition, priests involved in extended
leaves in the late 1960s were older than the average active priests, whereas
those in the early 1980s were younger than the average active priest. These
differences are partly due to changes in categories used for personnel records, a topic we return to in a concluding section of the chapter.

Rates

The data in table 8.11 standardize the raw numbers by size of the active
priest population and thus make them more comparable across time and
geographic region. As the standardized rates in the table illustrate, extended
leaves of absence and returns to active duty, though fewer in number than
other transitions, have not been unimportant demographic events in diocesan organizations. Subtracting leaves from returns to active duty produces an overall net decline of 2 percent during the census period, according to the data in row 1. Thus net leaves have had a noteworthy impact
on population change, because, as we saw in chapter 2, the overall decline
in the national clergy population during the historical period was just under
20 percent. So if leaves and returns to duty had been in balance, the total
decline would have amounted to about 18 percent, or one-tenth less than
was actually recorded.

The largest cumulative loss of manpower from temporary migration was
recorded by dioceses in the West Southcentral states, where the average

Table 8.11. Net leave rates of U.S. diocesan priests and percentage of gross change, 1966–84, by year, nation, and region (number of net leaves per 100 active priests)

	Average annual rate[a]				% gross change 1966–84[b]
	1966–69	1970–74	1975–79	1980–84	
United States	0.17	0.13	0.10	0.06	1.97
Regions					
New England	0.16	0.20	0.15	0.05	2.41
Middle Atlantic	0.14	0.07	0.15	0.10	1.98
East Northcentral	0.21	0.08	0.04	0.03	1.48
West Northcentral	0.18	0.16	0.04	-0.05	1.35
Mountain	0.01	0.09	0.15	0.18	2.11
Pacific	0.19	0.17	0.13	0.08	2.55
East South[c]	0.08	0.06	0.15	0.03	1.43
West Southcentral	0.31	0.25	0.05	0.15	3.36

Source: weighted census counts.

[a]Rate of return from temporary leave minus rate of temporary leave.

[b]Using the 1966 active population for the denominator and the cumulative number of returns minus leaves for the numerator.

[c]Combines the South Atlantic region and one diocese from the East Southcentral region.

imbalance of leaves over returns reached 3.4 percent between 1966 and 1984. Note, chapter 3 revealed that the overall decline in the active priest population during the entire 19 years was only 3.3 percent in West Southcentral states. If leaves and returns to duty had been in balance, dioceses in these states would have experienced no change in population size during the roughly two decades under observation.

The smallest loss was recorded in West Northcentral states, where, on the average, cumulative net leaves amounted to only 1.4 percent of the 1966 active diocesan priest population. The overall decline in West Northcentral dioceses was 23.4 percent, so net leave had minimal impact on the change process there.

Both raw numbers and standardized rates show that the importance of net leave has diminished throughout the country. During the historical period under study, the national average rate of exit due to net leave dropped by about two-thirds, from 0.17 percent annually during 1966–69 to 0.06 percent per year during 1980–84. Dioceses in the Mountain region experienced the most extreme deviation from this pattern, where the average annual net leave rate actually increased from 0.01 percent to 0.18 percent. The other regions, with minor exceptions, recorded steadily declining rates;

all, however, had significantly lower losses from net leaves at the end than they had at the beginning of the census period.

Part of the decline in net leave rates may have more to do with increased accuracy of record keeping than with less chronic illness and fewer incapacitating problems. For example, during the 1960s and early 1970s, resigning from the clerical ministry carried heavier overtones of scandal and stigma than nowadays. "Sick leave" was sometimes a euphemism for priests in the first stage of their resignation decision. This became apparent during data collection. Many times priests were originally reported in one source as on sick leave and then showed up in another source several years later as having resigned.[19]

Then, too, before retirement programs, priests beyond normal retirement age who became chronically ill were listed as sick, whereas in later years they would be reported as retirees. In other cases, someone who was mentally ill may have been cataloged as awaiting assignment instead of being listed on sick leave. Nowadays, awaiting assignment has become the preferred category in place of sick leave for irregular situations that prevent a priest from being given or from wanting to accept an official assignment. For example, if a priest should be suspended for disciplinary reasons, he is usually listed as awaiting assignment. For purposes of the study, a priest on inactive leave is categorized as awaiting assignment if he was not sick or had not resigned but had not participated in the active diocesan labor force for at least one year.

In any event, it appears that reporting procedures were more straightforward toward the end of the census period than during earlier years. Dioceses maintained systematic rosters of retirees and also reported withdrawals from the active priesthood more accurately as resignations rather than sick leaves or awaiting assignment. Note, however, in many instances there continues to be a "sabbatical" period for priests contemplating resignation. So awaiting assignment is still used, at least during years of uncertainty, to categorize priests who have left the active ministry and may or may not return. Obviously, a certain percentage of priests suffering from serious illness is inevitable. Dioceses now tend to use the sick leave category more uniformly solely for that purpose.

It should be apparent that changing category labels one way or another does not affect the overall attrition process as we have defined it demographically. We use standardized coding procedures across dioceses regard-

---

19. As one chancellor told us, "We finally had to take him off sick leave when his first child was born."

less of the inconsistency or variety of categories used at the local level.

Thus, according to our data, relatively high rates of net leave, once important for understanding the demographic transition, are definitely on the wane in the United States. As such, we did not pursue their analysis further. Nor would our sickness data, by themselves, be useful for actuarial statistics if, for example, the Catholic church were to wish to base its administration of sickness insurance on them. As we discovered, the criterion for identifying sickness is not at all uniform, even within the same diocese over two decades of observation, let alone across all the dioceses in the country.

Discussion and Conclusion

Both types of migration, permanent net immigration and temporary net emigration, have notable effects on growth and decline in the U.S. diocesan priesthood population. Net emigration has diminished in importance, so we limited its analysis to descriptive comparisons. The impact of net immigration, however, has been strong and has grown significantly in certain regions and dioceses.

We discovered that in some dioceses in the West Southcentral region and along the Pacific Coast the number of priests recruited through surplus incardinations almost equals and sometimes surpasses the number gained through ordinations. Recruitment through net immigration, however, is minimal in the Northeast and Northcentral dioceses. The contrast in net immigration rates coincides with the cleavage in decline trends. In the South and West, dioceses are experiencing low to minimal losses in the priesthood population but a large influx of priests through incardination. In the Northeast and Northcentral divisions, where clergy losses are high, gains through surplus incardinations are low to nonexistent.

Once again, through causal analysis we discovered that geographic region in and of itself does not explain why dioceses in one half of the country are so different from those in the other. Instead, organizational and environmental conditions, which differ by region, explain over half the variation in priestly immigration patterns. The causal model adds to our portrait of conditions explaining variation in recruitment trends.

What does the typical diocese with relatively high recruitment through immigration look like? The excess of incardinations over excardinations is higher in newly established dioceses with a relatively small Catholic population, small African-American population, effectiveness in attracting young Catholic males to the priesthood, and high demand for priestly services. High demand is reflected in a large parishioner-to-priest ratio resulting from low ordination rates.

In contrast, gains from priestly immigration are lower in old dioceses with relatively large Catholic and African-American populations, ineffectiveness in recruiting young Catholic males to the priesthood, and a large supply of priests. Higher supply is reflected in a relatively small ratio of parishioners to priests and high ordination rates.

In keeping with our findings on ordination rates, these results further disconfirm the hypothesis that the U.S. Catholic church is a loosely coupled system. Primarily, the forces of supply and demand and, secondarily, conditions affecting the attractiveness of the diocese seem to govern incardination trends throughout the system. Hence, regardless of the geographic location of the diocese, where demand for priestly services is high, so are net immigration rates, and where demand is low, surplus incardinations are minimal. Moreover, if the diocese appears attractive because it is new and innovative and is situated in an area with resources that enhance the quality of life, it has additional drawing power for incardinands.

Recruitment is the major issue in an organization with declining human resources, but poor retention is a closely related problem. Retention — measured by its opposite, resignation from the clerical ministry — is the topic we examine next.

9 Resignation

The driving force behind the decline and aging of the U.S. Catholic clergy is fueled not only by dwindling ordinations but also by moderately high and persistent resignations. In many professions, recruitment and retention are two sides of the same coin. When members of a profession are committed to their job, few resign. At the same time, individuals are attracted to a profession in which most members are satisfied and committed.[1] Thus, when retention is high, recruitment tends to be strong as well. Conversely, when retention is low, recruitment is weak too.

Empirical studies of the reciprocal effects of recruitment and retention of priests are nonexistent, principally because the data are hard to get and techniques for testing hypotheses are extremely complex. Nevertheless, the logical interconnection between a decision to be ordained and a decision to remain in the priesthood makes it reasonable to assume that ordination trends have an impact on resignations and vice versa. So we will point out the interrelationship between recruitment and retention in the treatment of resignations.

The aim of the present chapter is: to analyze the number, age at, and rate of past resignations; to examine the relationship between the rising age at both resignation and ordination; to assess the future direction of resignation and ordination trends; and to explain why resignation rates are different at the local and regional levels.

Highlights

1. Of the 13,631 men ordained for the diocesan clergy in the United States between 1966 and 1984, 51 percent were needed to cover positions vacated

---

1. In such cases screening the oversupply of candidates can become more important than recruiting them, as was true of Roman Catholic seminarians during the 1960s. Research on

by priests who resigned during the same period. During the "mass exodus" years (1968–73), 75 percent of ordinations were needed to fill vacancies created by resignations. The figure dropped to 38 percent during the late 1970s and early 1980s.

2. Nationally, resignations from the active ministry peaked in the early 1970s, when 4.6 percent of the active clergy ages 29–34 were resigning annually. The rates then dropped notably: resignations were cut in half during the census period. Resignations continued at moderately high rates, however, during the late 1970s and throughout the 1980s.

3. Regionally, dioceses in the East South and Pacific Coast states lost the largest proportions of their active clergy through resignation. In the East South, the cumulative loss from resignations between 1966 and 1984 was 25 percent of the 1966 number of active priests, on the average, and the loss in Pacific Coast dioceses was 24 percent.

4. Analysis of local variation reveals that dioceses in urban areas and those with more religious order priests lost relatively more diocesan clergy from resignation than dioceses in less urban areas with fewer religious order priests. Also, where Catholic church membership was growing faster, resignations were proportionately fewer than in dioceses where the Catholic population was growing more slowly.

Numbers

Data in earlier chapters described a "youth drain" in the U.S. Catholic clergy. The age distribution in most dioceses has grown significantly older during the past two decades, and the graying of the clergy is projected to continue as a national trend. The reason that the younger cohorts of priests are shrinking is twofold. First, fewer young men are being ordained and, second, declining recruitment is accompanied by a moderately high and steady exodus of young priests who resign.

Historical Period, 1966–84

Feelings among church leaders stretch from public joy at ordination ceremonies to quiet sorrow and pain over news of resignations from the priesthood. Table 9.1 is a sober reflection of two decades of recruitment and retention figures. The data are based on census counts from the 86 participating dioceses, weighted to estimate national parameters.

Figures in the first column give the number of ordinations each year. Column 2 lists the number of resignations from the active ministry. The

seminarians conducted around the time of the Second Vatican Council focused heavily on psychological screening techniques (see Menges and Dittes 1965).

Table 9.1. Number of ordinations, resignations, and net gains of U.S. diocesan priests, and percentage of gain lost by resignations, 1966–84

Year	Number		Net gain[a]	% lost by resignation[b]
	Ordination	Resignation		
1966	994	200	794	20
1967	1,062	338	724	32
1968	1,034	579	455	56
1969	847	750	97	89
1970	842	634	208	75
1971	692	667	25	96
1972	647	609	38	94
1973	831	499	332	60
1974	732	380	352	52
1975	768	296	472	39
1976	700	258	442	37
1977	667	295	372	44
1978	574	238	336	41
1979	647	223	424	34
1980	544	231	313	42
1981	544	176	368	32
1982	511	190	321	37
1983	530	194	336	37
1984	465	181	284	39
Total	13,631	6,938	6,693	51

Source: weighted census counts.
[a]Col. 1 - Col. 2.
[b](Col. 2/Col. 1)100.

third column shows the number of priests actually gained once resignations during the year are subtracted from the total number of newly ordained. The final column presents the percentage of newly ordained priests needed to fill positions vacated by recent resignees.

The national high-water mark for resignations was reached in 1969, when 750 U.S. diocesan priests left the active ministry. With 847 young men ordained that year, the net gain in active clergy was only 97 priests. Thus, 89 percent of the recruitment gain was lost by resignations in 1969.

In terms of net gain, however, 1971 and 1972 were the nadir of the census period. The balance of ordinations over resignations increased the number of active clergy in the country by 25 priests in 1971 and 38 priests in 1972. In the 1971–72 biennium, therefore, 95 percent of ordinations were needed to fill vacancies created by young priests leaving.

The years spanning 1968 through 1974 were the most critical for recruitment and retention recorded during the study, with resignation losses ranging from just over 50 percent to 96 percent; and for the following 10 years, from 1975 through 1984, resignation losses continued to reduce ordination gains substantially, with the proportion lost ranging from 32 percent to 44 percent.

The percentage figures in column 4 show that the retention problem reached alarming heights almost immediately after the Second Vatican Council. After persisting at critical levels for many years, the problem abated somewhat. Moderately high resignation losses continued without interruption to the end of the data-reporting period. The totals in the bottom row of the table show that of the 13,631 men ordained for the diocesan clergy in the United States between 1966 and 1984, 51 percent were needed to cover positions vacated by the 6,938 resignees during the same 19-year period.

Projection Period, 1985–2005

The historical data have been plotted in figure 9.1, along with the projected number of resignees based on optimistic, moderate, and pessimistic assumptions. The curve for 1966 to 1984 depicts the same data presented in table 9.1, but the annual fluctuations have been smoothed for four- and five-year cohorts and graphed at four- and five-year intervals; the projections follow the same procedures.

A striking aspect of the figure is that the annual number of resignations during the projection period is much lower than trends during the historical period. Resignations dropped from a peak of 558 per year during the early 1970s to a low of 194 per year in the early 1980s and have continued or will continue to fall during the projection period to 125 annually by 2005, under moderate assumptions.

Factors reducing the numbers of resignations in the U.S. priesthood are threefold. First, the active clergy is shrinking in size. Second, the clergy is steadily aging. And third, age-specific resignation rates have dropped, especially from the extreme highs experienced during the decade following the Second Vatican Council. All three demographic forces are incorporated in the assumptions that govern the projected number of resignations.

As we shall see later in this chapter, the high-risk period for resignation begins shortly after ordination and lasts until priests reach their mid-40s, which is represented by our 25–44-year-old age group. The proportion of 25–44-year-old priests dropped from 49 percent in 1966, or over 17,000 ac-

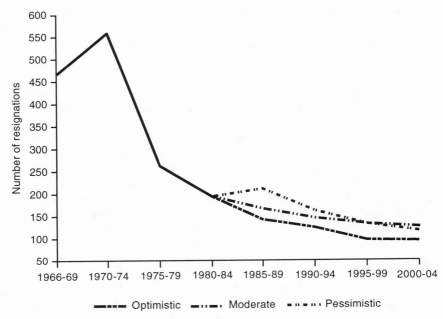

Figure 9.1. Average annual number of resignations of U.S. diocesan priests, 1966–2004

tive priests in absolute numbers, to 34 percent in 1985, or fewer than 10,000 active priests.

Inevitably, the number of resignations fell as the size of at-risk cohorts declined. The optimistic series assumes the size of the at-risk cohorts will continue to decline until at least 1995, and the moderate and pessimistic series assumes the number of priests in this age bracket will keep going down until 2005. Simply stated, the number of resignations must go down if the pool of priests at risk is getting smaller.

In addition to fewer at-risk priests, our projection models also take into consideration trends toward lower age-specific resignation rates. The moderate series assumes that the 1980–84 rates, which were the lowest of the entire census period, will continue for the next two decades.

The optimistic series, however, assumes the rates will continue to go down throughout the projection period because of the strength of past dampening trends.[2] We would not expect linear decline in the resignation rates, so we set the optimistic series at 84 percent of the 1980–84 rates between 1985 and 1994 and at 64 percent of the 1980–84 rates thereafter.

Because we do not believe the extremely high resignation rates experienced during the late 1960s and early 1970s will recur during the projection period, we do not follow our usual strategy of using the highest attrition rates from the historical period for our pessimistic resignation assumptions. Instead, for the most pessimistic scenario we assume future resignations will occur at approximately the average rate experienced over the entire historical period.[3]

The top two curves in the graph show that by the end of the period the models project a lower number of resignations under pessimistic than under moderate assumptions. This may seem unreasonable at first glance but is the result of interaction between assumed ordination and resignation trends.

The impact of relatively higher resignation rates under pessimistic assumptions is reduced by the complementary assumption of lower numbers of ordinations. The pessimistic series actually assumes higher rates of resignation than the moderate series. But there will be notably fewer at-risk priests in the pessimistic than in the moderate population, because the latter assumes higher ordinations than the former. Accordingly, the number of resignations will be smaller in the pessimistic than in the moderate model by the end of the projection period, because the pool of priests at risk will be relatively smaller owing to lower ordinations.

Age at Resignation

Age is one of the strongest correlates of resignation, and young priests resign more frequently than older ones. Figure 9.2 graphs the average age at resignation, along with the number of years between ordination and resignation, that is, the seniority of resignees. As the top curve demon-

2. Regressing resignation rates on time for the 19 years of the historical period yielded a negative correlation significant at the .01 level, so we concluded that further decline in the future would be a reasonable optimistic assumption.

3. Technically, we set the pessimistic assumption at a level which would correspond to the five-year average closest to the mean of the age-specific rates for 1966–84.

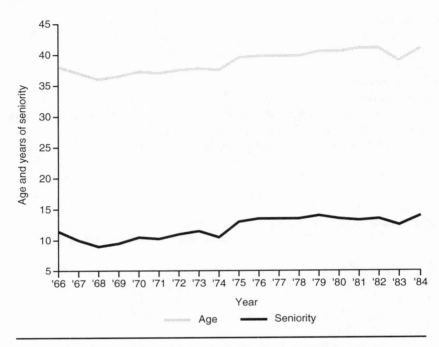

Figure 9.2. Age and seniority at resignation of U.S. diocesan priests, 1966–84

Source: weighted census counts.

strates, the average age at resignation has risen notably since the late 1960s.

The average age at resignation dropped from just over 38 to just under 36 in a few short years after the Second Vatican Council. Immediately, however, the age of resignees began to rise steadily and then appeared to level off in the early 1980s at approximately 41.

One question raised by the data is whether resignation was being postponed longer in the 1980s than earlier. Or does the older age simply reflect the rising age at ordination, such that the number of years between ordination and resignation are constant over the decades?

The bottom curve shows that trends in the number of years between ordination and resignation follow the same pattern as the aging trends. When the period began, the average was just over 11 years; it dropped to about 9 years in 1968 and then rose steadily to almost 14 years by 1984.

Apparently, the risk of resignation depends both on age and length of years in the ministry, and both are rising. Thus, currently, not only are priests older when they resign but they are also waiting longer before withdrawing.

A related issue concerns the consequence of older ages at resignation for altering manpower resources. In our discussion of ordinations we introduced the concept of man-years gained. The higher the age at ordination, the fewer the man-years of service *gained*. In contrast, as age and seniority at resignation rise, the years of service *lost* are reduced.

Rates

The raw numbers describe the magnitude of the resignation phenomenon, but focusing on rates adds a comparative perspective. *Crude rates* measure the number of resignees per 100 active priests, so allow us to compare resignation trends over time and across regions and dioceses.

Crude Rates by Region

The data in table 9.2 display the number of resignations per 100 active diocesan priests for the United States and census regions at four- and five-year intervals from 1966 to 1984. The period began with notably high attrition through resignations, as the national data in the top row of the table

Table 9.2. Crude resignation rates of U.S. diocesan priests and percentage of gross change, 1966–84, by year, nation, and region (number of resignations per 100 active priests)

	Average annual rate				% gross change
	1966 –69	1970 –74	1975 –79	1980 –84	1966 –84[a]
United States	1.32	1.71	0.85	0.65	19.50
Regions					
New England	0.70	1.50	0.73	0.65	15.52
Middle Atlantic	1.18	1.53	0.83	0.66	18.23
East Northcentral	1.53	2.15	1.05	0.66	22.26
West Northcentral	1.29	1.44	0.78	0.43	16.48
Mountain	1.58	1.54	0.73	0.64	20.63
Pacific	1.67	2.01	1.02	0.74	23.98
East South[b]	1.65	2.20	0.78	0.79	24.92
West Southcentral	1.77	1.44	0.67	0.72	20.51

Source: weighted census counts.
[a]Using the 1966 active population for the denominator and the cumulative number of resignations for the numerator.
[b]Combines the South Atlantic region and one diocese from the East Southcentral region.

indicate. The exodus peaked at an annual crude rate of 1.7 percent during the early 1970s and then dropped in the early 1980s to a level only half as high as that recorded at the beginning of the census.

The resignation drain, overall, averaged a gross loss of 19.5 percent of the 1966 number of active priests in 19 years. Although resignation rates have diminished considerably in the last decade or so, they appear to be bottoming out at a notably high level.

Regionally, the overall loss through resignations between 1966 and 1984 ranged from a low in New England, West Northcentral, and Middle Atlantic dioceses of about 16–18 percent of the active 1966 priest population to a high in East South and Pacific Coast dioceses of about 24–25 percent. West Southcentral, Mountain, and East Northcentral dioceses suffered medium losses from voluntary resignations of about 21–22 percent over the 19-year period.

The regional data reflect the national pattern with only minor exceptions. The most critical period, when losses from resignations were highest, was 1970–74 in all but the Mountain and West Southcentral regions of the country; resignation rates were highest in these last two regions during 1966–69. And, following the national trends, resignation rates declined steadily to the end of the historical period in all regions except the two in the South, where they bottomed out during 1975–79 and even went up slightly during 1980–84.

Resignation rates during 1980–84, which form the basis of the moderate projections, reflect the same variations as do the 1966–84 trends, with only one exception. The lowest cumulative loss through resignation during 1980–84 was recorded by priests in West Northcentral states, whereas the lowest cumulative loss between 1966 and 1984 was experienced in the average New England diocese.

Crude Rates by Diocese

The data in table 9.3 provide local annual crude resignation rates for the period, arranged alphabetically by state then diocese within census regions. So citing the extremes of diocesan resignation losses reveals the full range of differences in the data.

Northeast and Northcentral

In the Northeast the highest overall ratio of resignees to active clergy was reported by Newark, where resignations reduced the active priest roster by over 24 percent between 1966 and 1984. The lowest number of resignees during the period, in proportion to the size of the presbyterate in 1966, was registered in Altoona–Johnstown. In 19 years, the clergy there declined by only 7 percent through resignations.

Table 9.3. Crude resignation rates of U.S. diocesan priests and percentage of gross change, 1966–84, by year and diocese (number of resignations per 100 active priests; alphabetical order within region by state then diocese)

Region and diocese	Average annual rate				% gross change
	1966 –69	1970 –74	1975 –79	1980 –84	1966 –84[a]
Northeast					
New England					
Hartford CT	1.20	1.65	0.72	1.03	20.05
Norwich CT	0.89	1.98	1.49	0.17	20.22
Portland ME	0.52	0.75	0.72	0.32	9.18
Boston MA	0.89	1.54	0.74	0.62	15.92
Fall River MA	0.54	2.07	0.20	0.78	15.48
Worcester MA	0.41	1.16	0.65	0.67	13.46
Providence RI[b]	—	—	—	—	—
Burlington VT	0.56	2.06	1.54	1.00	22.78
Middle Atlantic					
Camden NJ	1.27	2.33	0.87	0.40	23.72
Newark NJ	1.85	1.92	1.09	0.92	24.37
Albany NY	0.81	1.72	1.79	0.88	20.24
Brooklyn NY	1.56	1.80	1.38	0.87	22.87
Buffalo NY	1.35	1.37	1.06	0.61	19.27
New York NY	1.21	1.39	0.48	0.62	14.88
Ogdensburg NY	1.04	1.98	0.35	0.58	17.89
Rochester NY	1.67	1.23	0.76	1.00	18.30
Rockville Centre NY	1.09	2.01	1.17	0.61	22.39
Allentown PA	0.97	0.88	0.74	1.07	16.82
Altoona–Johnstown PA	0.00	0.75	0.35	0.23	7.01
Philadelphia PA	0.87	1.22	0.51	0.52	13.29
Pittsburgh PA	1.49	1.37	0.68	0.62	18.76
Scranton PA	0.44	1.21	0.36	0.21	9.52
Northcentral					
East Northcentral					
Belleville IL	2.43	1.79	0.91	0.40	22.90
Chicago IL	1.86	2.14	1.43	0.51	23.83
Rockford IL	1.58	1.09	0.88	0.67	17.98
Indianapolis IN	1.71	3.15	0.79	1.67	28.73
Detroit MI	2.18[c]	3.19	1.57	0.96	29.70
Gaylord MI	1.61[d]	1.98	0.36	0.37	18.14
Grand Rapids MI	1.21[c]	2.40	0.50	0.50	17.88
Marquette MI	1.04	2.40	0.69	0.00	17.75
Saginaw MI	2.57[c]	3.34	1.74	0.53	34.86
Cincinnati OH	1.00	1.65	0.55	0.73	16.96
Cleveland OH	0.70	1.60	1.34	0.60	18.62
Columbus OH	1.28	1.86	0.58	0.74	19.15
Youngstown OH	1.32	2.07	1.60	0.91	23.53
La Crosse WI	1.38	1.93	0.59	0.10	16.40
Milwaukee WI	1.64	2.00	1.06	0.77	23.36

(continued on following page)

Table 9.3. Crude resignation rates of U.S. diocesan priests and percentage of gross change, 1966–84, by year and diocese (continued)

Region and diocese	Average annual rate				% gross change
	1966 –69	1970 –74	1975 –79	1980 –84	1966 –84[a]
Northcentral (continued)					
West Northcentral					
Des Moines IA	1.16	2.16	1.31	0.39	21.38
Dubuque IA	0.48	0.99	0.64	0.32	10.18
Sioux City IA	0.24	0.73	0.32	0.23	6.78
Dodge City KS	0.78	1.32	0.72	0.36	13.95
Salina KS	1.16	1.48	0.54	0.29	15.11
Wichita KS	1.32	1.15	0.32	0.17	11.84
New Ulm MN	1.39	1.02	0.94	0.22	14.96
St. Cloud MN	1.43	1.29	0.82	0.00	14.82
St. Paul–Minneapolis MN	2.07	1.78	1.67	0.55	24.59
Kansas City–St. Jos. MO	3.03	2.67	0.73	0.75	29.48
St. Louis MO	1.16	1.44	0.86	0.62	18.54
Springfield–C. Girard. MO	1.05	1.42	1.60	0.93	22.38
Lincoln NE[b]	—	—	—	—	—
Fargo ND	1.16	1.96	0.17	0.54	15.64
Rapid City SD	3.67	1.94	0.59	0.57	20.41
West					
Mountain					
Pueblo CO	0.84	3.18	0.94	1.22	29.91
Boise ID	1.27	0.77	0.98	0.94	19.48
Gallup NM	0.86[c]	0.00	0.00	0.41	7.14
Las Cruces NM	1.29	1.64	2.27	1.32	33.11
Santa Fe NM	2.48	1.72	0.32	0.00	18.62
Cheyenne WY	0.41	1.02	1.20	0.87	15.25
Pacific					
Fresno CA[b]	—	—	—	—	—
Los Angeles CA	1.68[c]	1.18	0.90	0.53	18.88
Monterey CA	2.08[e]	1.11	0.30	0.30	17.27
Oakland CA	2.76	3.40	0.77	1.21	34.34
Orange CA	1.68[d]	1.18	0.17	0.18	13.98
San Bernardino CA	1.48[d]	1.13	0.97	0.74	18.26
San Diego CA	1.48[c]	1.13	0.78	0.44	16.43
San Francisco CA	1.06[c]	2.91	1.48	0.76	26.03
San Jose CA	1.06[d]	2.91	1.48	0.99	26.78
Stockton CA	2.05	2.91	2.12	1.41	40.00
Baker OR	0.00	2.14	1.03	0.00	15.73
South					
East South[f]					
Wilmington DE	2.22	2.47	0.76	0.36	25.55
Orlando FL	0.65[g]	0.90	1.19	0.99	21.54

(continued on following page)

Table 9.3. Crude resignation rates of U.S. diocesan priests and percentage of gross change, 1966–84, by year and diocese (continued)

Region and diocese	Average annual rate				% gross change
	1966 –69	1970 –74	1975 –79	1980 –84	1966 –84[a]
South (continued)					
East South[f] (continued)					
St. Petersburg FL	0.60[g]	3.07	1.33	0.40	27.04
Atlanta GA	3.23	1.93	0.55	1.61	44.90
Covington KY	1.57	1.84	0.23	0.24	16.31
Baltimore MD	1.56	2.64	1.12	1.36	29.14
West Southcentral					
Little Rock AK	2.67	1.01	0.84	0.44	18.60
Alexandria–Shreveport LA	1.76	1.16	0.37	0.20	14.40
Baton Rouge LA	1.43	1.31	0.98	2.14	30.55
Lafayette LA	0.69[c]	1.49	0.71	0.70	16.88
Lake Charles LA	0.69[d]	1.49	0.71	0.00	13.50
Austin TX	2.25	1.14	1.13	0.00	20.22
Beaumont TX	0.00	3.85	0.37	1.21	29.21
Corpus Christi TX	0.00[c]	0.93	0.00	0.00	4.38
Dallas TX	2.48[h]	0.75	0.92	0.40	18.56
El Paso TX	1.19[c]	1.63	2.40	1.72	36.19
Fort Worth TX	0.00[h]	0.00	0.39	3.30	22.00
Galveston–Houston TX	2.77[c]	2.38	0.39	0.64	27.47
San Antonio TX	2.45[c]	1.44	0.42	0.34	20.44
Victoria TX	2.42[d]	1.51	0.41	0.11	19.24

Source: census counts.

[a]Using the 1966 active population for the denominator and the cumulative number of resignations for the numerator.

[b]Refused to participate.

[c]Divided during the census period. The division does not affect the rate, because it is standardized.

[d]Established during the census period by being divided from others in the sample. The annual rates prior to the year of the split are those of the parent diocese(s), weighted when necessary. See appendix D for year of establishment and parent diocese(s).

[e]Divided in 1967. The rate for 1966 is based on size of the active population as identifiable in 1966 (see appendix D).

[f]Combines the South Atlantic region and one diocese from the East Southcentral region.

[g]Established in 1968. The figure given for 1966–69 is the average of the 1969 and 1969 rates (see appendix D).

[h]Divided in 1969. The average given for 1966–69 is based on size of the active population as identifiable in years prior to and in the year of the split (see appendix D).

215

The highest losses from resignations in Northcentral dioceses reached almost 35 percent in Saginaw during the period. However, Saginaw will probably experience the second lowest overall decline in the Northcentral division, because exceptionally high ordination rates are offsetting these losses. With cumulative losses from resignations of just under 7 percent, Sioux City enjoyed the best retention record in the country for 1966–84.

West and South

In Stockton, the number of active priests recorded in 1966 was reduced 40 percent by 1984 because of resignations, for the high end of the range in the West division. At the low extreme, the Diocese of Orange would have lost only about 14 percent of its 1966 roster of priests through resignations if it had been in continuous existence between that year and 1984.[4]

In the South division, resignation losses reached their highest national level in Atlanta. Although Atlanta enjoys the fastest growing priest population in the sample, the archdiocese also suffered the largest recorded proportional loss from resignations in the country. Using the number of active priests in 1966 as the basis, the decline through resignations totaled almost 45 percent over 19 years.[5]

The smallest percentage of resignees was found in Lake Charles, but because the diocese was established in 1980, for the most part these data reflect trends in Lafayette, the parent diocese. Among the older dioceses of the South, Alexandria–Shreveport witnessed the fewest resignations, a cumulative loss of just over 14 percent of the 1966 number of active clergy.

Regional Patterns and Local Anomalies

The exodus of American priests began soon after the Second Vatican Council, peaked in the early 1970s, and then dropped in the early 1980s to a level only half as high as that recorded during the immediate postconciliar years (1966–69). Close examination reveals that dioceses in the Northeast

4. Orange was created in 1976. (See appendix D for procedures used to estimate resignations among priests residing in Orange County between 1966 and 1976.)

5. Resignation rates are affected primarily by entrance rates and the age structure of the priest population, so extremes of the distribution must be interpreted in view of these other demographic processes. Rapidly growing dioceses like Atlanta experience notably more resignations than rapidly declining dioceses like Sioux City, because the former have a relatively large and growing pool of young priests and the latter have relatively small and dwindling younger cohorts. As the data will show, younger priests are at substantially greater risk of resignation than older ones. Obviously, Atlanta is in a rare position of organizational growth, even though it suffered the highest cumulative resignation rate among the sampled dioceses.

and Northcentral half of the country followed this national resignation trend with few exceptions, whereas the majority in the West and South half deviated from the national pattern.

Thus in the Northeast and Northcentral states, resignation rates peaked during 1970–74 in almost three-fourths of the dioceses. In most of the remaining cases, which did not follow the national pattern, the highest levels of resignations were recorded, instead, immediately after the Second Vatican Council; but in two dioceses, Albany and Springfield–Cape Girardeau, the apex of the curve was reached during 1975–79.

Likewise, in keeping with the national pattern, fully nine-tenths of the Northeast and Northcentral dioceses experienced lower resignation rates during 1980–84 than during 1966–69. Among all 50 Northeast and Northcentral dioceses in the sample, only Fall River, Burlington, Albany, Allentown, and Altoona–Johnstown recorded relatively more resignations at the end than at the beginning of the census period.

Thus far our study has consistently uncovered strong contrasts between clergy populations in the West and South half of the country and those in the Northeast and Northcentral half. The same regional contrast is true of resignation trends.

In the average U.S. diocese, resignation rates peaked during 1970–74, but in 60 percent of West and South dioceses trends deviated from the national pattern. In the large majority of these dioceses, the highest levels of resignations occurred during 1966–69. In Las Cruces, Cheyenne, Orlando, and El Paso, however, resignation rates reached their zenith during 1975–79.

Additionally, in contrast with the national pattern, 26 percent of West and South dioceses experienced higher resignation rates in the early 1980s than they did during the late 1960s. In fact, Baton Rouge and Fort Worth recorded the highest resignation rates of the entire period during 1980–84.[6]

National Age-Specific Rates

A more complete picture of the national resignation phenomenon is provided in table 9.4, which presents rates according to age for the entire census period. Some of the same data are also summarized in different ways and graphed in figure 9.3 to facilitate comparisons.

The final column in table 9.4, which contains average rates for the 19 years, reveals the age differentials in the national data. Resignations were

6. The deviant resignation pattern has a strong impact on population projections for Baton Rouge and Fort Worth, because the moderate series is based on current (1980–84) trends.

Table 9.4. Age-specific resignation rates of U.S. diocesan priests, 1966–84 (number of resignations per 100 active priests)

Age cohort	Average annual rate				Grand mean 1966–84
	1966 –69	1970 –74	1975 –79	1980 –84	
25–26	0.8	0.5	0.0	0.0	0.5
27–28	2.0	1.9	0.8	0.7	1.5
29–30	2.8	4.5	1.3	1.5	2.7
31–32	3.4	4.8	1.8	1.5	3.0
33–34	3.2	4.5	2.0	1.3	2.8
35–36	2.7	3.6	2.0	1.5	2.5
37–38	3.0	3.6	2.0	1.6	2.6
39–40	2.1	2.7	2.0	1.2	2.0
41–42	1.4	2.2	1.2	1.1	1.5
43–44	1.1	2.1	1.1	0.8	1.4
45–46	0.7	1.3	1.0	0.7	1.0
47–48	0.7	0.7	0.7	0.7	0.7
49–50	0.5	0.9	0.5	0.4	0.6
51–52	0.3	0.6	0.5	0.4	0.5
53–54	0.3	0.6	0.4	0.3	0.4
55–56	0.3	0.3	0.2	0.4	0.3
57–58	0.3	0.2	0.4	0.1	0.2
59–60	0.1	0.1	0.1	0.2	0.1
61–62	0.1	0.1	0.1	0.1	0.1
63–64	0.0	0.0	0.1	0.0	0.0
65–66	0.1	0.0	0.0	0.1	0.0
67–68	0.0	0.0	0.1	0.1	0.0
69–70	0.0	0.0	0.0	0.1	0.0
71–72	0.0	0.0	0.1	0.0	0.0
73–74	0.0	0.0	0.0	0.0	0.0
75–76	0.1	0.0	0.2	0.1	0.1
77–78	0.0	0.0	0.0	0.0	0.0
79–80	0.0	0.0	0.0	0.0	0.0

Source: weighted census counts.

most prevalent among younger priests and rare among those over 50.[7]

Note, in the final column of the table, that at ages 27 and 28, two years or so after the usual age at ordination, resignations occurred at the rate of 1.5 percent annually. On the average, the national resignation rate peaked

7. The statistics demonstrate the differential impact of age on the risk of resignation. Thus, the age-specific rates in the table may be used to compute how many 30-year-old priests

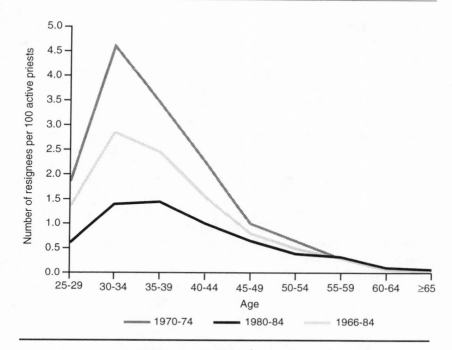

Figure 9.3. Average annual age-specific resignation rates of U.S. diocesan priests, 1966–84, by period

Source: weighted census counts.

at 3 percent annually by ages 31 and 32, or approximately five years after ordination.

Figure 9.3 presents the same data but switches to five-year cohorts of resignees, which smooths out the data and facilitates analysis. Comparing the top and bottom curves, we see that the highest risk of resignation was between ages 30 and 34 during 1970–74, but the high-risk period changed to ages 35–39 during 1980–84.

As the peaks of the same two curves indicate, over 4.5 percent of the

in contrast with 50-year-olds, for example, would resign over a certain period. If both age groups had begun with 100 priests and had been subject for 15 years to 1980–84 age-specific resignation rates (which are the basis of our moderate projection assumptions), the 30-year-old cohort would lose approximately 18 priests, whereas the 50-year-old group would lose only 3. If the 1970–74 rates were still operative, however, the 30-year-old cohort would witness 30 resignations during the 15 years, and the 50-year-olds would still lose only about 5 of their confreres through resignations.

highest-risk age group (30–34) resigned annually during 1970–74, but only 1.5 percent of the highest-risk age group (35–39) resigned each year during 1980–84. So even among younger priests, resignations are decreasing but the age group most at risk is rising. On the average, almost 3 percent of young priests in the overall highest-risk age group (30–34) resigned each year for a period of 19 years.

The figure further reveals that, during the time from 1966 to 1984, the relatively high-risk period for resignations continued throughout their 30s and began to subside when priests reached age 40. A significant level of resignations continued, however, throughout their 40s, diminished steadily during their 50s, and then virtually ceased when priests reached their 60s.

These trends lead to the following speculation. If the average age at ordination continues to rise, so will the average age at resignation, but only up to a point. Countervailing forces, such as diminishing career opportunities and marriage appearing less attractive to someone "set in his ways," seem to place limits on the age at resignation. Resignations are sharply reduced when priests begin to approach 55. As the demographic transition progresses, with a larger proportion of older priests, the result will likely be lower crude resignation rates.

How Losses Add Up

A different approach may help put the seemingly low resignation rates in proper perspective. Figure 9.4 shows how the small annual losses suffered by an ordination class add up over its career span, given three different hypothetical scenarios based on historical data. The top curve of the graph contrasts the loss that would result from resignation rates recorded during 1970–74 with the loss generated by the more recent 1980–84 rates, as revealed in the bottom curve.

The middle curve in the figure displays the loss that would result from the average of the resignation rates recorded over the entire census period, 1966–84. Thus, in dioceses affected by average resignation rates, by the time members of a typical class ordained in the late 1960s or early 1970s reached age 35, 19 percent would have resigned. By age 45, 34 percent would have resigned. And by the time the class celebrates its 25th anniversary, when most will have reached age 52, 37 percent would no longer be active in the priesthood. The cumulative result of the average of 1966–84 resignation rates reported in the last column of table 9.4 and the middle curve of figure 9.4, therefore, would reduce the average ordination class by almost two-fifths during the first 25 years of its career span.

The fluctuations by historical period in figures 9.3 and 9.4 reflect both

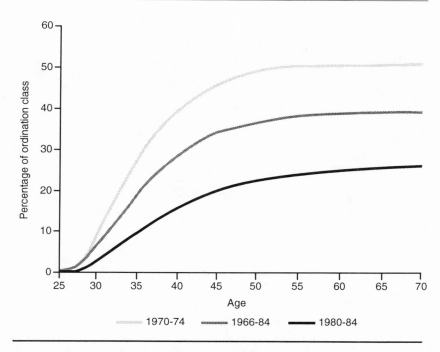

Figure 9.4. Loss from resignations of U.S. diocesan priests, by age and period

Source: weighted census counts.
Note: Formula for loss from resignation is:
    $X_j = (1-S_j)100$
where X_j is the cumulative percent loss due to resignation for age group j;
       S_j is the cumulative probability of surviving the risk of resignation for age
       group j; and
       $S_j = (1 - R_j)S_{j-1}$
where R_j is the age-specific resignation rate for age group j and
       S_{j-1} is the cumulative probability of surviving the risk of resignation for age
       group j-1. For this age distribution, $S_{24} = 1.0$.

good and bad news. The situation had improved considerably by the mid-1980s. If 1970–74 resignation rates were to continue to affect ordination classes, they would lose about 50 percent of their members, on the average, by the 25th aniversary of ordination. If ordination classes were affected by the 1980–84 rates, however, they would lose just under an average of 25 percent in that number of years. So the effects of resignations were reduced by half in a decade's time no matter how one looks at the data. The bad news is that resignations continue to be a major avenue of exit from the priestly population at the national and local levels.

Plausibility of Resignation Assumptions

Assuming recruitment and retention are interrelated, it is reasonable to suppose that a decision to participate in the priesthood, expressed through ordination, and a decision not to continue, expressed through resignation, are influenced by similar social forces. We will consider the available empirical evidence from related research that addresses this assumption. These studies help us understand why future trends will most likely follow those circumscribed by our moderate assumptions. Although our discussion focuses mainly on factors leading to resignation, it also applies *mutatis mutandis* to those affecting ordination.[8]

Earlier Studies of Resignation

The Second Vatican Council signaled the rethinking and reformulating of the theology of church and ministry and at the same time opened what some have called a Pandora's box of social change within the Catholic church (O'Dea 1968; Greeley et al. 1976). One facet of the aftermath of the council, documented in this report, is the exodus of young priests from the clerical ranks, especially during the late 1960s and early 1970s. In response to mounting concerns, the American Catholic bishops commissioned the National Opinion Research Center in 1969 to examine the state of the American priesthood on a wide array of issues, including the growing problem of resignations (NORC 1972).

Findings from the NORC study showed that resignations were more frequent among young priests who found loneliness a personal problem, who expressed a desire to marry if celibacy were declared optional, and who endorsed more modern rather than traditional statements of beliefs and values about church and priesthood (NORC 1972; Schoenherr and Greeley 1974). In terms of social exchange theory, the cost of forgoing marriage was the single most important explanatory factor in the model. A similar countrywide survey was sponsored by the Spanish hierarchy that same year. With minor differences, the same set of conditions (and principally the negative impact of celibacy) explained lack of commitment to the priestly role in Spain (Schoenherr and Pérez Vilariño 1979).

Recently, Verdieck and colleagues replicated relevant parts of the 1970 NORC survey in another national sample of American priests and tested whether the social forces explaining resignation had changed by 1985. They

8. According to March and Simon (1958), while some of the conditions influencing the decision to continue in an organization are different from the decision to participate in the first place, others are similar to it. See Schoenherr and Greeley 1974 and Schoenherr and Pérez Vilariño 1979 for an application of March and Simon's theory to priestly resignations.

conclude that "the dynamics underlying the role commitment process have changed very little. The cost of celibacy, although weaker than in 1970, is still a priest's principal consideration in the commitment process" (Verdieck et al. 1988, pp. 532–33). We may conclude, therefore, that the main reasons why priests leave the active ministry have not altered in a decade and a half.

If available research on the resignation phenomenon is correct, and thus far no other studies have contradicted or weakened the findings, then future trends in resignation rates will be related to developments in the church's stance regarding human sexuality and its theological views of ecclesial mission and ministry.

Growing Conservatism

Our assumptions regarding future resignations must first take into consideration certain period effects, beginning in the mid-1970s and continuing during the final decades of the century, that may be dampening resignation rates. Chief among them could be the growing conservatism in international Catholicism reinforced by the efforts of the Vatican.

Religion is conservative by nature, and the burden of conserving the sacred heritage of past traditions falls heaviest on church leaders (Eliade 1961; Schoenherr 1987a). We do not endorse a simplistic monocausal explanation of social trends, which would link them solely to leadership variables. At the same time, however, we recognize the pervasive influence of the papacy and Roman curia in this uniquely monocratic yet loosely coupled federation of local diocesan churches known as Roman Catholicism.

One notable conservative social force seemingly endorsed by Rome is a return to traditionalist views of human sexuality. Papal reinforcement of the teachings of *Humanae Vitae* and of the superiority of celibacy over marriage for priests, for example, comes at a historical period when the United States and many western European countries are undergoing extensive social change toward less restrictive sexual institutions (Richardson 1969; Greeley 1972).

Growing conservatism within Catholicism in general is the wider phenomenon of concern, of which John Paul II and his advisors may be the bellwether. Their renewed support for traditional values regarding sexuality is a primary example of conservative trends. Stressing traditional theological formulas in preference to those couched in the theories and terminology of modern hermeneutics and the social sciences is a second social trend of note. Championing conservative theology, especially if perceived as a reactionary movement, can greatly influence social change in organized religion, as O'Dea (1968) has argued in his analysis of the Second Vatican Council. Again, in this regard, John Paul II may be seen as a sign of the times.

Recently, for example, theologians across western Europe have begun challenging what they interpret as the overly conservative teaching and highly centralized leadership style of the current papacy. Among the complaints was the much publicized Cologne Declaration, signed by 485 theologians, including such prominent scholars as Hans Küng, Bernard Häring, and Edward Schillebeeckx. According to their statements, the growing concerns of theologians include: ". . . the overruling of local opinion in the naming of bishops, moves to silence independent and left-leaning theologians, the systematic weakening of national bishops' conferences, a narrow interpretation of sexual morality and the Pope's authoritarian style of rule" (Riding 1989). These and related developments in the church's official magisterium are bound to affect the driving force behind present and future resignations and ordinations.

Other conservative tendencies are now operative at the local level, which reinforce international trends. For instance, we can expect an increase in conservatism in the organizational climate of local dioceses as the age structure changes to a predominantly older clergy (Young and Schoenherr 1992). Further, Hoge, Shields, and Verdieck (1988) have documented that recent cohorts of young priests are more conservative theologically than those of the late 1960s and early 1970s. Finally, as fewer and older men are ordained, the probability increases that new ordinands will have well-examined and therefore more lasting commitments to the clerical ministry.

The cumulative impact of conservative forces argues for a decrease in priestly resignations and supports the plausibility of our optimistic assumptions. According to the research evidence, resignations have been and continue to be relatively more frequent among priests who espouse liberal Catholic beliefs and values. Given the conservative direction of the church's teaching authority and related developments at the diocesan level, the proportion of more conservative priests with stronger commitments to their ministry is likely to increase. Hence, we would expect fewer resignations to have occurred throughout the 1980s and to occur beyond than during the prior two decades.

Countervailing Forces and the Celibacy Issue

On the other hand, different social processes may continue to generate a driving force for resignations during the waning years of the century, which could make the moderate or pessimistic projection models more reasonable than the optimistic one. The data show that resignations peaked in the early 1970s and declined during 1975–84. As expected, and in keeping with the aging of the clergy and the trend toward conservatism just described, the average annual resignation rate during 1980–84 was much lower than that of recent prior years. The decline in the crude resignation rate, however, was apparently bottoming out during the 1980s.[9]

The moderate assumptions, therefore, are based on the level of resignations current in the early 1980s, which was a much lower rate than that of the peak years but, nevertheless, a moderately high one. We contend that the mid-1980s' rate will most likely continue in the future for several reasons. First among them, the emphasis on personalism and freedom of sexual expression in the wider American culture will continue to have its effect on priests' commitment to celibacy. And the closely related problem of loneliness can be expected to persist unabated.

Loneliness was a critical factor in the causal process leading to the decision to resign in 1970 and again in 1985. It can also readily be linked to the set of psychological and psychosexual factors describing "underdeveloped and developing" types of priests. As Kennedy and Heckler (1972) discovered, these two types made up the majority of Catholic clergy in the United States in contrast with the minority, whom they labeled the "maldeveloped" at one end of the continuum and the "well developed" at the other end.

Kennedy and Heckler base their analysis on Eriksonian developmental psychology, which calls attention to major crises facing maturing adults. This growing body of theory and research on the life cycle predicts that young priests face important adult crises in the early years after ordination in the form of not only a delayed identity crisis but also, more notably, the crisis of intimacy and mutuality (Levinson 1978; Whitehead and Whitehead 1979).

Data presented in table 9.4 provide indirect support for the prediction concerning normal transitional crises of priests. The evidence shows that resignation rates are highest approximately five years after ordination. It appears the new priest begins to resolve the appropriate life cycle challenges of identity, intimacy, and mutuality during the initial years of his career. The majority resolve the crises in favor of continuing in the priesthood, but the problems of loneliness and celibacy influence a significant minority of young clergy to opt for marriage and a different career.

Celibacy and living alone will probably continue in the foreseeable future as structural constraints that have to be met when adult transitional

9. Annual resignation rates for 1980–84 in the sample of 86 dioceses are: 0.78, 0.60, 0.65, 0.67, and 0.63. Those for 1985–88 in the subsample of 12 dioceses are: 0.67, 0.66, 0.76, and 0.56. The best-fitting curve through these points would be almost a straight line.

crises manifest themselves in priests' lives. And for young priests, as well as for candidates for the priesthood, the Christian value of marriage versus that of celibacy for meeting the challenge of intimacy and mutuality must now be weighed in light of the reaffirmation by the Second Vatican Council that celibacy and marriage may be considered equal but different paths to Christian holiness.

The theological nature of celibacy and marriage as ways of holiness was clarified in the council document *Pastoral Constitution on the Church in the Modern World.* The section on marriage (#48–52) formulated a new understanding of sex within marriage, stressing a more personalist understanding of the relationship and emphasizing that love between partners is the context in which children emerge (Abbott 1966, pp. 250–58). This understanding replaced the older terminology, which identified the primary and secondary ends of marriage as children and personal fulfillment, respectively. The new understanding emphasizes the relationships between Chrisitian love, sexuality, and friendship. It gave theologians — and priests themselves — the rationale for replacing the traditional claim that celibacy is the better, if not the only, road to perfection (see Fichter 1968) with the understanding that marriage and celibacy are different but equal paths of Christian perfection (cf. Nouwen 1979; Seidler and Meyer 1989).

The sociological issue involved is whether social change in cultural values regarding celibacy and marriage is pervasive enough to cause priests to continue resigning from the priesthood at approximately the same rate as assumed by our moderate forecast series. Additional data lead us to believe they will.

In 1966, Fichter (1968) polled a national sample of Catholic priests on the question, "If a married priesthood were permitted in the Roman rite, do you think that you would marry?" Thirty-eight percent of those under 35 thought they would. According to the U.S. Catholic Conference data gathered at NORC, in 1970 about 1 out of every 3 priests under 35 expressed a desire to marry if celibacy were declared optional and 8 out of 10 were in favor of such new legislation (NORC 1972). Potvin (1985) reports that in the mid-1980s exactly the same proportion of seminarians in theologates (33 percent) said they would want to be married as priests if celibacy were to become optional.

Most recently, Verdieck and colleagues (1988) discovered that the percentage of priests under 35 who said they would probably or certainly get married if priests were allowed had dropped from 37 percent in 1970 to 25 percent in 1985. The decline in the percentage makes us expect fewer resignations in the immediate future than during the exodus years of the early 1970s. Nevertheless, throughout the two decades following the Second Vatican Council large minorities of priests and seminarians persisted in stating a preference for marriage. These data demonstrate that celibacy remains not only an unsettling but also an unsettled issue for the American Catholic clergy. Hence, it will continue to play an important role in their developmental crises of maturity and have a negative impact on priestly retention. And, undoubtedly, through interaction effects and reciprocal causality, the same dynamics will also affect present and future ordination rates.

In summary, given the large proportion of "underdeveloped and developing" priests among the U.S. clergy, the pervasive influence of the wider culture's sexual norms, the uneasiness about the superior spiritual value of celibacy over marriage within Catholic theological and priestly circles, the large minority of priests who would prefer to be married, and the unavoidable challenge of every young priest to face the crises of intimacy and mutuality within his ministry and make them a passage for growth rather than regression, it is reasonable to expect that the driving force behind moderate levels of resignation and low levels of ordination will be sustained in the years ahead. The moderate assumptions regarding trends in resignation and ordination are based on these considerations.

Social forces surrounding the changing values of human sexuality impinge upon the countervailing trends of conservatism in the church. If the forces of ecclesiastical conservatism were not so pervasive, resignations could well increase to a level which would make the pessimistic assumptions the most realistic. However, conservative trends leading to lower resignation rates are balanced by an increasingly positive view of Christian marriage and sexuality, which, we argue, leads to higher resignation rates. Because the moderate assumptions about future resignation trends reflect a balance between these opposing social forces, the moderate projection series appears to us to be the most plausible of the three.[10]

The remainder of the chapter is devoted to an exploration of environmental and organizational conditions that explain variation in resignation rates experienced in United States dioceses at the beginning of the 1980s, the historical period upon which our moderate projection assumptions are based.

Causal Model of Resignation Rate

In discussing the plausibility of our projection assumptions we reviewed the three major social psychological studies of priestly resignations avail-

10. The same set of countervailing forces could have a major effect on the decision to participate, which could lower ordination rates below those experienced during 1980–84. In that case, with fewer young priests at high risk, resignation rates would also be lower than those assumed in our moderate projection series. The net effect on future population size, however, would remain unchanged, because one "forecast error" would balance out the other. For these reasons, priestly recruitment and retention should be treated as interrelated processes.

able in the literature. All three investigations reported the same consistent results, showing that the social action sequence leading to a decision to continue in the priestly role is most strongly affected by the negative impact of celibacy and modern values.

The researchers involved in these three studies tested a social exchange model reflecting two different historical periods and national settings. Verdieck and colleagues (1988) replicated the 1970 NORC study 15 years later and found the same pattern of effects among the variables. Schoenherr and Pérez Vilariño (1979) applied the model to data on U.S. and Spanish priests and reported that the same causal process leading to priestly role commitment was operative under different cultural conditions.

In a related study of "ex's," Ebaugh (1988) discovered that the stages of the exiting process were remarkably stable and consistent across time and across a wide variety of roles. The expectation of stability in the social psychological processes generating resignations among priests is supported by her more general data.

On the other hand, Seidler (1979) and Seidler and Meyer (1989) examined the resignation phenomenon from an organizational and environmental perspective, as reflected in local diocesan conditions during 1966–70. They focused on the diocese as the unit of analysis, so had to ignore social psychological processes. As Seidler and Meyer (1989) predicted from their conflict model, however, many structural conditions influenced diocesan resignation rates. The best fitting and most parsimonious empirical model showed that environmental conditions had the strongest impact, clergy climate only a modest effect, and episcopal policies hardly any influence on resignation rates. Surprisingly, resignations had no feedback effects whatsoever on diocesan conditions, including episcopal policies, which led Seidler and Meyer to explain the church's reaction to resignations during the 1960s and 1970s as that of a "lazy monopoly" (see Hirschman 1970).

In our causal analysis we address a question raised by Seidler and Meyer's findings about the impact of environmental and organizational conditions on diocesan resignation rates. As Verdieck and colleagues (1988) discovered, social psychological processes explaining priests' commitment have continued relatively unchanged for 15 years. Since individual-level processes leading to resignation have been so remarkably stable, we wish to examine whether ecological- and organizational-level processes likewise show continuous effects on priestly attrition over time.

Specifically, we ask whether the same environmental and structural processes that Seidler found operative in 1970 continued to explain variation in resignation rates of Catholic dioceses in 1980. Our current data set allows us to examine part but not all of the question, because we have no updated measures of clergy climate and episcopal policies. The most powerful explanatory variables in Seidler and Meyer's model, however, are the percentage of Catholic membership, regional dominance, and the proportion of staffing by religious clergy, that is, characteristics of the social context in which the decision to continue or resign is made. Measures of all three are available in our 1980 data.

In developing an empirical model of resignation rates from the variables available, we follow the same causal assumptions that guided the analysis in previous chapters: geographic region is an exogenous variable in the model; characteristics of the environment are the most antecedent conditions in the assumed causal sequence; and organizational conditions intervene between environmental antecedents and the dependent variable, diocesan resignation rate.

The environmental variables measure population characteristics of the counties that compose diocesan jurisdictions. The full set of environmental variables, which we tested in exploratory models, consisted of the percentage of urban population, racial-ethnic composition, age distribution, marital status, education, health, housing, occupation, family income, and religion. The organizational variables we examined included the year the diocese was established, regional dominance of the diocese, religious priest-to–diocesan priest ratio, permanent deacon-to–diocesan priest ratio, priest recruitment ineffectiveness, entrance and exit rates of the clergy population, and the parishioner-to-priest ratio. Sources and operational definitions of the variables are given in appendix C.

In 1980, the resignation rate in the average U.S. diocese was 0.67, as the grand mean in table 9.5 shows. Resignations were notably below the na-

Table 9.5. Resignation rates in U.S. Catholic dioceses, 1980, by region (mean number of resignations per 100 active priests)

Region	Rate
New England	0.62
Middle Atlantic	0.70
East Northcentral	0.63
West Northcentral	0.54
Mountain	0.67
Pacific	0.96
East South[a]	0.54
West Southcentral	0.69
Grand mean	0.67
Standard deviation	0.50

Source: weighted census counts.
[a]Combines the South Atlantic region and one diocese from the East Southcentral region.

tional rate in the average West Northcentral and East South diocese; the highest regional rates were recorded in Pacific Coast dioceses. Resignation rates in other regions hovered near the national average.

Table 9.6 displays the most effective model discovered during a systematic analysis of the available variables in their assumed causal sequence. As the adjusted R^2 statistic indicates, the model explains just over 13 percent of local diocesan variation in resignation rates. Despite notable variation in rates across the country, as reported in table 9.5, we discovered no net influence on resignation rates from geographic region. In fact, of the three dozen or so environmental and organizational variables tested, only three show net effects. The percentage of urban population is the most powerful predictor of resignation rates, followed by the religious priest–to–diocesan priest ratio and the percentage of Catholic growth.

Percentage of Urban Population

Dioceses where proportionately more of the general population lives in urban counties record higher resignation rates than those with less urbanization, after controlling for other variables in the model. Although the influence of urbanization is statistically strong, the substantive impact is relatively small. The cumulative net effect of a 10-point increase in percentage of urban population on diocesan resignation rates would be an increase in the number of resignees per 100 active clergy by about 1 extra priest every 20 years.[11] Though weak, the effect of urbanization raises several questions. Perhaps priests resign in relatively higher proportions in urban areas because stress factors in city parishes are greater than in rural communities. The finding may also imply that urban areas are more likely than rural areas to provide career options and diverse support groups for resignees. Or given that the endorsement of traditional rather than modern values is positively related to the decision to continue in the active ministry, perhaps the results reflect higher concentrations of conservative priests in rural than in urban dioceses.

Religious Priest–to–Diocesan Priest Ratio

Dioceses with relatively more religious clergy per active diocesan priest tend to have higher resignation rates, all other conditions being equal. Thus if Diocese A is staffed with 20 more religious order priests per 100 diocesan priests than Diocese B, each year it will experience 0.04 more resignations per 100 diocesan priests than Diocese B, or almost 1 additional resignee every 25 years.[12]

11. Precisely: $0.0053 \times 10 \times 20 = 1.06$.
12. Precisely: $0.0018 \times 20 \times 25 = 0.9$.

Table 9.6. Effects of environmental and organizational conditions on resignation rates in U.S. Catholic dioceses, 1980 (unstandardized regression coefficients)

Independent variable	b	Adjusted t-ratio[a]
% Catholic growth	-.0050	-2.035*
% urban	.0053	3.125**
Rel./dio. priest ratio	.0018	2.272*
n of dioceses	85	
Constant	.201	1.690
F-ratio	5.23**	
R^2	.162	
Adjusted R^2	.131	

[a]Adjustment is based on a finite population correction factor of 0.705 or the square root of 1 - (n/N) applied to the standard error of b; see Mendenhall et al. 1971.
 *$p \leq .05$.
 **$p \leq .01$.

At least two explanations must be considered in evaluating this finding. On the one hand, if a diocese has a relatively large staff of religious order priests, more diocesan clergy may choose to resign, because they perceive their exit will have fewer negative consequences for the organization. On the other hand, religious priests resign at higher rates than diocesan priests, as Shields and Verdieck (1985) discovered in their recent study and as the NORC researchers found in 1970. Thus, perhaps, dioceses with relatively large numbers of religious order priests provide the right climate for resignation for both types of clergy. Whatever the explanation, the differential impact is apparently slight: one additional resignee per 100 diocesan priests every 25 years.

Percentage of Catholic Growth

Dioceses experiencing higher growth in their church membership tend to have lower rates of resignation among their clergy than dioceses with lower growth. The impact of changing church membership on resignations is somewhat less than that of the percentage of urban population, and the influence is in the opposite direction. Nevertheless, if the Catholic population is growing 10 percent faster in Diocese A than in Diocese B, in 20 years the former should experience 1 fewer resignee per 100 active priests than the latter.[13] It seems that in dioceses where growing numbers of parishioners produce greater demands on the clergy, fewer priests leave the

13. Precisely: $-0.0050 \times 10 \times 20 = -1$.

active ministry. The direct influence of changing church membership appears to be part of a consistent pattern among the environmental and structural conditions affecting diocesan resignation rates.

Balancing Supply and Demand

The contrasting effects of staffing patterns and urbanism, on the one hand, and client growth, on the other, suggest that forces of supply and demand and diocesan resignation rates may interact favorably with regard to organizational goals. Thus, in urban areas where client concentration makes delivery of religious services more efficient, resignation rates among diocesan priests are relatively high. Additionally, when dioceses have a large staff of religious clergy, which increases the supply of sacramental ministers, diocesan priests are also more likely to resign than when fewer religious priests are available to take up the slack. In contrast, when diocesan organizations face growing demand because of rapid Catholic population growth, local priests are less likely to leave the active ministry.

In each situation, environmental and structural conditions tend to adjust the balance of supply and demand in favor of meeting organizational goals. Admittedly, the adjustment makes the best of a poor situation, because every resignation is a decrement to the overall priest supply. Nevertheless, the net result is that, given moderately high resignation rates across the country, variation around the mean tends to occur under environmental and organizational conditions where it will least affect the availability of sacramental ministry at the local level.

Explanatory Power

In models presented earlier—those analyzing priest population growth, parishioner-to-priest ratios, ordination rates, and net migration rates—we discovered that environmental and organizational variables explained from one-half to three-fourths of local variation around the national average. The regression equation in table 9.6, however, explains only about one-eighth of the variance in 1980 resignation rates.

The resignation model, however, is far from useless. In fact, the level of explained variance is not atypical in research literature and is low only in comparison to our previous models. As social scientists take pains to point out, social processes are highly complex. Oftentimes the most important causal conditions cannot explain a great deal of variance in the dependent variables (see Greeley 1989b). The power of any explanatory model lies in its ability to demonstrate the existence of important relationships among seemingly random processes and thus improve our ability to understand social reality.

Estimating the combined effects of the resignation model in terms of unit change in the dependent variable is one way to assess its explanatory power. If, for example, Diocese A were situated in an area where Catholic church membership growth is 10 percent lower, urban concentration is 10 percent higher, and religious priest staffing is 20 percent higher than in Diocese B, Diocese A would experience 1 extra resignation per 100 active priests every seven years in comparison to Diocese B. If the differences between the two dioceses were twice as great — a scenario that is possible given the range of environmental and structural conditions among the sampled dioceses — Diocese A, in contrast with Diocese B, would lose 1 additional priest per 100 active clergy every three and a half years. These are by no means trivial differences, given the recruitment and retention problems afflicting American Catholic dioceses.

Seidler's Model of Resignations Revisited

Given the interpretive power of the conflict model they used in other parts of their analysis, Seidler and Meyer (1989) expressed surprise that environmental and structural conditions rather than conflict measures were the strongest predictors of resignation rates in 1970. Indicators of conflict such as clergy climate and episcopal policies were somewhat helpful for understanding local variation in resignation patterns, but their influence was notably less than the impact from the more remote contextual conditions. In the Seidler and Meyer study, the percentage of Catholic church members, regional dominance, and the proportion of staffing by religious clergy explained approximately 21 percent of the variance in 1970 resignation rates.[14]

We found that three variables, which were similar to Seidler and Meyer's environmental and structural measures, explained 13 percent of the variance of 1980 resignation rates. The new results provide evidence for stability across time in the influence of wider social forces on resignations. Although minor differences between their model and ours raised a few questions, the discrepancies eventually pointed to measurement issues.

The most unambiguous similarity in the 1970 and 1980 models is the unchanging influence of staffing by religious clergy, which continued to inflate resignation rates throughout the decade. Seidler and Meyer's variable measures the percentage of parishes in the diocese that are staffed by

---

14. Seidler and Meyer (1989, p. 137) report an R^2 of .446 for their trimmed regression model of resignation rates. Of the total variance explained, 0.135 is ascribed to the influence of "control" variables, 0.019 to that of priests in nonparish work, 0.08 to that of clergy passivity, and 0.212 is attributable to the impact of the percentage of Catholic church members, regional dominance, and the proportion of staffing by religious clergy.

religious order priests, while ours measures the ratio of religious order priests to active diocesan priests residing in the diocese. We judge that both indices have minimal measurement error, and both reflect the same organizational trait. The similarity of effects over time lends credence to our judgment.

Although we found no effects from the percentage of Catholic population, a closely related measure, the percentage of growth in Catholic population between 1970 and 1980, produced the same effect in 1980 as did Catholic concentration in the 1970 Seidler and Meyer model. In our data, the zero-order correlation between the percentage of Catholic church members in 1970 and our 1970 resignation rate was −0.031, and the correlation between the same measures for 1980 was 0.022; the relationship did not increase when the percentage of Catholics and other independent variables were regressed on the resignation rate.

The disparate results from the percentage of Catholics in Seidler and Meyer's and in our model may be due to differences in operational measures, dissimilarities in the variables entered in the models, or genuine period effects. We suspect measurement error in Seidler and Meyer's data source for the percentage of Catholics. They took their measure from Luzbetak (1967), who relied on estimates from chancery officials for both the numerator and denominator. The numerator for our measure comes from Glenmary data. In comparing methods for estimating the size of the Catholic population used by Luzbetak and the Glenmary research team, we judge the latter's to be more trustworthy.[15]

With regard to the denominator, many estimates of the general population in Luzbetak's data are rounded to millions, implying they are indeed "rough guesses." Our denominator, however, is taken from U.S. census publications. Additionally, the only reliable estimates of the general population available to Luzbetak's diocesan contact person in 1967 would have been from the 1960 U.S. census. To the extent that Luzbetak's measure is valid, perhaps the relationship in Seidler and Meyer's data partly reflects conditions in 1960, which predated the Second Vatican Council, and are thus different from those captured by our 1970 and 1980 data. Longitudinal studies designed to include all relevant variables would be necessary to resolve the differences in our results.

Initially, we also found that the influence of regional dominance appeared to be different in 1980 from that of a decade earlier, but a critical comparison between our data and regression model and theirs reveals that

15. Compare the description of methods in Luzbetak 1967, Johnson et al. 1974, and Quinn et al. 1982.

regional dominance is a surrogate measure for urban concentration. So the positive effect of urbanization on clergy resignation was likewise constant over time.

In our data, the zero-order correlation between regional dominance and the 1970 resignation rate was 0.286, but the relationship with the 1980 rate was 0.113, perhaps indicating that period effects during the decade had weakened the impact of regional dominance. We ran separate regression models for 1970 and 1980, entering regional dominance, the percentage of Catholic church members, and the proportion of staffing by religious clergy, while controlling for the percentage of urban population. In each case the effect of regional dominance was washed out by the percentage of urban population.

Seidler and Meyer also tested for the joint effects of regional dominance and urban concentration and reported results different from ours; only the net influence of regional dominance persisted. Once again we suspect sizable measurement error stemming from Luzbetak's data sources. His respondents were asked to estimate the number of urban, suburban, and rural parishes in the diocese, a task that even a well-trained demographer would find daunting unless reliable and comparable census data were available. For our measure of urban population, we used aggregated county-level data provided by Glenmary, which was taken from U.S. census publications supplemented by data from Rand McNally field studies. We conclude from our critical comparison of Seidler and Meyer's and our results that regional dominance is a surrogate measure for urbanization.

Stability Amid Change

During the 1970s, structural innovation and change in the Catholic church was the order of the day (Greeley 1977; Seidler and Meyer 1989). The decade also witnessed steady growth in the Catholic population stemming from favorable demographic dynamics such as high birth and immigration rates and a young age pyramid (Roof and McKinney 1987). In contrast, our own data document an unprecedented change in the size and structure of the U.S. diocesan clergy during the same period. Nevertheless, a careful examination of the social forces behind the resignation phenomenon reveals that stability and continuity underlie the process generating the steady exodus of priests from the clerical ranks.

Verdieck and colleagues (1988) documented 15 years of stability in the social-psychological processes leading to the decision to resign. Ebaugh's (1988) study lends further credence to the expectation of stable patterns in the social-psychological stages of exiting from a role. Our analysis replicated the most powerful segment of Seidler and Meyer's 1970 model and discovered that essentially the same environmental and structural conditions facilitated and impeded resignations in 1980 as in 1970. Thus, the combined results of research to date confirm that a stable multilevel set of social forces has produced, and will probably continue to produce, moderately high levels of attrition from the active priesthood.

Within the local diocesan church, the process generating resignations takes place at the personal or social-psychological level. Given the persistence of the process, in years to come young priests who endorse modern values, find loneliness a problem, and prefer marriage over celibacy are more likely to resign than older clergy who hold traditional beliefs and values, are not troubled by loneliness, and are content with the celibate life style.

Between dioceses, the social forces generating higher or lower resignation rates will probably continue to be linked mainly to environmental and structural conditions. Our findings and those of Finke (1989) lend support to the assumption that social effects of ecological forces that have been stable across time will probably continue, all other things being equal. Thus, for the foreseeable future, rates of attrition are likely to be higher in urban areas and where religious order priests are concentrated, and are likely to be lower where Catholic church membership is growing.

Although research results from studies of priest resignations are trustworthy as far as they go, the explanations remain partial and incomplete. Further progress in understanding the relationship between priestly role commitment and social-psychological processes, organizational-level processes, and environmental conditions will require the formulation and testing of hypotheses involving data from all three foci of analysis.

Recent developments in the statistical theory of hierarchical linear models now provide appropriate techniques for simultaneously modeling within- and between-diocese differences in resignation behavior (Lee and Bryk 1989). In addition, hierarchical linear models should be applied to longitudinal data sets to determine whether changing period effects alter the multilevel process generating organizational role commitment over time. For example, we need to explore whether growing conservatism along with cohort and aging effects in the clergy population (see Hoge, Shields, and Verdieck 1988; Young and Schoenherr 1992) interact with urban-rural conditions at the diocesan level while shifts in the general population and Catholic membership occur over time.

We now switch our focus from the components of change affected primarily by social forces to attrition governed mainly by biological processes. Thus, in the next two chapters we treat retirement, preretirement mortality, and general mortality of U.S. diocesan priests.

10 Retirement and Preretirement Mortality

In most cases retirement is a definitive event which severs the work relationship between a person and an organization. For many Catholic priests, however, retiring from full-time ministry is not accomplished in one decisive step. In fact, up to the time of the Second Vatican Council, priests and bishops in the United States did not retire at all, except for serious illness or other incapacity. Traditionally, Catholic theology has stressed the permanent nature of priestly orders. The ordination ritual reminds the ordinand, "Thou art a priest forever . . ." (Hebrews 5:6).

The sacrificial nature of Catholic worship ascribes a unique role to the priest which undergirds the permanent character of ordination. Only an ordained priest may preside at the eucharistic sacrifice of the Mass, the church's central liturgical action. This privilege is not affected by retirement, though the responsibility for leading community worship is. An ambiguity prevails so that nowadays, even with formal retirement programs in full force, many retirees perform priestly duties. Indeed, in the face of the priest shortage, retired clergy may feel some moral obligation to continue celebrating Mass with a community.

According to diocesan sources, however, the average retiree performs parish-related duties a few hours a week at most. Some celebrate public Mass regularly, but most only occasionally. So, by and large, retirement may be considered a full decrement to the active priest population. For purposes of this study retirement means the priest is no longer a member of the active clergy. To assess the amount of time retirees spend in ministerial activity is beyond the scope of the project. If our informants are correct, however, the results of such an investigation would show that it is relatively small.

Retirement differs from the other organizational exit events considered so far in that it is subject to biologically linked actuarial forces. Excardination, resignation, and awaiting assignment are likewise decrements to the active population, but they are influenced more by psychological, interpersonal, and organizational processes than by those that are biological. Sick leave, if it becomes permanent, is indistinguishable from retirement. In fact, actuaries call it ill health or incapacity retirement (Benjamin and Haycock 1970). Diocesan policies vary, but the minimum retirement age is usually 65 and the maximum, 75. So the number of retirements per year is more or less fixed by the aging process and is predictable using actuarial statistics, with some exceptions for priests who postpone retirement or choose not to retire.

In terms of organization demography, retirement is similar to preretirement mortality, because both are components of natural loss. With regard to an organization's work force, if death occurs before retirement, it is a decrement to the active work population, but when it occurs after retirement it is not, because the retiree has already exited. This distinction is unnecessary in most organizational settings, but important in those, like the Catholic church, where custom blurs the line between retirees and active members of the work force.

Accordingly, in this chapter we examine retirement and preretirement mortality as organizationally related exit events. The analysis covers trends in retirement and preretirement mortality, changes in the age at which they occur, variation in their rates, and causal models explaining why these rates differ across dioceses.

Highlights

1. As the century wanes many U.S. dioceses will face relatively high numbers of retirements and preretirement deaths because of the aging of the clergy.

2. Manipulating retirement policies to extend years of priestly service generally results in only short-term gain, because lower retirement rates soon produce higher preretirement mortality rates. Natural attrition will quickly reach the same level experienced when priests were retiring at the usual age.

3. To the extent that the clergy enjoys exceptionally high longevity, as in the average West Northcentral diocese, postponing retirement can notably increase years of service.

4. Causal analysis of local variation reveals that dioceses in the South and those that are effective in recruiting young men to the priesthood experience relatively lower retirement rates. West dioceses and those with younger age distributions and lower resignation rates experience relatively lower preretirement mortality rates.

Numbers

The analysis of changing numbers of retirements and preretirement deaths begins with the period covered by our census. Once these tallies are presented, we pause to summarize our analysis of gains and losses in the priesthood population by showing how much each component of change contributed to the decline. We then project the number of retirements and preretirement deaths to the turn of the century.

Historical Period: 1966–84

Table 10.1 reports the number of priests who retired, the number who died on active duty, and the number of losses from natural attrition for 1966–84. Retirements averaged 476 per year and preretirement deaths 281 per year, for a total natural loss of 757 active priests annually during the cen-

Table 10.1. Number of retirements, preretirement deaths, and natural losses of U.S. diocesan priests, 1966–84

Year	Retirement	Preretirement death	Natural loss[a]
1966	291	444	735
1967	508	411	919
1968	627	362	989
1969	521	413	934
1970	554	334	888
1971	449	334	783
1972	488	265	753
1973	444	295	739
1974	465	269	734
1975	511	259	770
1976	399	236	635
1977	532	222	754
1978	509	225	734
1979	422	187	609
1980	394	202	596
1981	348	214	562
1982	565	242	807
1983	504	213	717
1984	505	211	716
Total	9,036	5,338	14,374

Source: weighted census counts.
[a]Col. 1 + Col. 2.

sus period. Exits through both transitions totaled 14,374 in 19 years.

Attrition from retirement and preretirement mortality declined almost 24 percent during the period, from an average of 894 active priests per year during 1966–69 to an average of 680 during 1980–84. The decline in natural attrition is due mainly to the shrinking of the priest population, which decreased by almost 20 percent between 1966 and 1984.

The second column shows that the number of preretirement deaths dropped dramatically during the first nine-year period, from an average of just over 400 annually during 1966–69 to about 300 per year during 1970–74. The biggest decline followed the formalization of priest retirement policies. In the late 1960s many dioceses did not have formal retirement programs, so older priests died while on active duty during those years. Once retirement programs were in place, however, older priests were listed as retired for some time before they died. Still, the decline in the number of deaths prior to retirement continued throughout the census period because of the diminishing size of the population.

With the presentation of numbers for retirement and preretirement mortality, we are now in a position to pause to summarize our analysis of the components of change in the priesthood population. Table 10.2 provides the total number of entrances to and exits from the population of active U.S. diocesan priests between 1966 and 1984. The data decompose the overall loss reported in chapter 2 into its component parts; they also clarify the contribution of each transition event.

The table shows that during the 19-year period entrances through ordination and incardination amounted to just over 15,000; exits through net leave, resignation, and natural loss totaled just over 22,000; and net loss, the difference between gains and losses, was a little under 7,000. According to our census counts, in round numbers, there were 35,000 active diocesan priests in the United States on January 1, 1966, and 35,000 minus 7,000, or 28,000, on January 1, 1985. The difference represents a 20 percent decline in population size.

Projecting Natural Attrition, 1985–2004

Retirement

Figure 10.1 displays the historical trends in retirement along with the optimistic, moderate, and pessimistic projections. Retirements steadily declined in number since the beginning of the census period, mainly because of the decline in the overall population. Hence, it may seem surprising that the number of retirees rises so abruptly at the beginning of the projection period in all three series. Why are retirements suddenly so much higher during the projection period?

Table 10.2. Number of entrances and exits in U.S.
diocesan priest population, 1966–84

Entrance	
Ordination[a]	13,631
Net immigration[b]	1,398
Total	15,029
Exit	
Net leave[c]	694
Resignation[d]	6,938
Natural loss[e]	14,374
Total	22,006
Net loss	6,977[f]

[a]Source: table 7.1.

[b]Incardinations minus excardinations; source: table 8.1.

[c]Sick leaves plus other leaves, minus returns from resignation and all other leaves; source: table 8.9.

[d]Source: table 9.1.

[e]Retirements plus preretirement deaths; source: table 10.1.

[f]Table 2.1 shows a net loss of 6,993 and table A.1 a net loss of 6,847 active priests between 1966 and 1985; the differences in the three estimates are due to discrepancies caused by our weighting and projection techniques.

Once again, the three forecast curves can be fully understood only in light of the complex assumptions underlying the projections. A full discussion of the assumptions is relegated to appendix B, but the main considerations behind the sudden surge of retirees can be summarized briefly here. The rise at the start of the projection period is the result of two factors: our research design and the rapid aging of the clergy.

The first is an artifact of our methodology. To simplify the projection procedures, we end the detailed one-year age cohorts at age 79; all priests still active at age 80 and beyond in 1985 are automatically placed in the retirement category, creating an arbitrary one-time increase in numbers. Hence from 1985 to 2004, the active population includes no priests older than 80. Second, because the priest population is aging rapidly, higher numbers will retire in the future.

The figure contains another seeming anomaly: retirements projected with optimistic assumptions are temporarily higher than those projected with moderate ones. New retirement programs which created one-time, artificially high retirement rates for very old priests and the constraints of our com-

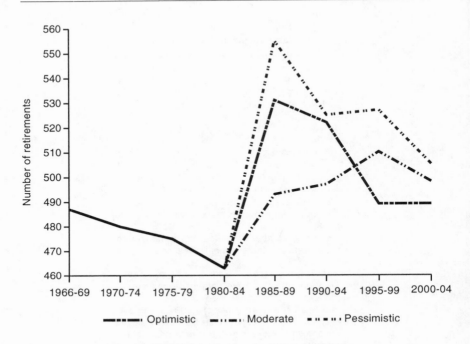

Figure 10.1. Average annual number of retirements of U.S. diocesan priests, 1966–2004

Year	Weighted census count	Projection series		
		Optimistic	Moderate	Pessimistic
1966–69	487			
1970–74	480			
1975–79	475			
1980–84	463			
1985–89		531	493	555
1990–94		522	497	525
1995–99		489	510	527
2000–04		489	498	505

parative methods are the main reasons for this aberration. How these factors interact is spelled out in appendix B.

Preretirement Mortality
Figure 10.2 depicts the historical trends in preretirement mortality along with future projections of the numbers. Preretirement deaths steadily declined in number from the beginning to the end of the census period for

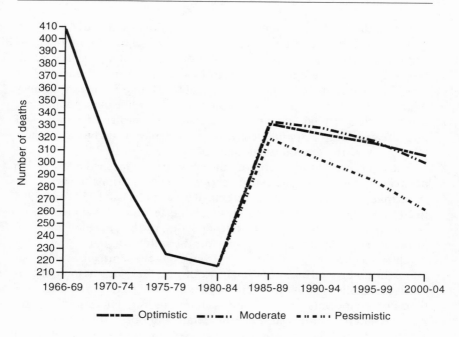

Figure 10.2. Average annual number of preretirement deaths of U.S. diocesan priests, 1966–2004

Year	Weighted census counts	Projection series		
		Optimistic	Moderate	Pessimistic
1966–69	408			
1970–74	299			
1975–79	226			
1980–84	216			
1985–89		332	334	320
1990–94		324	329	303
1995–99		317	319	287
2000–04		307	301	263

two reasons. First, formal retirement programs were established for the first time after the Second Vatican Council; second, the active priest population experienced steady decline in absolute numbers. Why does the number of deaths increase so dramatically at the beginning of the projection period? The answer likewise stems from the rapid aging of the clergy and is linked to the demographic techniques used, revealing some constraints we faced during the study.

Before this study was completed in 1989, national statistics on mortality rates for Catholic priests were nonexistent, so we had to use the most appropriate data available for our projection, namely, age-specific survival probabilities for white males provided by the U.S. Census Bureau.[1] It is apparent, from data to be presented in chapter 11, that the life expectancy of priests was more favorable than that of the U.S. white male population, at least between 1966 and 1984. As a result, our projected numbers of preretirement deaths are inflated, because they have been based on mortality rates of the general white male population.[2]

The figure shows that deaths among active priests reached a low of 216 per year by the end of the census period. The projections, however, assume that preretirement deaths will range between 263 and 332 from 1985 to 2004. Note that the number of deaths projected in the pessimistic series is lower than the optimistic and moderate series; further, the moderate projection curve is temporarily higher than the optimistic one.

These seeming irregularities result from using the same survival probabilities in all three series. Accordingly, we project fewer deaths under pessimistic assumptions because the projected number of those at risk is smaller than under moderate or optimistic assumptions. Similar reasons explain why the numbers projected under moderate and optimistic assumptions are so close and criss-cross at one point. (See appendix B for the detailed explanation.)

Second, not all the increase shown in the figure is the result of using survival probabilities of U.S. white males, because the priest population has been aging rapidly. Priests from the large ordination classes of the 1960s will have reached their 50s and 60s in the late 1980s and early 1990s. The large size of these cohorts accounts for our relatively high numbers of preretirement deaths in the projections for those years and beyond.

We are left with the question, What effects do the discrepancies between

1. Because the six-year research project had to develop in phases and the diocese was the basic unit of analysis, it was impossible to complete the data collection and cleaning procedures for the whole sample, derive survival probabilities based on the mortality experience of the national priest population, and only then begin the projections. The only way to use our resources rationally and meet intermediate deadlines was to perform the analysis for the diocese when each individual data set was completed.

Hence we had no alternative but to use the most appropriate survival probabilities available. Furthermore, we had to decide upon a uniform mortality assumption in order to maintain comparability across levels of analysis. We could not use one set of survival probabilities for dioceses and another for the regional and national projections without distorting comparability throughout the analysis.

2. The inflation is minimal; see the discussion in chapter 11. Rates for whites are chosen because the U.S. diocesan priesthood is 99 percent white (NORC 1972).

the mortality of priests and U.S. white males have on the overall projections? The consequences are small for the first part of the projection period and diminish as the demographic transition progresses, until they are practically imperceptible in 2004. The validity test for our projection models (in chapter 2) showed that in the subsample of 12 dioceses the actual size of the priest population in 1989 was only 2.2 percent higher than the moderate series forecasted. Because the greatest consequences will have taken effect in the earliest part of the projection period, we assume the effects will be around the 2 percent figure for 1990 and smaller thereafter.

Plausibility of Retirement Assumptions

Aside from the technical details of the projection assumptions, the plausibility of the forecasted number of retirements depends on several demographic and organizational considerations. First, the number of priests who retire is a direct result of the numbers in an age group and the aging process, so retirement rates are more or less fixed by actuarial processes — assuming priest retirement programs are here to stay.

Second, the upgrading and decentralization of diocesan personnel operations were some of the most important organizational reforms commonly associated with the Second Vatican Council (Szafran 1977). We discovered in a related area of research that "establishing or planning an acceptable diocesan retirement plan for priests" was, by far, the top priority in a list of 13 personnel issues facing church administrators in the mid-1970s (Schoenherr and Simpson 1978).

Prior to the council, retirement programs tied to age were nonexistent; only those whose illness or other impairment made it difficult or impossible to perform their priestly duties were allowed to retire. Today, however, with the establishment of democratically elected personnel boards in many dioceses and the strong emphasis on retirement programs throughout the U.S. Catholic church, it would be extremely difficult, if not impossible, to reverse firmly established retirement policies.

Retirement rates, in fact, have slowly increased over the 19 years under investigation, as the aging process dictates. Thus it is reasonable to use the current levels of 1980–84 for our moderate projection model. Moreover, the moderate assumptions balance forces not directly related to aging that might raise or lower retirement rates. Dwindling numbers of priests and the resulting high parishioner-to-priest ratios could motivate bishops, personnel directors, and clergy themselves to persuade one another to remain active longer.

On the other hand, the clergy might resist efforts to downplay retirement. They may argue, instead, that the strain caused by additional work resulting from fewer priests, coupled with the stress of organizational and pastoral changes (for example, some priests complain they are unaccustomed to laity participation in the decision-making processes of the parish), justifies the right to retire at the earliest allowable age. We believe that pressures raising the average age at retirement will most likely be countered by those that are lowering it. So, the most current trends, those of 1980–84, are the best basis for forecasting future retirement trends. We base our moderate assumptions on those trends.

Age

Table 10.3 reveals the average age at which priests retired and died in the United States during the 19 years covered by our population register. Once adjustments are made for differences preceding and following establishment of formal retirement programs, the data show almost no fluctuation in age at retirement and preretirement death. In the late 1960s, when relatively few dioceses had formalized their retirement policies, active priests retired at age 71, and those who died before retirement had reached age 63, on the average. For the remaining 15 years in the study, once formal retirement programs were widespread, age at retirement averaged around 69, and age at preretirement death averaged around 62.

Note: The mean age at retirement during 1980–84 was slightly higher than during the preceding decade, which might indicate that toward the end of the census period retirement was beginning to be postponed as the clergy shortage became more apparent. But the difference is slight and the time period too short to be conclusive. The evidence points to remarkable stability in the age governing natural attrition, once formal retirement programs were prevalent.

Although the data show almost no change in the average age at which clergy exit from the active population, the last column in the table reveals a trend toward greater longevity for priests. These data reflect the average age at death for all priests who died during the 19 years, whether active or retired. The life expectancy of priests increased from 72.6 years during the late 1960s to 73.9 during the late 1970s, and then went down very slightly to 73.8 during the early 1980s. Whether the slight decrease in recent years is the beginning of a downward trend or evidence that life expectancy is reaching a plateau is impossible to determine without further data.

Natural Attrition Rates

Describing the census data in terms of absolute numbers provides only part of the portrait of natural attrition and also limits the scope to the national level. The following rates standardize the numbers by size and

Table 10.3. Mean ages at retirement and at death of
U.S. diocesan priests, 1966–84

| | | At death | |
| | | --- | --- |
Year	At retirement	Preretirement priests	All priests
1966–69	70.9	62.9	72.6
1970–74	68.7	61.8	73.3
1975–79	68.7	61.9	73.9
1980–84	69.0	61.9	73.8

Source: weighted census counts.

permit us to continue the descriptive analysis by comparing differences over time, across geographic regions, and at the local diocesan level.

Crude Rates by Region

Table 10.4 contains retirement and preretirement mortality rates for active priests from 1966 to 1984 for the entire nation and by geographic region. The data in the top panel raise the question whether dioceses in the New England and East South regions were quicker to start retirement programs for aging priests than other dioceses. According to the statistics, the average retirement rates for dioceses in these two census regions were highest during 1966–69. Judging from this, new policies formalizing retirement in dioceses near the East Coast may have been put in place soon after the Second Vatican Council.

Apparently, dioceses in areas of the country other than the New England and East South regions were slower to develop formal retirement programs, although there were large pools of eligible older priests. Thus the typical diocese in other regions of the country — except those in the Great Lakes areas — experienced their lowest retirement rates of the entire period during 1966–69, which were followed by higher ones during the remaining period under observation. Dioceses in the East Northcentral region followed more closely the East Coast pattern than the trend prevalent in the other regions, beginning the period with relatively high retirement rates which declined during the 1970s but then peaked during the early 1980s. Note, the general trend from low to high retirement rates, discovered in the majority of geographic regions, sets the national pattern reflected in the first row of the table. Thus, although the number of retirements went down steadily between 1966 and 1984, the rates — the number of retirees per 100 active priests — actually increased just as consistently.

Retirement rates are also influenced by the age distribution of priests.

Table 10.4. Retirement and preretirement mortality rates of U.S. diocesan priests and percentage of gross change, 1966–84, by year, nation, and region (number of exits per 100 active priests)

Division and region	Average annual rate				% gross change
	1969 –69	1970 –74	1975 –79	1980 –84	1966 –84[a]
Retirement					
United States	1.40	1.49	1.56	1.59	25.77
Northeast					
New England	1.72	1.66	1.59	1.54	27.67
Middle Atlantic	1.06	1.31	1.59	1.44	23.37
Northcentral					
East Northcentral	1.86	1.75	1.76	1.93	29.47
West Northcentral	1.25	1.26	1.52	1.42	22.44
West					
Mountain	1.20	1.23	1.69	2.16	29.68
Pacific	1.21	1.66	1.50	2.00	28.21
South					
East South[b]	1.62	1.33	1.23	1.17	24.67
West Southcentral	1.03	1.46	1.21	1.28	22.89
Preretirement mortality					
United States	1.19	0.94	0.77	0.77	15.58
Northeast					
New England	1.13	0.91	0.74	0.79	15.08
Middle Atlantic	1.50	1.17	0.85	0.87	18.81
Northcentral					
East Northcentral	1.15	0.83	0.72	0.78	14.08
West Northcentral	1.10	0.92	0.67	0.74	14.13
West					
Mountain	0.94	0.53	0.83	0.54	13.04
Pacific	1.04	0.93	0.78	0.71	15.20
South					
East South[b]	0.81	0.78	0.60	0.60	12.90
West Southcentral	0.92	0.76	0.90	0.70	14.89

Source: weighted census counts.

[a]Using the 1966 active population for the denominator and the cumulative number of retirements or preretirement deaths for the numerator.

[b]Combines the South Atlantic region and one diocese from the East Southcentral division.

So it is possible that dioceses with relatively high retirement rates during 1966–69 also had high numbers of older priests. But when we reexamined the data that were used to produce figures 3.8–3.11 (specifically, the 65-and-over age category, which is not shown in the figures), we discovered that the situation wasn't quite that simple.

From the mid-1960s to the mid-1970s the proportion of priests 65 and over, the age at highest risk of retirement, ranged from about 11 percent to 13 percent in Northeast and Northcentral dioceses and from about 8 percent to 10 percent in West and South dioceses. The variation in average retirement rates across regions, however, did not follow a pattern that corresponds to these age differentials. For example, during the late 1960s the percentage of priests 65 and over in Middle Atlantic dioceses was one of the highest of any region in the country, and yet these same dioceses recorded one of the lowest average retirement rates for the period. The opposite is true of dioceses in West Southcentral states.

Natural Attrition: A Delicate Balance

The fact is, fluctuation in retirement rates is partly dependent on age structure and partly on management policy. Some dioceses may have decided to delay formal retirement procedures; others may have opted to set the retirement age of priests higher than usual. Either policy would have reduced retirement rates temporarily.

Delaying retirement, however, did not reduce the overall exit rate for aging priests, if one compares natural attrition over the two-decade period. Comparing rates in the last column of each panel of table 10.4 shows that, in five out of eight regions, when the cumulative percentage of loss through retirements was higher than the national mean, the cumulative loss through deaths among active priests was lower than the national mean. And vice versa: when preretirement mortality was higher, attrition through retirement was lower. The exceptions to the pattern occurred in the two South and the West Northcentral regions.

As table 10.5 reveals, in the average West Northcentral diocese, the cumulative loss from natural attrition between 1966 and 1984 was the lowest in the country. Yet the proportion of active West Northcentral priests age 65 or older was about 12 percent during the first 15 years of the period, among the highest percentages in the nation at the time. And the proportion of oldest priests reached almost 18 percent by 1985, about 2 percentage points higher than any other region for that year. It appears from the low retirement and death rates that, not only do priests in West Northcentral dioceses enjoy more favorable mortality rates, but also they are permitted to continue in the active ministry longer than priests elsewhere. A

Table 10.5. Attrition rates from retirement and preretirement mortality of U.S. diocesan priests and percentage of gross change, 1966–84, by year, nation, and region (number of exits per 100 active priests)

	Average annual rate				% gross change
	1966 –69	1970 –74	1975 –79	1980 –84	1966 –84[a]
United States	2.59	2.43	2.33	2.36	41.35
Regions					
New England	2.85	2.57	2.33	2.33	42.75
Middle Atlantic	2.56	2.48	2.44	2.31	42.18
East Northcentral	3.01	2.58	2.48	2.71	43.55
West Northcentral	2.35	2.18	2.19	2.16	36.57
Mountain	2.14	1.76	2.52	2.70	42.72
Pacific	2.25	2.59	2.28	2.71	43.41
East South[b]	2.43	2.11	1.83	1.77	37.57
West Southcentral	1.95	2.22	2.11	1.98	37.78

Source: weighted census counts.
[a]Using the 1966 active population for the denominator and the cumulative number of retirements and preretirement deaths for the numerator.
[b]Combines the South Atlantic region and one diocese from the East Southcentral division.

policy of delayed retirement seems to be paying off in terms of longer active careers.

The other two exceptions to the general pattern of one high biologically related exit rate balancing the other low one help to illustrate the underlying dynamic at work. In the two South regions, dioceses generally enjoyed both retirement and preretirement death rates below the national average for the entire 19-year period. At the same time, age distributions in those dioceses were among the youngest in the country. In dioceses throughout the rest of the country, excepting the West Northcentral region, combined exits through retirement and preretirement mortality resulted in natural attrition rates higher than the national mean; at the same time, age distributions in those dioceses were all among the oldest in the country. So aging raises natural attrition rates.

We conclude that attrition stemming from retirements and deaths among active priests is difficult to manipulate through organizational policy. Increasing the age of retirement results in a short-term gain. But soon after the age at retirement is increased, approximately the same overall rate of total attrition occurs, because death rates among active priests increase accordingly.

When the population is enjoying exceptionally favorable mortality rates, as in the average diocese in the West Northcentral region, raising the age of retirement to expand years of service will have longer-lasting effects. The combination of an older population with lower than average mortality rates appears to be rare, though.

Local Rates

The numbers in table 10.6 reflect natural attrition per 100 active priests experienced by dioceses between 1966 and 1984. We will cite the extremes in the cumulative loss from retirement and preretirement mortality within each geographic region (see the last column).

Northeast

The highest loss in *New England* was registered by Portland, where the active priest population was diminished by over 52 percent from 1966 to 1984 through retirement and preretirement mortality. At the other extreme, Hartford experienced a loss of about 31 percent during the same period.

In the *Middle Atlantic* states, Allentown suffered a cumulative loss from retirement and death among active priests of almost 55 percent for the high end of the range during the roughly two decades, and Camden recorded a decline of 24 percent at the low end. As we discovered in chapter 4, Allentown had one of the oldest and Camden one of the youngest age distributions in the country at the beginning of the census period, so the extreme high and low in natural attrition noted here is not surprising.

Northcentral

According to statistics for *East Northcentral* dioceses, the cumulative result of retirement and preretirement mortality in Grand Rapids amounted to just over a 47 percent loss in the number of active priests during the period, the highest decline from natural attrition in the region. The range in this area was relatively small; the lowest was a 37 percent decline in Belleville.

The natural attrition in *West Northcentral* dioceses ranged from 60 percent in Rapid City to just under 29 percent in Kansas City–St. Joseph. Rapid City is an anomaly in this region, because the diocese experienced the second highest natural attrition in the entire sample, whereas all other West Northcentral dioceses in the sample registered below the national average, making the average regional loss the lowest in the country.

West

The high figure for the range in the *Mountain* states — and the nation's high — is represented by a decline in Las Cruces of two-thirds (67 percent)

Table 10.6. Attrition rates from retirement and preretirement mortality of U.S. diocesan priests and percentage of gross change, 1966–84, by year and diocese (number of exits per 100 priests; alphabetical order within region by state then diocese)

Region and diocese	Average annual rate				% gross change
	1966 –69	1970 –74	1975 –79	1980 –84	1966 –84[a]
Northeast					
New England					
Hartford CT	1.96	1.84	2.01	1.33	30.88
Norwich CT	2.30	2.13	2.31	2.35	39.71
Portland ME	4.03	4.12	2.37	2.70	52.30
Boston MA	2.45	2.17	2.30	2.01	36.65
Fall River MA	3.15	2.54	2.93	2.34	45.59
Worcester MA	2.93	2.66	2.01	2.89	47.75
Providence RI[b]	—	—	—	—	—
Burlington VT	2.23	2.17	2.05	2.71	38.89
Middle Atlantic					
Camden NJ	1.27	0.95	0.92	1.87	24.00
Newark NJ	2.69	1.74	2.49	1.75	36.33
Albany NY	3.15	4.20	2.42	2.19	46.93
Brooklyn NY	2.79	2.00	2.79	2.52	40.17
Buffalo NY	2.55	2.39	2.08	2.29	40.44
New York NY	2.46	3.16	2.37	2.89	42.99
Ogdensburg NY	2.35	2.64	1.97	1.85	39.47
Rochester NY	3.08	2.53	3.10	3.44	47.12
Rockville Centre NY	2.07	2.10	1.95	1.98	36.80
Allentown PA	2.63	1.63	5.33	2.29	54.64
Altoona–Johnstown PA	2.42	2.01	1.30	2.33	39.49
Philadelphia PA	2.59	3.36	2.34	2.41	45.34
Pittsburgh PA	2.28	2.22	1.62	1.83	36.29
Scranton PA	2.76	3.09	2.50	2.37	45.02
Northcentral					
East Northcentral					
Belleville IL	2.14	2.05	1.95	2.82	37.43
Chicago IL	3.65	2.51	2.48	3.28	46.62
Rockford IL	3.15	0.97	2.51	2.26	37.64
Indianapolis IN	3.52	2.88	2.47	3.35	46.88
Detroit MI	3.48[c]	3.16	2.43	2.79	43.63
Gaylord MI	2.96[d]	2.80	2.52	2.24	43.93
Grand Rapids MI	3.20[c]	3.11	3.14	3.17	47.13
Marquette MI	3.29	2.10	2.07	3.24	42.32
Saginaw MI	2.40[c]	2.65	2.61	1.58	39.16
Cincinnati OH	2.17	3.34	2.41	2.38	44.49
Cleveland OH	3.37	2.82	2.34	1.90	44.86
Columbus OH	2.56	2.13	3.01	2.33	42.55
Youngstown OH	3.26	3.95	1.70	1.61	41.96

(continued on following page)

Table 10.6. Attrition rates from retirement and preretirement mortality of U.S. diocesan priests and percentage of gross change, 1966–84, by year and diocese (continued)

Region and diocese	Average annual rate				% gross change
	1966 –69	1970 –74	1975 –79	1980 –84	1966 –84[a]
Northcentral (continued)					
East Northcentral (continued)					
La Crosse WI	2.02	2.07	3.21	3.19	39.43
Milwaukee WI	1.97	2.06	2.02	3.00	37.80
West Northcentral					
Des Moines IA	2.71	2.00	2.25	2.14	37.40
Dubuque IA	2.57	1.62	2.55	2.83	38.34
Sioux City IA	2.92	1.77	1.94	1.80	36.32
Dodge City KS	1.55	2.31	1.80	1.09	29.46
Salina KS	2.33	1.97	2.72	2.62	40.70
Wichita KS	2.81	1.72	1.45	1.82	30.53
New Ulm MN	1.19	2.05	2.82	2.88	36.22
St. Cloud MN	2.43	1.42	1.23	2.55	31.34
St. Paul–Minneapolis MN	2.36	2.57	2.57	1.70	37.12
Kansas City–St. Jos. MO	2.17	1.87	1.74	1.34	28.90
St. Louis MO	1.39	2.63	1.95	1.63	34.92
Springfield–C. Girard. MO	1.05	2.27	4.17	1.54	40.56
Lincoln NE[b]	—	—	—	—	—
Fargo ND	1.49	2.26	2.33	3.41	37.13
Rapid City SD	8.15	6.78	3.52	2.29	59.86
West					
Mountain					
Pueblo CO	3.09	1.59	2.58	2.20	43.76
Boise ID	3.18	2.55	1.72	2.59	49.35
Gallup NM	0.86[c]	0.00	1.19	2.03	28.57
Las Cruces NM	1.82[d]	2.48	3.29	5.47	67.14
Santa Fe NM	2.13[c]	1.25	2.26	2.01	31.83
Cheyenne WY	0.83	2.71	4.39	4.34	52.54
Pacific					
Fresno CA[b]	—	—	—	—	—
Los Angeles CA	1.35[c]	2.79	1.95	2.26	37.95
Monterey CA	2.43[e]	3.87	1.48	3.56	54.67
Oakland CA	2.93	2.94	2.00	2.12	42.42
Orange CA	1.35[d]	2.79	3.17	1.79	41.60
San Bernardino CA	2.96[d]	1.63	3.17	4.26	50.11
San Diego CA	2.96[c]	1.63	2.60	2.83	43.23
San Francisco CA	2.06[c]	2.47	2.75	2.28	39.03
San Jose CA	2.06[d]	2.47	2.75	2.14	38.14
Stockton CA	2.56	3.33	1.27	4.69	54.74
Baker OR	0.54	2.14	3.08	2.02	35.95

(continued on following page)

Table 10.6. Attrition rates from retirement and preretirement mortality of U.S. diocesan priests and percentage of gross change, 1966–84, by year and diocese (continued)

Region and diocese	Average annual rate				% gross change
	1966 –69	1970 –74	1975 –79	1980 –84	1966 –84[a]
South					
East South[f]					
Wilmington DE	3.32	2.47	1.14	1.64	37.88
Orlando FL	0.00[g]	1.79	1.59	1.57	32.28
St. Petersburg FL	4.19[g]	1.65	1.77	2.04	41.11
Atlanta GA	1.38	1.29	0.55	0.46	22.45
Covington KY	1.57	2.17	2.79	2.55	37.41
Baltimore MD	3.67	2.30	1.78	1.63	40.06
West Southcentral					
Little Rock AK	1.85	3.02	1.67	2.19	32.56
Alexandria–Shreveport LA	1.96	1.49	2.59	2.59	34.85
Baton Rouge LA	1.79	1.05	2.44	2.85	43.05
Lafayette LA	1.51[c]	3.21	2.25	1.83	41.45
Lake Charles LA	1.51[d]	3.22	2.25	0.52	35.38
Austin TX	2.25	2.52	1.80	0.89	34.83
Beaumont TX	1.57	2.14	1.50	2.02	38.20
Corpus Christi TX	2.20[c]	2.80	1.47	2.66	42.41
Dallas TX	4.68[h]	1.76	2.54	2.01	46.39
El Paso TX	1.79[c]	2.56	3.36	3.06	56.26
Fort Worth TX	1.98[h]	2.87	1.16	2.64	44.00
Galveston–Houston TX	1.37[c]	1.85	2.19	1.91	34.44
San Antonio TX	1.55[c]	1.88	1.91	1.01	29.59
Victoria TX	1.55	1.90	1.92	1.33	30.92

Source: census counts.

[a]Using the 1966 active population for the denominator and the cumulative number of retirements and preretirement deaths for the numerator.

[b]Refused to participate.

[c]Divided during the census period. The division does not affect the rate, because it is standardized.

[d]Established during the census period by being divided from others in the sample. The annual rates prior to the year of the split are those of the parent diocese(s), weighted when necessary. See appendix D for year of establishment and parent diocese(s).

[e]Divided in 1967. The rate for 1966 is based on size of the active population as identifiable in 1966 (see appendix D).

[f]Combines the South Atlantic region and one diocese from the East Southcentral region.

[g]Established in 1968. The figure given for 1966–69 is based on size of the active population as identifiable in years prior to and in the year of the split (see appendix D).

[h]Divided in 1969. The average given for 1966–69 is based on size of the active population as identifiable in years prior to and in the year of the split (see appendix D).

of the 1966 active priest roster through natural attrition. The low in the Mountain region was established by a level of under 29 percent in Gallup.

Along the *Pacific Coast,* the 1966 active priest population in both Stockton and Monterey was diminished through retirements and preretirement deaths by just under 55 percent in 19 years, the highest loss from natural attrition in the region. The lowest decrease was registered in Baker: just under 36 percent.

South

The data in the *East South* reveal exceptionally favorable retirement and preretirement mortality rates for active priests. Although the 41 percent cumulative decrease from natural attrition in St. Petersburg was the high among East South dioceses, it was below the national average. The low in the region was found in Atlanta, where these losses amounted to a little over 22 percent during the entire census period. This is the lowest natural attrition in the sample. Recalling data from prior chapters, Atlanta seems to be triply blessed, with the lowest projected overall decline, the highest cumulative gain from ordinations, and the lowest loss through natural attrition of any diocese in the study.

In the *West Southcentral* states, the highest number of retirements and deaths before retirement, in proportion to the size of the 1966 priest roster, was registered in El Paso: 56 percent. The low figure in this region was established by San Antonio, with a loss of just under 30 percent.

Our interest lies not only in *describing* variation in the components of demographic change but also in *explaining* causes of the differences. In the next section we attempt to account for the variance in natural attrition rates.

Causal Models of Natural Attrition Rates

Table 10.6 described diocesan trends in natural attrition between 1966 and 1984. We now focus on its components, retirement and preretirement, and present regression models to explain conditions that account for variance in the 1980 rates.

As usual, in an exploratory analysis we examine the entire set of environmental variables from the Glenmary data as well as the organizational variables available from our data and other sources.[3] Additionally, because retirement and preretirement mortality are affected by age, we control for it by adding "percentage of priests 55 and older" to the models.

In developing the empirical models, we follow the same causal assump-

---

3. Appendix C lists and defines the full set of variables.

Table 10.7. Percentage of priests 55 and older, retirement rates, and preretirement mortality rates in U.S. Catholic dioceses, 1980, by region (means)

Region	% 55 and older	Retirement[a]	Preretirement death[a]
New England	37.9	1.43	0.72
Middle Atlantic	35.7	1.18	0.81
East Northcentral	36.7	1.66	0.73
West Northcentral	40.9	0.97	0.74
Mountain	39.9	1.70	0.36
Pacific	38.2	1.52	0.46
East South[b]	28.1	1.02	0.43
West Southcentral	35.0	0.78	0.86
Grand mean	36.8	1.24	0.69
Standard deviation	6.5	0.77	0.47

Source: weighted census counts.
[a]Number per 100 priests.
[b]Combines the South Atlantic region and one diocese from the East Southcentral region.

tions that guided the analysis in previous chapters: Geographic region is an exogenous variable; environmental variables are the most antecedent in the causal sequence; and organizational variables intervene between environmental antecedents and the two dependent variables, diocesan retirement rate and preretirement mortality rate.

Only one of the independent variables, percentage of priests 55 and over, was not included in previous causal models, so its descriptive statistics and those for the dependent variables are presented in table 10.7. This table gives summary figures by region as an overview of variation across dioceses.[4] In our sample of dioceses, the highest percentages of older priests were found in Mountain and West Northcentral states, where the proportions at age 55 and over averaged around 40 percent. Age distributions in East South dioceses were the youngest, with the proportional size of the oldest age group averaging only about 28 percent.

In 1980, the average diocesan retirement rate was 1.24 retirees per 100 active priests. Retirements were low in Middle Atlantic, West Northcentral, East South, and West Southcentral dioceses, where rates ranged from 0.78 to 1.18. They were high in the remaining regions, ranging from 1.43 retirements per 100 active priests in New England to 1.70 in Mountain dioceses.

---

4. Regional averages for percentage of priests 55 and over are based on the diocese as the unit of analysis, whereas those in chapter 3 are based on the priest as the unit of analysis; hence, the estimates here are slightly different from those given there.

Table 10.8. Effects of environmental and organizational conditions on retirement rates in U.S. Catholic dioceses, 1980 (unstandardized regression coefficients)

Independent variable	b	Adjusted t-ratio[a]
Northcentral	.1053	0.706
West	.2389	1.343
South	-.4318	-2.669**
Recruit. ineffectiveness	.000022	2.398*
n of dioceses	85	
Constant	1.0817	7.969***
F-ratio	3.037*	
R^2	.132	
Adjusted R^2	.088	

Note: The omitted category for division is the Northeast.
[a]Adjustment is based on a finite population correction factor of 0.705 or the square root of 1 - (n/N) applied to the standard error of b; see Mendenhall et al. 1971.
*p ≤ .05.
**p ≤ .01.
***p ≤ .001.

The preretirement death rate averaged 0.69 in 1980. Deaths per 100 active priests were highest in the Northeast and Northcentral divisions and the West Southcentral region, where they ranged from 0.72 to 0.86. The rate was lower in the rest of the country, ranging from 0.36 deaths per 100 active priests in Mountain-region dioceses to 0.46 in Pacific Coast dioceses.

Retirement Rate

Table 10.8 presents the most effective regression model explaining 1980 retirement rates given the available variables. As the adjusted R^2 shows, the model explains just under 9 percent of diocesan variation in the rate. Of the variables tested, only two have net effects: geographic division and priest recruitment ineffectiveness. Even the proportion of older priests in the diocese has no impact on the retirement rate once the two independent variables are accounted for. A brief discussion of how each independent variable affects the diocesan retirement rate follows.

Geographic Division[5]

The analysis suggests that dioceses located in the South will have lower retirement rates than dioceses in the other three geographic areas. So if

5. Although region was employed in previous models, we use geographic division here because it better explains the variance. The Northeast division is omitted as the comparison category.

two dioceses are similar with respect to priest recruitment ineffectiveness but one is located in a South state and the other in a Northeast state, the South diocese will experience almost 4 fewer retirements per 100 active priests every nine years.[6] Under the same conditions, the estimated difference for dioceses in the other two divisions is even greater. Compared with those in the Northcentral division, South dioceses will experience almost 4 fewer retirements per 100 active priests every seven years, and compared with those in the West, 4 fewer every six years.[7]

Recruitment Ineffectiveness

When the effect of geographic location is held constant, dioceses requiring larger numbers of young Catholic males to produce an ordination have higher retirement rates than those requiring smaller candidate pools. This relationship raises the question whether organizational climate and environmental conditions in certain dioceses produce both poor recruitment and high retirement rates. Are such dioceses characterized by some unknown traits hostile to priesthood candidates and older priests approaching retirement, such that the former do not want to join and the latter are eager to separate from the active ministry? This question deserves further research, particularly because retirement rates are not influenced by age distribution; as reported, the percentage of priests 55 and older has no effect on retirement rates.

Whatever the causes, the data show that if Diocese A requires 10,000 more 25–34-year-old Catholic males to produce an ordination than Diocese B, Diocese A will experience 1 additional retirement per 100 active priests every five years.[8]

The cumulative effect of geographic location and poor recruitment can be illustrated by comparing a Northeast diocese with poor recruitment results and a Northcentral diocese with average recruitment results. Assuming the Northeast diocese required 10,000 additional young Catholic males to produce each ordination, every three years it would experience nearly 2 extra retirements per 100 active priests compared with the Northcentral diocese.[9] This difference is substantial, because in 1980–84 the yearly rate for U.S. dioceses was 1.59 retirements per 100 active priests.

6. Precisely: $-0.4318 \times 9 = -3.89$.
7. Precisely, Northcentral: $(-0.4318 - 0.1053) \times 7 = -3.76$; West: $(-0.4318 - 0.2389) \times 6 = -4.03$.
8. Precisely: $0.000022 \times 10,000 \times 5 = 1.1$.
9. Precisely: $[0.4318 + (0.000022 \times 10,000] \times 3 = 1.956$.

Table 10.9. Effects of environmental and organizational conditions on preretirement mortality rates in U.S. Catholic dioceses, 1980 (unstandardized regression coefficients)

Independent variable	b	Adjusted t-ratio[a]
Northcentral	-.074	-0.806
West	-.437	-4.031***
South	.026	0.257
% priests ≥ 55	.019	3.363**
Resignation rate	.214	3.039**
n of dioceses	85	
Constant	-0.064	-0.280
F-ratio	3.085*	
R^2	.163	
Adjusted R^2	.110	

Note: The omitted category for division is the Northeast.
[a]Adjustment is based on a finite population correction factor of 0.705 or the square root of 1 - (n/N) applied to the standard error of b; see Mendenhall et al. 1971.
*$p \le .05$.
**$p \le .01$.
***$p \le .001$.

Preretirement Mortality Rate

Table 10.9 summarizes the most powerful model resulting from our exploratory analysis of environmental and organizational conditions that might explain diocesan variation in preretirement mortality. Overall, this model has slightly more explanatory power than the previous one: 11 percent versus 9 percent. Of those tested, only three variables help predict differences in the preretirement death rate: geographic division, percentage of active priests 55 and older, and diocesan resignation rate.

Geographic Division[10]

Table 10.9 shows that only dioceses located in West states experienced preretirement mortality rates that differ significantly from those in other divisions of the country. Thus if two dioceses are alike in other conditions tested, but one is located in the West and the other in the Northeast, every nine years the West dioceses will experience about 4 fewer preretirement deaths per 100 active priests than the Northeast diocese.[11]

10. The Northeast is the omitted category.
11. Precisely: $-0.437 \times 9 = -3.93$.

All other conditions being equal, divisional differences in preretirement mortality are similar when comparing West dioceses with those in Northcentral and South states. Compared with those in Northcentral states, West dioceses will experience about 4 fewer preretirement deaths per 100 active priests every 11 years, and compared with those in South states, about 4 fewer every 9 years.[12]

Percentage of Older Priests
Not surprisingly, we also discover that dioceses with older age distributions experience higher preretirement death rates. It is important to report this finding if only to note that the effect of age structure on death rates has been taken into account. When the age distribution of the active diocesan clergy shows an additional 10 percent in the 55 and older category, a diocese will experience 1 additional preretirement death per 100 active priests every five years.[13]

Diocesan Resignation Rate
The influence of the final variable in the model is completely unexpected: The higher the diocesan resignation rate, the higher the preretirement mortality rate. This finding raises an important concern. Do the same conditions that promote high resignation rates also increase the risk of preretirement mortality? The model estimates that if a diocese's resignation rate increases by 1 percentage point, it will experience 1 additional preretirement death per 100 active priests every five years.[14] Such an increase in preretirement mortality is plausible given that the 1980–84 average resignation rate for U.S. dioceses ranged from 0.0 to 3.3 (table 9.3).

The cumulative effect of location, age structure, and resignation rate on preretirement mortality may be illustrated by the following example: If a Northeast diocese has 10 percent more of its active clergy in the 55 and over category and an annual resignation rate 1 percentage point higher than that of a West diocese, then it also will expect 0.84 more preretirement deaths per 100 active priests each year, or almost six more every seven years.[15] This is a big difference, because the 1980–84 annual preretirement mortality rate for U.S. dioceses was 0.77 deaths per 100 active priests.

---

12. Precisely, Northcentral: $[-0.437 - (-0.074)] \times 11 = -3.99$; South: $(-0.437 - 0.026) \times 9 = -4.17$.
   13. Precisely: $0.019 \times 10 \times 5 = 0.95$.
   14. Precisely: $0.214 \times 1 \times 5 = 1.07$.
   15. Precisely: $[0.432 + (0.019 \times 10) + 0.214] \times 7 = 5.85$.

Conclusion

The census period began when preretirement deaths dominated natural attrition. In the late 1960s, the improvement of diocesan personnel practices inspired by the Second Vatican Council resulted in the formalization of retirement programs for diocesan priests. Thus, beginning in the mid-1970s, retirements began to account for the majority of natural losses in the priesthood population.

Because of these changing trends and the aging of the clergy, approximately the same number of deaths occurred annually during the entire 19 years. In the final decades of the century, therefore, death rates among retired priests have taken on increased significance for understanding mortality trends in the U.S. diocesan priesthood.

Rates of retirement and preretirement mortality vary across the dioceses of the U.S. Catholic church. Our analysis reveals notable regional differences in both rates. Northcentral dioceses experience lower retirement rates and West dioceses experience lower preretirement mortality in comparison to dioceses in other parts of the country. Additionally, we find that dioceses characterized by high levels of recruitment ineffectiveness also encounter higher rates of retirement, and dioceses with either high resignation rates or older age distributions experience higher rates of preretirement mortality.

In some respects these findings raise more questions than they answer. For example, all other things being equal, why would a diocese that has a difficult time recruiting new priests also lose proportionately more priests through retirement? Or, all other things — including age distribution — being equal, why would a diocese plagued by higher rates of resigning priests also experience higher rates of preretirement mortality? Unfortunately, answers to these questions are beyond the scope of this study and await further theoretical exploration and empirical research.

11 Mortality

Throughout the study we concentrate on priests who are active in the diocesan labor force. Hence, we limited the analysis of death in the previous chapter to preretirement mortality, because it touches only active priests. We now switch the focus to death rates over the entire life span, including the postretirement period. In this chapter we ask two questions: What are the trends in mortality of U.S. diocesan priests? And how does the mortality of priests compare with that of all U.S. white males and with subgroups categorized by education, occupation, income, marital status, and race?[1]

Highlights

1. At the beginning of the census period, deaths occurred more frequently among active priests, but by the early 1980s they occurred more frequently among the retired. Despite this shift and the aging of the population, the number of deaths remained stable from 1966 to 1984.

2. Along with those of all U.S. white males, priests' mortality rates declined during the period. The average life expectancy of priests rose from 72.0 in 1966 to 75.4 in 1984.

3. Mortality risks for priests are lower than those for U.S. white males in general. But they are not as favorable as would be expected on the basis of their education and occupation.

Mortality Trends of U.S. Diocesan Priests, 1966–84

Notable changes in mortality of the priesthood population have occurred since the Second Vatican Council. We examine the changing numbers of

---

1. We use whites because they are the most appropriate comparison group: in 1970 only 1 percent of U.S. diocesan priests were nonwhite (NORC 1972, table 2.6).

262

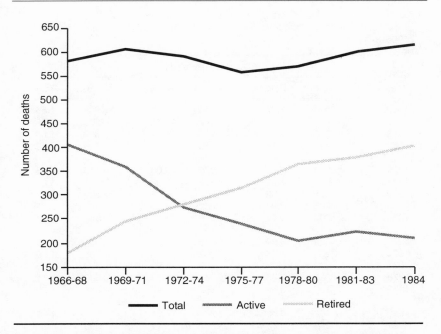

Figure 11.1. Average annual number of deaths of U.S. diocesan priests, 1966–84

Source: table 11.1.
Notes: "Retired" includes retired, sick, and absent priests. "Total" includes active, retired, sick, and absent priests.
The final point is for a single year.

deaths, crude death rates, and life expectancy of U.S. diocesan priests at the national level. This is followed by an analysis of regional variations in the crude death rate and an examination of trends in national age-specific mortality rates.

National Number of Deaths and Crude Death Rate

Figure 11.1 presents the average number of deaths from 1966 to 1984 for three-year intervals.[2] The population is divided into two categories: active priests and the retired, sick, and absent. The graph also plots information for the total population, which combines the two subgroups. Because retirees represent the vast majority in the second category, we will refer to it simply as retired. Corresponding data for single years, including crude death rates, are presented in table 11.1.

2. The period covers 19 years, so the final point in the graph is for a single year.

Table 11.1. Number of deaths and crude death rates of U.S. diocesan priests, 1966–84

Year	Active		Retired[a]		Total[b]	
	Number	Rate[c]	Number	Rate[c]	Number[d]	Rate[c]
1966	444	1.27	154	12.39	598	1.65
1967	411	1.17	167	11.51	578	1.58
1968	362	1.04	220	11.98	582	1.58
1969	413	1.20	256	11.21	669	1.82
1970	334	1.00	236	9.03	570	1.58
1971	334	1.01	239	8.02	573	1.60
1972	265	0.82	261	8.09	526	1.49
1973	295	0.94	282	8.09	577	1.65
1974	269	0.86	300	8.11	569	1.63
1975	259	0.84	278	7.08	537	1.55
1976	236	0.77	353	8.47	589	1.69
1977	222	0.73	317	7.55	539	1.55
1978	225	0.75	368	8.18	593	1.71
1979	187	0.63	352	7.49	539	1.56
1980	202	0.68	379	7.91	581	1.69
1981	214	0.73	392	8.18	606	1.77
1982	242	0.82	365	7.69	607	1.78
1983	213	0.74	387	7.76	600	1.77
1984	211	0.74	406	7.90	617	1.83

Source: weighted census counts.
[a]Includes sick and absent priests.
[b]Includes all priests: active, retired, sick, and absent.
[c]Number of deaths per 100 priests.
[d]Col. 1 + Col. 3.

As the middle and bottom curves of the figure show, between 1966 and 1984 the number of deaths steadily declined among active priests and increased among the retired. The curves crossed in the early 1970s. The net result of the contrasting trends is shown in the top curve: a steady number of deaths in the total population over the entire period.

Table 11.1 provides the yearly figures, but for this discussion we have arranged them by four- and five-year periods to reduce annual fluctuations. The average annual number of deaths among active priests declined from 408 in 1966–69 to 216 in 1980–84. During the same period, the number among the retired increased from 199 to 386. The average for the total population remained practically unchanged, decreasing slightly from 607 annual deaths in the late 1960s to 602 in the early 1980s.

Recall, we described similar contrasting trends in our analysis of retirement and preretirement mortality rates. Preretirement mortality accounted for most of the natural attrition that occurred in the late 1960s. But the introduction of formal retirement programs changed the balance between retirement and preretirement deaths as avenues of natural attrition. By the early 1980s, attrition from retirement dominated over preretirement mortality. The natural attrition rate, however, which combines the two, was relatively steady across the 19-year period.

From an organizational perspective, shifting the modal number of deaths from active to retired priests represents a rationalization of natural attrition, because death is an unpredictable exit whereas retirement is not. Moreover, as we shall see later, trends show a decrease in age-specific death rates for priests. This augments the rationalizing effect of formal retirement programs, because it increases the proportion of priests who survive past retirement age.

Table 11.1 calls attention to another change in mortality trends of U.S. diocesan priests. Although the pattern shows steady decline in the number of deaths among active priests, most of the decline took place before 1977. From 1977 to 1984, both the number of deaths and the crude death rates for active priests were relatively stable. This stability must be interpreted in the contexts of both the decline in size of the active priest population and the increasingly favorable mortality rates for priests and U.S. white males in general.[3]

Table A.1 indicates that the number of active priests declined from 35,087 in 1966 to 30,501 in 1977, a 13 percent loss.[4] At the same time, the number

3. The general population of U.S. white males is inclusive, covering those above and below age 25. Obviously, because the priest population excludes age groups below 25, the absolute values of crude death rates are not directly comparable across the two populations. To deal with the issue, we limited our analysis to *change* in the crude rates and ignored direct comparisons of their absolute values.

Comparisons of change in the rates are meaningful for two reasons. First, including those younger than 25 in the general male population has minimal impact on changes in the crude mortality rate, because a relatively small number of deaths occur among the young. Second, age-specific mortality rates among the young are much more stable than rates for older persons.

The effect of relatively few deaths and stable age-specific mortality rates among young age groups is illustrated in the following example based on data from table 1-3 of *Vital Statistics of the United States, 1984* (U.S. Department of Health and Human Services 1987b). If every age group had experienced the same decrease in number of deaths between 1966 and 1984 as those of ages 15–24, the crude death rate would have declined by 0.01 deaths per 100 white males. On the other hand, if every age group had experienced the same decrease in number of deaths as those of ages 65–74, the crude death rate would have declined by 1.2 deaths per 100 during the same period.

4. Table 2.1 and table 3.1 show 35,070 active priests in 1966, whereas table A.1 shows

of deaths was cut in half, from 444 in 1966 to 222 in 1977. By 1984 the size of the priest population had fallen to 28,618, a decline of 6 percent compared with the 1977 number. During the same period, the number of deaths declined from 222 to 211, a slightly smaller decline of 5 percent. The data clearly demonstrate that prior to 1977 the rate of decline in the number of deaths outpaced the rate of decline in the size of the active priest population. After 1977 the two rates were almost equal.

Much of the change in mortality trends of *active* priests is attributable to changing retirement policies. The same is not true, however, when we consider mortality in the total priest population. The diminishing size of the priest population and the decline in crude death rates for U.S. white males are more important than changes in retirement policies for interpreting mortality trends in the total population of priests.

For example, when compared with decline in the size of the total priest population, the number of deaths is not so stable. Table A.1 showed that the total population dropped from 36,330 to 33,756 between 1966 and 1984, a loss of 7 percent. During the same period, the number of deaths rose from 598 to 617, an increase of 3 percent. Crude death rates for U.S. white males dropped 13 percent between 1966 and 1984 (U.S. Department of Health, Education, and Welfare 1968, table 1-1; U.S. Department of Health and Human Services 1987b, table 1-1). Those for the total priest population, however, increased 11 percent during the same period.

The contrast in changing mortality rates for priests and all U.S. white males is undoubtably due to aging of the clergy population. During the census period, the median age of priests increased from 46 to 54; thus the population aged eight years in roughly two decades (table 2.1). The impact of aging on crude death rates is evident in table 11.1. Four of the five highest annual rates for the total population were recorded during the last four years of the census period. Moreover, the trend toward higher crude death rates observed in the early 1980s is likely to continue through the turn of the century, given the strong aging trends driving our projection models.

Life Expectancy

Even though the crude death rate of priests has been rising in recent years, table 11.2 shows that the mean age at death is also rising. Hence, although proportionately larger numbers of priests are dying each year because of aging trends, the typical priest is living longer than in prior decades be-

---

35,087; the discrepancy is due to different techniques used for handling the situation when a priest experienced two transition events in the same year (see appendix C, the subsection "Other Adjustments," for a full explanation).

Table 11.2 Mean ages at death
of U.S. diocesan priests, 1966–84

Year	Mean
1966	72.0
1967	72.3
1968	72.7
1969	73.2
1970	74.2
1971	72.7
1972	73.0
1973	73.3
1974	73.0
1975	73.1
1976	73.6
1977	73.4
1978	73.8
1979	74.7
1980	74.2
1981	75.1
1982	69.4
1983	75.0
1984	75.4

Source: weighted census
counts.
Note: Total priest population
used (active plus retired, sick, and
absent).

cause of increasingly favorable mortality rates. Between 1966 and 1984, the mean age at death increased from 72.0 to 75.4. Thus, the life expectancy of priests rose 3.4 years over the 19-year period. Furthermore, the trend has been generally monotonic. Only five of the years show a decrease in life expectancy compared with the previous year.[5]

Regional Crude Death Rate
Table 11.3 presents mortality rates of the total priest population from 1966 to 1984 for the United States and geographic regions. The top row shows that national trends followed a J-shaped curve. The curve begins at 1.66

5. In the previous chapter we presented these data for four- and five-year intervals to smooth annual fluctuations, reporting an increase in life expectancy of only 1.2 years. Thus during 1966–69, the age at death averaged 72.6, and during 1980–84, 73.8.

268   Part 3. Components of Population Change

Table 11.3. Crude death rates of U.S. diocesan priests and percentage of gross change, 1966–84, by year, nation, and region (number of deaths per 100 priests)

	Average annual rate				% gross change
	1966–69	1970–74	1975–79	1980–84	1966–84
United States	1.66	1.59	1.61	1.77	30.42
Regions					
New England	1.66	1.68	1.85	1.97	32.92
Middle Atlantic	1.83	1.66	1.66	1.84	32.09
East Northcentral	1.65	1.64	1.50	1.82	29.51
West Northcentral	1.71	1.54	1.64	1.81	29.19
Mountain	1.27	1.47	1.04	1.54	26.80
Pacific	1.41	1.67	1.49	1.34	28.06
East South[a]	1.38	1.27	1.29	1.56	27.43
West Southcentral	1.55	1.24	1.82	1.64	30.08

Source: weighted census counts.
Note: Total priest population used (active plus retired, sick, and absent).
[a]Combines the South Atlantic region and one diocese from the East Southcentral region.

deaths per 100 priests in the late 1960s, falls to its low point in the early 1970s, and then rises steadily to its high point in the early 1980s, 1.77.

Trends in mortality rates varied considerably by region. The J-shaped curve is repeated only in West Northcentral and East South dioceses, although Pacific dioceses followed an inverted J-shaped curve. Rates in the East Northcentral region remained stable for the first decade, dipped in the late 1970s, and rose to their high point in the early 1980s. They rose monotonically in New England dioceses and followed a U-shaped function in Middle Atlantic states. In the remaining regions, trends followed an S-shaped curve, rising and falling in each five-year period.

Despite variations, however, a consistent pattern governs the trends. In every region but two—the Pacific and West Southcentral—the highest mortality rates occurred at the end of the census period. In Pacific states the high point was reached in the early 1970s, while in West Southcentral states the high point was reached in the late 1970s. As noted above, this consistent trend toward higher crude mortality rates reflects the aging process.

Other differences in regional mortality rates for priests are similar to variations found in the rates for U.S. white males. For the general white male population, Rogot and colleagues (1988) report that the lowest crude mortality rates are found in the West and the highest in the Northeast. These differences persist when comparisons are limited to U.S. white males 65 and older.

The last column of table 11.3 shows that, nationally, mortality averaged a gross loss of 30.4 percent of the 1966 number of priests in 19 years. Cumulative losses in the Northeast were notably above the national average and were the highest in the country. Mortality losses in West dioceses were notably below the national mean and were the lowest, with one exception: losses in East South dioceses were equally low. Hence, for the most part, differences in mortality rates for priests reflect the same regional variations as those for the general white male population.

Further examination of regional differences in cumulative mortality losses shows that the range of variation was relatively small compared with the range for the other components of demographic change. Mortality losses were 23 percent higher in New England than in Mountain dioceses, the regions representing the extremes of the distribution.[6] The range in regional differences was notably higher for the other transition events. The range in gains from ordinations was 81 percent; in cumulative gains from net immigration, 3,083 percent; in cumulative losses from net leave, 135 percent; in losses from resignations, 61 percent; in losses from preretirement mortality, 46 percent; and in losses from retirements, 31 percent.[7]

Apparently, variation in cumulative gross change is greatest for those components most affected by social forces and least for those governed by biological forces. Losses from preretirement mortality and retirement are governed by biological processes of aging. Therefore, they show less regional variation than changes stemming from the other transition events, all of which are governed by social forces.

Furthermore, these two components, by themselves, show more regional variation than overall mortality in the total priest population. But when the two biologically based components of change are combined, their greater regional variation disappears. Cumulative losses from natural attrition, which include exits through retirement and preretirement mortality, show a regional range of only 19 percent. This is an even smaller range compared with the 23 percent of regional difference in cumulative losses from mortality in the total priest population. Combining retirement and preretirement mortality rates within regions controls for differences in retirement policy across regions. Thus, removing the effects of policy differences further reduces the regional variation in biologically based components of population change, because policy differences stem from social forces.

6. The percentage of gross change in New England minus the percentage of gross change in Mountain divided by the percentage of gross change in Mountain: $(32.92 - 26.80)/26.80 = 22.8$.

7. Computations using the formula described in the preceding note are based on data from the following tables: 7.3 for ordination, 8.3 for net immigration, 8.11 for net leave, 9.2 for resignation, and 10.4 for retirement and preretirement mortality.

National Age-Specific Mortality Rates

Table 11.3 showed that crude death rates for the total priest population generally increased between 1966 and 1984. Table 11.4 contains age-specific rates and shows the opposite: a trend toward lower mortality rates during the same period. Rising crude rates and falling age-specific rates reflect two changes occurring simultaneously. The priest population is aging and at the same time — along with the U.S. white male population — is enjoying increasingly favorable mortality risks. Aging in a population augments crude death rates, and increasing longevity reduces age-specific rates. Thus, although the proportion of priests dying in 1980–84 was larger than in any other five-year interval during the census period, the proportion dying in individual age groups tended to be at its lowest in 1980–84.

The rates in table 11.4 are for two-year age groups presented in four- and five-year periods from 1966 to 1984. Obviously, age-specific mortality rates increase with age. This relationship is apparent in column 5, which presents the grand means for 1966–84. The average annual rate for priests of ages 25–26 is 0.03 deaths per 100, and for priests 79 and over it is 12.3.

An examination of the rows shows that in all age groups mortality rates declined during the period. Regardless of age, mortality was lower in 1980–84 than in 1966–69. Furthermore, tracking the changes for each age group shows that 75 percent of the rates in successive five-year periods were lower than those in the preceding periods; hence the decline is generally monotonic.

We turn next to the question of how mortality rates of priests differ from those of the general U.S. white male population and subcategories within it. The general comparisons employ age-specific rates. For comparing differences that stem from social conditions we use standardized mortality ratios (Rogot et al. 1988).

Differences between Mortality Rates of
U.S. Diocesan Priests and All White Males, 1966–84

Table 11.5 contains age-specific mortality rates for five-year age groups of U.S. diocesan priests and U.S. males. Data are presented for the beginning, midpoint, and end of our census period. The sample in this table includes both active and retired priests. The data for the U.S. male population are taken from *Vital Statistics of the United States* (U.S. Department of Health, Education, and Welfare 1968, table 1-8; 1979, table 1-8; U.S. Department of Health and Human Services 1987b, table 1-8).

In 1966, priests generally experienced lower mortality rates than U.S. white males for ages 25–54. Rates for ages above 54, however, were notably higher for the total priest population than for white males. This was

Table 11.4. Age-specific death rates of U.S. diocesan priests, 1966–84 (number of deaths per 100 priests)

Age cohort	Average annual rate				Grand mean 1966–84
	1966–69	1970–74	1975–79	1980–84	
25–26	0.00	0.18	0.00	0.00	0.05
27–28	0.10	0.05	0.03	0.07	0.07
29–30	0.09	0.06	0.09	0.07	0.08
31–32	0.13	0.06	0.04	0.00	0.07
33–34	0.07	0.14	0.09	0.06	0.09
35–36	0.22	0.08	0.04	0.13	0.13
37–38	0.27	0.09	0.04	0.22	0.16
39–40	0.21	0.15	0.19	0.14	0.18
41–42	0.27	0.45	0.24	0.26	0.31
43–44	0.31	0.27	0.25	0.24	0.27
45–46	0.52	0.47	0.30	0.14	0.37
47–48	0.67	0.61	0.39	0.36	0.51
49–50	0.83	0.54	0.58	0.53	0.62
51–52	0.94	0.71	0.55	0.59	0.70
53–54	1.35	1.21	1.05	0.63	1.05
55–56	1.55	1.40	0.67	0.93	1.14
57–58	1.90	1.31	1.32	0.83	1.33
59–60	2.22	1.53	1.29	1.44	1.62
61–62	2.80	2.42	1.51	1.69	2.09
63–64	3.33	2.85	2.21	2.00	2.57
65–66	3.83	3.34	2.84	2.57	3.09
67–68	4.61	3.58	3.12	2.69	3.36
69–70	5.47	4.53	3.98	3.28	4.16
71–72	6.28	4.72	5.26	3.55	4.79
73–74	6.35	6.26	5.63	5.00	5.69
75–76	7.89	8.25	6.59	6.55	7.18
77–78	9.52	8.35	6.56	8.35	8.13
≥ 79	15.86	12.76	12.51	12.58	13.19

Source: weighted census counts.
Note: Total priest population used (active plus retired, sick, and absent).

especially true in the oldest age group. For the 75–79 cohort, the total diocesan priest population experienced 2.5 more deaths per 100 than the white male population in general.

By 1975, the disadvantages of older priests relative to white males had reversed. Whereas in 1966, mortality rates for ages above 54 were higher among priests than white males, in 1975 they were lower. On the other hand,

Table 11.5. Age-specific death rates of U.S. males and U.S. diocesan priests, 1966, 1975, and 1984 (number of deaths per 100 persons)

Age cohort	Males[a]		Priests[b]	
	All	White	Active	Total[c]
1966				
25–29	0.19	0.16	0.00	0.00
30–34	0.22	0.18	0.04	0.04
35–39	0.31	0.26	0.16	0.16
40–44	0.47	0.42	0.35	0.35
45–49	0.75	0.69	0.35	0.42
50–54	1.22	1.15	1.04	1.12
55–59	1.92	1.84	1.99	2.05
60–64	2.82	2.74	2.48	2.99
65–69	4.30	4.13	3.50	4.31
70–74	6.16	6.07	5.33	6.58
75–79	8.51	8.56	10.41	11.05
1975				
25–29	0.20	0.17	0.13	0.13
30–34	0.21	0.17	0.07	0.07
35–39	0.28	0.23	0.11	0.11
40–44	0.42	0.36	0.12	0.12
45–49	0.67	0.61	0.38	0.50
50–54	1.04	0.97	1.09	1.32
55–59	1.62	1.53	1.17	1.30
60–64	2.52	2.44	1.39	1.89
65–69	3.64	3.59	2.52	2.86
70–74	5.56	5.46	4.10	4.90
75–79	8.35	8.25	3.95	6.36
1984				
25–29	0.16	0.15	0.00	0.00
30–34	0.18	0.16	0.05	0.05
35–39	0.22	0.19	0.05	0.04
40–44	0.33	0.29	0.28	0.28
45–49	0.52	0.46	0.13	0.17
50–54	0.85	0.78	0.59	0.60
55–59	1.35	1.28	0.75	0.92
60–64	2.08	1.99	1.35	1.72
65–69	3.10	3.03	1.79	2.89
70–74	4.76	4.69	2.48	3.17
75–79	7.13	7.15	8.73	8.78

[a]Sources: U.S. Department of Health, Education, and Welfare 1968, 1979, table 1-8; U.S. Department of Health and Human Services 1987b, table 1-8.
[b]Source: weighted census counts.
[c]Active priests plus those retired, sick, and absent.

during the decade priests below 55 managed to retain most of their advantage over white males: 1975 rates in all but one of the younger age groups (50–54) were lower for priests than for the white male population. But the younger priests lost some ground. Rates in four of the six age groups below 55 were higher in 1975 than in 1966.

In 1984, the total priest population above 54 continued to experience favorable mortality rates compared with white males, except for the oldest age group. The magnitude of the advantage decreased, however, in three of the five older cohorts. Mortality rates for the 75–79 cohort changed dramatically, increasing by 2.5 more deaths per 100 in 1984 than in 1975. This increase meant that by 1984 the oldest group had begun to experience mortality rates substantially higher than for white males, thus reversing the advantage they enjoyed in 1975.

In 1984, not only did priests in all age groups under 55 continue to experience lower mortality rates than white males, but in five of the six younger cohorts the decrease between 1975 and 1984 was greater for priests than for white males.

Thus overall, priests enjoyed significant decline in their age-specific mortality rates between 1966 and 1984. The exceptions were insignificant: rates for the two youngest age groups remained practically stable. The most notable decline for older priests occurred between 1966 and 1975 and for younger priests between 1975 and 1984, except for those 40–44, which occurred in the first decade.

For the entire period, U.S. diocesan priests under 55 experienced lower mortality rates than the U.S. white male population. Furthermore, the advantage increased during the period for priests in several of the younger age groups. A different picture emerged for older priests. In age groups over 54, priests experienced higher mortality rates than white males at the beginning of our census period, but lower rates in all but the oldest category at the end of the 19 years.

Trends among older priests raise a number of questions. Did the improvements in mortality for older priests result from lifestyle changes? From better health care? To what extent have new retirement policies reduced stress among older priests and thus prolonged their lives? Why have priests of ages 75–79 suffered higher mortality rates in recent years? Has the priest shortage placed additional stress on this particular age group? If so, will the shortage lead to higher mortality rates for other age groups in the years ahead?

Unfortunately, the answers to these questions cannot be explored with the data at hand. The questions can be formulated more precisely, however, by comparing priests' mortality experience with that of other white males in various social settings. With few exceptions, age-specific mortality rates are lower for U.S. diocesan priests than U.S. white males. In the following section we attempt to show why the advantage exists by using comparisons that control for social conditions affecting mortality.

Effects of Social Conditions on Mortality

Large-sample studies of mortality that control for social forces are scarce. Only three were published in the last few decades. One is based on data for 1950 (Guralnick 1963a, 1963b) and another for 1960 (Kitagawa and Hauser 1973). Both data sets predate ours, so the studies are not useful for direct comparisons. The third, however, is an excellent study with a comparable time frame. Conducted at the National Institutes of Health (NIH), it pools eight different samples yielding 1 million observations for 1979–81 (Rogot et al. 1988).

The NIH study provides age-specific mortality rates by 10-year age groups for several categories of education, occupation, income, marital status, and race. The results are presented as standardized mortality ratios, or SMRs, a technique that controls the effects of social conditions in each age group. An SMR is the ratio of observed to expected deaths in a category of, say, education, assuming that the age-specific mortality rate is the same in all categories of education. An SMR score of 100 means the age-specific mortality rate of individuals within a particular category of education equals the average age-specific rate across all levels of education. Differences in mortality rates due to the effects of education are assessed by ranking categories on their SMRs, with the average (100) serving as the standard.

To continue the example of the effects of education on mortality: The million persons in the NIH study were divided into 10-year age groups and nine categories of education within each group. Then, SMRs were computed for each of the 90 subcategories. The effect of education on mortality was assessed by comparing the SMR for each subcategory with the age-specific mean ratio of 100. Rogot and colleagues (1988, p. 30) found that "mortality levels tend to decrease with increasing education." Thus, SMRs for lower levels of education usually exceed 100, and those for higher levels fall below 100.[8]

The NIH study provides a basis for comparing mortality rates of priests with those of other groups. For the comparative analysis we combined our data for 1979–81 with the NIH data and computed SMRs for 10-year age groups of priests. We followed the same techniques for our computations as

8. See Rogot et al. 1988, pp. 3–9, for a full discussion of methods.

those used by Rogot and colleagues (1988).[9] (Appendix G contains the results of calculating observed and expected deaths for priests by age and subsample; SMRs for priests in the following tables were derived from those results.)

Further Effects of Age

A preliminary examination of tables 11.6–11.10 provides an overview of how social forces affect mortality in different age groups and how this in-

Table 11.6. Age-specific mortality ratios for U.S. diocesan priests and U.S. white males, standardized by education, 1980

Number of years completed	Age group							
	10-year					Combined		
	25–34	35–44	45–54	55–64	65–74	≥ 25	25–64	≥ 65
Priests[a]								
College								
≥ 8 years	42	77	74	70	92	139	87	107
White males[b]								
Elementary								
0–4 years	—	—	124	131	124	118	133	115
5–7 years	—	170	170	138	114	121	145	114
8 years	—	177	115	116	107	104	119	99
High School								
1–3 years	246	185	114	125	98	115	132	102
4 years	114	89	102	89	92	93	94	91
College								
1–3 years	81	94	96	85	103	91	88	96
4 years	47	53	69	78	88	81	69	95
≥ 5 years	39	56	56	58	74	63	55	74
Unknown	—	—	—	—	—	96	99	95
Total sample	100	100	100	100	100	100	100	100

[a]Means of 1979–81 rates for total priest population (active plus retired, sick, and absent); source: weighted census counts.
[b]Source: Rogot et al. 1988, table 6, deaths of white males from all causes.

9. Age-specific SMR scores for priests vary in the tables presented because they are based on different subsets of our sample. In general, SMRs are based on the full sample of active and retired priests for examining the effects of education, income, marital status, and race and on a subsample of those who had been active in the ministry within the past five years for examining occupation. Additionally, to make the priests' SMRs comparable to those in the NIH study, we followed Rogot and colleagues' methods as closely as possible. Thus, varia-

Table 11.7. Age-specific mortality ratios for U.S. diocesan priests and U.S. white males, standardized by major occupation, 1980

	Age group							
	10-year					Combined		
Occupation	25–34	35–44	45–54	55–64	65–74	≥ 25	25–64	≥ 65
	Priests[a]							
Priesthood	50	85	78	86	121	195	106	135
	White males[b]							
Prof.-tech.	76	71	54	81	69	74	72	82
Mgr.-admin.	69	76	96	99	116	96	94	104
Sales	59	93	124	108	110	109	106	115
Clerical	101	119	102	109	127	113	108	129
Crafts	119	130	107	102	107	108	108	109
Operative	138	90	114	105	110	110	109	119
Transportation	122	143	127	82	127	107	107	106
Labor	159	127	122	149	110	135	141	116
Farming	—	—	73	76	68	73	73	74
Farm labor	—	—	—	155	54	89	109	59
Service	40	122	146	100	100	104	108	95
Total sample	100	100	100	100	100	100	100	100

[a]Means of 1979–81 rates for all active priests plus those retired, sick, and absent who have been in the labor force within the last five years; source: weighted census counts.
[b]Source: Rogot et al. 1988, table 11, deaths of white males from all causes.

formation helps understand variations in priests' mortality. Each table gives SMRs for 10-year age groups and, when possible, for three combined age categories: 25 and older, 25–64, and 65 and older.

For example, table 11.6 presents age-specific SMRs for all U.S. diocesan priests in our sample and all white males in the NIH sample with data on education. Examining the first five columns of row 1, we discover a curious effect of age: priests' SMRs are lowest at ages 25–34 and highest at 65–74. Additionally, all the scores are below 100, indicating that, controlling for education, priests' mortality is below the national average for white males in every age group.

Inspecting row 1 of the remaining tables (11.7–11.10) shows that this pattern is consistent for priests under all social conditions tested, with one

tions in the samples and age-specific rates produce unique sets of priests' SMRs for each socioeconomic condition tested.

Table 11.8. Age-specific mortality ratios for U.S. diocesan priests and U.S. white males, standardized by family income, 1980

Annual income	Age group							
	10-year					Combined		
	25–34	35–44	45–54	55–64	65–74	≥ 25	25–64	≥ 65
Priests[a]								
$28,651[b]	42	77	74	70	92	139	87	107
White males[c]								
< $5,000	200	—	220	214	137	132	214	118
$5,000–9,999	128	258	146	173	117	117	171	107
$10,000–14,999	112	120	158	122	95	106	128	96
$15,000–19,999	115	96	92	96	70	89	97	80
$20,000–24,999	95	79	88	71	87	83	78	92
$25,000–49,999	71	80	86	78	67	80	80	82
≥ $50,000	57	81	58	65	57	67	64	74
Unknown	75	85	97	80	95	92	84	95
Total sample	100	100	100	100	100	100	100	100

[a]Means of 1979–81 rates for total priest population (active plus retired, sick, and absent); source: weighted census counts.
[b]Source: Hoge, Carroll, and Scheets 1988, table 3.11 (1987 $).
[c]Source: Rogot et al. 1988, table 7, deaths of white males from all causes; family income (1980 $).

exception: when standardized for occupation, the mortality ratio for priests of ages 65–74 is 121 (see table 11.7). In contrast, examining the other rows of the same tables reveals that the relationship between age and SMRs shows little if any discernible pattern in the general white male population. Why should the advantageous impact of social conditions on mortality be stronger for younger priests than older ones, especially since young white males in the general population experience no similar advantage?

One possible reason is that a gatekeeping mechanism prevents those with high mortality risks from entering the priesthood. Perhaps the demanding formation program discourages those with notable illness from entering and persevering in the seminary. This explanation is supported by rows 8 and 9 of table 11.6, which show that in the general population young white males with a college education or graduate study enjoy the same lower SMRs as priests.

Thus, higher education generally may account for the effect. Further examination of the same three rows (1, 8, and 9) provides additional evi-

Table 11.9. Age-specific mortality ratios for U.S. diocesan priests and U.S. white males, standardized by marital status, 1980

	Age group							
	10-year					Combined		
Marital status	25–34	35–44	45–54	55–64	65–74	≥ 25	25–64	≥ 65
Priests[a]								
Celibate	40	82	75	72	91	141	89	106
White males[b]								
Married	78	86	93	93	96	94	92	97
Separated	–	–	–	148	171	171	191	147
Never married	134	154	137	135	111	125	137	113
Widowed	–	–	–	155	114	112	169	107
Divorced	136	207	122	159	123	133	154	110
Unknown	–	–	–	–	–	89	35	142
Total sample	100	100	100	100	100	100	100	100

[a]Means of 1979–81 rates for total priest population (active plus retired, sick, and absent); source: weighted census counts.
[b]Source: Rogot et al. 1988, table 9, deaths of white males from all causes.

dence for the more general explanation. The data consistently show that the impact of a gatekeeping mechanism diminishes over time for priests as well as for college- and university-educated U.S. white males. For some reason, once young males are ordained or complete their college or university training and continue to age, their mortality risks increase and gradually approach the national average.

An alternative explanation for lower SMRs in younger cohorts is that seminaries and other colleges are admitting and retaining healthier individuals nowadays. This period effect would account for the increasingly high SMRs in the older age groups. Of course, the pattern may result from a combination of the gatekeeping and period effects.

The highest SMRs for priests — but still below the national average — appear consistently for the 65–74 age group in tables 11.6 through 11.10, with the exception noted above. When they enter the oldest age category, priests still enjoy lower mortality rates compared with their counterparts in the white population, but the magnitude of the advantage decreases significantly.

Recall, table 11.5 showed that in 1984 priests in the 75–79 age group, but in no other, experienced higher mortality rates than U.S. white males. Note, too, the one exception to the overall pattern we are discussing is for priests of ages 65–74; once standardized for occupation, their mortality ratio is 121, notably above the national average for white males. Taken together, these findings raise the question of whether the demands of priestly ministry produce higher mortality risks among older priests relative to both younger priests and the white male population. And if so, why? Again, data limitations do not allow us to pursue the questions.

Continuing the overview of this group of tables, we discover in columns 6 to 8 of row 1 that priests' SMRs are generally higher in the combined age categories than might be expected, given the scores for each 10-year age group. For example, in table 11.6 the SMRs for the 25 and over and the 65 and over age groups are above the national average for white males, even though they are well below it in all the 10-year age groups. The apparent discrepancies have a simple explanation. The SMRs are higher than the national average for white males in the two aggregated age groups mainly because the priest population is highly skewed toward older members.

Examining the SMRs in column 7 of these tables shows that when the aggregated age group is more comparable, the age effect is diminished but does not disappear. Among U.S. white males of ages 25–64 — roughly the active labor force — the SMR for priests is below 100 but not as low as scores for white males with a college education or graduate study. Thus, even though mortality rates for every 10-year cohort are below the national average for white males, the priesthood population as a whole suffers from higher mortality rates than white males with comparable education. Most of this effect probably results from priests' age distribution, which is notably older than the general population.

Effects of Socioeconomic Forces

Socioeconomic status is generally ascribed according to one's level of education, occupation, and income. Examining the impact of each of these indicators, we ask, To what extent do lower mortality risks of priests result from socioeconomic forces?

Education

We have already noted Rogot and colleagues' finding that higher education lowers mortality risks for U.S. white males (table 11.6). We discovered, accordingly, that because priests receive at least eight years of education beyond high school their mortality rates, standardized for education, are lower than the national average for white males in every age group. On the other hand, comparing rows 1 and 9 of table 11.6 shows that the advantage from education is not as great for priests as for white males with comparable education.

Occupation

Table 11.7 gives mortality rates standardized by occupation for U.S. white males and diocesan priests. The samples for both groups represented in the table are adjusted to improve measurement validity. The NIH sample includes only white males who were currently working, were temporarily unemployed, or had worked within the past five years. Consequently, without adjustments neither the active nor the total priest population is an appropriate comparison group. So we limited our sample for this table to those who had been active in the priestly labor force within the past five years. [10]

The first five columns of row 1 show that, once standardized for occupation, mortality rates are lower for priests than for the vast majority of U.S. white males, but only up to age 65. For the oldest category (65–74), priests' SMRs are substantially higher than the national average for white males. Likewise, columns 6–8 reveal that in two of the aggregated age groups (25 and over and 65 and over) the SMRs of priests are the highest and second highest of the occupations represented. The magnitude of these scores, however, is largely due to the age distribution, which is skewed toward older priests. In the more comparable age group (25–64) the difference is greatly reduced.

The professional-technical and managerial-administrative occupations, shown in rows 2 and 3, are the most appropriate comparison groups for priests. The data show that in every age group — except those 65–74, as noted above — SMRs for priests hover above and below those of white males with comparable occupations. Looking only at professional and technical occupations, SMRs for priests are less favorable in all but one age group (25–34).

Thus, combining these with the results from testing the effects of education we conclude that, although priests experience lower mortality rates than the white male population, the advantage is not as great as that experienced by other highly educated professionals. In addition, the advantage priests enjoy relative to the white male population regardless of socioeconomic status diminishes as they age. Furthermore, the high SMR for priests in the 65–74 age group again raises the question of occupational stress on older priests. Only workers in clerical and transportation jobs experience higher rates of mortality in this age group.

Income

Mortality rates standardized by income are presented in table 11.8. Examining rows 2–8 for the white male population shows, not surprisingly, that

10. The sample includes those who were currently active and those who had retired or otherwise left the labor force within the past five years.

the higher the income, the lower the mortality rate for every age group.

According to Hoge, Carroll, and Scheets (1988, p. 58), the annual compensation package for priests in 1987 was $28,651. The first five columns of row 1 reveal that, up to age 45, priests experience more favorable mortality rates than white males in any income category; from 45–64, only those with family income greater than $50,000 experience lower ratios than priests; and, once again, the favorable mortality of priests is diminished in the oldest age group. The relative standing of priests aged 65–74 places their mortality rates at approximately the same level as those with family income of $10,000–$14,999.

Along with those of education and occupation, the advantageous effects of income on mortality decrease when priests enter the final years of their career. The same question reappears: Does perhaps the positive impact of socioeconomic conditions on mortality wane as priests grow older because of increased occupational stress and deteriorating lifestyle?

Because they are highly educated professionals, priests may be able to adopt a lifestyle that reduces mortality in their earlier years, albeit not one that reduces it as much as other comparable groups. Maybe their relatively low income prohibits priests from utilizing health care options to the same degree as other highly educated professionals. If such a relationship could be demonstrated, it would help explain the somewhat higher mortality ratios of priests compared with similar educational and occupational groups in the earlier stages of their careers. Furthermore, the impact of limited financial resources might increase as priests grow older, accounting for the deterioration in their mortality rates observed for the oldest age group. Once again, data limitations do not permit us to test these hypotheses.

Effects of Marital Status and Race

Other social conditions besides socioeconomic forces affect mortality. Our data allow us to examine two of them, marital status and race.

Marital Status

Table 11.9 presents mortality rates standardized for marital status for U.S. diocesan priests and U.S. white males. Comparing the rows of columns 1–5 shows that, regardless of age, priests experience lower mortality risks than married white males or any other group in the table. Their mortality ratios are dramatically lower than those for the never-married category, the most comparable group.

It might appear that celibate priests have been able to mitigate the mortality risks associated with nonmarriage. Before drawing this conclusion, however, we would need to control for the effects of socioeconomic conditions. The mortality risks of priests should be compared with other never-married, highly educated professionals. Similarly, much if not all of the seeming advantage of lower mortality rates for celibate priests compared with married men may be due to socioeconomic status, which is higher for priests than the average married white male in the United States.

Race
The final table presents mortality rates standardized by race for priests and the total U.S. male population. We raise two issues with these data. First, is the population of white males used in most of the previous tables a more valid comparison group for priests than the total U.S. male population? Second, to what extent was using mortality rates of white males in the projection models presented in earlier chapters an improvement over using those of the total male population?

Examining columns 1–5 in table 11.10 shows that, regardless of age, priests experience lower mortality risks than either white or African-American subgroups of the general male population. The data answer both questions affirmatively. Because they experience lower mortality ratios than

Table 11.10. Age-specific mortality ratios for U.S. diocesan priests and U.S. males, standardized by race, 1980

| | Age group | | | | | |
| | 10-year | | | | | Combined[a] |
Race	25–34	35–44	45–54	55–64	65–74	≥ 65
	Priests[b]					
Predominately white[c]	37	73	70	68	92	107
	Males[d]					
White	91	92	95	96	100	101
African American	201	197	161	156	110	96
Other	70	85	76	55	44	72
Total sample	100	100	100	100	100	100

[a]Data on race of U.S. males are availabe for only one combined category.
[b]Means of 1979–81 rates for total priest population (active plus retired, sick, and absent); source: weighted census counts.
[c]In 1970 U.S. diocesan priests were 99 percent white (NORC 1972, p. 29).
[d]Source: Rogot et al. 1988, table 1, deaths of males from all causes.

African Americans, white males are the more appropriate comparison group for our analysis of mortality than the total male population.

Likewise, utilizing age-specific mortality rates of white males rather than those of the total population in our projections of the priest population at least minimizes overestimations of deaths. The more appropriate rates would be those for white college-educated professionals, but they are unavailable. Note, however, the data show that the gap between the mortality ratios of priests and those of white males is substantially narrowed once priests reach age 65 (column 6). Because most deaths occur at older ages, the wide differences noted in table 11.10 between mortality ratios of younger priests and U.S. white males had only minimal impact on our projections.

Conclusion

Changes in death rates of U.S. diocesan priests have marked the decades since the Second Vatican Council. In the late 1960s, death occurred most frequently among active priests, but by the early 1980s it occurred most frequently among retirees. The introduction of retirement programs rationalized attrition patterns, because retirement is a planned exit from the priestly work force but death is not. Overall, age-specific mortality rates declined during our census period. They fell below those for the U.S. white male population in every age group except the oldest.

Although age-specific rates declined, crude rates increased. This happened because mortality rates had become more favorable for both U.S. white males and priests, but, at the same time, the priesthood population was aging rapidly. Thus, in the mid-1980s proportionately more priests were dying, but the typical priest was living longer than in the mid-1960s. Their average life expectancy increased from 72.0 to 75.4 during the census period.

Although U.S. diocesan priests experience lower mortality rates than U.S. white males, their mortality risks are higher than expected given their level of education and occupation. They also enjoy lower mortality than white males in comparable income brackets and lower death risks than those who never married. The advantages from income and marital status must be interpreted with caution, however, until controls for education and occupation are included in the analysis. This examination of mortality completes our investigation of the components of demographic change. In Part Four we address the consequences of change.

4   Consequences of Change

12 Replacement

Organizational growth and decline may also be gauged using replacement rates, which provide a useful tool for summarizing our complex data. Replacement issues also draw attention to some of the consequences of population change in the priesthood. The diocese, from a sociological perspective, is a religious organization with personnel needs that are being seriously jeopardized by internal demographic trends of the past two decades. The problem comes down to low replacement rates. Defined simply, a replacement rate is the ratio between the number of gains in the priestly work force through entrances and the number of losses through exits.

Sustained deficits and poor replacement of professional resources provide the foreground of supply and demand problems facing diocesan organizations. Swelling layperson-to-priest ratios furnish the background for the complete picture.[1] In this chapter we discuss trends in the net loss created by more exits than entrances in the priest population and examine the projected number of net losses from 1985 to 2005. Net losses are then translated into replacement rates in order to focus more specifically on recruitment-retention ratios, natural replacement, and overall replacement problems.

We also present the contours of shrinking supply and growing demand for priestly services, especially in light of the rapidly increasing Hispanic population. Finally, scope and depth are added to the descriptive analysis by including religious priests in our assessment of the expanding clergy deficit.

---

1. See footnote 6, chapter 4, for the difference between the layperson-to-priest ratio and the parishioner-to-priest ratio.

Highlights

1. Currently, for every 10 priests who leave the active ministry by resignation, sick leave, retirement, or death, only 6 are being replaced by ordination. Four of every 10 vacant positions are going unfilled in dioceses that rely on native clergy.

2. Because of steady growth in church membership, the layperson-to-priest ratio in the United States will double in size from 1,100 Catholics per active priest in 1975 to 2,200 in the year 2005. This is a conservative estimate, because the calculations could not take into account the future effects of rapid growth in the Catholic Hispanic population.

3. If the U.S. Catholic church wishes to maintain the same level of sacramental service in 2005 as was prevalent in 1975, it will need twice as many priests in 2005 as are forecasted under our moderate projection series.

Losses in Need of Replacement

During periods of sustained decline, subtracting exits from entrances yields what is called the net loss in organizational manpower. Table 12.1 presents net losses from 1966 through 1984. (Entrances include the number of ordinations plus surplus incardinations; exits represent resignations, retirements, preretirement mortality, and excess leaves of absence.)

Historical Period, 1966–84

Except for 1966, the U.S. clergy population suffered net losses for roughly two decades, peaking at 853 in 1969. As we saw in chapter 9, the years from 1968 to 1972 were a "mass-exodus" period because of resignations. During this five-year stretch the church witnessed extremely high attrition in comparison to recruitment, with net losses averaging 685 priests a year. Net losses leveled off during the mid-1970s but continued at moderately high numbers, averaging 280 priests annually from 1973 to 1984. Note, however, that attrition was going up again at the end of the census period.

Projection Period, 1985–2005

Net losses are plotted in figure 12.1, which also shows projected numbers based on our optimistic, moderate, and pessimistic projection series. The curve depicting the historical period, 1966–84, groups the data in column 3 of table 12.1 in four- and five-year periods to reduce annual fluctuations. The projection curves are likewise based on grouped data.

In all three projections, net losses are forecasted to rise considerably throughout the 1980s. Higher attrition for the immediate future is mainly the result of large numbers of priests reaching the age of retirement and highest risk of preretirement mortality. The pessimistic series captures the

Table 12.1. Number of entrances, exits, and
net losses or gains of U.S. diocesan priests,
1966–84

Year	Entrances[a]	Exits[b]	Net losses or (gains)[c]
1966	1,028	1,022	(6)
1967	1,108	1,305	197
1968	1,092	1,613	521
1969	901	1,754	853
1970	924	1,576	652
1971	746	1,484	738
1972	728	1,391	663
1973	917	1,276	359
1974	807	1,159	352
1975	853	1,078	225
1976	771	867	96
1977	757	1,132	375
1978	670	1,048	378
1979	737	844	107
1980	615	814	199
1981	614	736	122
1982	592	1,048	456
1983	629	935	306
1984	540	924	384
Total	15,029	22,006	6,977

[a]Ordinations plus net immigrations;
sources: tables 7.1 and 8.1, respectively.
[b]Resignations, retirements, preretirement
deaths, and net leaves; sources: tables 9.1,
10.1, and 8.9, respectively.
[c]Col. 2 - Col. 1.

potential impact of the aging clergy population, projecting net losses during the latter half of the 1980s that exceed the historical extremes of the late 1960s and early 1970s. If pessimistic assumptions were to hold true, attrition would drop below 500 priests per year only after the turn of the century.

The bottom curve represents the most optimistic scenario, given past trends. Even in an optimistic forecast, we project net losses at well over 300 priests annually during the late 1980s. The losses will dip slightly below the 200 mark by the end of the projection period. In the most likely future trends — the middle curve — net losses continue to rise, peaking at

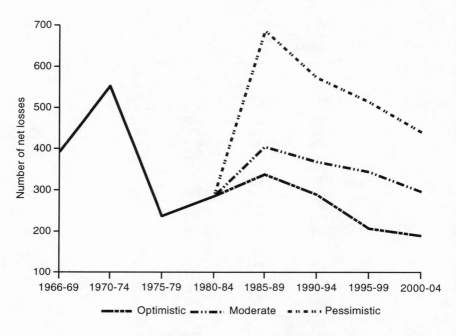

Figure 12.1. Average annual number of net losses of U.S. diocesan priests, 1966–2004

Year	Weighted census counts	Projection series		
		Optimistic	Moderate	Pessimistic
1966–69	393			
1970–74	552			
1975–79	237			
1980–84	285			
1985–89		338	404	686
1990–94		289	368	572
1995–99		207	344	513
2000–04		189	296	440

400 priests per year in the second half of the 1980s, then will decline slightly below 300 at the turn of the century.

The reason net losses will decline after they crest again at the end of the 1980s is that the priest population will be shrinking. But are losses relative to the changing size of the priesthood population declining? As indices that standardize for changing size, replacement rates help address this question. They allow us to examine trends in the ability of the Catholic church to replace losses in its priestly labor force.

Replacement Rates, 1966–84

We find it useful to distinguish various types of rates. The first criterion for categorizing replacement rates is whether or not the individual was recruited and ordained for the local presbyterate, or the "native population," and remained a member until the end of his career. A second criterion distinguishes the different ways an individual leaves the active population.

Types of Replacement

Using the different exit events as distinguishing factors, we focus on three different rates: (1) the recruitment-retention rate, derived by dividing the ordination by the resignation rate; (2) the natural or biological replacement rate, calculated by dividing the ordination rate by the sum of the retirement and preretirement mortality rates; and (3) the total replacement rate, determined by dividing the ordination rate by the sum of all exit rates, namely, resignation, retirement, preretirement mortality, and net leave rates.

The three replacement rates may be computed for the native clergy population and for the combined native and incardinated population. One enters the native clergy, obviously, only through ordination. Exit events remain the same in both types of populations.

To illustrate how to interpret replacement rate scores, a 100 percent replacement rate means that for every 10 priests lost another 10 are gained. At a 150 percent replacement rate, every 10 exits from the active priesthood are offset by 15 entrances. And at a 50 percent rate, every 10 exits are matched by only 5 replacements. Thus the population is stable at 100 percent replacement, growing at any rate above 100 percent, and declining at any rate below 100 percent.

Why Different Types?

One reason for distinguishing between types of replacement rates is that they have different causes, consequences, and policy implications. Knowing the total replacement rate is most useful for providing an overview of growth or decline. Componential replacement rates, such as the recruitment-retention rate and the natural replacement rate, focus on other issues. For example, replacement in an organizational population can be affected by either social forces or biological conditions, each of which have unique implications for strategies of intervention and change.

If, for example, resignation rates are high or unacceptable in relation to low ordination rates, church officials could examine the social causes of the ensuing net loss, intervene to change those structural conditions over which they have control, and thereby attempt to stem the decline. On the other hand, an abnormally low natural replacement rate likewise leads to

decline, but if the primary cause is an aging work force, an organization
has very few options for intervention that could reverse the downward trend
once it is underway.

Needless to say, a recruitment-retention rate can be improved by raising
either or both recruitment and retention. Recruiting and retaining active
members of an organization, of course, go hand in hand. For example,
it is very difficult to attract an individual to a profession in which almost
as many are resigning each year as are choosing to enter. This was the situation in the national priest population during the early 1970s, as the data
have shown. The good news, mentioned in chapter 9, is that resignations
decreased notably by the end of the census period. Ordinations, however,
continued to drop. As we shall see, this combination of trends adds up
to a serious replacement problem.

Each of the replacement rates is calculated for the native population
and the combined native and incardinated population. This distinction
draws attention to the transnational nature of the priest shortage. The
U.S. Catholic church is part of a global religious organization and is
not alone in facing long-term decline in its priest population. Though a
loosely coupled organization in some respects, the international church
is a closed system with regard to clergy migrations. Every incardination
in one diocese represents an excardination in another diocese or in a religious order.

According to some observers, redistributing priests through incardination as an answer to the clergy shortage raises the question of global or
regional equity. In fact, internationally conscious Catholics may agree that
"by global standards the United States does not have a shortage of priests"
(Hoge 1987, p. 108). Countries like the United States that enjoy relatively
high net immigration from religious orders and foreign countries despite
a comparatively "favorable" layperson-to-priest ratio may soon have to face
the equity issue. Accordingly, we provide data on replacement rates for
both native and combined native and incardinated clergy populations to
help define the parameters of the situation in this country.

Advantages of High Incardinations

The percentages in tables 12.2, 12.3, and 12.4 allow us to examine three
types of replacement rates. Each table presents two different rates, one that
includes ordination and net immigration (combined population) and another that does not include net immigration (native population). A comparison of rates with and without immigration in all three tables reveals
the advantage of incardinations for raising replacement rates.

Hence all the rates in the odd-numbered columns are higher than those in the even-numbered columns of each table, with only a few exceptions.[2] According to the final figure in row 1 of all three tables, national replacement ratios for active diocesan priests are about 9 percent more favorable when net immigration is included than when it is not.

Regional differences depict the familiar contrast between the Northeast and Northcentral half of the nation, on the one hand, and the West and South half, on the other. The differences between replacement rates with and without incardinations given in the final column in each table show that the advantage from incardinations ranges from only about 2 percent to 7 percent in the Northeast and Northcentral divisions, but from about 15 percent to 26 percent in the West and South. High gains from incardinations translate into more favorable replacement rates especially well along the Pacific Coast. The advantage of replacement rates that include incardinations is around 1.5 times more favorable for Pacific Coast dioceses than for other West and South dioceses, and about 4–15 times more favorable than for dioceses in the remaining half of the country.

Recruitment-Retention Rate

The data in table 12.2 reflect the relationship between entrances and resignations for both types of priest population. Our analysis here, however, is limited to the native clergy, ignoring the impact of net immigration. The national average shows a recruitment-retention rate of 210 percent at the beginning of the census period, which indicates that for every 10 priests who resigned during 1966–69, an average of about 21 were ordained. Put another way, every two ordinations had a net yield of roughly one priest for active duty.

During the peak resignations of 1970–74, the ordination-resignation replacement rate dropped to 133 percent; for every 10 priests who resigned, an average of about 13 were ordained, for a net gain of roughly 1 active priest from 4 ordinations. Between 1975 and 1979, the rate rose to 259 percent and continued climbing to 271 percent during the early 1980s. These ratios translate to 10 priests resigning for about every 26 or 27 being or-

---

2. The exceptions are rates in New England dioceses for 1980–84, West Northcentral dioceses for 1966–69 and 1975–79, and Mountain dioceses for 1980–84; in each case the replacement rate without net migration is equal to or greater than the rate with net migration. The exceptions occur because of two possibilities. First, excardinations were equal to or greater than incardinations, so that net migration is zero or negative. When negative, net migration reduces rather than supplements the number of entrances from ordinations, so replacement rates with net migration are lower than those without. Second, the difference results from our adjustment procedures, whereby we removed from both the numerator and the denominator those priests who had incardinated from or excardinated to dioceses outside the region.

Table 12.2. Recruitment-retention rates of U.S. diocesan priests, with and without immigration, and percentage of difference, 1966–84, by year, nation, and region (number of entrances per 100 resignations)

	Average annual rate										% diff.
	1966–69		1970–74		1975–79		1980–84		1966–84		
	w/	w/o	w/	w/o	w/	w/o	w/	w/o	w/	w/o	1966
					immigration[a]						–84[b]
United States	221	210	148	133	289	259	308	271	217	197	9.2
					Regions						
New England	374	354	162	150	310	281	204	200	238	222	6.7
Middle Atlantic	253	241	175	164	264	246	264	244	226	213	5.8
East Northcentral	195	191	110	105	239	231	243	233	173	167	3.5
West Northcentral	187	190	112	108	193	195	440	413	185	182	1.6
Mountain	235	222	162	118	614	455	395	410	295	250	15.3
Pacific	202	163	158	118	269	204	462	329	234	175	25.2
East South[c]	217	198	164	141	480	362	371	308	259	216	16.6
West Southcentral	162	145	203	158	534	433	386	302	268	218	18.7

Source: weighted census counts.

[a]With immigration: $r = (o + i)/s$; without immigration: $r = o/s$;
where r is the recruitment-retention rate,
         o is the ordination rate,
         i   is the net immigration rate, and
         s is the resignation rate.
[b][(Col. 9 - Col. 10)/Col. 9]100.
[c]Combines the South Atlantic region and one diocese from the East Southcentral region.

dained, or a net gain of 5 active priests from every 8 ordained. The final rate column shows that during the census period the typical American diocese experienced an average recruitment-retention rate of 197 percent. Thus, for 19 years every 2 ordinations had a net yield of roughly 1 priest for active duty.

With only two exceptions, trends in the various regions followed the pattern of the national data, namely, steady growth in replacement rates between 1966 and 1984, except for the sharp dip during the peak exodus years of 1970–74. New England dioceses differed in that replacement was less favorable at the end than at the beginning of the census period. In West Southcentral dioceses the lowest ratios were recorded during the late 1960s rather than between 1970 and 1974.

Natural Replacement Rate

Natural replacement is the ratio of entrances to retirements plus preretirement deaths. As table 12.3 reveals, the natural replacement rate for native

Table 12.3. Natural replacement rates of U.S. diocesan priests, with and without immigration, and percentage of difference, 1966–84, by year, nation, and region (number of entrances per 100 natural losses)

	Average annual rate										%diff.
	1966–69		1970–74		1975–79		1980–84		1966–84		1966 –84[b]
	w/	w/o	w/	w/o	w/ immigration[a]	w/o	w/	w/o	w/	w/o	
United States	115	109	106	95	108	96	88	78	105	95	9.5
	Regions										
New England	96	91	95	88	100	88	60	60	89	83	6.7
Middle Atlantic	118	112	110	103	92	85	79	73	100	94	6.0
East Northcentral	102	100	92	87	103	101	61	59	90	87	3.3
West Northcentral	103	104	77	74	72	72	90	86	85	84	1.2
Mountain	166	152	142	104	167	123	99	108	141	121	14.2
Pacific	156	124	125	94	121	91	138	93	134	99	26.1
East South[c]	152	138	173	149	207	160	171	147	175	148	15.4
West Southcentral	156	142	141	111	171	148	139	115	152	128	15.8

Source: weighted census counts.
[a]With immigration: $r = (o + i)/(t + d)$; without immigration: $r = o/(t + d)$;
where r is the replacement rate,
        o is the ordination rate,
        i is the net immigration rate,
        t is the retirement rate, and
        d is the preretirement mortality rate.
[b][(Col. 9 - Col. 10)/Col. 9]100.
[c]Combines the South Atlantic region and one diocese from the East Southcentral region.

clergy hovered at slightly below or above 100 percent for most of the period under study. Thus, on the average from 1966 through 1979, each priest who retired or died was replaced by another who was newly ordained.

By the early 1980s, however, the natural replacement rate had dropped to 78 percent, so that every 10 priests who retired or died were replaced by an average of fewer than 8 newly ordained. The natural replacement rate dropped because the ordination rate had continued to fall, whereas, at the same time, retirement rates had started to climb because of the aging of the clergy.

Total Replacement Rate

The ratio of entrances to exits is accurately reflected only in the total replacement rate. Trends in national and regional overall replacement rates for 1966–84 are presented in table 12.4. During the census period, true replacement in the national native clergy population fluctuated from a high of 69 percent for 1966–69 to a low of 54 percent for 1970–74. For 1975–79,

Table 12.4. Total replacement rates of U.S. diocesan priests, with and without immigration, and percentage of difference, 1966–84, by year, nation, and region (number of entrances per 100 exits)

	Average annual rate									
	1966–69		1970–74		1975–79		1980–84		1966–84		% diff.
	w/	w/o	w/	w/o	w/	w/o	w/	w/o	w/	w/o	1966 –84[b]
						immigration[a]					
United States	73	69	60	54	76	68	67	59	68	62	8.8
					Regions						
New England	73	70	57	53	72	64	46	46	62	58	6.5
Middle Atlantic	78	74	66	62	65	60	59	54	67	63	6.0
East Northcentral	64	62	49	47	72	70	48	46	58	56	3.4
West Northcentral	63	64	44	42	52	52	77	73	57	56	1.8
Mountain	96	89	74	54	124	92	74	80	92	78	15.2
Pacific	84	68	67	51	80	60	103	71	82	61	25.6
East South[c]	88	80	83	71	137	107	117	101	102	86	15.7
West Southcentral	73	66	79	62	126	108	96	78	91	76	16.5

Source: weighted census counts.
[a]With immigration: $r = (o + i)/(s + t + d + l)$; without immigration: $r = o/(s + t + d + l)$;
where   r is the replacement rate,
         o is the ordination rate,
         i   is the net immigration rate,
         s is the resignation rate,
         t   is the retirement rate,
         d is the preretirement mortality rate, and
         l   is the net leave rate.
[b][(Col. 9 - Col. 10)/Col. 9]100.
[c]Combines the South Atlantic region and one diocese from the East Southcentral region.

the total replacement rate returned almost to the previous high but stopped short at 68 percent. It then dropped almost to the previous low but stopped at 59 percent for 1980–84.

At 69 percent replacement, for every 10 priests who leave the active ministry through resignation, retirement, or death, an average of about 7 priests are ordained. At 54 percent replacement, for every 10 who exit fewer than 6 enter. And at 59 percent replacement — the rate at the end of the census period — for every 10 who leave the active ministry only about 6 are ordained. At this replacement rate, if the bishop ordains 6 men in any given year, 4 of the 10 positions vacated that year go unfilled.

Growing Demand and Shrinking Supply

Low replacement rates among the clergy are exacerbated by a growing demand for priestly services. A steady increase in membership has marked the history of the Catholic church in the United States. Immigration accounted for much of the growth during the last two centuries. Favorable birth rates, a relatively young age pyramid, and continued high immigration account for recent and projected steady growth (Roof and McKinney 1987). During the 20th century, for example, the number of American Catholics has more than tripled from fewer than 20 million to over 60 million. Catholicism's share of the total U.S. population also has increased from under 20 percent to over 25 percent during the same period.

Growth and Decline in U.S. Catholic Population, 1965–2005

Table 12.5 summarizes data on church membership growth for the decades covered by our investigation. The table's first four columns consistently indicate steady growth in the number of Catholics. The last three columns of statistics, however, provide opposing views of the proportion of the U.S. population represented by Catholics. The Gallup estimates show an increase from 23 percent in 1965 to 27 percent in 1985. In contrast, during the same period both the Official Catholic Directory and the Glenmary estimates show slow but steady decline in the proportion.

While the discrepancies in the figures reflect weaknesses in different estimation techniques, they also highlight a potential danger for church planners. Estimates based on national surveys such as the Gallup poll are generally considered more accurate than "educated guesses" of church officials, upon which the Official Catholic Directory and Glenmary compilers must rely. In a poll, Gallup interviewers ask a national sample of individuals their religious preference along with other relevant questions that permit pollsters to check for consistency. The total number of Catholics in the country is then extrapolated from the number in the sample. Following the same probability techniques, independent surveys produce remarkably consistent and valid results.[3]

The sources for the numbers provided by the Official Catholic Directory and the Glenmary Research Center are contact persons in each diocese. Few if any of their estimates are based on a scientific diocesan-wide

---

3. Although Gallup polls are usually from 1 to 3 percentage points higher in their estimates of the percentage of Catholics than are the General Social Survey results (Greeley 1988), for example, one can be systematically adjusted in view of the other, as Hoge (1987) has done in preparing the Gallup estimates cited in table 11.5. Two other recent surveys further demonstrate the consistency of estimates based on national probability samples. On the basis of a sample of 13,017 U.S. adults in 1987–88, the National Survey of Families and Households estimated that 27 percent of Americans identify themselves as Roman Catholic (Young 1991). In a study of 113,000 U.S. adults conducted in 1989–90, the National Survey of Religious Identification placed the figure at 26 percent (Kosmin 1991).

Table 12.5. Estimates and projections of U.S. general and Catholic populations, 1965–2005 (numbers in thousands)

| | | Catholic | | | | | |
| | General | Number | | | % of total U.S. population | | |
Year	1^a	2^b	3^c	4^d	5^e	6^f	7^g
			Estimates				
1965	194,303	44,790^h	45,648	—	23.1	23.5	—
1970	205,052	50,355^i	47,455	44,863^j	24.6	23.1	21.9
1975	215,973	56,030	48,268	46,183^k	25.9	22.3	21.4
1980	227,757	61,344	49,865	47,502	26.9	21.9	20.9
1985	239,279	64,341	52,107	49,905^l	26.9	21.8	20.9
			Projections				
1990	250,410	67,334	54,531	52,227	26.9	21.8	20.9
1995	260,138	69,950	56,649	54,255	26.9	21.8	20.9
2000	268,266	72,135	58,419	55,951	26.9	21.8	20.9
2005	275,604	74,109	60,017	57,481	26.9	21.8	20.9

[a]Source: U.S. Bureau of the Census 1989a: for estimates, report nos. 519, 917, 1022; for projections, report no. 1018. Figures include armed forces overseas.

[b]Source for estimates: Gallup polls; figures cited in Hoge 1987, table B-1. Projections: Col. 1 × Col. 5 (before rounding).

[c]Source for estimates: the Official Catholic Directory, 1966, 1971, 1976, 1981, 1986; volumes dated the year of publication contain data for one year prior. Figures exclude eastern rite Catholics but include those under the military ordinariate. Projections: Col. 1 × Col. 6 (before rounding).

[d]Sources for estimates: Glenmary Research Center; figures cited in Johnson et al. 1974 and Quinn et al. 1982. Projections: Col. 1 × Col. 7 (before rounding).

[e]Col. 2/Col. 1.

[f]Col. 3/Col. 1.

[g]Col. 4/Col. 1.

[h]Figure for 1965 not available; the one shown is interpolated from 1962 and 1967 data.

[i]Figure for 1970 not available; the one shown is interpolated from 1967 and 1972 data.

[j]Figure for 1970 not available; the one shown is for 1971.

[k]Figure for 1975 not available; the one shown is interpolated from 1971 and 1980 data.

[l]This figure for 1985 is a projection rather than an estimate.

census or sample survey. In addition, dioceses may be motivated to under-estimate, because they are taxed by the U.S. Catholic Conference on the basis of church membership size.

What are the organizational consequences of divergent estimates of church membership size? If national church officials and planners had re-lied on the Official Catholic Directory or Glenmary estimates instead of Gallup figures, for example, they would have been unaware in 1985 of the presence of some 12 million to 14 million adult Americans who claimed Catholicism as their preferred religion. Apart from the difficulty of making accurate diocesan estimates, the discrepancy occurs because surveys try to count all who claim Catholicism as their religious preference, whereas official estimates may wish to count only those who are more or less active adherents. Which definition of the population is more useful is debatable. When differences range in the several millions, though, the distinction is far from trivial.

In any case, the proportion of Americans who claim to be Catholic is growing while the proportion the church recognizes as Catholic is declining. Pursuing the definitional question is beyond the scope of the present report. The additional 12 million to 14 million Catholics, however, represent a potential demand for priestly services, and thus should be included in a discussion of consequences of the demographic transition of the clergy.

Growth in U.S. Hispanic Population, 1980–2005

We believe that Hispanic Catholics constitute a sizable portion of the "invisible" church membership not represented in official data. According to the U.S. Census Bureau, the nation's Hispanic population "has been growing about five times as fast as the rate of the non-Hispanic population since 1980" (U.S. Bureau of the Census 1989b, p. 1). Undoubtedly it is extremely difficult for diocesan officials to improve the accuracy of their educated guesses of the size of the Catholic population in dioceses with high concentrations of Hispanics.

There has been an unprecedented 39 percent growth in the U.S. Hispanic population since 1980; immigration accounts for about half the overall gain.[4] Table 12.6 gives the U.S. census estimates and projections of the total Hispanic population, and attempts to provide parallel data on the Catholic Hispanic population. The official projections show that the num-

4. A U.S. Bureau of the Census release (1989b) provides the following geographic distribution of the Hispanic origin population as of March 1989: California, 34 percent; Texas, 21 percent; New York, 10 percent; Florida, 8 percent; New Mexico, 8 percent; Illinois, 4 percent; New Jersey, 3 percent; and the remainder of the United States, 12 percent. According to Pablo Sedillo of the U.S. Catholic Conference, national Hispanic leaders claim that the U.S. Census Bureau undercounted the Hispanic population in 1980 by 6–7 percent (personal communication). In addition, estimates of undocumented Hispanic immigration range from 2 million to 6 million nationwide, which exacerbates the problem of accurate estimations. Diocesan officials, particularly in the states mentioned, should be aware of the probability of underestimating their Catholic population if they rely on past procedures for calculating current numbers.

Table 12.6. Estimates and projections of U.S. Hispanic population and U.S. Catholic Hispanic population, and percentage of Hispanics in the U.S. Catholic population, 1980–2005 (numbers in thousands)

Year	Number of Hispanics		% Hispanic in U.S. Catholic population[c]
	Total[a]	Catholics[b]	
Estimates			
1980	14,458	12,289	20.0
1985	17,322[d]	14,724	22.9
Projections			
1990	20,638[e]	17,542	26.1
1995	22,550	19,168	27.4
2000	25,223	21,440	29.7
2005	28,009[f]	23,808	32.1

[a]Sources: for estimates, U.S. Bureau of the Census 1989b; for projections, U.S. Bureau of the Census 1986; includes armed forces overseas. Projection data are from the moderate series.

[b]Col. 1 × 0.85; the U.S. Catholic Conference estimates that approximately 85 percent of U.S. Hispanics are Catholic (personal communication with Pablo Sedillo).

[c]Col. 2 divided by Gallup estimates of U.S. Catholic population (see col. 2, table 12.5).

[d]Figure for 1985 unavailable; the one shown is interpolated from 1984 and 1986 estimates.

[e]1989 estimate multiplied by 102.8; estimated annual rate of growth for 1985–90 is 2.8 percent (see U.S. Bureau of the Census 1986, table Q).

[f]Interpolated from 2000 and 2010 projections.

ber of U.S. Hispanics will almost double, from about 14.5 million in 1980 to about 28 million in 2005.

According to U.S. Catholic Conference estimates, about 85 percent of Hispanics are Catholic (Pablo Sedillo, personal communication). On the basis of that estimate, the number of Catholic Hispanics would almost double, from 12.3 million in 1980 to about 23.8 million in 2005.[5] Again,

5. The USCC estimate (85 percent) may be too high. The General Social Survey reports 71 percent (see Greeley 1988) and Gallup 70 percent (American Institute of Public Opinion 1987) of Hispanics claiming Catholicism as their religious preference. Many Catholic Hispanics are switching to Protestant fundamentalist and evangelical churches. During the period of transition from their traditional to their new religion, some may claim allegiance and indeed participate occasionally in both churches. We use the USCC percentage as a way to balance undercounts of the Hispanic population mentioned in the preceding footnote.

assuming that 85 percent of Hispanics in the United States claim Catholicism as their religious preference, the proportion of American Catholics who are of Spanish origin would increase from approximately 20 percent to 32 percent between 1980 and 2005.

Given the demographics affecting Catholic Hispanics, projections of the Catholic population provided in table 12.5 are too low across the board. In light of contrasting counts of the Catholic population, we made three projections and used the most recent percentages available as the basis for projecting the number of Catholics in each series. Thus for the Gallup and Official Catholic Directory projections, we assume the proportion of Catholics in the U.S. population in 1985 (26.9 percent and 21.8 percent, respectively) will continue to 2005. Because the latest available Glenmary estimates are for 1980, we used the percentage for that year (20.9) to project the numbers for 1985 to 2005. In none of the projection series, however, do we take into account that the Hispanic population is growing five times faster than the non-Hispanic population. As a result, in all three projections, the number of Catholics from 1990 to 2005 is too low by some unknown but undoubtedly notable amount.[6]

For all the reasons stated, we feel that the Gallup estimates and projections, although probably somewhat conservative, represent the best data available upon which to base comparable calculations of past, present, and future layperson-to-priest ratios in the Catholic church. Ratios based on Gallup estimates will, of course, be higher than those presented in table 4.2, which were calculated from Glenmary estimates. The Glenmary data have the advantage of being available at the county level, so can be aggregated by diocese, unlike the Gallup results, which are not available for diocesan-level analysis. The Gallup data, on the other hand, provide at least a partial correction of U.S. census undercounts and the rapidly growing Hispanic population.

Assets and Deficits of Population Change

Losses in the number of priests represent one way to view the extent of the priest shortage, but this view ignores the growing number of Catholic laypersons. Table 12.7 gives estimates and projections of the layperson-to-

6. Of the three given, the Gallup estimates probably reflect the faster growth rate of Hispanics most accurately, because they are based on current random samples, but only up to 1985. In that year the proportion of Catholics who were Hispanics was 22.9 percent. This proportion is held constant in the Gallup series throughout the projection period, though it is growing steadily and will probably reach 32.1 percent by 2005. Obviously, if 32 percent rather than 23 percent of the Catholic population is growing five times faster than the rest of the population, by 2005 the forecasted number of 74 million Catholics will be substantially lower than the "true" figure.

Table 12.7. Estimates and projections of U.S. lay Catholic and diocesan priest populations, and the adjusted diocesan priest population and diocesan priest deficit, 1975–2005

Year	Unadjusted number			Adjusted number[a]		
	Lay-persons[b] (thousands)	Priests[c]	Lay-persons/ priest[d]	Priests needed[e]	Priest deficit[f]	Deficit rate[g]
			Estimates			
1975	56,030	30,808	1,819	30,808	0	0.0
1980	61,344	29,667	2,068	33,705	4,038	13.6
1985	64,341	28,240	2,278	35,352	7,112	25.2
			Projections			
1990	67,334	26,062	2,584	36,997	10,935	42.0
1995	69,950	24,230	2,887	38,434	14,204	58.6
2000	72,134	22,511	3,204	39,634	17,123	76.1
2005	74,109	21,030	3,524	40,719	19,689	93.6

[a]Sherry Index: Rev. Robert Sherry (1985) suggests the 1975 parishioner-to-priest ratio as a minimum standard for assessing the severity of the priest shortage; see chapter 4.
[b]Source: Gallup polls (see col. 2, table 12.5).
[c]Source: for estimates, table A.1; for projections, table 2.1 (moderate series).
[d]Col. 1/Col. 2.
[e]Col. 1/1,820: the 1975 modified parishioner-to-priest ratio, or Sherry Index.
[f]Col. 4 - Col. 2.
[g]Col. 5/Col. 2.

priest ratio, adjusted numbers of priests needed on the basis of Rev. Robert Sherry's 1975 standard, along with the corresponding deficit in the priest population if the church were to maintain the 1975 standard of priestly service.[7]

The statistics in the middle column show that if our moderate projections for the priest population and the Gallup-based projections for the lay population hold true, the layperson-to-priest ratio in round numbers will almost double, from 1,800 Catholics per active diocesan priest in 1975 to 3,500 in 2005. Suppose, however, the layperson-to-priest ratio were to remain constant at the 1975 level of 1,819 (column 3, row 1) in keeping with Sherry's proposed minimal standard of availability of priestly ser-

7. See chapter 4 for a description of the Sherry Index, which sets a national standard for comparative purposes.

vices.[8] The fourth column reveals that the number of priests needed to maintain the 1975 ratio would have to increase from about 31,000 in 1975 to about 41,000 in 2005.

The difference between the number of clergy needed to maintain the 1975 standard of priestly service and the number available is the priest deficit (column 5). Given the 1975 standard, the U.S. Catholic church faces a 1990 deficit rate of 42 percent, a shortage of some 11,000 priests. Between 1990 and 2005, the priest deficit would practically double. According to our moderate projections, there will be about 21,000 active diocesan priests in 2005. To maintain the arbitrary 1975 standard of priestly service, however, the church would need an additional 20,000 diocesan priests at the beginning of the 21st century. Furthermore, these are conservative estimates of the deficit, because the rapid growth of the Hispanic Catholic population is not accounted for.

To recapitulate the national data on active diocesan priests: Given our moderate projection series, the U.S. church will probably continue to experience a net loss of about 330 active diocesan priests every year. Hence, the overall replacement rate will average about 65 percent between 1990 and 2005, leaving an average of 35 percent of the vacant priestly positions unfilled year after year.

In terms of a standardized ratio of Catholics to priests, however, the situation is even more extreme. The U.S. Catholic church was operating at a 25 percent deficit in diocesan priestly manpower during the mid-1980s. Just one decade later the projected deficit will approach 59 percent. And as the new century gets underway, the deficiency in the number of priests needed to supply sacramental services at the 1975 level will most likely skyrocket to almost 94 percent.

A Look at Religious Order Priests

Throughout this report we have focused on diocesan priests. We pointed out in chapter 4, however, that the overall priestly staff includes religious order priests. The final set of data to be presented, therefore, includes information on religious priests. Given a staff that includes active diocesan and religious priests, how fast is the layperson-to-priest ratio growing, and how many priests would be needed to maintain the 1975 ratio?

Table 12.8 gives three separate estimates and projections of the statistics presented in the previous table, with slight modifications in the presen-

8. Sherry (1985) based his index on the parishioner-to-priest ratio. For the reasons discussed above, we modify the Sherry Index by basing it on the layperson-to-priest ratio.

Table 12.8. Estimates and projections of U.S. lay Catholic and diocesan and religious priest populations, layperson-to-priest ratio, adjusted combined priest population, and overall priest deficit, 1975–2005

		Unadjusted					
	Laypersons[a] (thousands)	Active priests			Laypersons/ priest		
		Dio.[b]	Rel.[c]	Total	Dio.[d]	Rel.[e]	Total[f]
Year	1	2	3	4	5	6	7
1975	56,030	30,808	20,023	50,831	1,819	2,798	1,102
1985	64,341	28,240	18,588	46,828	2,278	3,461	1,374
2005	74,109	21,030	12,749	33,779	3,524	5,813	2,194

		Adjusted[g]							
	Priests needed			Priest deficit			Deficit rate (%)		
	Dio.[h]	Rel.[i]	Total	Dio.[j]	Rel.[k]	Total[l]	Dio.[m]	Rel.[n]	Total[o]
Year	8	9	10	11	12	13	14	15	16
1975	30,808	20,023	50,831	0	0	0	0	0	0
1985	35,352	22,995	58,347	7,112	5,875	12,987	25.2	34.3	28.6
2005	40,719	26,486	67,205	19,689	13,737	33,426	93.6	107.7	99.0

[a]Source: table 12.7.

[b]Sources: for 1975 and 1985, table A.1; for 2005, table 2.1.

[c]Sources: for 1975 and 1985, the Official Catholic Directory for 1976 and 1986, respectively; the OCD gives only totals, which were multiplied by the percentage of active among diocesan priests derived from table A.1. The forecast for 2005 was calculated as follows:

$$r = (d/p) - d$$

where r is the projected number of active religious priests in 2005,

d is the number of projected active diocesan priests in the same year, and

p is the percentage of diocesan priests in the total number of active clergy $(d + r)$;

d is given in table 2.1, and for p we use the mean of five-year intervals between 1965 and 1988, derived from data given in the OCD, assuming p in 2005 would be the same as during 1965–88.

[d]Col. 1/Col. 2.

[e]Col. 1/Col. 3.

[f]Col. 1/Col. 4.

[g]Sherry Index: Rev. Robert Sherry (1985) suggests the 1975 layperson-to-priest ratio as a minimum standard for assessing the severity of the priest shortage; see chapter 4.

[h]Col. 1/1,819: the 1975 national layperson–to–diocesan priest ratio, or Sherry Index; discrepancies are due to rounding.

[i]Col. 1/2,798: the 1975 national layperson–to–religious priest ratio, or Sherry Index; discrepancies are due to rounding.

[j]Col. 8 - Col. 2.

[k]Col. 9 - Col. 3.

[l]Col. 10 - Col. 4.

[m]Col. 11/Col. 2.

[n]Col. 12/Col. 3.

[o]Col. 13/Col. 4.

tation. The data for diocesan priests are repeated, new information on religious order priests is added, and the totals are given to complete the picture.

Estimates and projections of the religious priest population are based on two assumptions. First, we assume that the same proportion of religious priests is active as in the diocesan population and, second, that the same ratio of diocesan to religious priests that characterized the total priest population in the United States from 1966 to 1988 will exist in 2005. The resulting estimates of the active religious priest population are crude but, nevertheless, useful. Obviously, they are not made with the same precision as the projections for the diocesan clergy; the numbers for religious order priests are ballpark figures and must be interpreted with caution. Additionally, the same caveat affecting the size of the lay population, noted above, also applies. The number of lay Catholics in 2005 is underestimated, because the large growth of the Hispanic Catholic population cannot be accounted for in the available data. Therefore, the layperson-to-priest ratios and priest deficit figures for 2005 in the table are conservative.

According to columns 2–4, the number of religious clergy is projected to decline around 35 percent, from about 20,000 active priests in 1975 to just under 13,000 in 2005. During the same time frame, the total clergy population will drop about 34 percent, from roughly 51,000 to 34,000 active priests. The data show religious priests declining at a slightly faster rate than diocesan priests.[9]

Calculating layperson-to-priest ratios separately for diocesan and religious priests is somewhat artificial, because both types of clergy represent resources for a diocesan church. Column 5 reveals how many Catholics each active diocesan priest would have to serve if there were no religious priests available; column 6 shows how many a religious priest would serve if no diocesan priests were available. The ratios based on the total number of active clergy, given in the next column, are more realistic but still do not reflect the situation with complete accuracy, because many religious order priests are not assigned to parish ministry, and of those who are, many do not work full-time in the parish. Despite their shortcomings, however, these are the best data obtainable. They reveal that in just three decades the layperson-to-priest ratio for the total active priest population will have doubled, from about 1,100 to 2,200 Catholics per priest.

Increased membership size is usually a benefit to a service organiza-

9. Note, the moderate projections presented in chapter 2 forecast a 40 percent decline between 1966 and 2005, roughly a four-decade period; the 34 percent decline cited here is for the three-decade period, 1975–2005. Additionally, the former percentage refers exclusively to the active diocesan priest population, and this one refers to the combined active diocesan and religious priest population.

tion, because growth represents reinforcement of the organization's social mandate. But the assets of high church membership in the Catholic church contrast with staggering deficits in professional resources and create a strain on the organization. Furthermore, the perception of the deficits would be greatly exacerbated if, as Rev. Robert Sherry suggested, the church were to attempt to provide the same ratio of lay Catholics to priests in 2005 that was prevalent in 1975. The table indicates, in round numbers, that the diocesan clergy in 2005 would need to stand at 40,500 and the religious clergy at 26,500, for a total of 67,000 active priests, to maintain the 1975 layperson-to-priest ratio. These figures translate into deficits of almost 19,700 diocesan priests and over 13,700 religious priests, or an overall deficiency of about 33,400 active priests by the year 2005.

The deficit rates in the last three columns show how large a percentage of increase in clergy size would be needed to achieve the arbitrary standard of the 1975 layperson-to-priest ratios. By 2005, the deficit rate for the diocesan clergy would be approaching 100 percent, and for the religious clergy it would exceed 100 percent. Thus, the total number of active priests in the United States would need to be twice that forecasted by our moderate projections if sacramental services are to be as available at the beginning of the 21st century as they were in 1975.

Most likely, this scenario of diminishing supply and increasing demand will unfold as projected. The interaction of these conflicting population trends portends extensive social change for the Roman Catholic church at the dawn of the third Christian millennium.

13 Priest Shortage as Demographic Transition

This project began on the premise that, in balance, theoretical and applied research enrich each other. Lawler and colleagues (1985) testify, however — on the basis of considerable consulting experience — that doing research which is useful for both theory and practice is like walking a tightrope. As part of the balancing act, social analysts remain devoted to standards of theoretical and methodological rigor but at the same time become attracted to canons of practical usefulness. Leaning too far either way causes one to lose equilibrium and fall into one or the other camp or, worse, into oblivion.

Striking a proper balance in research begins by choosing a practical problem for study. It's a truism that the more practical the research problem, the more policy-oriented the theory explaining it. The purpose of this and the remaining chapters, therefore, is to consolidate and assess our contributions to theory, methodology, and practical-minded policy. Additionally, we consider what needs to be done next to corroborate and extend theory and put it into practice. Hence, we propose some priorities for further research grounded in solid theory and practical issues.

Declining numbers of U.S. Catholic priests have created a shortage in key religious services. Shortages affecting critical needs are cause for practical concern. The more critical the need, the more serious the concern. From a theoretical viewpoint, the decline has launched a demographic transition. Transitions imply movement, a beginning and an end. This may connote a less threatening situation than the concept of "critical shortage," but only if the end of the transition is a better stage than the beginning. If not, a transition, too, becomes a cause for practical concern. In this chapter we will reexamine the loss in priestly manpower as a shortage and a transition, trying to balance the practical knowledge and theoretical insights the study has provided from the two different viewpoints.

Shortage as Practical Problem

A severe priest shortage is a practical problem not only for committed Catholics but also for anyone aware of the power and influence of organized religion. Like any shortage, there are two sides to the problem, supply and demand. The severity of clergy decline (the supply side) and strength of membership growth (the demand side) are both disputed issues in the Catholic church. Accurately documenting the growing imbalance in supply and demand for priestly services is *the* first and major contribution of the study for policy-oriented readers.

Assessing Growth

Prior to this study, the full force of the trends could be disputed because of poor information. Even the amount of growth in demand is contested (Greeley 1991). Seemingly reliable data are available, but they do not tell a consistent story. As a result, membership growth is greatly underestimated by church officials (table 12.5). The Official Catholic Directory (OCD) and Glenmary Research Center (GRC) report 12 million to 14 million fewer U.S. Catholics than Gallup polls and other national surveys. Although some of the discrepancy is due to the difference between practicing and nominal Catholics, a substantial part of the huge "invisible church" is accounted for by the Hispanic population, which is growing five times faster than the rest of the U.S. population.

We consider the Gallup estimates of the demand side of the priest shortage to be more accurate than those provided by the OCD or GRC for two reasons. First, those who report Roman Catholicism as their religious preference in Gallup polls were probably baptized and initially reared as Catholics. They are not included in official diocesan estimates, although they represent a potential claim on priestly services. If the church were to honor their preference with some sort of pastoral attention, these non-practicing Catholics could not be ignored in assessing the severity of the priest shortage.[1]

Second, the higher Gallup estimates compensate somewhat for the rapidly increasing Hispanic population. The vast majority of Hispanics are Roman Catholics, but because of rapid growth they are difficult to enumerate by diocesan officials, who provide the estimates given in the OCD and Glenmary reports. Thus, for example, the Archdiocese of New York (with a relatively large Hispanic population) estimates that the number of Catho-

---

1. Ignoring the existence of several million adherents may be an unconscious way of minimizing the severity of the shortage.

lics reported in the OCD is at least 300,000 too low for that archdiocese alone.[2]

Poor enumeration methods and different strategies for defining the population result in an irony of massive proportions: Nonpracticing Catholics together with "invisible" Hispanic Catholics represent the third or fourth largest religious body in the country. Quinn and colleagues (1982) report that the vast majority of U.S. churches have fewer than 300,000 total adherents in their entire denominations. Furthermore, according to the same Glenmary data, in 1980 only three U.S. denominations claimed more than 10 million adherents: United Methodist (11.6 million), Southern Baptist Convention (16.3 million), and Roman Catholic (47.5 million).

Dwindling professional services for some 50 million known adherents plus an additional 12 million to 14 million occasional or unknown practitioners would be considered a critical problem in most human service organizations. We have documented that this problem exists for the U.S. Catholic church. Furthermore, it is getting worse with each passing year while membership grows and the priesthood population declines.

Assessing Decline

Our study calls attention to the need for greater accuracy in assessing the severity of growing demand, but, more important, we have provided a systematic analysis of clergy decline, the supply side of the shortage. We offer our data as the most accurate and definitive information available to document the extent, speed, components, and outcome of decline in the U.S. diocesan priesthood population. The data set describes the main thrust and variation in the losses at the national, regional, and local levels. The analysis also provides an explanation of some of the major causes of the variation across regions and dioceses.

Our data leave no doubt about the historical trends behind the decline. Between 1966 and 1984 the U.S. Catholic church witnessed a 20 percent loss in the number of active diocesan priests. These results are based on the best evidence available: official personnel records provided by participating dioceses and verified name by name with the help of diocesan officials. The 86-diocese sample represents 68 percent of the U.S. diocesan priest population. The census registry we created includes names of over 36,300 priests with 19 years of demographic information on each.

The projections to 2005 forecast continued losses, leading to a total de-

---

2. Personal communication with Ruth Doyle of the Archdiocese of New York research office, Nov. 20, 1989.

cline of 40 percent of the 1966 number of active diocesan priests. To assess their accuracy we tested the projections with new data from 12 dioceses, a subsample of the 86 that represents 19 percent of U.S. diocesan priests. We discovered that the historical trends during the additional four years (1985–88) were only 2 percent higher than our moderate projection. The test strongly corroborates the short-run accuracy of the projections.

The sobering message of our research is that declining numbers of U.S. Catholic priests are virtually unavoidable, at least over the next decade or two. The inevitability of the downward trend is not based on overly pessimistic assumptions about future ordination and resignation trends. The demographics show that rapid aging is becoming the force for decline at the turn of the century. As older age groups grow in size, any conceivable increase in ordinations or decrease in resignations will do little to stem the effects of large numbers exiting the active priesthood through retirement and death. For example, even if ordinations were to increase by 25 percent — while other entrances and all exits occur as forecasted by our moderate assumptions — the decline in the priesthood population between 1966 and 2005 would still be 34 percent.

Thus, while the Catholic lay population will probably grow more than 65 percent between 1966 and 2005, the priesthood population will decline 40 percent in the same period (table 12.5 and table 2.1). This knowledge is eminently practical as church leaders face the growing dilemma of full pews and empty altars.[3]

Shortage as Theoretical Problem

Inasmuch as anyone can count noses, most people understand statistics on population growth and decline. In this sense demographic data have

3. We contend that our estimates of national parameters for the U.S. diocesan priesthood population are the most reliable ones currently available. Nevertheless, we also want to remind readers of the margin of error in some of our estimates of regional parameters. Given large sample sizes, however, margins of error are small enough to ignore in all but the East South and Mountain regions. Some of our estimates may differ from other statistics that are based on the full population in the East South and Mountain regions because of the smaller number of dioceses in our sample from those areas. We expect the differences to be minimal and note further that, for the most part, our regional data are likewise the best available.

In our sample, which was originally drawn using data for 1968, the East South (combining the South Atlantic and East Southcentral regions) is represented by 6 out of 20 dioceses (30 percent) and by 964 out of 2,972 diocesan priests (32 percent), and the Mountain region by 5 out of 11 dioceses (45 percent) and by 471 out of 1,171 diocesan priests (40 percent). Even these are proportionately large samples by most standards, so the margins of error should be relatively small.

"a voice of their own." Even demographic reports, however, contain hidden messages. The truth of the matter is that the full impact of any data set cannot be felt or understood outside a theoretical framework.

Therefore, the priest shortage is not just a practical problem but a theoretical one as well. Ideally, theory construction involves deducing hypotheses from logical propositions and testing them against rival hypotheses with empirical evidence in controlled settings. We endorse this type of theorizing — when it is appropriate for the task at hand. But we have set out to tell a complex story about critical demographic trends. This calls for other priorities. A sociological story can be successful in two ways: by satisfactorily explaining a complex chain of unique events, or by developing a generalizable theory that explains a repeatable pattern of events. The two approaches are interrelated, although usually pursued sequentially.

Our overriding concern has been to document one key element in the complex process generating social change in the Catholic church. Nevertheless, for part of the story we draw on available theory to help explain the causes, concomitants, and consequences of the degeneration process. Theory development in the strict sense, however, is a secondary goal. Obviously, we think this is an important set of data that cries out for a fuller theoretical and historical treatment than we can provide here.

In addressing the priest shortage as a theoretical problem we pose two limited questions: How does organization theory and research help explain the priest shortage? And how does our study contribute to that literature? The response to these questions becomes part of the dialogue necessary for theory development in the strict sense.

For organization theorists, shortage in human resources is a perennial issue. Simply put, it is the problem of change in organization size. Changing size, along with its causes and consequences, is one of the oldest and most extensively researched topics in organization science. Our study addresses the perennial problem with a novel approach — that of organization demography and the population perspective.

Organization demography (Pfeffer 1983) as a newly emerging subdiscipline is best subsumed under the population perspective (Hannan and Freeman 1989; Carroll 1988). Together these theoretical frameworks represent a new and powerful approach to an old question (McKelvey and Aldrich 1983): Why do organizations and populations of organizations grow, remain stable, or decline? We place the population perspective, broadly conceived, at the center of our theoretical framework, because it embodies a comprehensive approach which builds solidly on other major works in the field. As Aldrich (1979, p. 2) notes, an aim of the population approach is "to show that the literature on organizations can be recast into an organization-environment framework that brings together research on internal organization structure *and* organizational environments."

Two areas in organization science have been of particular interest to us: (1) the extensive investigations of the relationship between organization size and structural change, and (2) a more recent and smaller set of studies focused specifically on organizations in decline. The research on these topics helps place the priest shortage in a useful theoretical background. Furthermore, explaining the demographic transition of the clergy within this background helps recast these earlier studies and our research in an organization demography mold and thus within the broader population perspective.

Organization Size and Social Change

Changing size as an antecedent or concomitant of other forms of social change is one of the most widely discussed and documented relationships in organizational sociology (Pugh et al. 1963, 1968; Aiken and Hage 1968; Klatzky 1970; Blau and Schoenherr 1971; Meyer 1972; Blau 1977). Kimberly (1976) diagnosed the conceptualization of size in most organization studies as too atheoretical and, for the most part, his criticism is correct. On the other hand, the sheer number of participants in a social system and its subunits — the general definition of size adopted in most studies — has been analyzed in theoretical detail by classical writers, notably Simmel (1950) and, most recently, Blau (1977). From another viewpoint, Hirschman (1970) and Zald (1970) have paid theoretical attention to the number of organizational members in conceptualizing them as human resources, that is, as part of the economy subsystem of an organization.

We find these conceptions of size complementary to that employed in demographic studies, where change in the size of a population is analyzed in terms of its consequences for changing the population's structure. Following Keyfitz (1973), Matras (1975) demonstrates the usefulness of the demographic approach for organization studies. He shows that organizational transformation, like population transformation in general, is a process whose net effect is to alter an organization's size and compositional structure over time.

The sustained interest in organization size, evident in recent editions of popular textbooks on organizational sociology (Hall 1987; Scott 1992), is advanced by its integration in the population perspective. According to its chief proponents, the overriding concerns guiding research on the evolution and population ecology of organizations are "why populations of organizations have the form that they do, how they came to have it, and why they are declining, remaining stable, or growing in size" (McKelvey and Aldrich 1983, p. 117). The question of decline, stability, or growth of the priest population has been posed in the context of these wider theoretical concerns.

A further review of the literature reveals that fluctuation in population size and alteration in composition are integral parts of many prevalent theories of social change, including Marxist analyses and others interested in historically based processes whereby purposive actors construct and reconstruct social reality. As Bottomore (1975, pp. 161–62) explains:

> One obvious source of variation in the social structure is the continued circulation of the membership. . . . By the elaboration of new ideas and values, younger generations clearly play a part in the de-structuring and restructuring of society; but they may also do so . . . by interpreting roles differently and . . . by forming new groups which engage in different types of action.

This view of the size variable emphasizes the fact that the size of a membership population fluctuates through history, thus creating compositional changes when old members exit and new ones enter the system.

The process of changing size has a structure of its own. Because growth and decline of the priesthood population are the focus of our research, we have examined in detail the structural process that generates changing size. Hernes (1976) provides a number of concepts useful for the analysis. To analyze structural models of social change, he distinguishes among output, process, and parameter structures. As he explains:

> . . . in analyzing structural change it is crucial to note that we are dealing with structures at different levels, and that these levels are interrelated in such a way that the structure at one level is the output of a process which itself has a structure. . . .
>
> Thus it seems useful to distinguish among structures at three levels. The first is the *output structure* or distribution of results, such as that given by a population pyramid. The second is a specification of the logical form of the process generating these results, which I will call a *process structure*. The simplest and most compact way of expressing a process structure is by a mathematical model or formulas which give its functional form, such as the equations for the birth and death process of a population. . . . Finally, the parameters governing the process, such as age-specific birth and death rates, take on definite values in concrete situations, and their configuration may have a certain constancy. Hence it is natural to speak of a *parameter structure*. (Hernes 1976, p. 519)

Aldrich (1979) incorporates Hernes' model into the population perspective, specifically as a tool for analyzing organizational persistence and transformation under changing environmental conditions. He argues that populations of organizations like species of biological organisms emerge, grow, and survive or fail by competing for resources in an ecological niche. Ecological or "environmental *niches* are distinct combinations of resources and other constraints that are sufficient to support an organization form" (Aldrich, 1979, p. 28).

Organizational forms evolve in cyclical stages involving variation, selection, and retention processes. Sufficient *variation* within and between organizations and across environments is the first requirement for organizational change to occur. *Selection* of new or changed forms occurs when organizations compete amidst the variety of resources and constraints of their common environment. *Retention* of certain structures and activities within an organization, which serves to reproduce or transform its basic structural elements, is a function of external environmental and internal organizational characteristics. As Aldrich (1979, p. 31) summarizes:

> Variation, selection and retention thus constitute the three stages of the organizational change process. Variation generates the raw materials from which selection, by environmental or internal criteria, is made; retention mechanisms preserve the selected form. The model can be applied to the selective retention or elimination of entire organizations or their components.

Our research questions deal not with organizational survival — although the creation and suppression of dioceses in the history of the Catholic church would be a very informative research project — but with the retention or elimination of certain internal structural components of the Catholic church at the local diocesan level.[4]

We need to clarify the definitions of organizational "form" and "population," because they are the object of confusion in the population perspective. Regarding organization form, we follow Aldrich's broad view, given above, that the natural selection "model can be applied to the selective retention or elimination of entire organizations or their components." Thus we consider not only an entire Catholic diocese an organizational form but also one of its key structural components, the male celibate priesthood, an organizational form. Indeed an entire organization, such as a

---

4. The sample frame for a study of mortality rates of dioceses is potentially very large, with the occurrence of sampling units extending over two millennia and most of the globe. The death of diocesan organizations has been relatively frequent in some periods and regions and very infrequent in others. No dioceses have been suppressed in the history of the United States, for example, but many were eliminated in North Africa after the patristic age.

diocese, changes over time only as a result of change within its component structural forms. Inclusively defined, organizational forms are "organized activity systems oriented toward exploiting the resources within a niche" (Aldrich 1979, p. 28).

Theoretical confusion also arises over different uses of the term "population." Organization demography as an analytical framework focuses on a population of members within organizations and studies how change in that population affects change in the organization's structure. Population ecology as a theoretical approach focuses on populations of organizations and studies the capacity of the whole population to survive in its present organizational form.

We use both terms, "form" and "population," in their different meanings. The diocese as unit of analysis is an organizational form competing for new priests in its ecological niche. Dioceses' inability to select and retain sufficient numbers of priests is threatening the survival of the present sociological form of the priesthood. Thus we distinguish among (1) the priesthood as a concrete organizational form, that is, a structural component of an organization, (2) the population of priests who have the necessary traits to allow the diocese to select and retain the current sociological form of priesthood, and (3) the population of dioceses that is undergoing transformation in its organizational form because the componential organizational form of the male celibate priesthood is undergoing structural change.

Following Hernes' and Aldrich's approach, to assess the extent and consequences of decline in size of the clergy population in the U.S. Catholic church, we first studied the structural components of changing size. That is, we explained how the change is generated, because the structural form of the change affects its organizational and environmental causes and consequences. So, for example, in this book we examine how historical changes in the parameter structure of the clergy population have resulted in changes in the output structure, that is, growth or decline of organizational size. We also investigate how observed changes in size may be accompanied by other critical changes in output structure, such as alterations of the composition of the clergy, particularly their age distribution. Then we analyze the individual components of the change process — each entrance and exit event — to describe and explain how and why they differed across regions and dioceses.

The Wider Theoretical Question

The broad research problem addressed in our analysis is: What processes account for the generation, persistence, or decline of organizational forms? We ignore the historical analysis of the question, that is, how the organizational form of male celibate priesthood was generated, selected, and retained in dioceses of the Western church throughout prior centuries. We focus instead on the ongoing processes that account for its continued generation, persistence, or decline. Population ecology theory identifies three mechanisms, namely, ecological, generational, and isolating processes, that explain the emergence and persistence of organizational forms.

Ecological processes are those forces *external* to organizations that produce constraints and resources which cause Catholic dioceses, for example, to adapt to them and thereby evolve forms that insure their survival. Chief among these forces are other organizations that form an organizational ecological community with Catholic dioceses. Given the large regional differences in the clergy shortage, this question arose: In South and West dioceses are new organizational forms evolving that are tapping new resources or adapting to new constraints in a new ecological community?

Generational processes are the activities of those social forces internal to the organization, such as competence elements (McKelvey 1982), that explain why a population of organizations like Catholic dioceses becomes associated with a particular pool of resources. Therefore, we asked whether certain environmental and organizational conditions are responsible for dioceses being associated with an advantageous pool of resources in the South and West, where the clergy decline is low, but not in the Northeast and Northcentral divisions, where the clergy decline is high.

Isolating processes are those that prevent competence elements from being interchanged and adopted by all organizations in an environment; unrestricted interchange and uniform adoption would remove all differences in organizational forms and make all organizations alike. Are U.S. Catholic dioceses a homogeneous population of organizations? Or do those situated in the different halves of the nation form subspecies or two distinct local populations or dioceses? Is there some traditional approach to recruitment and retention of priests deeply rooted in the two different geographic regions that isolates and separates the two subspecies? Do regional differences in the demographic transition provide evidence of loose coupling in the U.S. Catholic church?

Ecological, generational, and isolating mechanisms along with the principles of variation, selection, and retention explain the process of natural selection. Natural selection, however, occurs amidst competition. Darwin (1859) clearly recognized the "struggle for life" in the biological sphere. Similarly, according to the growing literature on the topic, successful organizational forms evolve and persist as a result of the competitive struggle among organizations (Hannan and Freeman 1977, 1989; Pfeffer and Salancik 1978; Brittain and Freeman 1980; Carroll and Delacroix 1982;

Singh 1990). Thus Catholic dioceses compete for recruits to the male celibate priesthood among a pool of young Catholic men who are also potential recruits for a wide variety of careers and life styles in the same organizational ecological community.

In a full research agenda—which extends much beyond the aim of our present study—the structural analysis of changing size would lead to a variety of theoretically related issues. Fundamentally, we are interested in whether and to what extent an observed decline in the clergy population results in organizational transformation, that is, changes in goals, technologies, or activity systems of the church (Aldrich 1979, p. 203). For us, the social demography of organizations in the population perspective includes determining the effects of population transformations for altering seemingly distant elements of the system such as the power distribution and the culture or normative structure of the organization. We were content at this point, however, to address empirically a limited but significant part of the question.

Theory Merging with Practice

Some of the practical implications of our theoretical analysis of changing size were specified in a preliminary examination of the clergy shortage (Schoenherr and Sørensen 1982). In that report the authors argued that sustained decline and aging of the priesthood population would probably lead to notable modifications in the belief structure as well as changes in the internal political economy and control structure of the diocesan church.

This earlier analysis of changing beliefs attempted to show that three aspects of changing size would cause the overall pattern of beliefs and values to reflect a retreat toward more conservative ground. As a result, the clergy would become more conservative as a group. It was hypothesized that this would occur because (1) proportionately more liberal than conservative priests were resigning, (2) younger ones were mellowing with age and responsibilities, and (3) the newly ordained were beginning to reflect the neo-conservatism of the John Paul II papacy.

The technique Schoenherr and Sørensen used to test the hypotheses was to project distributions of attitudes into the future. This method, however, cannot capture historical events that may intervene to change beliefs and values. Catholic clergy may undergo notable changes from period effects (such as the John Paul II papacy), which would warrant a more complex analysis than Schoenherr and Sørensen performed. In fact, Hoge, Shields, and Verdieck (1988) recently criticized Schoenherr and Sørensen's (1982, p. 45) conclusion that "a series of events all linked to age will result in cohorts of priests becoming progressively more conservative as they enter and move through their career cycle."

Despite the shortcomings of the early study, the 1985 data on attitudes of Catholic priests reported by Hoge, Shields, and Verdieck explicitly confirmed one of Schoenherr and Sørensen's (1982, p. 46) speculations, namely, that young neo-conservative cohorts of priests would enter the clergy population during the late 1970s and early 1980s. Indeed, Hoge and colleagues discovered that younger priests were notably more conservative in 1985 than their age-peers were in 1970. Nevertheless, their analysis showed that as clergy aged they did *not* become more conservative, at least between 1970 and 1985.

In a further reanalysis of the same data, however, Young and Schoenherr (1992) found evidence for an aging effect as groups of priests move through their career cycle. They noted that Hoge, Shields, and Verdieck had not carried their analysis far enough. The aging effect, however, could not be disaggregated into its component parts, namely, the direct effects of aging and the structural results of resignation. Limitations of the data set were such that Young and Schoenherr could not perform a complete analysis either; however, their results show that the aging process, when it includes the effects of resignation, leads to a more conservative priesthood.

The upshot of the ongoing debate, thus far, is that Catholic priests as a whole were probably *not* more conservative in 1985 than they were in 1970.[5] On the basis of the interchange, however, we now understand more clearly that changes in clerical conservatism are the combined result of at least three factors: cohort effects, aging effects, and the effects of continuous resignations. It still remains to be shown how much of the change toward conservatism is the direct effect of each individual factor and whether conservatism will decline, remain stable, or increase in the future.

New insights from the dialogue and from data presented in previous chapters lead us to conclude that the three mechanisms appear to be generating a new wave of conservatism among the Catholic clergy in the waning years of the century. Regarding the cohort effect, for example, Hoge, Shields, and Verdieck (1988) report that priests aged 26–34 in 1985 were significantly more conservative on a modern values index than those of the same age in 1970. If this trend toward neoconservatism continues as new cohorts enter and older ones leave, the cohort effect will change the belief structure of the clergy in the direction of conservatism. Furthermore, the positive effect of aging on clerical conservatism, suggested by Young and Schoenherr, will reinforce the cohort effect.

---

5. This does not necessarily disconfirm the hypothesis of growing conservatism in the U.S. priesthood. The time span was probably too short for the full effects to have occurred.

Concerning the impact of resignations, studies have shown that the selection process influencing who remains active and who resigns from the clerical ministry contributes to overall conservatism among the clergy (chapter 9). Prior research reported that, regardless of age, a decision to resign is more likely among priests with modern values and those who support changes in restrictive church regulations (such as rescinding the rule of mandatory celibacy) than among priests with traditional views who endorse the status quo (Schoenherr and Greeley 1974; Schoenherr and Pérez Vilariño 1979; Verdieck et al. 1988).

Thus, the trend toward a conservative distribution of beliefs and values caused by both cohort and aging effects would be even greater, because priests who resign are relatively more liberal than members of their own cohorts who stay in the active ministry. And as the data in chapter 9 have shown, priests have continued to resign at high to moderately high rates throughout the two and a half decades since the close of the Second Vatican Council.

This excursus into theoretical and methodological debates over consequences of changing size highlights the close connection between theory and methods, on the one hand, and practical policy-oriented research, on the other. The extent to which Catholic religious leaders as a group will hold more conservative beliefs and values at the turn of the century than they did in recent decades is a serious question in view of the growing momentum for social change in the Catholic church.

The systematic information on age cohorts and resignation statistics available in the present report provides an essential part of the data set needed for a definitive explanation of the causes and extent of clerical conservatism in the changing American church. Change in the size of an organization is rarely inconsequential, particularly when it produces sustained decline, another topic that has captured our theoretical interests.

Organizational Decline

Empirical studies of organizations in decline are relatively few but have been gaining in number and importance recently.[6] We call attention to Whetten's (1987) excellent review of the growing literature on the topic.

6. See, for example, Cyert 1978, on managing universities of decreasing size; Hannan and Freeman 1978, on internal politics of growth and decline; Levine et al. 1981, on the politics of retrenchment; Miles and Cameron 1982, on decline in the tobacco industry; Greenhalgh 1983, on organizational decline in general; the work of Whetten (1980, 1981, 1987); McKelvey 1988, on organizational decline from the population perspective; and Ludwig 1993, on decline in a religious order. The entire issue of *Organization Science* (Spring 1993) is devoted to the problem and is titled "Organizational Decline, Adaptation, and Turnaround: Current Controversies."

In his early studies of failing organizations, Whetten (1980) makes the useful distinction between organizations that are declining because of poor management ("decline as stagnation") and those that are failing because of environmental entropy ("decline as cutback").

We see dioceses as organizations in decline because the variation, selection, and retention mechanisms that assured them a relatively abundant supply of priestly resources in the past do not seem to be operating effectively in recent and perhaps future decades. Theoretically, the priest shortage could be the result of stagnation, purposive cutback, random ecological factors, or a combination of all three.[7]

The shortage of priests in contrast with growing church membership points to a lean environment in one area of the church's ecological niche, namely, the priest recruitment candidacy pool, and a rich environment in another area, the religious market favoring Catholic lay growth. Our data on organizational decline raise the question of whether the causes can be traced to variables manipulable by church policymakers or to environmental conditions outside the control of organizational actors. Whatever the full causal source of the shortage—which, as we have shown, is at least a combination of internal and environmental forces—the decline is sure to trigger continued cutbacks and alterations in the mix of religious services at the diocesan and parish levels.

In a study of responses to decline in a population of Jesuit religious organizations, Ludwig (1984, 1993) raises many theoretical issues relevant to dioceses facing priest shortages. His investigation analyzes the extent to which cutbacks and alterations in the mix of services enabled the organizations to buffer their technical core. As Thompson (1967, p. 20) demonstrated, "organizations subject to rationality norms seek to seal off their core technologies from environmental influences."

Ludwig's longitudinal data on the 10 provinces of U.S. Jesuits suggest that the technical core of their provincial organizations was maintained fairly intact despite prolonged decline in the active Jesuit population. He discovered, further, that narrow, deep cuts at the departmental level of the organization (college, parish, retreat center) may have dampened resignation rates. But similar cuts at the divisional level (sixfold mission of the

7. As an example of purposive cutback (albeit from the viewpoint of revisionist history), some church leaders state that the priest population had grown too large and that cutting the slack is producing positive effects of increasing lay participation in the ministry. For example, Rev. Eugene Hemrick of the U.S. Catholic Conference research office says, "Maybe we had too many priests in the past. There's much more relying on lay people than before, which could be a good thing. This may be why all this is happening" (quoted in Cornell 1990).

provinces) may have increased the rates of exit. Ludwig's extended analysis of how reallocation processes are linked to slack resources, members' uncertainty, tenure or age distribution, political maneuvering, and commitment to the organization provide hypotheses that would help understand organizational change in diocesan organizations while the demographic transition of the priesthood progresses.

Further Applied Research

Falling entrance and rising exit rates of the diocesan clergy affect the changing economy, or resource structure, of the church. A sure sign of an organization in the state of decline is a sagging internal economy. The steady loss resulting from resignations combined with the precipitous decline in ordinations (documented in Part Two) may be properly described as a youth drain. Not only does the sheer number of personnel constitute economic strength for service organizations like the church, but characteristics of the staff such as energy and idealism, mastery of the latest professional literature, and openness to new ideas and procedures (all of which are generally associated with youthful new members) are likewise valuable organizational resources.

With its human resources greatly reduced in size and presumably in quality, the church will undergo some drastic changes in its program priorities, which reflect how an organization cuts back and reallocates its economic resources in response to decline.[8] While the number of qualified full-time professionals dwindles, the sacramental ministry or "means of justification," which is a defining characteristic of Catholicism (Troeltsch 1960; Johnson 1957), will inevitably be curtailed. In addition, the parochial system of administration, which is not only the liturgical center of Catholic religiosity but also the organizational force behind a host of related social and community-oriented services (Fichter 1951), will necessarily change its thrust when it is manned by fewer and older clergymen.

In an extensive study utilizing a large national sample, Leege and Gremillion (1989) profiled U.S. Catholic parishes of the early 1980s, a period when the priest shortage was beginning to be noticed in some areas but not in others. Their findings show that lay leadership is extensive, generally welcomed, but not without problems. The Notre Dame Study of Catholic Parish Life, as it is called, may serve as a benchmark for future com-

---

8. Schoenherr and Simpson (1978) report the amount of time and effort spent in 1974 by U.S. dioceses on a selected set of personnel, administrative, and community or national issues and programs. The data provide a partial view of program priorities at the beginning of the demographic transition, which could be used for comparisons with new priorities as the decline progresses and continues to affect cutbacks and reallocations of manpower.

parative research when more severe cutbacks and reallocations begin to affect the political economy of the church at the parish level.

The interaction between an organization's economic and political subsystems during periods of decline brings into play the "politics of scarcity" (Pettigrew 1983). Program priorities of organizations are not rearranged solely by the forces of rational decision, as March and Olsen (1976) demonstrate with their "garbage can" model of decision making, or even by the forces of idealistic religious vision, as Wood (1981) discovered in his study of controversy over social-action programs in Protestant churches. Setting new goals and priorities is part of an organization's political process.

Reallocation of declining resources takes place among units in a shifting power equilibrium. As Salancik and Pfeffer (1974) discovered, more powerful units are able to secure more resources than less powerful units during periods of scarcity. Furthermore, as we point out below, Hirschman (1970) and Zald (1970) demonstrate that the mutual influence of the polity and economy of an organization is inextricably linked to changes in its normative structure. Systematic research is needed that spells out other implications of the interrelationships between the priest shortage and the changing economic, political, and normative structures of U.S. Catholic dioceses.

We gained further theoretical and practical insights from examining the changing balance between the supply and demand of priestly services as a demographic transition. In the next section, we assess those gains and then integrate the contributions of this viewpoint of the shortage with other major works in organization science.

Transition as Theoretical Problem

Viewing the priest shortage as a demographic transition is a new theoretical and methodological approach that helps systematize the understanding of structural change in formal organizations. The structural form of an organization is not static but dynamic, because it is always in the process of either reproducing or transforming itself. For example, to know that changing size is a dynamic process that unfolds according to a systematic pattern rationalizes and so lessens the threatening aspects of change. To our knowledge, analyzing organizational change as a demographic transition is an original and pathbreaking contribution to the field.

The conceptual and methodological tools provided by Hernes' (1976) model and by demography allow us to observe, analyze, and explain the structural process of changing size. For example, the process of change is systematized when its structure can be mapped with the formulas of a multiple increment and decrement life table. The magnitude of change can be assessed by comparing the parameter structure and outcome structure of the change process over time. These complex dynamic processes and comparisons can be simplified by summarizing them in the five stages of a demographic transition. Graphs allow the untrained observer to see the change process unfold before her or his eyes (chapter 5).

As a preliminary step toward understanding social change in organized religion, we try to demonstrate that the theory of the demographic transition and the stable population models are useful tools for organizational analysis. Trends in recruitment and attrition serve as the basis for projections depicting the stages of a dramatic population change. Our data describe the movement of a large, young, and growing population of diocesan priests through theoretically predictable phases of evolution which include, midway, a stage delineating an old declining population and, eventually, a final stage with a pyramid reflecting a small, young, and stable population. We conclude that the well-known structure of the societal demographic transition characterizes, *mutatis mutandis,* the process of population change that takes place in organizations undergoing sustained membership decline.

In his discussion of organizational persistence and transformation, Aldrich (1979) attempts to specify types of change. His typology of organizational change is based on Hernes' (1976) structural model, which identifies an output, process, and parameter structure in every change process. An organizational transition like the one we have described is different from simple reproduction or a full-scale transformation. In an organizational transition, the output structure and the parameter values change but the process structure is not altered. In simple reproduction, however, all three remain fixed, whereas in an organizational transformation the structures change at all three levels.

In our analysis of social change in the Catholic church we have discovered an organizational transition in process. We are able to document that the output structure — the size and shape of the priesthood population — is being dramatically altered over time and in a predictable pattern given certain reasonable assumptions. Likewise, the parameters of the change process — the values of the entrance and exit rates — are changing notably, with entrance rates dominating the transition during the first several decades, then exit rates becoming more prominent in later decades.

The process structure itself, however, has remained unchanged, because all entrance rates (ordination, incardination, and return from leave) and all exit rates (excardination, resignation, leave of absence, retirement, and death) continue to be the components of change in all phases of our demographic transition model. Should the defining characteristics of any of the transition events change, however—for example, if entrances were to expand from ordinations of male celibates to ordinations of celibate and married men and women—the priesthood and church would be altered significantly. In that event the change process would be labeled an organizational transformation, because the parameter and outcome structures as well as the process structure would all change.

Transition as Practical Problem

That alterations in population size and age distribution of priests follow a predictable pattern over the decades can be a very useful discovery. The pattern, which we call the demographic transition of the priesthood, is very similar to stages of transformation that have created population explosions in many areas of the world. Demographic transitions ending in overpopulation are cause for practical concern. The transformation of the Catholic clergy, however, is different from societal demographic change in that clergy populations are on a trajectory of decline rather than growth. Underpopulation, too, is a practical problem.

By applying straightforward demographic theory, we now have a working knowledge of the extent, speed, stages, and duration of a complex population transition underway in the U.S. Catholic priesthood. The graphs in chapter 5 exhibit a full range in the extent to which diocesan priest populations will undergo a demographic transition. Dioceses can be classified in descending order from Class A transitions, all of which are expected to run the full gamut of decline and aging in priest populations, to Class E, most of which are expected to decline in size but remain practically unchanged in age composition.

If the recruitment and attrition trends of the early 1980s continue unaltered, according to our theoretical model we can expect three-fourths of the dioceses in this country to reach Stage 3, the most extreme phase of the aging process, by the turn of the century. Each phase of the transition has its problems, but Stage 3 is probably the most critical, because it represents the most top-heavy, or oldest, age pyramid of all the phases. Class C priest populations may face unusual difficulties, because they are projected to stabilize in Stage 3 by the turn of the century and remain very old for as long as the moderate projection trends are operative.

In addition to clarifying how much change to expect, the analysis also provides a rough estimate of how fast the stages of the demographic transition will unfold and how long they will last. Thus, dioceses are rank ordered within each class by the speed with which their priest populations pass from Stage 1 to Stage 3 (table 5.2).

The analysis provides sufficient detail on variations in the demographic transition that make the results useful not only for further basic research in organization demography but also for policy and planning. Adapting to change is hard under any circumstances, but planning for the organizational consequences of rapid decline and aging of key personnel is exceptionally difficult.

Foreknowledge of the extent, speed, stages, and duration of a demographic transition, once there is evidence that it is underway, should enable organizational leaders to anticipate and perhaps mitigate some of its consequences. With the help of table 5.2, personnel officers in each diocese can identify the approximate year when the transition process will change the population from a young, to an aging, and then to an old pyramid. For several years in advance, they can estimate the number of priests available by age category.

Such prior information is valuable for policy and planning. For example, devising new diocesan programs, a different division of labor at the parish level, and suitable decision-making rules for successful priest–laity collaboration would be areas of concern. How to fill important administrative and pastoral vacancies as they grow in number, anticipate new promotion policies when normal channels begin to dry up, or reprogram when the politics of scarcity replace the politics of abundance may be on the agenda for planning sessions during periods of organizational decline (Pettigrew 1983; Pfeffer 1983).

Situating Related Research in the Population Perspective

Organization size, as some have argued, is basically an economic variable. But the issues of "why populations of organizations have the form that they do, how they came to have it, and why they are declining, remaining stable, or growing in size" (McKelvey and Aldrich 1983, p. 117) are much more than economic in nature. We contend that many of the causes and consequences of changing size in diocesan organizations are better understood using the population perspective, because it helps integrate several theoretical approaches.

For example, Hirschman (1970), an economist, and Zald (1970), an organization sociologist, both developed frameworks for understanding organizational change that emphasize not only economic but also political and cultural forces. We consider them next, then discuss how their insights are enriched by emphasizing the interaction between internal organizational processes and external forces in the environment, the central focus of the population perspective.

Exit, Voice, and Loyalty

Hirschman's (1970) model for explaining how declining organizations either deteriorate further or regenerate themselves is both insightful and parsimonious. In his well-known work he analyzes the relationships between three fundamental determinants of organizational change, namely, economic, political, and cultural variables. *Exit* — the rate of leaving an organization — affects the organization's internal economy, because it reduces the level of human resources. Exit, in a word, is an economic pressure for change.

Voice is the level of active participation in the political processes of the organization. As Hirschman (1970, p. 30) explains, voice is "any attempt at all to change, rather than to escape from, an objectionable state of affairs, whether through . . . petition to the management directly in charge, through appeal to a higher authority . . . , or through various types of actions and protests." Voice, therefore, represents a political pressure for change.

Loyalty is defined by Hirschman simply as "attachment to the organization." Thus, generally speaking, loyalty deters exit and activates voice. In a more complex conceptualization, however, loyalty is based on the constellation of beliefs and values defining the organization in an ideal sense. So loyalty is part of the cultural heritage or normative structure of the organization (Selznick 1957; Pettigrew 1979). Given the fact that coalitions within organizations generate competing normative ideals, the question becomes: To whose vision of the organization is the loyalty directed? Depending on one's coalitional leanings, loyalty may motivate exit or voice or both.

If Hirschman's model is correct, priests and would-be seminarians may be voting with their feet and so generating economic pressure for change. Large numbers of potential clerics and committed clergy seem to sense that the priesthood is in a state of decline. According to recent studies, the vast majority of young Catholic males in the United States declare that for them compulsory celibacy is not a meaningful eligibility requirement for priesthood (Hoge 1987). Few enter the clerical ranks and, of those who do, many leave the ministry during the early years of their career, citing compulsory celibacy as a major reason for their actions.[9]

---

9. According to Brazilian sociologist of religion Pedrinho Guareschi (personal communication, June 18, 1991), seminarians in his country are voting with their feet even before ordination. Some are "exiting" by not stepping forward for ordination, informing superiors they will delay or even refuse ordination unless the hierarchy allows married priests. They have completed training for the priesthood but prefer to practice a limited pastoral ministry as lay brothers in protest against the exclusivity of the celibate priesthood.

Demographic reality—low entrances and high exits—becomes a signal that the current organizational form of priesthood is in a state of degeneration. When church leaders become aware of the signal, they may realize that this form of exit is nothing other than the slow hemorrhaging of a valuable economic resource: the ordained priesthood. The persistence and growing awareness of exit provide pressure to regenerate the declining organization.

Further Applied Research

As Birch (1975) has pointed out, there are four options for members facing deteriorating organizational performance: (1) stay and be silent; (2) stay and be vocal; (3) exit and remain silent; and (4) exit and be vocal. Thus, for example, the reciprocal relationship between exit and voice is mediated by priests' loyalty to the church. Nowadays, however, many contested "visions" and models of the ideal church and priesthood are rampant within Catholicism (Dulles 1974). If certain members of the church and priesthood view the status quo as "an objectionable state of affairs," it is a matter of empirical research whether loyalty leads to exit or voice and whether exercising the voice option as a mechanism for reversing organizational decline is more effective within or outside the formal structures of the priesthood.

A growing social movement in the Catholic church, spearheaded by priests who have left the clerical ministry and married, would provide an excellent opportunity for analyzing the relationships between exit, voice, and loyalty. National organizations, composed mainly of Catholic priests who have resigned but still consider themselves members of the priesthood, have formed over the last two decades in more than a dozen countries. Their publicly stated aim is to foster a married clergy in the Catholic church. As an example of the interaction of exit, voice, and loyalty and their affects on social change, this movement warrants careful research.[10]

Political Economy and Organizational Power

Zald's (1970, 1981) political economy framework focuses attention on how various aspects of the organization and its environment affect the distribution of power, formation of coalitions, determination of goals, and other political processes. Although organizational politics are of primary inter-

---

10. Recently, they banded together to form a cross-national roof organization as an outcome of several international meetings—one in the shadow of the Vatican. Most of these organizations hold yearly national meetings and are becoming increasingly vocal in their local media (see, for example, *Corpus Reports,* the newsletter of the U.S. organization now in its 16th volume).

est, he identifies four broad aspects of the organization which directly affect the "interplay of power, the goals of power-wielders and productive exchange systems" (Zald 1981, p. 238). The major components of an organization's political economy are the external political and economic environments, the internal polity, and the internal economy.

The political economy approach, which is more a loose conceptual scheme than a systematic theory, helps organize an extensive literature on power, domination, and control in organizational settings. Weber's analysis of the institutionalized forms of domination in the bureaucracies of modern society informs much of this literature. His extensive studies of world religions, the interaction between culture, economy, and polity, and the institutionalization of values anticipate the theoretical foundation of middle-range models such as Hirschman's and Zald's (Weber 1963, 1978).

The recent interest in organizational culture, for example, derives from Weber's insight that institutionalized beliefs and values are a latent mechanism of control (Pettigrew 1979; Perrow 1986; see also the entire September 1983 issue of *Administrative Science Quarterly*). Organization culture defines the values of those who determine the operative goals, the legitimate use of resources, and the rewards and sanctions motivating members. The controlling aspects of culture operate from within individual members to the extent that they have internalized aspects of the organization's culture; as such, culture is a most *unobtrusive* mechanism of control (Perrow 1986). Zald speaks of culture in terms of "constitutions": "Just as nation-states and primitive societies have constitutions, so do complex organizations. . . . An organization's constitution is its fundamental normative structure . . . a set of agreements and understandings which define the limits and goals of the group (collectivity) as well as the responsibilities and rights of participants" (Zald 1981, p. 240). Organizational constitutions normatively regulate the economic and political behavior of organizations.

Central to Zald's view is that change originating in any one sector of the organization—whether in the economy, polity, or constitution—necessarily impinges on the other sectors. Our present analysis has focused primarily on the economy of the Catholic church. The priest shortage is an imbalance between supply and demand, aspects of the internal and external economy of the church. A diocese's inability to select and retain sufficient professional resources from its ecological niche is an internal economic problem. It is affected by aspects of its external economic environment, such as membership growth, the concentration of Hispanics, and the level of affluence characterizing the diocese's ecological niche (chapters 6–9).

At first glance, the problem may seem to be primarily economic but, as both Hirschman and Zald insist, the diocesan economy affects and is affected by the polity and the normative or cultural structure of the church and wider society. Schoenherr and Sørensen's (1982), Hoge, Shields, and Verdieck's (1988), and Young and Schoenherr's (1992) analyses of the impact of changing size and age distribution on the attitudinal structure of the priesthood fit this theoretical framework. Their research explains the effects of change in the organization's internal economy on its normative or constitutional structure.

Social change, therefore, is a process or, better, a chain reaction. If the church's economy and normative systems are changing, so are its internal and external polities. This brings us back to Zald's primary interest, organizational politics. Our empirical analysis ignores the church's polity, but our theoretical interests lead inevitably to the question of conflict and change in internal and external church politics — in Zald's words, the "interplay of power, the goals of power-wielders." To repeat, although we begin with one important aspect of the question — change in the organization's economy — we are interested in the distribution of power, formation of coalitions, determination of goals, and other political processes in the Catholic church (see Schoenherr forthcoming).

Conclusion

In reality, change of any type includes conflict, even when analytic models ignore its impact. These earlier studies of social change in organized religion, though cast in a political economy framework, do not explicitly treat power and conflict. Many sociologists identify the term "political economy" with Marxist analysis of social change and restrict its usage to describe societywide processes involving class conflict (Hymer 1972; Gilpin 1976; Burawoy 1990). Class conflict as a catalyst for change, however, is operative within modern organizations and not just at the societal level (Braverman 1974; Goldman and Van Houten 1977, 1981). Indeed, Weber's theory of the rise of capitalism and rational-legal bureaucracy is the story of how modern organizations became the mechanisms of domination and control in the hands of the capitalist class (McNeil 1978).

Further theoretical and empirical research is sorely needed to recast the partial models of changing size, organizational degeneration, and internal political economies in a broader theoretical mold. We believe the population perspective is a significant step in that direction. It too, however, needs to be expanded to include other issues, particularly social conflict, raised by Marxist and Weberian models of social change. Population research should focus, not only on random ecological forces as a natural selection process, but also on organizational actors and groups as participants in voluntaristic institutional operations and purposive control processes.

Hannan and Freeman's (1989) latest compilation of their theoretical and empirical efforts brings the population ecology model closer to a full sociological theory, that is to say, one that recognizes technical, legal, political, and other social processes along with the natural or organic variation-selection-retention mechanisms of social change. Perrow's (1986) designation of organizations as "tools in the hands of their masters" captures the major thrust of the Marxian and Weberian legacies. For us, Perrow's qualified power model provides an integration of the most important contributions of bureaucratic, class conflict, institutional, environmental, and political economic approaches to organizational analysis. Furthermore, the population approach is strengthened considerably by integrating it with the qualified power model.

The next step in explaining the demographic transition of the priesthood is to develop a systematic middle-range theory of social change in organized religion, the task undertaken in the companion volume to this report (Schoenherr forthcoming). In this second treatise the discussion moves beyond integrating the population approach with studies treating the impact of size on structure, organizations in decline, the exit, voice, and loyalty model of organizational regeneration, and organizational political economy. Systematic attention is given to how the demographic transition interacts with other historical forces, intervening causal conditions, and the influence of conflict and coalitional politics to effect social change in the Catholic church.

14 Understanding the Components and Consequences of Change

From the standpoint of social demography, decline in the priesthood is the outcome of the population change described in Part Two. The change process was characterized in terms of systematic stages of a demographic transition. In Part Three we gained a better understanding of the complexity of population change by examining individual components of the process. And in Part Four we are considering the consequences of change. In this chapter we evaluate our analysis of the components and consequences of change in terms of practical and theoretical gains.

Major Components of Change

Our attempt to assess theory and practice in our study uses the analogy of a balancing act. Hence we reexamine our analysis of each component of change, first as a contribution toward understanding it as a practical problem, and then as a theoretical issue. In the presentation we walk a tightrope, trying to strike a balance between the two.

Recruitment and Retention

Our analysis identifies ordination and resignation rates as the key components of the demographic transition. In the terminology of organization demography these rates reflect the primary increments and decrements governing change in the priesthood population. From the viewpoint of church executives, they represent the problem of recruitment and retention of key professional personnel.

It is not an oversimplification to understand decline in the priesthood population as primarily a crisis of poor recruitment and retention. If dioceses were able to recruit and retain priests in sufficient numbers, the other components of change — immigration, leave of absence, retirement, and death — would be of much less concern. Basically, the impact of all the other transition events are determined by the rates of ordination and resignation.

This is obvious regarding retirement and mortality. Usually, organizational stability or growth results from successful recruitment and retention of members, such that entrances balance or outweigh natural attrition. The same is true for immigration and leave of absence. Under conditions of an abundant supply of clergy, immigration and leave rates would fluctuate moderately with little strain on the organizational well-being of the church. But the long-standing persistence of poor recruitment and retention of priests is one of the gravest problems facing the contemporary Catholic church.

It is primarily because of two and a half decades of poor recruitment and retention that U.S. dioceses face a declining and aging priesthood population. While the aging process gains momentum, however, retirements and preretirement deaths will increase in importance as components of decline. The growing impact of natural attrition was only beginning to be noticed in the 1980s. Its full force will be felt at the turn of the century.

Because the demographic transition is now governed by inevitable biological forces, policymakers have little power to alter its direction, at least for the next couple decades. Improvement in recruitment and retention is the only effective antidote to a declining work force. Normally, reversing long-term trends of poor recruitment and retention is a slow and difficult process.

Recruitment as Practical Problem

Recruitment is more critical than retention. If ordination rates were high, low or even moderate resignation rates, though inefficient, would not be so worrisome. Indeed, chapter 2 demonstrates that the impact of ordination on overall decline is three to four times greater than that of the next most powerful transitions, namely, resignation and retirement. Once again, merely documenting the extent of the drop in ordinations has considerable value for evaluating the severity of the recruitment problem.

How bad is recruitment to the U.S. Catholic priesthood? We discovered that since the end of the Second Vatican Council the number of ordinations in the United States has dropped well over 20 percent per decade. During the late 1960s, recruitment to the U.S. diocesan priesthood stood at 984 ordinations per year. This figure was cut almost in half by the early 1980s, to 519 ordinations per year.

Is it possible that comparisons with the 1960s are spurious because of unusually high growth in the number of ordinations during those years? This question can be answered only by extending the comparisons over a longer period. Hoge (1987) presents data documenting stability or growth in ordinations from 1920 to the mid-1960s.

The 1950s and early 1960s saw notable growth in the number of ordinations, leading some observers to interpret the period as one of unusual expansion of the clergy supply. Consequently, the recent trend of declining ordinations reported in this book might be interpreted as a return to more normal patterns of recruitment. Such an interpretation of the data is incorrect. Hoge rightly observes that the relative stability of the layperson-to-priest ratio — the only accurate index of supply and demand — illustrates that growth in ordinations merely kept pace with growth in the number of Catholics during the 15 years preceding the Second Vatican Council.

It follows that the dynamics of recruitment during the 1950s and early 1960s were similar to the forces governing ordinations going back to at least 1920. Therefore, the steady drop in ordinations over the past 25 years is something entirely new. The recent trend deviates significantly from the norm experienced by the Catholic church during most of the prior decades of the 20th century. Furthermore, we believe low ordination rates will continue in the foreseeable future.

Our projections of continuously low ordinations are in keeping with a steep and steady decline in the number of U.S. seminarians. For example, the number of seminarians in theology studies, the last step before ordination, dropped 58 percent between 1965 and 1990. The relentless downward trend in priesthood candidates has not yet bottomed out. In fact, it has shown signs of worsening since we completed our empirical analysis.

High school seminary enrollment fell 35 percent in the last two years (1988–90), and college enrollment dropped 33 percent in the last four years (1986–90).[1] Bishop James P. Keleher, head of the Committee on Priestly Formation, warned U.S. bishops that college seminaries are facing "imminent demise," even though they are widely recognized as the "finest form" of preparation for theology studies (Filteau 1991).

In the six years prior to the 1990–91 academic year, the total number of seminarians (in high school, college, and theology studies) fell 35 percent, from 11,591 to 7,523. Given the force of these trends it is safe to conclude that, even with pronounced efforts, the steady decline in ordinations to the male celibate priesthood could not be stopped, reversed, and then the numbers increased significantly in less than two or three decades. In view of the causes for poor recruitment, it is more likely that concerted effort could not reverse the trends in less than two generations.

---

1. The source for seminarian statistics is the Center for Applied Research in the Apostolate; it was cited by the Catholic News Service in Filteau 1991.

Why are vocations to the priesthood drying up? Strong and consistent empirical evidence that comes from one of the largest series of studies on recruitment of professionals in the social sciences points to two factors. Reflecting on his comprehensive review of the literature, recently updated surveys, and his own recent contributions, Hoge (1987, p. 132) concludes that the consistent evidence over time shows "the two principal determinants of interest in vocations remain . . . the encouragement factor and the deterrence of celibacy." He continues: "Most important: the shortage of vocations is not a temporary thing which is self-correcting or a short-term low point in a cyclical pattern. It is a long-term situation with no end in sight. No large increases in the number of seminarians can be expected, even if recruitment efforts are expanded and improved" (Hoge 1987, p. 119). Hoge's pessimism about the chronic nature of poor recruitment stems largely from consistent findings about the negative impact of mandatory celibacy.[2] This complicated issue receives further attention in a related attempt to develop a model of social change in organized religion (Schoenherr forthcoming).

Retention as Practical Problem
Poor retention also has serious consequences for the church. As we demonstrated in chapter 9, recruitment and retention are two sides of the same coin. Our data show that, along with dismal recruitment trends, moderately high resignation rates continue to plague U.S. dioceses. Currently, each year 35–40 percent of the newly ordained priests are needed to fill vacancies created by priests who resign. Improving recruitment is very difficult in the face of such poor retention.

Although the overall record is poor, retention has improved notably since the "mass exodus" years (1968–74), when resignation losses reduced ordination gains by 75 percent annually. Despite the improvement, however, resignees continue to leave the active ministry in moderately high numbers relative to those being ordained.

Our interpretation that resignations have bottomed out at a moderately high level since the Second Vatican Council is based on comparisons with the extremely high rates of the mass exodus years and the low numbers reported earlier by Fichter (1968). According to his data, resignation rates averaged approximately 0.1 percent annually for the 25 years prior to the council. Annual rates are currently at 0.65 resignees per 100 active priests, or six times higher than during preconciliar decades.

2. For his review of that literature see Hoge 1987.

Diocesan officials ought not to overlook significant improvements in the retention record since resignations peaked in the early 1970s. More important, however, they should be well aware that poor retention has been a persistent problem for the entire 25-year period following the Second Vatican Council. All the studies conclude that the major reasons why young priests resign are adherence to modern values and problems with loneliness and celibacy. Additionally, the data show that the impact of these same causal conditions has persisted for 15 years. Given all this evidence, we conclude that, along with continued low ordinations, moderately high resignations will most likely continue in the foreseeable future.

Recruitment as Theoretical Problem
We approach recruitment as a substantive issue from a strictly limited focus. The questions raised are posed within the theoretical framework of organization demography and the population approach. Though restricted to organizational and ecological variables, the causal model explaining differences in ordination rates across dioceses is powerful, accounting for well over half the variance. The analysis reveals that ordination rates tend to be lowest where concentrations of Hispanics are highest. Also, younger dioceses have higher rates than older ones, all other things being equal. The second finding has theoretical implications regarding the assets and liabilities of newness.

Stinchcombe's (1965) celebrated insight about the liabilities of newness is modified by our analysis. In support of his hypothesis, recent studies have shown that new organizations are subject to higher risks of dying, so that organizational mortality decreases with age (Freeman et al. 1983). In Catholic dioceses, however, newness is an asset, not a liability, because it raises recruitment rates, helping to insure survival. Newly established dioceses may reflect Hannan and Freeman's (1984) findings that structural inertia is less operative in newer than in older organizations. Perhaps younger dioceses enjoy the structural leeway to develop administrations that "grow information-processing and decision-making structures toward the source of information about the critical uncertainties of their work" (Stinchcombe 1990, pp. 339–40).

In the last few decades, recruiting priests has become a major source of uncertainty for the Catholic church as a whole. But finding sufficient human resources in an unknown and uncertain ecological niche is the primary problem of all new organizations. Recruitment success is a life or death struggle for new dioceses. So they seem to develop structures that exploit the "source of information about the critical uncertainties" they face. If Stinchcombe's recent hypothesis is correct for religious organizations, new dioceses probably have better information-processing structures than older ones, so are more successful in their recruitment efforts.

We also did a related analysis of recruitment effectiveness, measured by the number of young Catholic males it takes to yield one ordained priest. The causal model shows that the proportion of Hispanics, the proportion of Catholics, and Catholic membership growth all have the net positive effect of increasing the size of the candidacy pool relative to the number of ordinations and thus making a diocese less effective in recruiting priests.

These results corroborate the findings of a growing body of literature on the performance of monopoly versus minority organizations (Hirschman 1970; Westhues 1971; Seidler 1979; Seidler and Meyer 1989; Stark and McCann 1989; Iannaccone 1990). The more a Catholic diocese is in a minority situation and is growing slowly, the more effective it is in recruiting priests. Dioceses where the Catholic population is a majority perform like Hirschman's "lazy monopoly," that is, with ineffective recruitment. Our data provide further empirical evidence for the weakness of monopoly churches.

High proportions of Hispanics have the consistent effect of dampening recruitment, whether it is measured by ordination rates or by the relative size of the candidacy pool. These results raise more questions than they answer. They are consistent with Hemrick and Hoge's (1986) data showing that Hispanics are underrepresented in U.S. seminaries. But our limited analysis begs the question of why proportionately larger Hispanic populations in a diocese's ecological niche lowers recruitment results there. Is it because of the traditional way Hispanic men view the priesthood? Or is it perhaps because the church does not aggressively approach or adequately adapt itself to young bicultural Hispanic males who might be interested in ordination? These and the related issues of the assets of newness and the greater success of minority in comparison to majority churches need to be explored in further research on recruitment effectiveness.

Retention as Theoretical Problem
Resignation rates were likewise subjected to regression analysis to determine the influence of organizational and environmental variables on retention. We discovered that resignations are higher in urban areas and where religious order priests are concentrated, and are lower where Catholic church membership is growing rapidly. The findings raise some interesting speculations.

We wonder whether urbanism, staffing patterns, and client growth act as an "invisible hand" to balance the forces of supply and demand. Perhaps client concentration in urban areas, which makes delivery of religious services more efficient, and a relatively large staff of religious order priests, who can provide the Mass and sacraments, combine to increase the availability of priestly services. Under these conditions resignations of diocesan priests is high. In contrast, when rapid membership growth increases demand, clergymen are less likely to leave the active ministry.

This combination of conditions and effects tends to make the best of a bad situation by keeping as optimal a balance of supply and demand as possible during a period of decline. Admittedly, explanations appealing to blind forces are opposed to social theories based on purposive action assumptions. The population approach, however, allows us to raise the question of how much organizational change is due to random forces and blind chance and how much stems from the purposive behavior of organizational actors. The data needed to answer these questions for Catholic dioceses are not yet available.

We have also examined related research to determine whether the social forces affecting resignations have been consistent over time. We find remarkable stability at the environmental, organizational, and social psychological levels of behavior. Seidler and Meyer (1989) discovered that the same environmental and structural conditions explained variation in resignation rates in 1970 as those we find operative in our 1980 data. Similarly, Verdieck and colleagues (1988) demonstrated that the social psychological process leading to the decision to resign in 1985 was practically the same as that discovered by Schoenherr and Greeley (1974) for 1970.

In brief, a stable multilevel set of forces has produced and will probably continue to produce moderately high levels of resignation from the active priesthood. At the individual level, priests who endorse modern values, find loneliness a problem, and prefer marriage over celibacy will tend to resign in years to come just as confreres like them have resigned ever since the end of the Second Vatican Council. At the organizational and environmental levels, future resignation rates — like those in the past — will tend to be higher in urban areas and in dioceses with relatively large concentrations of religious order priests, and rates will tend to be lower where the Catholic lay population is growing relatively fast.

We wish to underscore several related facts. Ordinations have been declining steadily for 25 years. Resignations have been alarmingly high or moderately high over the same period. Compulsory celibacy has had a persistent negative impact on both recruitment and retention during the same two and a half decades. Our data and analysis have succeeded in laying bare and explaining some of the relationships among these facts. Undoubtedly, they add up to a practical and theoretical problem of great proportions.

Immigration

Net immigration, or the excess of incardinations over excardinations, is a minor component of population change in comparison to ordinations and resignations. Nevertheless, it plays a major role in the demographic transition of Catholic clergy in some regions and dioceses of the United States. We uncovered some surprising features of priestly migration patterns in a combination of descriptive and causal analyses. The findings have both practical and theoretical implications.

Practical Problem

We have discovered that net immigration is moderate to high in half of the United States and low to almost nonexistent in the other half. During the census period, the cumulative gain from surplus incardinations ranged from 9 percent to 17 percent in the South and West compared with a range from 0.5 percent to 2.5 percent in the Northeast and Northcentral divisions.

Gross regional differences in patterns of incardinations prompted us to reexamine our population projections, controlling for net immigration. We have removed the effects of surplus incardinations to concentrate on a diocese's ability to recruit and retain its own native clergy. We discover, first, that the drop in native clergy between 1966 and 2005 would be 45 percent of the 1966 active U.S. priesthood population, a decline which is notably larger than the 40 percent decline projected for the combined native and incardinated populations. Second, we find that when gains from surplus incardinations are removed, South and West dioceses are suffering serious decline, just like other dioceses in the rest of the nation.

The highest gains from excess incardinations are realized in the West Southcentral region and along the Pacific Coast, areas with the heaviest concentrations of Hispanics and the fastest growth in the Catholic population. Raising the level of incardinations is one answer to population shifts and the subsequent growing demand for priestly services. But where do the incardinations come from? The only sources are other dioceses and religious orders, whether in the United States or foreign countries. These sources, however, are finite and shrinking. In the United States the priesthood population in religious orders is declining faster than in some dioceses (Shields and Verdieck 1985). Likewise, attracting priests from foreign countries can be only a short-term solution, because the priest shortage is a growing worldwide problem (figure 1.1).

In view of the pervasive decline, national bishops' conferences are negotiating guidelines for balancing the flow of incardinations and excardinations across international borders. When U.S. dioceses continuously incardinate priests from Africa and Latin America, for instance, it raises problems of equity or even parasitic behavior. On these populous continents, where there are only 2.4 and 1.4 priests per every 10,000 Catholics, Mass and other priestly services are rare events.

Should Catholic communities in the United States further drain the life out of the eucharistic tradition in these already deprived areas? Yet what is a U.S. Catholic community to do in the face of its own dwindling supply and growing demand, especially if foreign priests are eager to join the diocese permanently through incardination? This is a genuine dilemma that is particularly acute in West Southcentral and Pacific Coast dioceses.

Theoretical Problem

We examine local diocesan differences in net immigration rates against the theoretical background of the population approach. The narrowly focused causal model allows us to explain almost half the variation in terms of organizational and ecological conditions. We find that when holding all other conditions constant, the higher the parishioner-to-priest ratio and the growth in the Catholic population, the higher the net immigration rate. Also the newer the diocese, the higher the rate. But the higher the percentage of Catholics, the percentage of African Americans, the recruitment ineffectiveness, and the ordination rate in a diocese, the lower the level of net incardinations.

The most powerful explanatory conditions in the model reflect the forces of supply and demand. Priests tend to migrate to where the shortage is the greatest, namely, where dioceses are growing relatively fast and have high parishioner-to-priest ratios. Both conditions raise the demand for priestly services. Additionally, where ordination rates are low and thus not capable of replenishing the supply of priests, net incardinations are also high. Net immigration, therefore, is basically a rational adjustment that increases supply where it is shortest.

The relationship between net immigration rates and recruitment ineffectiveness, measured by the size of the candidacy pool relative to the number of ordinations, creates constraints against improving the balance of supply and demand. The net impact of recruitment ineffectiveness is to lower priestly immigration. Dioceses with that combination of traits are twice afflicted. They need a relatively large candidacy pool per ordination, and they have low incardination rates. Perhaps such dioceses are unattractive to young men who might aspire to be priests as well as to priests looking for a new community in which to practice their ministry. Thus, although migrating priests settle in relatively large numbers in dioceses with high Catholic population growth, high parishioner-to-priest ratios, and low ordination rates, even more would come if the conditions producing recruitment effectiveness were also present.

The negative relationship between a high concentration of Catholics and net incardination rates is another indication of the weakness of monopoly churches. As noted above, monopoly conditions lower diocesan ordination rates. In areas where Catholics are a minority, dioceses try harder to survive by raising not only their ordination rates but also their incardination rates. Likewise, newness is a double asset for increasing the supply of priestly services. The younger the diocese the higher both the ordination and net incardination rates.

We have no further explanation for the negative impact of the percentage of African Americans on net immigration of priests other than the observation that African Americans are located disproportionately in areas lacking resources that enhance the quality of life (Wilson 1987). We speculate that dioceses with poor living conditions attract migrating priests in relatively low numbers, but we would need to test the hypothesis with more appropriate data.

Natural Attrition: Retirement and Mortality

As a component of demographic change, natural attrition is easiest to understand and predict. Retirement and mortality are tied to biological processes and can be determined with considerable accuracy by actuarial projection techniques. The study uncovers some practical facts and raises some theoretical issues about natural attrition.

Practical Problem

In young growing organizations, entry-level recruitment, horizontal transfer, and retention are the most powerful forces governing population change. In old declining organizations, retirement and mortality dominate the change process. From the mid-1960s to the early 1980s ordination and incardination rates along with resignation rates, which reflect the diocese's ability to retain the personnel it recruits, told most of the story of the transition from a young growing population to an old aging one. But during the final two decades and into the turn of the century, mounting retirement and mortality rates dramatize the inevitability that the priesthood population will continue to decline and age.

The study deals with a practical issue facing aging organizations: How many person-years of service are gained by extending the age at retirement?

According to the data, in 1980–84 the average age at retirement was 69.0, and average age at death, 73.8. So eliminating retirement altogether would add almost five years to the average career span.

Completely suspending retirement is most unlikely, but postponing it a few years is an obvious mechanism for achieving a small increment in manpower. By examining the relationship between the rates, however, we find that attrition stemming from retirement and death among active priests is hard to manipulate through organizational policy. Postponing the age of retirement results in a short-term gain. But soon after the age is increased, approximately the same overall rate of total attrition occurs, because death rates among active priests increase accordingly.

In certain situations, such as those we find in dioceses in the West North-central region, raising retirement age to expand years of service has longer-lasting effects. To achieve the effects, however, the aging population must be enjoying exceptionally favorable mortality rates, a combination that is rare in our sample of dioceses.

Providing accurate mortality statistics on U.S. priests is a unique con-tribution of this study. To our knowledge these data are available for the first time. We have learned, for example, that the average life expectancy of priests increased by more than three years during the census period. It rose from 72.0 in 1966 to 75.4 in 1984.

Theoretical Problem

A rapidly aging population creates a growing imbalance in the age distri-bution. Older cohorts looking forward to retirement are less likely to seek ways to innovate, improve, or expand programs. New recruits in large young cohorts are a mechanism for incorporation of diversity or variation from the environment (Aldrich 1979). When the weight of the clergy population shifts from predominantly young to predominantly old members, the dio-cese is gradually shutting itself off from diversity and, therefore, from rele-vance in its environment.

Organizations exert pressures that encourage internal stability and har-mony. "Thus any social organization tends to move in the direction of in-ternal compatibility, independently of increased external adaptiveness," as Campbell (1969, p. 76) notes. Dioceses with large aging cohorts who are readying themselves for retirement are organizations seeking internal har-mony and stability, a situation that calls for minimal exertion of energy. Under these conditions, dioceses are protected from the environment and so may be moving away from external relevance to become so-called ossi-fied organizations.

Regarding mortality differentials, we discover that age-specific death rates of priests are consistently lower than those of U.S. white males. But the relative advantage of priests over U.S. white males diminishes with age. Indeed, the oldest priests — those 65–74 — experience higher mortality rates than the national average. Comparisons with age groups standardized for education, occupation, and income reveal, not surprisingly, that priests enjoy lower mortality risks largely because they are highly educated professionals. At the same time, however, we discover that priests have higher mortality risks than are expected given their education and occupation.

Priests experience much lower mortality rates than U.S. white males who are unmarried. Data are not available, however, to control for the influence of education, income, and occupation while comparing the net effect of marital status. The advantage enjoyed by celibate priests may also be due to their professional status, education, and income, which are higher than the general population of unmarried U.S. white males. The analysis produces several important findings about priest mortality. Many questions, however, must remain unanswered until more extensive data are available, permitting multivariate comparisons.

Consequences of the Demographic Transition

While the priest shortage unfolds according to predictable stages of the demographic transition, certain concomitants and consequences are inevitable, some highly probable and others more or less likely (see Hoge 1987; Schoenherr forthcoming). Because our primary aim is to analyze the structure and extent of demographic change, we have limited our empirical investigation of its concomitants and consequences to two issues. The first, the problem of low replacement rates, is inevitable. Indeed, poor replacement is as much a gauge defining organizational decline as a problem that inescapably accompanies it.

The second issue, expanding parishioner-to-priest ratios, is likewise unavoidable given the countervailing demographic trends documented in this report. The contraction of the priest supply and expansion of the laity's demand for priestly services are captured by increases in the number of parishioners to be served by each active priest. The practical questions we will yet examine are: How bad are the inevitable consequences? And how likely is the projected severity? Research that acknowledges the interaction of theory and practice cannot avoid a discussion of their mutual applications. So this section also includes some speculation about organizational drift and myopia, other highly probable consequences of the demographic transition.

The average U.S. diocese faces a 60 percent replacement rate of its native clergy. That is to say, for every 10 priests lost by resignation, sick leave, retirement, or death, only 6 are being replaced by ordination. Put the other way around, 4 out of 10 vacant positions are going unfilled every year in dioceses that rely on native clergy. Annual net losses (entrances minus exits) will fluctuate between 300 and 400 between 1985 and 2005. So replacement will continue to be a severe problem through the turn of the century.

To complete the analysis we examine the growing imbalance between supply and demand by including religious order priests in the calculations. Though many are not directly involved with pastoral ministry, religious priests regularly celebrate Mass, making that uniquely priestly service available to the laity. According to the data presented here, steady growth in church membership and precipitous decline in the diocesan and religious clergy are practically inevitable. Consequently, it is highly probable that the layperson-to-priest ratio in the United States will double in size from 1,100 Catholics per active priest in 1975 to 2,200 in 2005. This is a conservative estimate. The figures do not take into account the effects of rapid growth in the Catholic Hispanic population, which is increasing five times faster than the general population.

We suggest the modified Sherry Index as a gauge of the severity of the priest deficit. If the Catholic church wants to maintain the same level of sacramental service in 2005 as was available in 1975, the average diocese will need twice as many priests in 2005 as we forecast in the moderate projection series. That's a deficit rate of 100 percent. In terms of absolute numbers, the church will be facing a deficit of some 33,400 active diocesan and religious priests when the new century dawns.

Combining Theory and Practice

Orchestrating organizational change with foreknowledge and planning is the exception in the world of complex organizations. Organizational drift and myopia are more commonly the rule. For example, here are some facts uncovered by our analysis:

> — The three most important environmental conditions affecting variation in the U.S. priest shortage are Catholic population growth, Hispanic population size, and priestly migrations.
>
> — Differences in parishioner-to-priest ratios reveal that dioceses in areas of the country with the least decline in the priesthood population, namely, the South and West, suffer from as bad a priest shortage or worse than dioceses in the Northeast and Northcentral divisions, where the clergy decline is greatest in absolute numbers. Texas and California, for example, have the worst priest shortages of any areas in the

country. The average diocese in these states is characterized
by the highest parishioner-to-priest ratios and highest net incardination rates recorded. They are also among those dioceses with the highest percentage of Hispanics and the highest percentage of Catholic growth.

— East Coast dioceses[3] are the most advantaged in the country
in that they suffer the least strain from the priest shortage.

What do these facts say, if anything, about organizational change, drift,
or myopia in the Catholic church?

The timing of organizational change is critical. If an organization begins to sense degeneration and discovers that conditions in its ecological
niche are just beginning to change, a reasonable reaction is to take a wait-
and-see approach. Perhaps the organization can weather the decline. If
organizational leaders discover that change in the niche is far advanced
and probably irreversible, however, immediate action is necessary. Not
transforming the core technology and/or internal political economy of the
organization may result in drift into a societal backwater or even extinction.

The story of Facit AB is an instructive example of organizational drift,
myopia, and irreversible degeneration instead of transformative change.
In his analysis of organizations in crisis, Starbuck (1983) describes how
Facit lost its unrivaled first place in the international calculating machine
market in a relatively short time. By ignoring the electronics revolution,
which was transforming its ecological niche, and insisting on maintaining
the status quo, top managers allowed the organization to go beyond the
point of no return. They were never able to recover from the rapid degeneration process.

Starbuck warns that although older, larger, and bureaucratically complex organizations are more likely to survive, nevertheless "even elderly
organizations are far from immortal" (1983, p. 101). Studies of organizational mortality cited earlier bolster the warning. Death rates are higher
among newer organizations, but older organizations also die. Nonetheless, we contend that the demographic transition at work in the church
will most likely lead not to its demise but rather to some kind of regeneration and structural transformation. Thus, implicit in our argument is a
further assumption that the Roman Catholic church, though a "lazy monopoly" (Hirschman 1970; Seidler 1979), is still a robust and flexible
organization. It has sufficient slack to react positively to the extended decline in human resources it will most likely experience.

Although extinction is improbable, drift and myopia are not. Dioceses

---

3. Those in the Middle Atlantic and East South regions.

in the West Southcentral and Pacific Coast regions, for example, could ignore or minimize the decline, even though they suffer from the worst priest deficits in the nation. Leaders could shortsightedly look at only the absolute figures and discover that their active priesthood populations are not declining nearly as much as those in the rest of country. Indeed, in some dioceses the clergy roster is actually growing. They may conclude, "The priest shortage is not our problem!"

This conclusion is myopic, because — as the list of facts reveals — environmental conditions mask the true nature of the decline. Because of rapid growth in the Catholic population and the high concentration of Hispanics, West Southcentral and Pacific Coast dioceses actually suffer from the highest parishioner-to-priest ratios in the country. In terms of supply and demand the shortage is worse there than elsewhere.

Officials may be further blinded from the facts by heavy reliance on the short-term solution of surplus incardinations. For when the shortage is couched in terms of ability to recruit and retain an adequate supply of native clergy, again, it is worse in the incardination-rich dioceses of the West Southcentral and Pacific Coast regions than anywhere else.

Another blind spot might be created by basing the prognosis for the future on increases in the absolute number of ordinations while ignoring the complex causality governing changes in recruitment rates. One reason for higher ordination rates may be better recruitment techniques, but another, as our data have shown, is growth in the size of the candidacy pool. If the number of young Catholic males were increasing rapidly in an area, the diocese would inevitably increase its number of ordinations just by maintaining its accustomed level of recruitment effectiveness. Even if recruitment efforts were improved, without carefully controlled comparisons it is impossible to know whether higher numbers of ordinations would be the result of better recruitment techniques, growth in the size of the candidacy pool, or a combination of both.

The Archdiocese of Los Angeles, for example, recently denied that it faces a serious priest shortage (Mahony 1990). Yet, our data show that Los Angeles not only has the worst recruitment effectiveness score but also is one of the fastest growing dioceses with the highest parishioner-to-priest ratio and concentration of Hispanics in the sample. Archbishop Roger Cardinal Mahony, ordinary of the archdiocese, bases this denial on the hope of rising ordinations, which, he claims, will result from improved recruitment efforts.[4]

---

4. Among them he lists greater faith, prayer, and sacrifice as well as more sophisticated vocation program efforts. In criticizing our projections he compares his much higher forecast

The insidious nature of organizational myopia is highlighted by this example. Higher numbers of ordinations in Los Angeles are practically inevitable for two reasons. First, the candidacy pool is growing in size, and, all other things being equal, a larger candidacy pool yields more ordinations. Second, the poorer the record, the easier it is to improve. Because the recruitment record in Los Angeles is the poorest in the sample, there is nowhere to go but up, so improvement should be relatively easy. An important lesson for Los Angeles and similar dioceses is that it may be disastrous to celebrate an inevitable improvement when the rejoicing becomes a distraction from the real forces at work, which are leading to degeneration.

At the other extreme, organizational myopia could also afflict dioceses where the priest shortage is considered to be least advanced once organizational and environmental forces are taken into account. Our findings reveal, for example, that Middle Atlantic and East South dioceses suffered the lowest decline in terms of standardized losses. Additionally, many dioceses in these regions had the lowest and none had above average standardized parishioner-to-priest ratios.

In this case, knowing that environmental forces account for local differences in the shortage could lead church leaders to conclude falsely that the East Coast has been spared the effects of decline and aging of the priesthood. The truth is, dioceses of the Northeast division are suffering the greatest losses in the country. Environmental conditions explain why, but understanding their impact does not alter the situation.

This form of misunderstanding might exacerbate the subtle forms of regional cleavages in the political processes of the U.S. Catholic church. In discussing geographic differences in the shortage, Hoge (1987, pp. 7–8) writes: "One frustrated bishop offered a revealing explanation of why the U.S. bishops have not been more aggressive in searching for alternatives in coping with the priest shortage: 'Nothing will happen until the Eastern seaboard dioceses begin to feel the crunch.'"[5]

The overall trends of the demographic transition are plain to see from the data in this report. There is no guarantee, however, that policymakers will take the time to read and understand the general thrust of the transition or the variations in regional and environmental conditions that affect

---

of future ordinations with ours. Unfortunately, he bases the comparison on the wrong figures taken from the second respondent report (the number of ordinations standardized for rising age at ordination; see Schoenherr 1988). Using the correct figures, his optimistic estimate of future ordinations in Los Angeles falls between our moderate and optimistic projections.

5. The bishop's quote is cited by Wilson (1986, p. 450).

it. Case studies of organizations in decline lead us to believe many will not. This body of research teaches us that, normally, organizations seek solutions to problems from among their stock of tried-and-true procedures and programs (Starbuck et al. 1978; Starbuck 1983). The studies show that organizations act unreflectively and nonadaptively most of the time. Especially during times of stress it is reassuring to turn to programs and procedures that offer some relief but "require no information-bearing stimuli because they are activated through job assignments, clocks and calendars" (Starbuck 1983, p. 93). The usual solutions, therefore, are to keep doing the things an organization knows how to do. These are often stopgap remedies.

For example, increasing the local priest supply through more incardinations is a ready-made, though short-term and probably short-sighted, solution to a long-term, pervasive recruitment and retention problem. Beefing up vocation programs and prayer efforts is also part of the stock approach to sagging priestly recruitment. Such efforts can appear to be successful even though increased vocations may result as much or more from population shifts as from the tried-and-true approaches. Even new insights, such as those provided by this study, may be used to further regional rivalry and struggles for domination that are also part of the traditional approach to handling threatening problems. And postponing retirement is another handy stopgap solution. It works by the calendar and requires no change in the status quo — but produces minimal gain and exacerbates drift and myopia.

Conclusion

Indeed, the timing of social change is critical. Has the hour come for seizing new alternatives to cope with the priest shortage, or should policymakers continue to wait? Taking the wait-and-see attitude is the usual approach. It is strongly reinforced by structural inertia (Hannan and Freeman 1989), the general nonadaptability of organizations (Starbuck 1983), and what we call organizational myopia. The probable consequences of inaction or support of the status quo are further drift and degeneration.

The contribution of applied theoretically based research is to shed light on the kinds of change processes at work and their likely causes, concomitants, and consequences. It is for recognized organizational leaders to decide upon solutions to stem the decline and for informal leaders to apply pressure for change in the direction of their values.

15 Advances in Theory and Practice

We have evaluated the practical and theoretical knowledge gained in the study by weighing the contributions of each part of this report. In the concluding chapter we wish to assess the more general advancements in theory and practice for the newly emerging fields of organization demography, for policymakers and other church leaders, for organization science, and for those who believe in the grace of God.

For Organization Demography

We think the main contribution of this book is the documentation of historical trends and presentation of population projections delineating priest decline in the late 20th-century American Catholic church. In many ways this contribution stands on its own, for demographic data have a voice of their own as few other kinds of data do. Demographic data, however, often have highly contested policy implications, and information on priest populations is no exception. Therefore, we also situate the analysis in a framework of applied theoretical research.

Mapping the contours of demographic transitions in organizations is a first step toward explaining the causes and consequences of historical events that may be transforming organizations unbeknownst to their members. So, for example, social forces that are creating other sorts of structural transformation in diocesan organizations may be indistinguishable from mechanisms creating decline and aging of the clergy population. Sorting out conditions that cause social change from those that are its consequences and determining precisely how one condition affects another in the causal process belong to the collective work of social science. Analyzing population change has always been a part of that serious business.

While we use straightforward demographic techniques that are tried and true, their creative application represents a genuine and, we believe, im-

348

portant innovative step forward in methodology. We apply life table analysis to a relatively large sample of populations over a 40-year and an 80-year period, a design that is seldom used in the field. Furthermore, the populations are distinctive in size and social characteristics compared with biologically reproducing populations studied by most demographers. For example, the life table was adapted to handle four increments and six decrements to the population.

Other adaptations were needed to treat problems that emerged from studying comparatively small populations (ranging in size from 27 to 1,340 members) with techniques usually applied to much larger ones. Thus, for most comparisons we use five-year instead of three-year averages to reduce fluctuations in the data. We also constructed an inconsistency index to gauge the impact of fluctuating trends on our projection models. This index helps researchers and practitioners judge the usefulness of the projections for a particular diocese.

We had to develop strategies for handling modifications in organizational boundaries, which are more fluid than those of counties, states, and nations. Changes in jurisdictions affected 24 priesthood populations in our sample when new dioceses were created and old ones divided during the census period; to trace movement from one population to another, we had to gather data from six dioceses not included in the study. Appendix D describes the techniques devised to maintain comparability of cases amidst considerable fluctuation in boundaries.

Births and deaths in a biologically reproducing population are different from entrances to and exits from an organizational population. To handle those differences we turned to the concept of man-years gained and lost by transitions. Calculating the years of service gained by an entrance or lost by an exit takes into account age differences at the time of the event. Thus, for example, we relied on years of service gained or lost to adjust for age differences across dioceses when setting our projection assumptions. Appendix B describes the procedures we followed for these adjustments. Similarly, in chapter 7 we report the number of ordinations standardized by man-years gained to insure comparability over time despite the rising age at ordination.

These and other important refinements are necessary if the organization demography approach is to gain momentum in the field. As Stewman (1986) and other analysts are beginning to realize, in a society dominated by large and powerful organizations, organization demography must take its place along with other forms of social demography and population studies. This study is among the pioneering efforts in that direction.

For Policymakers and Other Church Leaders

Oftentimes social groups move and drift in unpredictable directions, such that proponents of the natural selection model of organizational analysis claim that social change is 90 percent blind. Nevertheless — and many other sociologists feel natural selection theory exaggerates the forces of random change — committed participants in most organizations hope to channel change in the direction of their cherished beliefs and values. In other words, everyone wants a piece of the action, even if it amounts to only a share of the 10 percent of change governed by purposive intervention.

We recognize that different groups of clerical and lay leaders in the church would champion one or another of the variation, selection, and retention options expressed or implied in this research. The general practical contribution made by this book to the ongoing struggle over change in the Catholic ministry is to provide all the actors in the social-change process with accurate, definitive, and up-to-date demographic information on the priest shortage. We also help distinguish the variables that may be subject to manipulation by organization members from those conditions in the church's environment that are the result of inexorable ecological forces. In addition, by way of examples and illustrations, we point out possible and probable directions the change might take.

Thus we have accepted the challenge to improve the practicality of empirical studies of organizations. McKelvey and Aldrich (1983, p. 101) note with regret, "A spirit of application pervades most sciences . . . [but] in organizational science . . . application is much less visible." We hope the strengths of applied research are very visible to our readers.

For Organization Science

We also endorse the proposition that not only policy but also theoretical implications of research conducted on one population of organizations become more useful across types if they are spelled out in a comprehensive theoretical context. The population perspective has provided background theory for our research whenever possible, although demographic theory and techniques govern the bulk of the actual analysis. Accordingly, at several junctures we tie our demographic analyses to concerns of the population approach, which we integrate with the study of declining organization size, the political economy framework, and the qualified power model. Thus, for example, the structural consequences of changing size — one of the most pervasively studied topics in organization science — may now be understood in a much more comprehensive theoretical background.

Besides advancing the balance between pure and applied research, our study has implications at the nexus that joins theoretical and empirical investigation. To test complex causal theories one needs a complex, multi-level, longitudinal data set. For example, Lee and Bryk (1989, p. 172) used the newly developed hierarchical linear models in their study of "*why* some schools are better able to induce academic outcomes among a broad social and racial distribution of students." Similarly, as an illustration from our own study, the longitudinal data on priests may allow us to distinguish causal factors leading to priestly resignations at the social-psychological level (see Schoenherr and Greeley 1974) from those operative at the organizational and environmental levels, a topic we addressed in chapter 9. Our research should increase the store of new and old techniques for theoretical and empirical organization studies with explicit policy applications.

For Believers

We are left with a particularly thorny question: What do we say to those who ask, "Can believers learn anything from a reductionistic model of religion?" Targeted policymakers may dismiss the findings by saying, "Your explanations ignore the fact that the church is basically a mystery of God's never-failing grace." After attending a three-day workshop on some of the data and reading the private respondent report sent to each participating diocese and archdiocese, one archbishop wrote:

> I reject [the study's] pessimistic assessment and feel that the Catholic church in our country has been done a great disservice by the . . . report.
> . . . The study presumes that the only factors at work are sociology and statistical research. That is nonsense. We are disciples of Jesus Christ, we live by God's grace, and our future is shaped by God's design for his church — not by sociologists. . . Had sociologists studied the life of Jesus up through his crucifixion and death, I can just imagine the projections that would have resulted. But the resurrection and God's grace are not the products of research and surveys. (Mahony 1990)

Although we find it short-sighted and extreme, the archbishop's reaction touches a sensitive nerve among not only committed believers but also dedicated participants in any organization.

Organization analysts attempt to generalize their findings from one population of organizations to another, and yet, at the same time, they wish to produce knowledge that is applicable to policymakers in unique organizations. Furthermore, most policymakers imagine that theirs is truly a *unique* organization. Thus the frequent admonition to eager M.B.A.'s fresh from graduate school is to forget all the general principles and get down to "learning the business."

The claim to uniqueness is especially strong in religious organizations, which assert that their activity systems center on supernatural, nonempirical realities. Indeed, a supernatural being by definition is *totaliter aliter.* That is to say, a divine being is not just *somewhat* different but *wholely* different; there is absolutely nothing like it in the material human world, as Otto (1969) explains in his classic analysis of the "Holy." In addition, many religious groups feel their form of organized religion is the "only true church."

Serious attempts both to generalize and to apply research results create a dilemma. Social scientists exaggerate the situation by assuming that organizations are all alike, and managers do likewise by asserting that organizations are all unique. A way out of the dilemma may be to note that all empirical models are reductionistic, not just those used to explain the behavior of religious organizations. Every explanatory model used in social science is a conscious attempt to sharpen one's focus, reduce complexity, and thus explain some part of reality. No model ever claims to explain all reality, so in this sense all models are reductionistic by nature. Hence, organization theorists would do well to substantiate carefully every claim to generalizability, and managers ought to test the utility of research findings before rejecting them out of hand.

A fully comprehensive theory, in contrast with an empirical explanatory model, may claim to encompass all the major aspects of reality. Yet, theorists should take to heart Borges' warning in his tale of the missing moon. He notes that in every attempt at ". . . making an abridgement of the universe . . . The essence is always lost. . . ."[1] Some sociological theories of religion are more blatantly reductionistic than others. In fact, however, all empirical models are partial and in that sense reductionistic — not just in the study of religion, but in the study of all other social institutions as well.

Let it be noted that we draw from a phenomenological *theory* of religion that attempts to be as nonreductionistic as possible. The theory holds that religion, in all its organized forms, is ultimately grounded in a definitive, nonverifiable faith event (Schoenherr 1987a).[2] At the same time we

1. From "The Moon," by J. L. Borges; quoted in Blau and Schoenherr 1971, p. v.

2. In the same essay, the author also suggests a research agenda for studying the phenomenological core of religion. The models proposed are empirical, thus partial and reductionistic, but the variables included in the models attempt to describe living faith grounded

contend that empirical models, though partial and so reductionistic, are useful within a nonreductionistic theory. Admittedly, no explanatory model says it all. It is enough if it says *something* true and worthwhile.

What we offer believers is a partial explanation of some aspects of the truth about diocesan organizations. Policymakers and committed participants who have "ears to hear" will want to know the empirical truth, even though it doesn't touch the essence of religion as they know it. Knowledge of demographic and organizational facts can help them search for that "survival path" which may lead the ancient church in the direction of their own living faith and cherished values.

Discussion and Conclusion

The loss of numbers and the rapid aging of the priesthood population is a severe crisis but not the only problem confronting the contemporary Roman Catholic church. The priest shortage is singularly critical, however, because it is the driving force for pervasive social change. Arguably, the demographic transition spells the radical transformation of the Catholic ministry in all its forms.

The priesthood in its present organizational form represents the key economic resource and power elite of the hierarchical church. Change in the church's core technology embodied in the priesthood inevitably leads to transformation of other elements of its political and economic structures. Furthermore, once unleashed, the transformation process spills over into cultural and normative structures (Hirschman 1970; Zald 1970; Pettigrew 1979). Hence Catholic sacramental piety and other forms of religious expression along with the doctrines supporting them are also being threatened and transformed. The far-reaching ramifications of the priest shortage are a study in themselves. We shall limit our concluding discussion of the social consequences of the priest shortage to the more obvious and likely forms of transformation.

Beginning with the most visible and volatile issue, we believe the church is being confronted with a choice between its sacramental tradition and its commitment to an exclusively male celibate priesthood. One of the most critical aspects of this confrontation is that most church leaders have failed to accept responsibility for the choice. Instead they focus on stopgap solutions to the ever-worsening priest shortage while hoping for a dramatic increase in vocations.

Church leaders continue to prefer a wait-and-see strategy coupled with

---

in a unique religious experience that cannot be reduced to any other psychological or social categories.

a belief that unpredictable historical events will intervene to restore pre–Second Vatican Council growth rates in the priest population. The future will bring a "restoration," thus obviating the need for radical structural changes such as optional celibacy or the ordination of women.[3] Clearly, if the hoped-for restoration were to occur, the demographic transition would take a different course, and its impact on structural change would be greatly altered.

The probability that future events will create a regeneration process which would restore high levels of recruitment and retention of male celibate clergy, however, seems low for at least two reasons. First, the Second Vatican Council has effectively undermined the social pattern of thinking and acting that supported earlier high rates of ordination and low rates of resignation. Official pronouncements regarding the value of sacramental marriage as an alternative path to true Christian holiness which is equal though different from vowed celibacy (Abbott 1966; Schillebeeckx 1985) and the council's emphasis on lay participation in the ministry (Leege 1986) serve to reduce vocations and increase resignations.

Second, the feminist movement, particularly among nuns and laywomen in church-related careers, has eroded male hegemony over the church's ministry and established a growing sense of female equality (Gilmour 1986; Wallace 1992). Thus, while it is entirely possible for the Roman Catholic church to return to previous high levels of male celibate ordinations and successful retention of young priests, we argue that social forces are relentlessly weakening the probability. At the same time these forces are strengthening the alternative probability that regeneration will occur through a process of more radical structural change.

Without a fundamental restoration of the selection and retention mechanisms that produced an adequate supply of male celibate priests, the shortage will continue. Because undoing history is unlikely, the Roman Catholic church will undergo a process of protestantization. Most notably, the growing emphasis on scripture-based worship will dim the eucharistic sacrificial tradition. Furthermore, the control over ministry held by the clergy will be weakened as lay leadership gains legitimation during the transition. The ordination of married men and eventually of women would preserve the priesthood and along with it both the eucharistic tradition and the mechanisms of control over the central belief system and modes of worship.

3. Küng and Swidler (1987) present the opinions of noted theologians and other Catholic scholars that John Paul II administers a repressive regime bent on "restoring" the church to its pre–Second Vatican Council state.

Some believers may view such a discussion of the costs of maintaining a male celibate priesthood as bordering on heresy. Other critics may consider the argument about the importance of preserving priesthood as a reinforcement of patriarchy. We believe both critiques fail to appreciate fully the nature of organized religion and the strength and complexity of the forces of transformation that are underway.

Those who decry tendencies toward protestantization because they imply that Catholicism would be lapsing into heresy need to consider that failure to face the choice does not make it go away. The need to decide whether to preserve the eucharistic tradition or to maintain compulsory celibacy and male exclusivity looms ever larger as the priest shortage grows. In fact, as Rev. Gerard Broccolo (1985) has cogently argued, each day that an exclusively male celibate priesthood is retained in the face of sustained clergy decline, the choice is being made to sacrifice the ancient sacramental traditions of Catholicism in favor of male celibate hegemony.

Those concerned primarily with patriarchalism may need to explore more deeply the nature of organized religion lest what is essential is lost in the name of reform. A willingness to sacrifice the sacramental priesthood in order to dismantle the oppressive patriarchal structures of control can easily lead to further degeneration of religion. Sacrament and deeply structured ritual are essential to religious expression (Wach 1944; Langer 1961; Turner 1969; Deflem 1991). The production, reproduction, and transformation of sacred ritual and the cosmogonic myth system underlying ritual are inherently difficult processes (Eliade 1961). Likewise, the organizational requirements necessary to transmit a religious tradition across space and time involve complex mechanisms of centralized control (Schoenherr 1987a).

Most agree that heresy should be avoided and oppressive patriarchical forms dismantled in the church. Will sacrament, priesthood, centralized control, compulsory celibacy, and male exclusivity be weakened or even eliminated in the transformation process? We contend that sacrament, priesthood, and control are more critical to the organizational well-being of Catholicism than either compulsory celibacy or male exclusivity. We speculate further that, to preserve the more essential elements of Roman Catholicism, the nonessentials — first compulsory celibacy and later male exclusivity — will need to be eliminated as defining characteristics of priesthood. Whatever direction is taken, the Roman Catholic church bears careful scrutiny over the next several decades while conflict and change emerge in the wake of a major demographic transition.

Appendices
Bibliography
Indexes

Appendix A
National Census Counts and Category Definitions

This appendix presents a table of raw counts derived from a 19-year register of the U.S. diocesan priest population and the category definitions that guided the data collection. Readers interested in a history of the project, a description of the methodological procedures used to create the population register, and an executive summary of the findings presented in this book may contact the Center for Demography and Ecology at the University of Wisconsin–Madison.[1]

Census and Vital-Statistics Register, 1966–85

Table A.1 displays counts of the U.S. diocesan priest population for each year from January 1, 1966, to January 1, 1985. Examining the finished product provides an overview of the population register. The census table is presented here both for illustrative purposes and to record the data; we comment in detail on its contents in the chapters of this report.

The figures presented are the result of careful enumeration techniques described in the methodology addendum.[2] The top panel of the table shows the status of the priesthood population at the beginning of each year by categories used in the Kenedy Official Catholic Directory. The middle panel presents counts of the tran-

1. Request "Full Pews and Empty Altars: History of the Project and Summary of Results," by Richard A. Schoenherr and Lawrence A. Young; Center for Demography and Ecology, 4412 Social Science, University of Wisconsin–Madison, Madison, Wis. 53706. Among other things, the paper describes the population registration system through which the data were created, sponsorship and funding of the project, design of the data collection campaign, and details about the data processing.

2. See the previous footnote.

Table A.1. Census of U.S. diocesan priest population, 1966–85

	Year								
	1966	1967	1968	1969	1970	1971	1972	1973	1974
	Status at beginning of year[b]								
Active	35087	35107	34915	34402	33555	32914	32182	31518	31163
Retired	904	1060	1436	1886	2190	2544	2791	3059	3250
On sick leave	311	351	364	338	377	379	380	370	382
Other leaves	28	40	35	58	47	57	55	59	65
Total population	36330	36558	36751	36685	36169	35894	35407	35005	34860
	Transitions during year								
Entrances									
Ordinations	994	1062	1034	847	842	692	647	831	732
Incardinations	56	62	95	100	105	239	111	107	110
Returns from									
Resignations	0	1	2	0	4	6	6	14	15
Other leaves	23	34	41	39	46	48	47	36	34
Exits									
Excardinations	22	16	37	46	23	185	30	21	35
Resignations	200	338	579	750	634	667	609	499	380
Retirements	291	508	627	521	554	449	488	444	465
Deaths among									
Inactives	154	167	220	256	236	239	261	282	300
Actives	444	411	362	413	334	334	265	295	269
Sick leaves	96	71	60	95	79	68	64	61	71
Other leaves	14	12	28	14	25	20	18	27	23
	Net changes during year[c]								
Total population	230	193	-67	-518	-276	-487	-401	-146	-127
Active population	20	-191	-514	-841	-640	-730	-660	-354	-346

sition events that occurred during the year. And the bottom panel lists net changes in population size during the year.

The figures in the table are weighted estimates based on a data file which combined the population registers prepared for each diocese in the sample. A local census table, with the same format as table A.1, was included in "Respondent Report I" (Schoenherr 1987b) sent to each diocese so that data could be verified before we proceeded with the analysis.

Categories and Definitions

To produce and interpret table A.1 and the equivalent table for each diocese, it was essential to provide a standard set of definitions:

1. *Diocesan priest population:* all and only Roman Catholic priests ordained for or later incardinated into the diocese and who were alive on January 1, 1966,

Table A.1. Census of U.S. diocesan priest population, 1966–85 (continued)

					Year					
1975	1976	1977	1978	1979	1980	1981	1982	1983	1984	1985[a]

Status at beginning of year[b]

1975	1976	1977	1978	1979	1980	1981	1982	1983	1984	1985[a]
30808	30595	30501	30126	29773	29667	29472	29354	28925	28618	28240
3474	3747	3826	4085	4229	4337	4398	4383	4599	4754	4880
380	352	312	306	339	327	296	277	277	283	288
70	69	60	109	132	124	101	88	111	101	101
34733	34763	34698	34626	34473	34456	34267	34103	33912	33756	33510

Transitions during year

1975	1976	1977	1978	1979	1980	1981	1982	1983	1984
768	700	667	574	647	544	544	511	530	465
118	201	126	344	132	159	256	311	140	123
9	11	5	8	10	4	5	13	7	12
57	36	26	64	76	91	37	53	59	67
33	130	36	248	42	88	186	230	41	48
296	258	295	238	223	231	176	190	194	181
511	399	532	509	422	394	348	565	504	505
278	353	317	368	352	379	392	365	387	406
259	236	222	225	187	202	214	242	213	211
60	13	49	89	60	52	32	65	64	70
18	8	65	59	38	30	8	52	26	36

Net changes during year[c]

1975	1976	1977	1978	1979	1980	1981	1982	1983	1984
30	-65	-72	-154	-14	-194	-164	-192	-157	-246
-214	-84	-372	-348	-100	-179	-110	-428	-296	-373

Sources: census registers from 86 U.S. dioceses; the number of priests registered in the 19-year census is 36,370. Diocesan census counts are weighted to estimate national parameters.

[a]Data on transitions during 1985 are incomplete because data collection terminated before the end of the year.

[b]Because of weighting and rounding some totals in the top panel and net changes in the bottom panel do not compute from their component parts.

[c]"Net changes" equal entrances minus exits. For "Total population," entrances include ordinations, incardinations, and returns from resignation; exits include resignations, deaths of active and inactive members, and excardinations. For "Active population," entrances include ordinations, incardinations, and all returns to active duty; exits include resignations, retirements, deaths of active members, excardinations, and all temporary leaves.

or after. Religious order and Eastern rite priests are excluded, as are priests who resided for any period of time in the diocese but who were never officially incardinated there.

2. *Active priests:* those who have an official work assignment either inside or outside the diocese; the assignment includes but is not restricted to specifically priestly functions such as presiding at Mass. Priests on study leave, on loan outside the diocese, on duty as military chaplain, and so on, are included.

3. *Total population:* the total number of incardinated diocesan priests alive on January 1 of a given year.

4. *Active population:* the total number of incardinated diocesan priests with an official work assignment either inside or outside the diocese as of January 1 of a given year.

5. *Retired:* those so designated by the diocese. Retired priests do not have a full-time diocesan work assignment, though they may preside at Mass regularly and help out with other pastoral activities on a part-time basis.

6. *Sick leaves:* those so designated by the diocese. Sick priests do not have a full-time diocesan work assignment but are in good standing, meaning they are permitted to celebrate Mass and help out if their health allows. The leave must last a minimum of 12 months to be counted.

7. *Other leaves/absences:* those so designated by the diocese; labeled "awaiting assignment" for purposes of the population register. Normally, priests awaiting assignment do not have a diocesan work assignment but are in good standing, meaning they are permitted and perhaps expected to celebrate Mass and help out if an occasion arises. The leave must last a minimum of 12 months to be counted.

8. *Ordination:* receiving the order of priesthood either directly from, or under the auspices of the Ordinary, which includes incardination in the diocese.

9. *Incardination:* a process which includes receiving official permission from all superiors involved to change one's canonical affiliation from another diocese or a religious order to the present diocese. No priest may be incardinated in two dioceses or be affiliated with a religious order and incardinated in a diocese at the same time.

10. *Return to active duty:* receiving an official full-time work assignment either inside or outside the diocese after being on any type of leave for at least 12 months.

11. *Excardination:* a process which includes receiving permission from all superiors involved to change one's canonical affiliation from the present diocese to another diocese or a religious order. After excardination, a priest is no longer a member of the diocesan clergy population of the original diocese.

12. *Resignation:* not having a diocesan work assignment by choice, permission, or other circumstance (including suspension). Normally priests who have resigned would not be expected or permitted to carry out priestly functions such as presiding at Mass. A "resigned" priest may or may not be dispensed from the obligations of Holy Orders, may or may not be married, or may or may not have been granted an official leave of absence.

13. *Death while inactive:* death while on sick leave, awaiting assignment, official leave of absence, or in retirement.

14. *Death while active:* death while in an official work assignment either inside or outside the diocese.

15. *Date of transition event:* the year in which the entrance or exit event occurred or began. A transition event must last for a minimum of 12 months; the year in which the event began is recorded, not the year in which the 12th month ended.

Appendix B
Projection Assumptions

In the first section of this appendix we discuss the assumptions governing our models of overall population change. Later we specify how the general assumptions apply to certain components of change, specifically resignation, migration, retirement, and preretirement mortality.

Assumptions about Overall Population Change

Our comparative design dictates that we employ one generalizable set of assumptions to be used uniformly in the projection models for every diocese. Admittedly, making population projections is an art, even though it relies upon the most suitable empirical evidence and advanced mathematical techniques. The assumptions we have chosen incorporate the following organizational, historical, mathematical, and statistical considerations:

1. We distinguish between transition events mainly related to factors "internal" to the priesthood population itself (e.g., resignations or retirements) and events related to factors that are "external" to that population (e.g., the size of the local Catholic population to be drawn upon in recruitment efforts). Ordinations, incardinations, and returns from temporary leave are most closely related to factors other than the number of active priests already in the clergy population. So we base our assumptions about entrance events on age-specific numbers (e.g., the numbers of incardinations or returns to active duty in specific age groups) rather than rates; in equations calculating rates, the number of active priests is the denominator.

Clearly, assumptions regarding entrances into the active diocesan clergy would be strengthened if closely linked to mechanisms operating within the populations governing these events. For example, assumptions about future ordination levels could incorporate data on fertility rates of Catholic females and on population size and age structure of single Catholic males within the diocese or data on his-

364

torical trends in the number of young men entering and graduating from the diocesan seminaries.

Likewise, data on migration (in- and excardination) within the national and international priestly labor markets would increase the validity of our assumptions governing future trends in incardinations. Collecting such data, however, is well beyond the scope of this study. Furthermore, we question whether the gains in improving the validity of our entrance assumptions would justify the additional costs of obtaining the data.[1]

All other transition events are related to the number of active priests at risk in each age cohort within the diocese. Thus, assumptions concerning these internally dependent events are based on past trends in their age-specific rates, using the number of active priests as the denominator.

2. Because we are dealing with organizational rather than natural life spans of priests, we set the lower limit of a priestly career at 26 (usual age at ordination) and the upper at 71 (usual age at retirement) in order to calculate the number of man-years gained or lost for the organization by a transition event. The concept of organizational man-years allows us to take into account age differentials in the entrance and attrition events when setting assumptions about their future trends.

Accordingly, we set assumptions about expected recruitment levels by examining past trends in the number of man-years gained through ordination, incardination, and returns from temporary leave rather than changes in the raw numbers of new priests entering the population each year. Likewise, in setting attrition assumptions we focus on the rate of man-years lost rather than the usual unstandardized attrition rates. This relatively simple procedure standardizes for age and thus increases the appropriateness of the assumptions.

3. Instead of the three-year averages traditionally used by demographers, we calculated five-year moving averages from 1966 to 1984 for the number of man-years gained by recruitment events and returns from leaves of absence and for the rates of man-years lost by attrition. Using five- instead of three-year averages helps reduce more of the noise in the data from these relatively small populations.

4. When demographic trends of growth or decline continue during an entire period of observation, it is reasonable to assume that future events will reflect even more growth or decline than that already experienced. To help decide whether past experience or probable future events should govern the projection assumptions, we regress each entrance and attrition measure and its log on the year of occurrence, then use the statistics from the equations to calculate probable future values of the variables through the year 1994, 10 years after the end of the census period.

If either of these models is statistically significant, we use data for 1990–94 to set either the optimistic or pessimistic assumption for the given change event, because, of all the moving five-year averages covering 1966–94, they would be clos-

1. As noted in the full version of appendix A (see footnote 1, appendix A), the demands of our data-collection campaign so strained the cooperating dioceses' resources — and ours as well — that we had to abandon our attempts to gather 19 years of information on the number of seminarians in each diocese.

est to the peak or nadir of the presumed true curve. If both models are significant, we use the one that explains more variance in the variable under consideration.

We have arbitrarily set the range of values for the Y term of the regression equation so that future trends do not fall below half or rise above twice the level of the trend experienced in 1980–84, the last five-year interval covered by the observed data. This strategy results in a conservative approach while still including in the models consistent tendencies of growth and/or decline.

5. Optimistic, moderate, and pessimistic assumptions have been chosen on the basis of an examination of the complete set of five-year moving averages calculated from the observed data for 1966–84 and, when relevant, the regression-based estimates for 1985–94. With the exceptions discussed below, we have chosen the highest average entrances and lowest average attritions for the optimistic assumptions and the lowest average entrances and highest average attritions for the pessimistic assumptions.

For the moderate assumptions we have chosen the five-year averages for 1980–84, which reflect the most recent trends in the historical data. Exploratory analyses show that using assumptions based on the most recent levels of entrances and exits produces a reasonable projection curve at approximately the midpoint between the optimistic and pessimistic curves.

6. For the national and regional projections, we focus on the net migration effect of incardinations and excardinations. That is to say, assumptions for these events are based on the imbalance of incardinations over excardinations. First we examine the complete set of moving five-year averages between 1966 and 1994; the 1966–84 averages are based on historical data and the 1985–94 averages on regression-based projections of the regional data sets. For the optimistic assumptions we use the five-year average that produces the largest net gain in man-years from the imbalance of incardinations over excardinations, and for the pessimistic assumption, the five-year average that produces the smallest net gain from migrations during the entire period. Thus, although the five-year period selected for the optimistic assumption might not correspond to the most optimistic average of either incardinations or excardinations, it does capture the most optimistic five-year average for net migration. The same holds true for the pessimistic assumption, *mutatis mutandis*. As noted, moderate assumptions for net migration are based on the 1980–84 five-year average.

For local diocesan projections, we treat incardinations and excardinations separately. Accordingly, for incardinations, we have selected the five-year average that produces the largest gain in man-years from incardinations for the optimistic assumptions and the five-year average that produces the smallest gain in man-years for the pessimistic assumptions. For excardinations, the optimistic assumptions are based on the five-year average with the smallest rate of loss in man-years due to excardinations, whereas the pessimistic assumptions are based on the five-year average with the largest rate of loss in man-years.

Obviously, the rules governing assumptions about diocesan-level incardinations and excardinations differ somewhat from the national and regional-level rules. As noted, we treat the two events separately at the local level, whereas at the national and regional levels we focus on the net-immigration effect of incardinations and excardinations. Implicit in the differing approaches is the fact that local incardinations are less constrained by the number of local excardinations than is the case at the national and regional levels. That is, any given diocese operates as an open system so that it can experience simultaneously many incardinating priests and few excardinating priests or vice versa. The priest population at the national and regional levels, however, tends toward a closed system. Thus much of the migration is between dioceses within the nation or the region; the closed nature of the system produces constraints which tend to stabilize and balance the overall net effect of incardinating and excardinating priests.[2] So our assumptions attempt to capture the different migration dynamics at work at the national, regional, and local levels of the organization.

7. Past research (Schoenherr and Sørensen 1982) as well as the data in this report indicate that most diocesan clergy populations are undergoing sustained decline. It appears unlikely that the trend has bottomed out, such that, under optimistic assumptions, the highest past growth tendencies should have been set in motion immediately in 1985. Therefore, we lag the optimistic assumptions 10 years by using 5-year moving averages that are closest to the midpoint between the moderate and highest entrance events and between the lowest and moderate attrition events to fit the optimistic curve for 1985–94. The most optimistic assumptions deemed reasonable then start in 1995. In effect, this results in an optimistic projection that incorporates moderately optimistic assumptions for the first 10 years, followed by fully optimistic assumptions for the remaining decade of the model.

8. We further modify the optimistic assumptions by basing the projections beginning in 1995, not on the highest five-year averages for ordinations, but on the five-year average closest to the midpoint between the moderate and highest five-year averages. Furthermore, in establishing the optimistic ordination assumptions for regional projections, we set a minimum level of increase over the moderate assumption of 17.8 percent, which is the national increase in ordinations under optimistic assumptions.

A long period of declining recruitment in the United States has resulted in a 58 percent drop in the number of diocesan seminarians preparing for ordination; the bottom of the downward cycle is not yet evident. Further, the trend is worldwide and does not permit a simple or quick solution (see Statistical Yearbook of the Church, 1969–86; Schoenherr and Pérez Vilariño 1979).

Therefore, assuming that during the foreseeable future the most reasonably optimistic recruitment levels will not exceed the five-year moving average selected by following these procedures, we continue to use it for the optimistic assumptions governing ordinations throughout the projection period.

9. We also modify the pessimistic assumptions with regard to resignations. Again, according to earlier research (Schoenherr and Sørensen 1982) as well as

2. In addition to switching dioceses within the United States, migrating priests come from and go to religious orders and foreign dioceses. Thus, the national priest population can experience a net increase or decrease as a result of migration dynamics (see chapter 8).

the data presented here, Catholic dioceses in the United States suffered an exodus from the active ministry soon after the close of the Second Vatican Council.

The extremely high rates receded by the mid-1970s, however, when the pool of resignation-prone clergy declined. We contend that the rates observed during that early period were due to unique historical events and are highly improbable in future decades. Thus we set the pessimistic assumptions for resignations at the moving average closest to the mean instead of at the highest of the five-year moving averages.

10. Priests are not classified as retired until so designated by their diocese. We encountered difficulty in establishing a uniform measure of retirement rates, because some dioceses continued to list older priests as nonretired, even though they no longer had full-time work assignments. Consequently, beginning with the first year of our projections (1985), we treat all priests older than 80 as retired, and remove them from the active priest population. This technique increases comparability across dioceses by introducing a uniform maximum age at retirement for the projections, thus making regional and local comparisons more accurate. Even though a small number of active priests who are older than 80 have been arbitrarily removed, in projecting the size and age of the active population their cumulative full-time equivalent positions are balanced by other priests between 75 and 80 who still remain active and are counted as full-time equivalents though they work only part-time.

11. Because we are dealing with relatively small populations, we have encountered other difficulties in making the projections. A problem arises, for example, when small age cohorts do not survive beyond a specific age during the years covered by an attrition assumption. Unless remedied, this situation could result in projecting an age-specific attrition rate of 1.0 into the future, making it impossible for any cohort to survive past that particular age.

To reduce this problem we have changed pessimistic survival probabilities of less than 0.6 to 0.6. At the diocesan level of analysis, this results in 196 changes in 4,730 survival probability cells; all but 5 of the changes, however, occur in age groups older than 65. Thus, the changes made affect 4 percent of the probabilities considering all age groups, but only 0.1 percent of the probabilities among age groups 65 and under. Following the same rules, we have modified one cell in the probability matrix for the national data set, namely that for 76-year-olds, which has a minuscule effect on the analysis. When using region as the unit of analysis, we have changed 22 out of 440, or 5 percent of the cells; all the modified probabilities correspond to age groups over 70.

12. Assumptions regarding three transition events are held constant for all the projection models; that is, the same values are used to calculate the optimistic, moderate, and pessimistic curves. First, assumptions about future re-entrances into the population from leaves of absence and returns from resignation, and second, assumptions about future attrition through leaves of absence are not allowed to vary. We base our single assumption for these events on a 10-year average for 1975–84. The means for this period are used because the reliability of the data in several dioceses is suspect for 1966–74. In addition, our exploratory analysis revealed that

when the data are reliable such events occurred more frequently in recent years. We also learned from the exploratory analysis that none of these events has much impact on the projection models.

Third, the single assumption governing the death rate is based on the 1983 life tables (the $_1L_x$ version) for white males in the United States (U.S. Department of Health and Human Services 1987a). We have chosen mortality rates based on national instead of local diocesan data because of the false impressions that can be conveyed by such small organizational populations, and have chosen only whites instead of the total male population because the subcategory more accurately reflects the U.S. priest population (see chapter 11).

To recapitulate: With the exceptions described above, the five-year period between 1966 and 1984 — or 1994 if regression data are used — during which each entrance event was highest and each exit event was lowest has been used for the optimistic assumptions. And vice versa, the historical five-year period in which each entrance event was lowest and each exit event was highest has been chosen for the pessimistic assumptions. The moderate assumptions are always based on data reflecting transition events experienced during 1980–84. (Table B.1 summarizes the projection assumptions used at the national, regional, and local levels of analysis.)

Assumptions about Future Migrations

Incardinations and Excardinations

Several observations provide a context for interpreting the data in figure 8.1. From the perspective of organizational resources, the age at migration is as important in determining the effects of net immigration as is the number of migrations. If, for example, a diocese were to have an equal number of incardinations and excardinations but the incardinands were all younger than the excardinands, the diocese would be experiencing a net gain in organizational resources.

By focusing on man-years gained or lost in setting assumptions about net immigration, we take into consideration both the age at migration and the number (or rate) of migrations. Recall that we set the lower limit of a priestly career at 26 and the upper limit at 71 to calculate gains or losses in years of service due to an entrance or exit event.[3]

The net immigration assumptions used in this study are based on five-year averages of man-years gained between 1966 and 1984.[4] Nationally, the five-year period with the smallest net immigration gain was 1971–75. During those years, net im-

3. For example, if a population of 100 priests were to have an average age of 45, it would have 2,500 expected man-years of future human resources available for ministry. If a 45-year-old priest were to exit the population through excardination, both the number of priests and number of man-years would be reduced by 1 percent. However, if a 65-year-old were to exit the population through excardination, the number of priests would still be reduced by 1 percent, but the number of man-years would be reduced by only 0.2 percent.

4. Data after 1984 are not used in setting the national net migration assumptions, because there was no significant linear trend in the 1966–84 data. However, five-year averages

Table B.1. Summary of assumptions for national and regional projection models

Assumptions that vary by projection series

Optimistic, 1995–2005

Ordination — Numbers of ordinations from the five-year period in which number of annual man-years gained is closest to the midpoint between the moderate and highest five-year averages[a]

Net migration — Numbers of incardinations and rates of excardination corresponding to the five-year period with the largest gain in man-years from net migration

Resignation — Rates corresponding to the five-year period with the smallest loss in man-years from resignation

Retirement — Rates corresponding to the five-year period with the smallest loss in man-years from retirement

Optimistic, 1985–1994

Ordination — Same as optimistic assumption for 1995–2005

Net migration — Numbers of incardinations and rates of excardination corresponding to the five-year period in which number of man-years gained from net migration is closest to the midpoint between man-years gained under optimistic assumptions in effect for 1995–2005 and those gained in 1980–84 (i.e., moderate assumptions)

Resignation — Rates corresponding to the five-year period in which number of man-years lost due to resignations is closest to the midpoint between man-years lost under optimistic assumptions in effect for 1995–2005 and those lost in 1980–84 (i.e., moderate assumptions)

Retirement — Rates corresponding to the five-year period in which number of man-years lost due to retirements is closest to the midpoint between man-years lost under optimistic assumptions in effect for 1995–2005 and those lost in 1980–84 (i.e., moderate assumptions)

Moderate, 1985–2005

Ordination — Numbers of ordinations for 1980–84

Net migration — Numbers of incardinations and rates of excardination for 1980–84

Resignation — Rates of resignation for 1980–84

Retirement — Rates of retirement for 1980–84

(continued on following page)

Table B.1. Summary of assumptions for national and regional projection models (continued)

Assumptions that vary by projection series (continued)	
Pessimistic, 1985–2005	
Ordination	Numbers of ordinations corresponding to the five-year period with the smallest gain in man-years from ordinations
Net migration	Numbers of incardinations and rates of excardination corresponding to the five-year period with the smallest gain in man-years from net migration
Resignation	Rates corresponding to the five-year period in which the annual number of man-years lost through resignation is closest to the 19- or 29-year average
Retirement	Rates corresponding to the five-year period with the largest loss in man-years due to retirement
Assumptions that remain constant[b]	
All series, 1985–2005	
Mortality	Survival rates based on the 1983 $_1L_x$ life table for U.S. white males
Return from leave	Numbers of returns for 1975–84
Leave	Rates of leave for 1975–84

Notes: Diocesan projections are based on identical assumptions, except that incardinations and excardinations are treated separately; see item 6 in text section "Assumptions about Overall Population Change" for a more complete discussion.

All assumptions are based on historical data for 1966–84. In addition, if the regression-based projections of entrance or exit events were statistically significant, future trends through the year 1994 were incorporated in setting the optimistic or pessimistic assumption; see item 4 in text section "Assumptions about Overall Population Change" for a more complete discussion.

References to 19-year averages refer to 1966–84, 29-year averages to 1966–94.

All numbers and rates used in the assumptions are age-specific averages.

[a]For regions, a minimum increase over the moderate assumption was set at 17.8 percent.

[b]Assumptions for optimistic, moderate, and pessimistic series do not vary.

migrations increased the national clergy resource pool by an average of 1,120 man-years. Accordingly, for the pessimistic series we assume that future net immigrations will be equal to the average number of age-specific incardinations and the average age-specific excardination rates between 1971 and 1975.[5]

---

of man-years gained between 1966 and 1994 are used for regional populations of priests in those regions where there was a statistically significant trend.

5. In making assumptions about future events, we project numbers for entrances and rates for exits. Thus, after establishing the five-year period with the lowest man-years gained

In the moderate series, we assume that future immigrations will follow the pattern in the number of incardinations and rate of excardination for 1980–84, when the national clergy experienced an average net gain of 1,576 man-years through the combined effects of incardinations and excardinations.

For the optimistic assumptions, we assume that future immigrations will be patterned after the age-specific number of incardinations and rates of excardination for 1977–81, when national clergy resources increased by an average of 1,848 man-years because of net migrations.[6]

We project a static number of incardinations in each series but a fluid number of excardinations; the latter is based on the changing size of the clergy population. Because all three series project decreasing numbers of clergy, they also project decreasing numbers of excardinations, so the net result is rising numbers of net immigrations under all three projection assumptions.

Leaves of Absence

Figure 8.2 displays the annual number of national net leaves for 1966–2004. Net leave, like net migration, consists of two separate components, leaves and returns from leave. Just as our assumptions about future net immigration focus on age-specific numbers and rates, those for net leave utilize age-specific number of returns and age-specific rate of leave. Unlike net immigration, however, we use a single net leave assumption for all three projection series, based on the age-specific averages in leaves and returns for 1975–84.

The difference in number of net leaves in the three projection series results from the different population sizes in interaction with the single assumption. Because the pessimistic series projects the smallest population, it also projects the smallest number of net leaves, even though we use the same assumption about the number of future leaves and rate of return as those in the other series. Ironically, the number of net leaves is therefore most advantageous under the pessimistic assumption and least advantageous under the optimistic assumption. The overall trend toward fewer net leaves is due to the decreasing size of the priest population in each series.

Assumptions about Future Resignations

As described in chapter 9, the high-risk period for resignation begins shortly after ordination and lasts until priests reach their mid-40s, which is represented by our 25–44-year-old age group. The proportion of 25- through 44-year-old priests dropped from 49 percent in 1966, or over 17,000 active priests in absolute numbers, to 34

---

from net migrations, we project the number of age-specific incardinations and the rate of age-specific excardinations associated with this period.

6. We lag the fully optimistic assumptions 10 years. Between 1985 and 1994, the optimistic net migration assumption corresponds to the five-year average closest to the midpoint between man-years gained under moderate and optimistic assumptions. For the national population of priests, this period is 1979–83, when there was an average annual gain of 1,700 man-years due to net migrations.

percent in 1985, or fewer than 10,000 active priests. Inevitably, the number of resignations fell when the size of at-risk cohorts declined. The optimistic series assumes that the size of the at-risk cohorts will continue to decline until at least 1995, and the moderate and pessimistic series assume the number of priests in this age bracket will keep going down until 2005. Simply stated, the number of resignations must go down if the pool of priests at risk is getting smaller.

In addition to fewer at-risk priests, our projection models also take into consideration trends toward lower age-specific resignation rates. The moderate series assumes the 1980–84 rates, which were the lowest of the entire census period, will continue for the next two decades. The optimistic series, however, assumes the rates will continue to go down throughout the projection period because of the strength of past dampening trends.[7] We would not expect linear decline in the resignation rates, so we set the optimistic series at 84 percent of the 1980–84 rates between 1985 and 1994 and at 64 percent of the 1980–84 rates thereafter.

Because we do not believe the extremely high resignation rates experienced during the late 1960s and early 1970s will recur during the projection period, we do not follow our usual strategy of using the highest attrition rates from the historical period for our pessimistic resignation assumptions. Instead, for the most pessimistic scenario we assume that future resignations will occur at approximately the average rate experienced over the entire historical period.[8]

The top two curves in figure 9.1 show that by the end of the period the models project a lower number of resignations under pessimistic than under moderate assumptions. This may seem unreasonable at first glance, but it is the result of interaction between assumed ordination and resignation trends. The impact of relatively higher resignation rates under pessimistic assumptions is reduced by the complementary assumption of lower numbers of ordinations. The pessimistic series actually assumed higher levels of resignation than the moderate series. There will be notably fewer at-risk priests in the pessimistic than the moderate population, however, because the latter assumes higher ordinations than the former. Put another way, the number of resignations will be smaller in the pessimistic than in the moderate model because the pool of priests at risk will be relatively smaller owing to lower ordinations.

Assumptions about Future Natural Attrition

Retirement

The following comments provide a context for interpreting the data in figure 10.1. As with the other transition events, age at retirement is as important as the number of retirements in determining the magnitude of clergy loss. Two dioceses with the same crude retirement rates do not suffer the same loss in clergy resources if the

7. Regressing resignation rates on time for the 19 years of the historical period yields a negative coefficient significant at the .01 level; so we conclude that further decline in the future is a reasonable optimistic assumption.

8. Technically, we set the pessimistic assumption at a level which would correspond to the five-year average closest to the mean of the age-specific rates for 1966–84.

average age at retirement in one diocese is substantially younger. Hence, in setting assumptions about future retirements we consider man-years lost over the standardized 45-year career; rates of man-years lost take into account both age at retirement and number of retirees per 100 active priests.

Thus, a diocese of 100 priests whose average age is 55 has 1,500 man-years of human resources available for ministry. If a 55-year-old priest were to retire, both the number of priests and the number of man-years of service would be reduced by 1 percent. If a 65-year-old priest were to retire, however, the number of priests would be reduced by 1 percent but the man-years by only 0.3 percent.

The retirement assumptions used in this study are based on five-year averages of man-years lost during 1966–94.[9] The five-year period with the smallest loss was 1966–70, when retirements reduced national clergy resources by 0.19 percent of man-years available for priestly service. So for the optimistic series we assume that future retirements will be equal to the average age-specific retirement rates of 1966–70.

The moderate series assumes that future retirements will follow the pattern of age-specific rates of loss for 1980–84, when the clergy experienced a 0.21 percent loss in man-years because of retirements.

The pessimistic assumptions incorporate past and future trends. Analysis of retirements during 1966–84 shows continuous and statistically significant increases, so we extrapolate the trend to 1994. Accordingly, the 1990–94 period would show an annual loss of approximately 0.27 percent of available man-years, the highest loss during the 29 years; for the pessimistic series, we assume this rate will continue to 2005.

Note: the annual rate of loss in man-years is small in comparison to the crude retirement rates presented in table 10.4. Crude rates indicate the percentage of active priests lost, whereas rates of man-years lost indicate the percentage of years of service lost because of retirement.

As figure 10.1 reveals, until the turn of the century we project more retirements under optimistic than under moderate assumptions. This is reasonable because the annual number of retirements projected is a function of the size and age distribution of the active priest population in any given year. Size and age distribution, in turn, are determined by the entire set of assumptions governing each projection series. Thus, because the size of the older age groups is larger under optimistic than under moderate assumptions, the number of retirements is larger in the former than in the latter series.

Preretirement Mortality

Figure 10.2 summarizes the number of national preretirement deaths projected for 1985–2004. Because preretirement deaths are governed by a single assumption based on the 1983 $_1L_x$ life table for U.S. white males, interpreting the variation in projected deaths is straightforward.

9. Data after 1984 are based on the results of regressing rates of man-years lost from retirement on the year of retirement for 1966–84.

All three models are based on the same age-specific death rates, so variation in projected deaths is a function of differences in size and age structure of the active priest population. For example, even though the overall decline is larger in the pessimistic than in the other series, the number of projected deaths is smaller, because fewer priests are subject to the risk of preretirement mortality.

Appendix C
Notes on Methodology

In this appendix we discuss the standardization techniques used to handle problems of comparability; describe sources and definitions; describe adjustments to the data that are not treated in the main text; comment on the statistical techniques used in the analysis; and discuss our causal assumptions governing the regression models.

Problems of Comparability

Standardized Measures

A well-known example of standardizing a measure is adjusting the value of the dollar to the purchasing power it had in some prior year to remove the effects of inflation. Similarly, because ages at ordination, resignation, and retirement changed over the census period, we have to standardize the rates to allow reasonable comparisons from one decade to the next.

Because we are dealing with organizational rather than natural life spans, we define the lower limit of a priestly career as 26 (usual age at ordination) and the upper as 71 (usual age at retirement). All entrance and exit events are then adjusted for a constant number of man-years gained or lost by the diocese. The adjusted age-specific measures allow us to take into account age differences when setting projection assumptions (see appendix B).

Similarly, statistics in table 7.1 report the number of ordinations standardized by man-years gained, in order to control for the rising age at ordination. Just as 1990 dollars do not have the same purchasing power as 1966 dollars, so too today's newly ordained priests do not contribute the same number of man-years to the diocesan work force as the ordinands of 1966. In practice, therefore, standardization reduces the number of ordinations in each year of the study but makes the estimates for all years comparable in terms of man-years gained through ordination.

Age-Specific and Crude Rates

Another methodological issue is age-related. Not surprisingly, resignation rates are higher among younger priests, and retirement and death rates are higher among older ones. To examine these differentials, we use age-specific rates and compare them with the averages for the entire population, which are called crude rates. A 1966 age-specific resignation rate for priests 30–31 years old, for example, tells how many resignees per 100 active priests of that age there were in 1966. The 1966 age-specific rate for the youngest group is notably higher than the 1966 crude resignation rate, because the latter is based on the average for the entire active population 25–80 years old.

For example, table 2.2 displays crude growth and decline rates, and table 9.4 presents age-specific resignation rates. The point is, crude rates and unstandardized measures do not account for changes in age composition over time. Our methods adjust for these changes whenever it is necessary for the analysis.

Other Data Sources and Definitions

Most variables used in the analysis are constructed from original demographic data gathered for this research; these are described in the various chapters and clarified in appendix A. Other data, employed mainly in the regression analysis presented in chapters 6–10, are taken from the following sources.

Environmental Data

Diocesan jurisdictions are drawn along county lines, which makes it possible to use county-level data from the U.S. census. We obtained some county data already aggregated by diocese from the Glenmary Research Center in Atlanta, which had been obtained, for the most part, from the U.S. Census of Population and Housing 1980, Advance Reports PHC 80-V, table 1 (Quinn et al. 1982). These variables describe urban-rural, racial, ethnic, age, marital status, education, health, housing, occupation, family income, and religion characteristics of the general population living within diocesan jurisdictions.

We have constructed another set of variables on the size of five-year age groups of adult males on the basis of county data taken from a resource file tape of the U.S. Bureau of Health Professions (1987). Procedures for aggregating county data to the diocesan level are tedious and further complicated, because 17 counties are bisected by diocesan boundaries. To handle these situations we weight the data for each bisected county by the proportion of its population falling within the affected diocese's jurisdiction. The Glenmary Research Center provided reliable population figures which divided the totals for bisected counties between the affected dioceses.

The following environmental variables are used in the regression analysis:

1. *Geographic region:* the nine U.S. census regions; the South Atlantic and

East Southcentral regions are combined in one, which we call the East South, because only one diocese from East Southcentral states falls into the sample.

2. *Catholic population size:* number of Catholic parishioners in 1970 and 1980 residing in those counties that compose the diocese's jurisdiction.[1]

3. *Catholic population growth:* difference between the 1970 and 1980 number of Catholic parishioners residing in counties that compose the diocese's jurisdiction.

4. *Percentage of Catholics:* percentage of the total 1980 population in the diocesan territory that is Catholic.[2]

5. *Percentage of Catholic population growth:* percentage of difference between the 1970 and 1980 number of Catholic church members residing in counties that compose the diocese's jurisdiction.[3]

6. *Percentage of urban population:* percentage of the total 1980 population in the diocese that is urban; the urban population of counties is computed by adding the population of the Rand McNally Metropolitan Areas, if any, to the population of towns of 10,000 or more that are not included in Rand McNally areas.[4]

7. *Percentage of Hispanics:* percentage of the total 1980 population in the diocese that is Hispanic; persons of Spanish origin or descent are those who classified themselves in one of the specific Spanish-origin categories listed on the U.S. Census of Population and Housing 1980 questionnaire—Mexican, Puerto Rican, or Cuban—as well as those who indicated that they were of other Spanish/Hispanic origin.

8. *Percentage of affluent families:* percentage of all families in the diocese in 1980 with annual income of $25,000 or more.[5]

9. *Percentage of high school graduates:* number of persons in the diocese 25 years of age or older in 1980 who have completed at least four years of high school divided by the 1980 total population, multiplied by 100.

10. *Percentage of African Americans:* percentage of the total 1980 population in the diocese that is African American; the category "African American" includes persons who indicated their race as black or Negro on the census questionnaire. Included also are persons who did not classify themselves in one of the specific race categories listed on the questionnaire but who reported entries such as Jamaican, black Puerto Rican, West Indian, Haitian, or Nigerian.

1. County membership figures for the Roman Catholic church are from Quinn et al. 1982.

2. See footnote 1.

3. See footnote 1.

4. A Rand McNally Metropolitan Area is a large city, along with built-up areas whose boundaries are determined by Rand McNally field studies. Population figures used by Rand McNally to aggregate the metropolitan population are from the 1980 U.S. Census. The population of towns of 10,000 was obtained by the Glenmary Research Center staff from the 1980 U.S. Census. Population figures are from the U.S. Census of Population and Housing 1980, Advance Reports PHC 80-V, table 1 (Quinn et al. 1982).

5. Source: U.S. Census of Population and Housing 1980, Summary Tape File 3, tables 73 and 86 (Quinn et al. 1982).

Organizational Data

The impact of organizational characteristics of dioceses is tested in several causal models. A few variables describing staffing patterns and regional dominance, for example, are taken from the Kenedy Official Catholic Directory (annual).

The following organizational variables are used in the regression analysis:

1. *Year established:* year the diocese was established as reported in the Official Catholic Directory.

2. *Priest population size, 1970:* mean number of active diocesan priests as of January 1 of 1969, 1970, and 1971; the mean is used to minimize data fluctuation in small populations.

3. *Priest population growth:* difference between mean number of active diocesan priests in 1970 and 1980; the means are based on data for 1969–71 and 1979–81, respectively.

4. *Religious priest–to–diocesan priest ratio:* number of priests from religious orders who reside in the diocese per 100 active diocesan priests; the ratio is calculated from the mean figures for 1979–81.[6]

5. *Permanent deacon–to–diocesan priest ratio:* number of permanent deacons in the diocese per 100 active diocesan priests; the ratio is calculated from the mean figures for 1979–81.[7]

6. *Recruitment ineffectiveness:* number of Catholic males of ages 25–34 residing in the diocese in 1980 per newly ordained priest; the ratio is calculated using the mean number of ordinations for 1978–82.[8]

7. *Parishioner-to-priest ratio:* number of Catholic church members residing in the diocese in 1980 per active diocesan priest; the ratio is calculated using the mean number of priests for 1979–81.[9]

Adjustments to the Data

New Diocesan Boundaries

During the census period, splits occurred in 16 of the dioceses under investigation, and 14 dioceses were newly established, which necessitates various adjustments to the data. (See appendix D, which identifies the dioceses and explains the modifications.) These adjustments are based on the assumption that the priest population, which eventually composed the diocesan clergy in the new jurisdictions, already existed on January 1, 1966.

6. Data for the numerator are from the Kenedy Official Catholic Directory, 1980–82; volumes dated the year of publication contain data for one year prior. For dioceses established during or after 1979–81, data are for the three years subsequent to establishment closest to 1979–81.

7. See footnote 6.

8. County-level age-distribution data are from a resource file tape of the U.S. Bureau of Health Professions (1987); the number of Catholic males is estimated by the product of the male population in the age category and the percentage of Catholics in the diocesan territory.

9. For number of Catholic church members, see footnote 1.

By avoiding missing values, the adjustments permit a full range of comparisons among the new dioceses, parent dioceses, and all others. The adjustments also allow us to estimate size and other parameters of the entire diocesan priest population in the United States without being affected by artificial growth or decline during those years when parent dioceses were divided and new ones created.

Other Adjustments

Most missing values in the population registers are replaced by appropriate cohort means at each level of analysis. For example, when the year of birth is known but not the year of ordination, the missing value is replaced with the mean year of ordination of all those born the same year; and vice versa, if the ordination year is known but not the birth year, the missing value is replaced with the mean year of birth of all those ordained the same year. Missing values for all other transition events are substituted using similar procedures.

Cohort means are calculated only when three or more observations are present; otherwise missing values are replaced with population means. A separate substitution program has been used to calculate missing values for each diocese and region, and again for the total national population. Given these procedures, the smaller the population, the greater the number of missing values that are replaced with population rather than cohort means.

In order to create an annual census count in which the population is broken down into several exclusive categories (see table A.1), we have to adjust the data whenever two transition events occurred in the same year. Thus, for example, if a priest was ordained and also resigned in the same year, we change the date of resignation to one year after ordination. Similarly, if a priest retired and died in the same year, we change the date of retirement to one year earlier. In like manner, when two events of any type of transition occurred in one year we follow logical decision rules to adjust one or the other event so as to maintain exclusive categories in the census counts.

In calculating transition rates and survival probabilities, however, we follow different procedures from those used to substitute for missing values in census registers. When rates and probabilities are used in designing the projection models, we calculate them on the basis of midyear population figures. Thus, for example, when ordination and resignation—or two of any other paired entrance and exit events—occurred in the same year, the individual is classified as active for the first half and inactive for the second half of the year.

Analytic Techniques

The bulk of our analysis is descriptive in keeping with most demographic research. Thus we follow standard demographic methods described, for example, in Shryock, Siegel, and Associates' (1971) popular two-volume manual. We are also interested, however, in explaining variations at the local level in terms of cause and effect, or, in other words, dependent and independent variables. Given the nature of our data and the theoretical issues raised, the most appropriate statistical technique is ordinary least squares regression, which we use for testing cross-sectional and time-series models.

In examining the effects of regionalism we perform an analysis of covariance without interaction terms. We then compare adjusted means that have been standardized by equalizing the covariates in the regression model. These techniques are explained in chapter 14 of Agresti and Finlay (1986).

Causal Assumptions

The causal assumptions for the model presented in figure 6.1 and table 6.2 are relatively straightforward; they are presented in chapter 6. Similarly, the assumed order of causal precedence is forthright in all our other regression models if we concentrate on three blocks of variables, namely, geographic location (or region), ecological environment, and organizational traits. Region is an exogenous variable for the reasons explained in chapter 6. Thus, geographic region logically precedes all causal processes affecting organizations like Catholic dioceses and is always entered first in the models. We assume the unmeasured characteristics that define region have a direct impact on traits describing the population living in the region, on characteristics describing diocesan organizations, and on any ultimate dependent variable in our models.

Priorities among distinct segments within the other two categories (ecological environment and organizational traits) are not always fixed by a time sequence and thus are debatable (cf. Duncan 1975). A time sequence does apply to some, however, and the other causal priorities have been assumed on the basis of widely accepted evidence or our own understanding of the social forces at work in the contemporary Catholic church. Because the analysis of all the regression models is limited to the ultimate dependent variable (one model—table 6.4—also includes the penultimate variable), there's no need to present detailed assumptions about causal precedence among the intervening variables. A full discussion of all our causal assumptions, however, is available upon request.

Appendix D
New and Divided Dioceses

Dioceses Established after January 1, 1966

As a comparative analysis of 86 dioceses, the technical design for this study must take into account a wide range of conditions specific to individual dioceses. Fourteen of the dioceses were established after January 1, 1966, the starting date of the census registry, so their data do not cover the full 19 years under investigation. These fall into four categories for the purposes of this study. The dioceses of Fresno, Monterey, Beaumont, Dallas, and Fort Worth compose the first category; Orange, San Bernardino, San Jose, and Lake Charles, the second; Gaylord, Las Cruces, and Victoria, the third; and Orlando and St. Petersburg, the fourth.

Category 1: Beaumont, Fresno, Monterey, Dallas,
and Fort Worth

Beaumont was separated from Corpus Christi and established as an autonomous diocese during 1966. Fresno–Monterey formed a combined jurisdiction until 1967, when each became an autonomous see. And Dallas and Fort Worth were a single diocese until 1969, when they were established as separate corporate entities.

The reason for combining them in a single category is that all dioceses involved in these splits had been included in a series of interrelated studies begun in 1969 which form a single longitudinal data base. Also, they were established shortly after January 1, 1966.

In order to include them in all aspects of the present study, we assume the separate and continuous existence of their diocesan priest populations as of January 1, 1966. That is to say, those diocesan priests who were *ipso facto* incardinated on the date of the dioceses' establishment were already identifiable in the former diocesan jurisdictions on January 1, 1966. Because accurate sources were available, we constructed the registry for the new dioceses from that date onward.

Thus, even though a diocese was established during or after 1966, all the graphs

382

and tables for the new dioceses include data from 1966 onward. The reader must note, however, that only entrances in the populations are fully reflected in the data that cover the period prior to the dioceses' creation. No exits other than sick leave or retirement could be recorded for the obvious reason that if a priest resigned, excardinated, or died, he would not have been *ipso facto* incardinated into the new diocese on the date it was established. Apart from these exceptions, the dioceses in Category 1 are handled the same as dioceses that were not divided during the census period.

Some exit rates are slightly underestimated for the period between January 1, 1966, and the date the diocese was founded. This adjustment has negligible consequences for the projection models; it overestimates growth and underestimates decline very slightly.

Category 2: Orange, San Bernardino, San Jose, and Lake Charles

The diocese of Orange began in 1976 with 100 priests (according to our census counts) who were formerly of the Archdiocese of Los Angeles. San Bernardino began in 1978 with 139 priests formerly of San Diego. San Jose began in 1981 with 87 priests formerly of San Francisco. Lake Charles was created in 1980 with 34 priests from Lafayette, Louisiana.

These newly established dioceses are alike in that each was created from a single parent diocese at least 10 years after the census period began. Likewise, all the parent dioceses had been included in the series of interrelated studies which began in 1969 and thus, of course, are part of the present sample.

As part of the overall design, we constructed a complete registry for each of the parent dioceses for 1966–84. Therefore, from the beginning of the census onward, we can assume the separate and continuous existence of and identify that population of diocesan priests who would eventually become the clergy of the new diocese on the date of its creation.

Thus, the historical data, namely statistics in the tables and graphs covering 1966–84, are taken from the parent dioceses' information up to the separation and from the newly established dioceses' records after the latter's creation. In like manner, the projection assumptions are based on the experience of the parent dioceses before the split and on the newly established dioceses' own experience after they began.

For the newly created dioceses in Category 2, then, the reader must bear in mind that the historical data for the years prior to date of establishment are assumed to be the same, *mutatis mutandis,* as the data for the parent dioceses.

To be specific, changes in the historical data for those years prior to the establishment of the new dioceses are handled in the following manner: First, the size of the population and the number of transition events are calculated by multiplying the corresponding numbers recorded in the parent diocese by the percentage of the parent population that was transferred to the new diocese the year of the split. Second, rates and other statistics used in the projection models are taken directly from the data for parent dioceses for the prior years and data for the new dioceses for the years following the division.

Category 3: Gaylord, Las Cruces, and Victoria

The Category 3 dioceses were established from multiple parent dioceses, and all the latter were included in earlier related studies as well as the present investigation. Gaylord began in 1971 with 41 priests from Grand Rapids and 17 from Saginaw. Las Cruces was created in 1982 with 30 priests from El Paso and 2 from Santa Fe. Victoria was also established in 1982 with 47 priests from San Antonio, 5 from Galveston–Houston, and 1 from Corpus Christi.

Here again we use the same strategy as for the other newly established dioceses but take into account multiple dioceses of origin. We assume that the aggregated priest population that made up the new clergy in these dioceses had existed as an identifiable group since January 1, 1966. Because we have constructed a complete registry for each of the parent dioceses, we are able to calculate weighted estimates of the size and transition rates of the combined population of diocesan priests that would eventually become the clergy of the new diocese. The estimates cover the period from January 1, 1966, to the date of establishment of the new diocese and are based on the combined experience of the multiple parent dioceses weighted by the proportion of the population contributed by each one.

So the historical data, namely, statistics in the tables and graphs covering 1966–84, are taken from the parent dioceses' weighted data up to the separation and from the newly established dioceses' records after their creation. In like manner, the projection assumptions are based on the weighted experience of the multiple parent dioceses before the split and on the newly established dioceses' own experience after they began.

For the newly created dioceses in Category 3, then, the reader must remember that the historical data for those years prior to the date of establishment are assumed to be the same, *mutatis mutandis,* as the weighted data for the combination of parent dioceses. The projections, too, rely upon the combination of parent dioceses' weighted assumptions for the early years and the new dioceses' assumptions for the later years of the historical period.

Category 4: Orlando and St. Petersburg

The diocese of Orlando and St. Petersburg were created from the Diocese of St. Augustine in 1968. Because St. Augustine was not part of the sample for the earlier related studies, we cannot include its data as a parent diocese in this investigation.

For these two newly established dioceses, therefore, we project the data from their 1968 registries backward to January 1, 1966. This strategy allows us to estimate the probable size of the clergy populations and the number of entrances through ordination and exits through retirement and sick leave for 1966 and 1967.

The two dioceses in Category 4 are unique in that their parent diocese was not included in the earlier data which form part of the data base for the present study. Thus we have no reasonable estimates of entrance and exit rates for the first two years and for half of the third year of the census period. Accordingly, for Orlando and St. Petersburg, when the information is available, we include reasonable estimates in those tables and graphs containing historical data, but we base the assumptions for their projection models only on the complete data for 1969–84.

Summary

The uniform assumption for all dioceses established after January 1, 1966, including Orlando and St. Petersburg, therefore, is that the priest population that eventually composed the new diocesan clergy already existed on January 1, 1966. Furthermore, in each case, except Orlando and St. Petersburg as noted, the population size and all transition events can be estimated from the data in existing census registries, which all begin on that same date.

Along with permitting a full range of comparisons between the new dioceses and all the others, this strategy also allows us to estimate the size and other parameters of the entire diocesan priest population in the United States without showing artificial growth or decline during those years when parent dioceses were divided and new dioceses created.

Parent Dioceses Divided after January 1, 1966

As you have seen, during the census period, splits occurred in 16 of the dioceses and archdioceses under investigation. These fall into two categories. The first includes Los Angeles, San Francisco, San Diego, Lafayette, Saginaw, Santa Fe, San Antonio, Corpus Christi, El Paso, and Galveston–Houston. The second includes Pueblo, Orlando, St. Petersburg, Detroit, Grand Rapids, and Gallup.

Category 1: Los Angeles, San Francisco, San Diego, Lafayette, Saginaw, Santa Fe, San Antonio, Corpus Christi, El Paso, and Galveston–Houston

The divisions occurring in these dioceses resulted in movements to other dioceses included in the study. Thus, despite significant losses in some of the parent dioceses, the sample of diocesan priest populations from which we estimate national population parameters remains intact. That is, the organizational divisions in this set of dioceses caused "migrations" within the sampled national population but no "emigrations" outside it. Table D.1 describes the divisions, showing the parent diocese of origin, the new diocese of destination, and the number of priests transferred in the year of the split.

Two adjustments in our data files are necessary to take these organizational "migrations" into account. The first affects the projection assumptions for the individual dioceses in which the splits occurred. In the diocese of origin, for the year in which the division occurred, we replace the abnormally high excardination rate with the mean excardination rate of all other years for 1966–84. In the case of Saginaw, which also gained seven priests from Grand Rapids in the year of the population shifts, we also replace the high incardination rate with the mean incardination rate of all other years for 1966–84. This avoids projecting a one-time exogenous event into the future.

The second adjustment is made in the concatenated national data file created from the census registries of the 86 responding dioceses. (The concatenated file is used to estimate national population parameters.) In each new diocese of destination, for the year in which it was created, we code an incardination event for every priest in the registry. Thus, in the national data file each excardination event

Table D.1. Division of dioceses without emigrations, 1966–84

New diocese	Year created	Diocese(s) of origin	Number transferred
Beaumont	1966	Galveston–Houston	44
Gaylord	1971	Saginaw	17
		Grand Rapids	41
Orange	1976	Los Angeles	100
San Bernardino	1978	San Diego	139
Lake Charles	1980	Lafayette	34
San Jose	1981	San Francisco	87
Victoria	1982	Corpus Christi	1
		Galveston–Houston	5
		San Antonio	47
Las Cruces	1982	El Paso	30
		Santa Fe	3

in the diocese of origin is matched by an incardination event in the diocese of destination, thereby avoiding any artificial growth or decline in our estimates of the national population parameters in any years of the splits.

Category 2: Pueblo, Orlando, St. Petersburg, Detroit,
Grand Rapids, and Gallup

The divisions occurring in this set of dioceses resulted in movements of relatively large numbers of priests to other dioceses not included in the study. Thus, the losses suffered by the parent dioceses alters the sample of diocesan priest populations from which we needed to estimate national population parameters. Table D.2 summarizes the pertinent information, showing the parent diocese of origin, new dioceses of destination, and the number of priests transferred in the year of the split.

Three adjustments in the data are needed to handle these organizational "emigrations." The first is similar to the adjustment made for the divisions described in Category 1, namely, replacing the abnormally high excardination rates for the dio-

Table D.2. Division of dioceses with emigrations, 1966–84

Old diocese	Year divided	Diocese(s) of destination	Number transferred
Gallup	1969	Phoenix	13
Detroit	1971	Lansing	27
Grand Rapids	1971	Gaylord	41
		Kalamazoo	8
		Saginaw	7
Pueblo	1984	Colorado Springs	3
St. Petersburg	1984	Venice	36
Orlando	1984	Palm Beach	7
		Venice	3

cese of origin in the year of the split with the mean excardination rate of all other years from 1966 to 1984. Again, this adjustment avoids projecting a one-time exogenous event into the future.

The second adjustment affects the concatenated national data file which we created from the census registries of the 86 cooperating dioceses. In each diocese of origin we suppress the excardination event the year in which the division occurred for those priests who were transferred to a diocese outside the sample. In effect, this adjustment ignores the organizational division in favor of keeping the original sampled population intact, so it avoids an artificial decline in the national population size for the years of the splits.

The third adjustment required gathering new data from three of the dioceses of destination, namely, Phoenix, Lansing, and Kalamazoo. Through direct contact with these dioceses and official archival sources, we were able to code all further transition events for each priest that occurred after his excardination to the new diocese and add the information to the data files for the dioceses of origin.

Because the splits in Pueblo, Orlando, and St. Petersburg occurred in 1984, we already had the relevant data for all transition events that year, so no additional coding is needed. (Note: For Grand Rapids the transfers to Gaylord and Saginaw are handled the same way as for the divisions described in Category 1 at the beginning of this section.) The third adjustment eliminates under- or overestimation of exit rates for the period after the splits occurred.

Appendix E
Diocesan Projections

This appendix is devoted primarily to table E.1, which provides the projected size of the priest population for each diocese in the sample. Sizes are given for the optimistic, moderate, and pessimistic series at five-year intervals beginning in 1990 and ending in 2005.

Inconsistency Index

To help assess the usefulness of the projections, we have constructed an inconsistency index which measures the amount of fluctuation in the trends.[1] The lower the score, the more consistent the trends and the more powerful the projection models. Low scores are in the 20–40 range, which indicate consistent trends, and more reliable projection models. Scores approaching and exceeding 60 signify less consistent trends and weaker but useful projection models. When scores reach 100 and over, they indicate strong fluctuations in the historical trends and very erratic and much less useful projections.

Inconsistency scores in the sample of dioceses range from a low of 17 in Fargo to a high of 153 in Fort Worth (table E.1, last column). (In Gallup, a small diocese that relies heavily on religious order priests and that underwent an organizational split in 1969, the score is 513; this is clearly a deviant case about which our projection models have little to say.)

Cautionary Note about New and Small Dioceses

Projections of small populations have severe limitations. The analysis indicates that smaller dioceses (generally those of 75 or fewer active priests) have experienced the most fluctuation in their historical data, so their projection models as

---

1. The index is calculated by:

$$I = [(O - P)/E] \, 100$$

where I is inconsistency index,

   O is the size of population in 2005 based on the optimistic projection series,

388

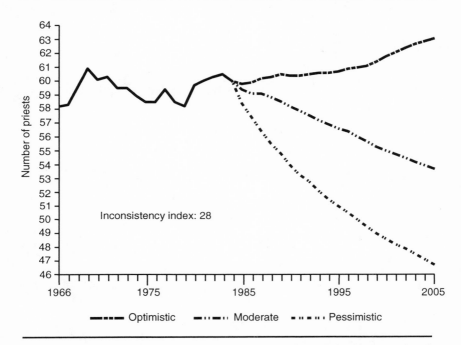

Figure E.1. Average size of U.S. diocesan priest population in 11 small dioceses, 1966–2005

a group are less useful. In addition, newly established small dioceses tend to show both erratic change and unusual growth because of their size as well as their newness (see chapters 7 and 8). Thus most, but not all, inconsistency scores for small dioceses approach or exceed 100.

An attempt to control for the effects of strong fluctuations in the historical data for small dioceses is reflected in figure E.1. The results provide a more consistent projection model, which is based on 660 active priests in 11 dioceses and has an inconsistency score of 28, well within the range of reliability.[2] The figure may be read as a graph of consistent trends and projections for the "typical" or "average" small diocese and can be used for comparisons with data in table E.1.

P is size of population in 2005 based on the pessimistic series, and

E is estimate of the 1966 population based on census counts.

2. The subset includes the 11 sampled dioceses with 75 or fewer active priests in 1966 (therefore excluding any small dioceses created later) that did not undergo an organizational division during the census period — namely, Atlanta, Baker, Baton Rouge, Beaumont, Cheyenne, Corpus Christi, Dodge City, Fort Worth, Monterey, Springfield–Cape Girardeau, and Stockton. Although the Dallas–Fort Worth split occurred in 1969, we include Fort Worth in this subset under the assumption that the clergy there existed more or less intact as a separate population between 1966 and 1969.

Table E.1. Projected size of U.S. diocesan priest population, 1990–2005, by year and diocese (alphabetical order within region by state then diocese)

| Region and diocese | Year | | | | | | | | | | | | Incon-sistency index |
| | 1990 | | | 1995 | | | 2000 | | | 2005 | | | |
	Opt.	Mod.	Pes.	Opt.	Mod.	Pes.	Opt.	Mod.	Pes.	Opt.	Mod.	Pes.	
New England						Northeast							
Hartford CT	433	395	361	406	340	293	381	291	239	358	245	189	30
Norwich CT	119	116	99	118	112	87	120	107	75	121	101	65	41
Portland ME	169	167	141	160	152	116	154	138	96	149	124	81	27
Boston MA	919	848	794	880	751	665	828	655	545	783	569	437	26
Fall River MA	173	153	139	167	138	117	150	120	94	131	101	72	25
Worcester MA	296	253	243	301	229	213	308	207	189	312	190	172	45
Providence RI[a]	–	–	–	–	–	–	–	–	–	–	–	–	–
Burlington VT	135	116	103	129	99	79	120	81	63	117	68	49	38
Middle Atlantic													
Camden NJ	352	322	295	352	296	253	350	264	210	338	222	162	49
Newark NJ	725	674	580	724	631	482	731	583	400	732	528	316	47
Albany NY	299	273	244	294	245	204	295	219	169	293	196	137	34
Brooklyn NY	671	608	545	641	527	440	641	478	369	631	428	302	32
Buffalo NY	493	452	417	481	405	350	477	359	293	468	318	240	36
New York NY	772	740	654	728	671	546	696	612	457	669	560	377	24
Ogdensburg NY	167	155	138	165	142	117	168	131	100	170	122	85	45
Rochester NY	246	231	206	237	210	170	223	186	140	215	166	115	25
Rockville Centre NY	442	406	358	446	390	312	447	371	268	451	358	232	49
Allentown PA	278	254	233	296	251	222	323	244	206	342	238	192	52
Altoona–Johnstown PA	174	156	156	174	142	144	179	133	136	181	123	125	35
Philadelphia PA	821	729	671	835	668	578	877	627	507	911	590	445	45
Pittsburgh PA	537	492	433	540	469	376	558	452	332	572	432	288	50
Scranton PA	355	344	327	338	317	290	336	298	266	336	285	248	19

(continued on following page)

Table E.1. Projected size of U.S. diocesan priest population, 1990–2005, by year and diocese (continued)

Region and diocese	Year												Incon-sistency index
	1990			1995			2000			2005			
	Opt.	Mod.	Pes.	Opt.	Mod.	Pes.	Opt.	Mod.	Pes.	Opt.	Mod.	Pes.	
East Northcentral													
Belleville IL	134	129	119	131	115	97	129	104	81	129	95	68	34
Chicago IL	959	845	712	958	765	588	971	702	500	989	657	429	42
Rockford IL	136	122	115	130	105	93	133	88	73	133	73	57	43
Indianapolis IN	176	145	133	181	129	110	185	113	88	185	97	71	43
Detroit MI	495	410	330	508	372	256	515	339	205	510	310	168	47
Gaylord MI	53	52	40	53	48	33	59	45	28	62	41	23	59
Grand Rapids MI	115	102	92	118	95	78	123	89	67	127	81	57	60
Marquette MI	96	84	76	94	71	58	97	63	46	99	57	37	42
Saginaw MI	122	115	90	132	114	77	141	112	67	147	108	58	66
Cincinnati OH	380	331	302	375	304	264	375	282	235	376	266	212	36
Cleveland OH	554	514	457	557	498	411	560	478	373	561	460	340	36
Columbus OH	186	171	153	183	157	130	184	146	112	182	136	96	36
Youngstown OH	191	174	151	184	155	125	181	138	108	178	126	95	32
La Crosse WI	171	164	149	154	137	111	143	114	83	139	101	64	24
Milwaukee WI	463	410	369	445	351	289	441	306	228	437	268	181	38
West Northcentral													
Des Moines IA	102	93	76	106	91	62	106	84	49	103	73	37	48
Dubuque IA	260	238	225	226	193	172	200	154	129	177	117	93	20
Sioux City IA	159	153	145	152	139	124	151	122	103	142	107	83	28
Dodge City KS	51	50	37	47	47	27	48	45	22	48	43	18	46
Salina KS	68	58	54	68	53	45	70	48	36	71	43	29	49
Wichita KS	118	113	97	117	107	78	114	100	59	114	97	46	41
New Ulm MN	76	76	63	73	68	46	75	62	33	76	56	24	39
St. Cloud MN	130	122	116	122	111	96	118	101	78	114	94	63	29
St. Paul–Minneapolis MN	357	322	287	361	307	251	363	293	217	368	280	190	41

(continued on following page)

Table E.1. Projected size of U.S. diocesan priest population, 1990–2005; by year and diocese (continued)

Region and diocese	1990			1995			2000			2005			Incon-sistency index
	Opt.	Mod.	Pes.	Opt.	Mod.	Pes.	Opt.	Mod.	Pes.	Opt.	Mod.	Pes.	
Northcentral (continued)													
West Northcentral (continued)													
Kansas City–St. Jos. MO	139	131	105	145	127	85	147	121	71	154	115	62	53
St. Louis MO	533	478	446	536	447	403	531	419	362	531	390	327	37
Springfield–C. Girard. MO	74	72	49	76	74	40	79	75	34	82	76	30	72
Lincoln NE[a]	–	–	–	–	–	–	–	–	–	–	–	–	–
Fargo ND	95	94	85	86	82	68	79	75	57	75	69	49	17
Rapid City SD	41	41	25	44	44	20	49	47	15	51	49	13	49
West													
Mountain													
Pueblo CO	84	71	64	84	63	50	90	58	42	98	56	36	73
Boise ID	84	73	62	83	67	54	82	62	50	85	60	45	52
Gallup NM	66	53	42	78	52	34	91	54	30	101	53	24	513
Las Cruces NM	28	23	24	27	19	22	27	17	19	29	15	17	44
Santa Fe NM	113	109	97	108	103	86	109	100	81	110	98	76	24
Cheyenne WY	49	44	36	52	44	30	56	43	27	59	45	26	56
Pacific													
Fresno CA[a]	–	–	–	–	–	–	–	–	–	–	–	–	–
Los Angeles CA	597	527	457	637	521	411	675	509	370	692	495	333	63
Monterey CA	76	60	43	85	55	31	99	51	27	111	50	24	126
Oakland CA	138	133	113	143	131	105	151	131	101	159	129	96	43
Orange CA	146	135	96	169	146	84	198	153	75	222	161	66	153
San Bernardino CA	109	106	74	116	109	59	121	111	48	127	113	41	64
San Diego CA	186	169	152	194	158	131	209	148	112	227	140	95	63

(continued on following page)

Table E.1. Projected size of U.S. diocesan priest population, 1990–2005, by year and diocese (continued)

Region and diocese	Year												Incon-sistency index
	1990			1995			2000			2005			
	Opt.	Mod.	Pes.	Opt.	Mod.	Pes.	Opt.	Mod.	Pes.	Opt.	Mod.	Pes.	
Pacific (continued)				West (continued)									
San Francisco CA	225	206	167	240	207	143	255	207	121	269	206	104	68
San Jose CA	90	86	66	95	85	53	104	84	43	108	82	36	65
Stockton CA	45	34	33	50	29	26	57	25	23	62	24	20	88
Baker OR	45	38	30	50	38	23	52	35	17	54	33	13	91
South													
East South													
Wilmington DE	118	110	87	123	109	73	126	107	61	127	104	53	66
Orlando FL	104	97	83	113	97	75	125	94	65	135	90	55	111
St. Petersburg FL	114	113	80	135	128	77	157	142	72	172	152	68	125
Atlanta GA	108	97	89	120	102	86	136	106	85	144	109	82	127
Covington KY	169	157	148	169	143	129	178	133	115	179	130	105	35
Baltimore MD	287	255	216	284	232	175	287	211	143	286	189	119	50
West Southcentral													
Little Rock AK	81	75	63	77	68	52	79	63	44	81	59	35	36
Alexandria–Shreveport LA	77	76	75	69	61	58	70	50	45	71	42	33	28
Baton Rouge LA	88	74	77	92	70	74	106	67	71	117	64	67	69
Lafayette LA	139	132	120	139	127	111	143	121	105	146	117	99	33
Lake Charles LA	46	45	34	50	48	31	57	52	28	62	53	25	112
Austin TX	94	87	74	97	84	60	104	77	50	107	70	40	74
Beaumont TX	56	48	37	62	45	30	65	44	23	70	43	20	114
Corpus Christi TX	76	70	48	84	72	38	90	71	29	91	67	24	99
Dallas TX	116	108	85	130	116	78	143	122	71	155	128	66	91

(continued on following page)

Table E.1. Projected size of U.S. diocesan priest population, 1990–2005, by year and diocese (continued)

Region and diocese	Year															Incon-sistency index
	1990			1995			2000			2005			
	Opt.	Mod.	Pes.	Opt.	Mod.	Pes.	Opt.	Mod.	Pes.	Opt.	Mod.	Pes.	
				South (continued)									
West Southcentral (continued)													
El Paso TX	72	58	52	79	56	45	90	57	40	96	56	38	109
Fort Worth TX	70	54	47	77	50	38	92	48	32	102	46	27	153
Galveston–Houston TX	161	150	130	165	141	111	176	133	98	182	127	87	62
San Antonio TX	158	143	128	168	139	115	178	133	103	182	126	88	63
Victoria TX	49	45	39	49	40	30	45	37	24	44	34	19	53

Note: Sizes of local priest populations in 1966 and 1985 are given in table 4.1.
[a]Refused to participate.

As a guideline for interpreting the data, readers interested in statistics for small dioceses should note the following: In the roughly four-decade period under study, the typical small diocese would register growth of 8 percent under optimistic assumptions, as the top line in the figure shows. Pessimistic assumptions yield an average decline of 20 percent, according to the bottom curve. And the middle line shows that the average small diocese would endure a loss of 8 percent in a moderate projection model. All these projections fall notably below the national average (see table 2.1).

Note: These caveats about small dioceses apply to projections of not only the size of the priesthood population (table E.1 and table 4.1, column 3) but also the age distribution (table 4.3, column 3); likewise, they apply to the combined projection models in table 5.2, columns 4–9. They do not pertain to the analysis presented in table 4.2 or to any other analysis in the book, all of which are limited to historical data on dioceses or national and regional projections.

Appendix F
Sampling Methodology

Because it is well suited to our needs and we wished to integrate some of the relevant data based upon it, we use the same sample as that created for the National Opinion Research Center (1972) survey of diocesan and religious priests. The NORC study used a two-stage sampling procedure, first drawing a sample of dioceses and religious orders and then drawing a sample of individual priests from within each primary sampling unit. For this study, we limit ourselves to their first-stage sample of dioceses and ignore religious orders.

From the standpoint of sample design, the aim of the NORC study was twofold and is identical to ours. A major goal is the accurate description of demographic characteristics of the entire population of Roman Catholic dioceses in the United States. Of equal importance, however, is the analysis of variation in the demographic trends in terms of other independent variables measured for each diocese. Furthermore, our study has explicit policy implications which are also well served by the sample design.

We believe that size of the diocese and geographic location will doubtless be correlated with other characteristics of the diocese and their ecological environment as well as with the various aspects of population growth and decline. In keeping with these assumptions, the NORC sampling frame, which was constructed with data for 1968, was stratified by size and region. The size categories were defined as small (1–100 priests), medium (101–200), large (201–500), and extra large (501 and above). After separation into size strata, the dioceses were arranged in geographical order by the four major U.S. census divisions, and 85 cases were drawn.

All dioceses with populations above 500 priests were automatically included in the NORC sample. This feature is retained and serves to strengthen the applied nature of our research. Another primary goal of the project is to make the reports available to policymakers in the Catholic church who are concerned with declining numbers of priests. Because officials in the larger dioceses are likely to be among

396

those policymakers, we wanted to insure that all of them would be included in the study.

The NORC sample also included four Eastern-rite dioceses. These are eliminated from our sample, because we believe the set of social forces affecting structural change in them is different from that in Latin-rite dioceses; the latter compose the vast majority of Catholic dioceses in this country. Some dioceses were divided during the period under investigation; these and the newly created dioceses that split from them are retained, bringing the sample size to 89 (see appendix D for a list of the divided and newly created dioceses).

The sample design requires the weighting of variables when we wish to estimate national parameters.[1] In such instances we use the following weight:

$$(P_s/p_d)n_s$$

where P_s is the total population of priests in the stratum;

p_d is the population of priests in the selected diocese; and

n_s is the number of dioceses selected within the stratum.

The following exceptions apply:

1. All extra-large dioceses have a weighting factor of 1.0.

2. Because in the stratum for small dioceses some units were grouped before the sample was drawn, the formula for dioceses in the small stratum becomes:

$$(P_s/p_g)n_g$$

where P_s is the total population in the stratum;

p_g is the population of priests in the selected group of dioceses or single diocese; and

n_g is the number of groups of dioceses and single dioceses selected within the stratum.

3. When a new diocese was divided from a single diocese, the same weighting factor is used in both. When a new diocese was created from two or more parent dioceses, the weighting factor is a weighted mean. (See appendix D for other adjustments to methods necessitated by the creation of new dioceses during the historical period.)

4. The design involves sampling without replacement, with the consequence of potentially biased estimates of variance.

Table F.1 presents the names of the dioceses that make up the sample, priest population size as reported by the Official Catholic Directory, 1969, for the year the sample was designed, and the weighting factors used in this study.

1. Data are weighted in all other tables except the following: 1.1, 2.4, 5.2, 6.4–6.7, 7.4–7.6, 8.4, 8.8, 9.3, 9.6, 10.6–10.9, 12.5, 12.6, D.1, D.2, E.1, and F.1. Data are weighted in all figures except those without quantitative data.

Table F.1. Size in 1968 and unadjusted and adjusted weight for sampled dioceses (alphabetical order within region by state then diocese)

Region and diocese	Size, 1968[a]	Unadjusted weight[b]	Adjusted weight[c]
	Northeast		
New England			
Hartford CT	594	1.000	
Norwich CT	155	2.115	
Portland ME	272	2.161	3.233
Boston MA	1,435	1.000	
Fall River MA	243	2.419	3.619
Worcester MA	316	1.860	2.783
Providence RI	412	1.427	0
Burlington VT	187	1.753	
Middle Atlantic			
Camden NJ	384	1.531	
Newark NJ	909	1.000	
Albany NY	475	1.238	
Brooklyn NY	1,094	1.000	
Buffalo NY	654	1.000	
New York NY	1,250	1.000	
Ogdensburg NY	205	2.868	
Rochester NY	426	1.380	
Rockville Centre NY	458	1.284	
Allentown PA	296	1.986	
Altoona–Johnstown PA	176	1.863	
Philadelphia PA	1,071	1.000	
Pittsburgh PA	593	1.000	
Scranton PA	484	1.215	
	Northcentral		
East Northcentral			
Belleville IL	199	1.648	
Chicago IL	1,419	1.000	
Rockford IL	190	1.726	
Indianapolis IN	290	2.027	
Detroit MI	840	1.000	
Gaylord MI	—[d]	2.405	
Grand Rapids MI	222	2.648	
Marquette MI	149	2.200	
Saginaw MI	176	1.863	
Cincinnati OH	462	1.272	
Cleveland OH	626	1.000	
Columbus OH	241	2.439	
Youngstown OH	275	2.138	
La Crosse WI	350	1.680	
Milwaukee WI	700	1.000	
West Northcentral			
Des Moines IA	134	2.447	2.821

(continued on following page)

398

Table F.1. Size in 1968 and unadjusted and adjusted weight for sampled dioceses (continued)

Region and diocese	Size, 1968[a]	Unadjusted weight[b]	Adjusted weight[c]
Northcentral (continued)			
West Northcentral (continued)			
Dubuque IA	454	1.295	
Sioux City IA	223	2.636	
Dodge City KS	68	1.998	
Salina KS	93	1.461	
Wichita KS	169	1.940	2.237
New Ulm MN	129	2.542	2.930
St. Cloud MN	195	1.681	1.938
St. Paul–Minneapolis MN	507	1.000	
Kansas City–St. Jos. MO	195	1.681	1.938
St. Louis MO	568	1.000	
Springfield–C. Girard. MO	75	1.811	
Lincoln NE	151	2.171	0
Fargo ND	166	1.975	2.277
Rapid City SD	61	2.227	
West			
Mountain			
Pueblo CO	94	1.445	1.668
Boise ID	86	1.579	1.823
Gallup NM	37[e]	1.617	0
Las Cruces NM	—[d]	1.588	
Santa Fe NM	194	1.690	
Cheyenne WY	60	2.264	2.613
Pacific			
Fresno CA	137	2.393	0
Los Angeles CA	718	1.000	
Monterey CA	62	2.191	
Oakland CA	177	1.852	3.286
Orange CA	—[d]	1.000	
San Bernardino CA	—[d]	1.568	
San Diego CA	375	1.568	
San Francisco CA	346	1.699	
San Jose CA	—[d]	1.699	
Stockton CA	52	2.612	
Baker OR	47	1.617	
South			
East South[f]			
Wilmington DE	121	2.710	
Orlando FL	96	1.415	
St. Petersburg FL	94	1.445	
Atlanta GA	64	2.122	

(continued on following page)

Table F.1. Size in 1968 and unadjusted and adjusted weight for sampled dioceses (continued)

Region and diocese	Size, 1968[a]	Unadjusted weight[b]	Adjusted weight[c]
South (continued)			
East South[f] (continued)			
Covington KY	218	2.697	
Baltimore MD	371	1.585	
West Southcentral			
Little Rock AK	134	2.447	
Alexandria–Shreveport LA	131	2.503	
Baton Rouge LA	81	1.677	
Lafayette LA	194	1.690	
Lake Charles LA	—[d]	1.690	
Austin TX	92	1.476	
Beaumont TX	51	2.663	
Corpus Christi TX	77	1.764	
Dallas TX	—[g]	2.230	
El Paso TX	87	1.561	
Fort Worth TX	—[g]	2.230	
Galveston–Houston TX	182	1.801	
San Antonio TX	228	2.578	
Victoria TX	—[d]	2.490	

[a]Source: the Official Catholic Directory, 1969.

[b]Assuming 100 percent response in all regions.

[c]The dioceses of Providence in the New England region, Lincoln in the West Northcentral, and Fresno in the Pacific did not respond. Thus, weights for the other three large dioceses in the New England region are adjusted for a response rate of 0.669; for the other six medium dioceses in the West Northcentral, of 0.867; and for the other one large diocese in the Pacific, of 0.564. We use adjusted weights in all tables and figures in which we estimate national and regional parameters.

[d]Established after 1968; see appendix D for parent diocese(s).

[e]The Diocese of Gallup in the West region is included in the descriptive analysis but is dropped from the regression analysis. Thus, we use unadjusted weights for small dioceses in the West in all weighted tables and figures except tables 6.1 and 6.2. In the two excepted tables, weights for the other three small dioceses in the West are adjusted for a response rate of 0.866.

[f]Combines the South Atlantic region and one diocese from East Southcentral region.

[g]Divided in 1969; see appendix D for adjustments made to standardize measures.

Appendix G
Standardized Mortality Ratios

This appendix presents the results of tabulating observed and calculating expected deaths for priests by age and subsample. The standardized mortality ratios (SMRs) presented in tables 11.6–11.10 are derived from these calculations. An SMR is the ratio of observed to expected deaths in a category of age and social condition. The mean value of SMRs across categories of a particular control variable is equal to 100. SMRs below 100 indicate lower than average mortality risks, and values above 100, higher than average.

For example, the SMR of priests aged 25–34, given in the first cell of column 1, table 11.6, is calculated for comparison with subcategories of U.S. white males aged 25–34 classified by level of education, given in column 1, rows 2–9, of the same table. This SMR is derived from data given in table G.1, column 1, rows 3 and 4, and is computed as follows: $(2.26382/5.33832) \times 100 = 42$. Comparing the SMR score of 42 with the other data in column 1 of table 11.6 reveals that priests aged 25–34 experience slightly higher mortality risks than U.S. white males in that age group with comparable education.

Table G.1. Data on U.S. white males and U.S. diocesan priests, for computing standardized mortality ratios in tables 11.6–11.10

| | Age group | | | | | | | |
| | 10-year | | | | | Combined | | |
Standardized by	25–34	35–44	45–54	55–64	65–74	≥ 25	25–64	≥ 65
Education								
Annual rate[a]	0.00117	0.00252	0.00613	0.01688	0.03801	0.01205	0.00582	0.05286
Exp. deaths	5.33832	17.2679	50.4867	117.687	202.935	414.548	154.946	411.216
Family income								
Annual rate[b]	0.00117	0.00252	0.00613	0.01688	0.03801	0.01205	0.00582	0.05286
Exp. deaths	5.33832	17.2679	50.4867	117.687	202.935	414.548	154.946	411.216
Marital status								
Annual rate[c]	0.00124	0.00237	0.00604	0.01634	0.03867	0.01183	0.00568	0.05340
Exp. deaths	5.65771	16.2400	49.7454	113.922	206.459	406.980	151.219	415.416
Race								
Annual rate[d]	0.00133	0.00265	0.00644	0.01726	0.03828	–	–	0.05286
Exp. deaths	6.06835	18.1587	53.0398	120.337	204.377	–	–	411.216
No. of priests[e]	4,563	6,852	8,236	6,972	5,339	34,402	26,623	7,779
Obs. deaths[e]	2.26382	13.2528	37.1429	81.9238	187.273	575.056	134.583	440.473
Occupation								
Annual rate[f]	0.00105	0.00229	0.00525	0.01315	0.02566	0.00553	0.00455	0.02786
Exp. deaths	4.55770	15.6850	42.9520	90.2221	123.390	177.137	119.357	161.356
No. of priests[g]	4,341	6,849	8,181	6,861	4,809	32,032	26,232	5,792
Obs. deaths[g]	2.26048	13.2597	33.5626	77.5548	149.567	345.034	126.638	149.567

Sources: for U.S. white males, Rogot et al. 1988; for priests, weighted census counts.

Notes: Expected deaths equal the age-specific annual mortality rates (R) of all U.S. white males (except for occupation) multiplied by the number of priests; R is based on deaths from all causes as reported by Rogot et al. (1988, tables identified in the footnotes below). For occupation, R is limited to deaths of white males employed within the past five years. R varies by social condition, because it is based on samples that differ in composition and size, with one exception: it is the same for education and family income. Discrepancies are due to rounding.

[a]Table 6, mortality, by education.
[b]Table 7, mortality, by income.
[c]Table 9, mortality, by marital status.
[d]Table 1, mortality, by race.
[e]These numbers represent age-specific means for 1979–81, based on the total priest population: active priests, plus those retired, sick, and absent.
[f]Table 11, mortality, by major occupation.
[g]These numbers represent age-specific means for 1979–81, limited to active priests plus those who were active within the past five years.

Bibliography

Abbott, Walter M. (ed.). 1966. *The Documents of Vatican II.* New York: America Press.

Agresti, Alan, and Barbara Finlay. 1986. *Statistical Methods for the Social Sciences.* 2nd ed. San Francisco: Dellen.

Aiken, Michael, and Jerald Hage. 1968. "Organizational Interdependence and Intraorganizational Structure." *American Sociological Review* 33:912–30.

Aldrich, Howard E. 1979. *Organizations and Environments.* Englewood Cliffs, N.J.: Prentice-Hall.

Alterman, Hyman. 1969. *Counting People: The Census in History.* New York: Harcourt, Brace and World.

American Institute of Public Opinion. 1987. *Gallup Opinion Index.* No. 259. Princeton, N.J.: Princeton Religion Research Center.

Argyris, Chris. 1972. *The Applicability of Organizational Sociology.* London: Cambridge University Press.

Barclay, George W. 1958. *Techniques of Population Analysis.* New York: Wiley.

Benjamin, Bernard, and H. W. Haycock. 1970. *The Analysis of Mortality and Other Actuarial Statistics.* London: Cambridge University Press.

Berger, Peter L. 1967. *The Sacred Canopy: Elements of a Sociological Theory of Religion.* Garden City, N.Y.: Doubleday.

Berger, Peter L. 1980. *The Heretical Imperative: Contemporary Possibilities of Religious Affirmation.* Garden City, N.Y.: Anchor.

Birch, A. H. 1975. "Economic Models in Political Science: The Case of 'Exit, Voice and Loyalty.'" *British Journal of Political Science* 5:69–82.

Blau, Peter M. 1965. "The Comparative Study of Organizations." *Industrial and Labor Relations Review* 18:323–38.

Blau, Peter M. 1977. *Inequality and Heterogeneity: A Primitive Theory of Social Structure.* New York: Free Press.

Blau, Peter M., and Richard A. Schoenherr. 1971. *The Structure of Organizations.* New York: Basic Books.

Bottomore, Tom. 1975. "Structure and History." In *Approaches to the Study of Social Structure,* ed. Peter M. Blau, pp. 159–71. New York: Free Press.

Braverman, Harry. 1974. *Labor and Monopoly Capital: The Degradation of Work in the Twentieth Century.* New York: Monthly Review Press.

Brittain, Jack, and John Freeman. 1980. "Organizational Proliferation and Density Dependent Selection." In *Organizational Life Cycles,* ed. John Kimberly and Robert Miles, pp. 291–338. San Francisco: Jossey-Bass.

Broccolo, Gerard T. 1986. "Can We Have Prayer Without Father?" *Journal of the Catholic Campus Ministry Association* 1:22–24.

Bühlmann, Walbert. 1986. *The Church of the Future: A Model for the Year 2001.* Maryknoll, N.Y.: Orbis Books.

Burawoy, Michael. 1990. "Marxism as Science: Historical Challenges and Theoretical Growth." *American Sociological Review* 55:775–93.

Campbell, Donald. 1969. "Variation and Selective Retention in Sociocultural Evolution." *General Systems* 16:69–85.

Carroll, Glenn R. (ed.). 1988. *Ecological Models of Organizations.* Cambridge, Mass.: Ballinger.

Carroll, Glenn R., and Jacques Delacroix. 1982. "Organizational Mortality in the Newspaper Industries of Argentina and Ireland: An Ecological Approach." *Administrative Science Quarterly* 27:169–98.

Castelli, Jim. 1989. "New Breed of Foreign Priests Descends." *National Catholic Reporter* (Kansas City, Mo.), Sept. 29, pp. 1, 8–9.

Catholic News Service. 1990. "U.S. Seminarian Number Down for Fifth Year in a Row." *The Catholic Herald* (Madison, Wis.), Feb. 8, p. 10.

Cleary, O.P., Edward. 1989. "Flocking to Seminaries in Latin America." *National Catholic Reporter* (Kansas City, Mo.), November 10, p. 10.

Clouse, Bonnidell, and Robert G. Clouse. 1989. *Women in Ministry: Four Views.* Downers Grove, Ill.: InterVarsity Press.

Coriden, James A. 1972. "Celibacy, Canon Law and Synod 1971." In *Celibacy in the Church,* ed. William Basset and Peter Huizing, pp. 109–24. New York: Herder and Herder.

Coriden, James A., Thomas J. Green, and Donald E. Heintschel. 1985. *The Code of Canon Law: A Text and Commentary.* New York: Paulist Press.

Cornell, George W. 1990. "Priest Decline May Be Useful, Analyst Says." *Houston Chronicle* (Houston, Tex.), Sept. 1.

Corpus Reports. Vols. 1–17. Edited and published by Terence Dosh, 4124 Harriet, Minneapolis, Minn., 55409.

Cyert, Richard. 1978. "The Management of Universities of Constant or Decreasing Size." *Public Administration Review* 38:344–49.

Darwin, Charles. 1859. *The Origin of Species.* London: J. Murray.

Deflem, Mathieu. 1991. "Ritual, Anti-Structure, and Religion: A Discussion of Victor Turner's Processual Symbolic Analysis." *Journal for the Scientific Study of Religion* 30:1–25.

Dolan, Jay P., R. Scott Appleby, Patricia Byrne, and Debra Campbell. 1989. *Trans-*

forming Parish Ministry: The Changing Roles of Catholic Clergy, Laity and Women Religious. New York: Crossroad.

Doohan, Leonard. 1986. *Grass Roots Pastors: A Handbook for Career Lay Ministers.* San Francisco: Harper and Row.

Dulles, Avery Robert, 1974. *Models of the Church: A Critical Assessment of the Church in All Its Aspects.* Garden City, N.Y.: Doubleday.

Duncan, Otis D. 1975. *Introduction to Structural Equation Models.* New York: Academic Press.

Ebaugh, Helen Rose Fuchs. 1988. *Becoming an Ex: The Process of Role Exit.* Chicago: University of Chicago Press.

Ebaugh, Helen Rose Fuchs (ed.). 1991. *Vatican II and U.S. Catholicism.* Greenwich, Conn.: JAI Press.

Edwards, Richard. 1979. *Contested Terrain: The Transformation of the Workplace in the Twentieth Century.* New York: Basic Books.

Eifert, Carl. 1990. "Trend Is for Religious Priests to Leave Parish Work." Catholic News Service (U.S. Catholic Conference, Washington, D.C.), June 8.

Eliade, Mircea. 1961. *The Sacred and the Profane: The Nature of Religion.* Trans. Willard R. Trask. New York: Harcourt, Brace and World.

Ellis, John Tracy. 1971. *The Catholic Priest in the United States: Historical Investigations.* Collegeville, Minn.: St. John's University Press.

Fee, Joan L., Andrew M. Greeley, William C. McCready, and Teresa A. Sullivan. 1981. *Young Catholics: A Report to the Knights of Columbus.* Los Angeles: Sadlier.

Fichter, Joseph H. 1951. *Dynamics of City Church: Southern Parish.* Vol. 1. Chicago: University of Chicago Press.

Fichter, Joseph H. 1968. *America's Forgotten Priests: What They Are Saying.* New York: Harper and Row.

Fichter, Joseph H. 1989. *The Pastoral Provisions: Married Catholic Priests.* Kansas City, Mo.: Sheed and Ward.

Filteau, Jerry. 1991. "Seminary Numbers Down Again for Sixth Straight Year." (For the Catholic News Service, Washington, D.C.) *The Catholic Herald* (Madison, Wis.), Jan. 10, p. 9.

Finke, Roger. 1989. "Demographics of Religious Participation: An Ecological Approach, 1850-1980." *Journal for the Scientific Study of Religion* 28:45-58.

Finke, Roger, and Rodney Stark. 1986. "Turning Pews into People: Estimating 19th Century Church Membership." *Journal for the Scientific Study of Religion* 25: 180-92.

Finke, Roger, and Rodney Stark. 1988. "Religious Economies and Sacred Canopies: Religious Mobilization in American Cities, 1906." *American Sociological Review* 53:41-49.

Finke, Roger, and Rodney Stark. 1989. "How the Upstart Sects Won America: 1776-1850." *Journal for the Scientific Study of Religion* 28:27-44.

Finke, Roger, and Rodney Stark. 1992. *The Churching of America, 1776-1990.* New Brunswick, N.J.: Rutgers University Press.

Freeman, John. 1982. "Organizational Life Cycles and Natural Selection Processes." In *Research in Organizational Behavior,* ed. Barry M. Staw and L. L. Cummings, pp. 1–32. Greenwich, Conn.: JAI Press.

Freeman, John, and Michael T. Hannan. 1983. "Niche Width and the Dynamics of Organizational Populations." *American Journal of Sociology* 88:1116–45.

Freeman, John, Glenn R. Carroll, and Michael T. Hannan. 1983. "The Liability of Newness: Age Dependence in Organizational Death Rates." *American Sociological Review* 48:692–710.

Fuguitt, Glenn V., and Stanley Liebersen. 1974. "Correlation of Ratios or Difference Scores Having Common Terms." In *Sociological Methodology, 1973–74,* ed. Herbert L. Costner, pp. 128–44. San Francisco: Jossey-Bass.

Gargan, Edward T., and Robert A. Hanneman. 1978. "Recruitment to the Clergy in Nineteenth-Century France: 'Modernization' and 'Decline'?" *Journal of Interdisciplinary History* 9:275–95.

Gilmour, Peter. 1986. *The Emerging Pastor: Non-Ordained Catholic Pastors.* Kansas City, Mo.: Sheed and Ward.

Gilpin, Robert. 1976. "The Political Economy of the Multinational Corporation: Three Contrasting Perspectives." *American Political Science Review* 70:184–91.

Glassman, Robert. 1973. "Persistence and Loose Coupling." *Behavioral Science* 18:83–98.

Goldman, Paul, and Donald R. Van Houten. 1977. "Managerial Strategies and the Worker: A Marxist Analysis of Bureaucracy." *Sociological Quarterly* 18:108–25.

Goldman, Paul, and Donald R. Van Houten. 1981. "Bureaucracy and Domination: Managerial Strategy in Turn-of-the-Century American Industry." In *Complex Organizations: Critical Perspectives,* ed. Mary Zey-Ferrell and Michael Aiken, pp. 189–216. Glenview, Ill.: Scott, Foresman.

Greeley, Andrew M. 1972. *Unsecular Man: The Persistence of Religion.* New York: Schocken.

Greeley, Andrew M. 1977. *The American Catholic: A Social Portrait.* New York: Basic Books.

Greeley, Andrew M. 1988. "Defection among Hispanics." *America* 159(3): 61–62.

Greeley, Andrew M. 1989a. *Religious Change in America.* Cambridge, Mass.: Harvard University Press.

Greeley, Andrew M. 1989b. "Protestant and Catholic: Is the Analogical Imagination Extinct?" *American Sociological Review* 54:485–502.

Greeley, Andrew M. 1991. "The Demography of American Catholics: 1965–1990." In *Vatican II and U.S. Catholicism,* ed. Helen Rose Ebaugh, pp. 37–56. Greenwich, Conn.: JAI Press.

Greeley, Andrew M., William C. McCready, and Kathleen McCourt. 1976. *Catholic Schools in a Declining Church.* Kansas City, Mo.: Sheed and Ward.

Greenhalgh, Leonard. 1983. "Organizational Decline." In *Research in the Sociology of Organizations,* vol. 2, ed. Samuel B. Bacharach, pp. 231–76. Greenwich, Conn.: JAI Press.

Guralnick, Lillian. 1963a. "Mortality by Occupation Level and Cause of Death among Men 20 to 64 Years of Age." Washington, D.C.: U.S. Public Health Service, National Vital Statistics Division, Mortality Statistics Branch.

Guralnick, Lillian. 1963b. "Mortality by Industry and Cause of Death among Men 20 to 64 Years of Age." Washington, D.C.: U.S. Public Health Service, National Vital Statistics Division, Mortality Statistics Branch.

Gusfield, Joseph R. 1957. "The Problem of Generations in an Organizational Structure." *Social Forces* 35:323–30.

Hagan, Jacqueline M. 1990. "The Legalization Experience of a Mayan Community in Houston." Ph.D. dissertation, University of Texas at Austin.

Hall, Richard H. 1987. *Organizations: Structure and Process.* 4th ed. Englewood Cliffs, N.J.: Prentice-Hall.

Hannan, Michael T., and John Freeman. 1977. "The Population Ecology of Organizations." *American Journal of Sociology* 82:929–64.

Hannan, Michael T., and John Freeman. 1978. "The Population Ecology of Organizations." In *Organizations and Environments,* ed. Marshall W. Meyer, pp. 131–71. San Francisco: Jossey-Bass.

Hannan, Michael T., and John Freeman. 1984. "Structural Inertia and Organizational Change." *American Sociological Review* 49:149–64.

Hannan, Michael T., and John Freeman. 1989. *Organizational Ecology.* Cambridge, Mass.: Harvard University Press.

Hastings, Adrian. 1972. "Celibacy in Africa." In *Celibacy in the Church,* ed. William Basset and Peter Huizing, pp. 151–56. New York: Herder and Herder.

Hegy, Pierre (ed.). 1993. *In the Spirit of Vatican II: Issues for the 1990s.* Collegeville, Minn.: Liturgical Press.

Hemrick, Eugene F., and Dean R. Hoge. 1986. *Seminarians in Theology: A National Profile.* Washington, D.C.: U.S. Catholic Conference.

Herberg, Will. 1955. *Protestant, Catholic, Jew: An Essay in American Religious Sociology.* Garden City, N.Y.: Doubleday.

Hernes, Gudmund. 1976. "Structural Change in Social Processes." *American Journal of Sociology* 82:513–47.

Hirschman, Albert O. 1970. *Exit, Voice and Loyalty: Responses to Decline in Firms, Organizations and States.* Cambridge, Mass.: Harvard University Press.

Hoge, Dean R. 1987. *Future of Catholic Leadership: Responses to the Priest Shortage.* Kansas City, Mo.: Sheed and Ward.

Hoge, Dean R., Jackson W. Carroll, and Francis K. Scheets, O.S.C. 1988. *Patterns of Parish Leadership: Cost and Effectiveness in Four Denominations.* Kansas City, Mo.: Sheed and Ward.

Hoge, Dean R., Raymond H. Potvin, and Kathleen M. Ferry. 1984. *Research on Men's Vocations to the Priesthood and the Religious Life.* Washington, D.C.: U.S. Catholic Conference.

Hoge, Dean R., Joseph J. Shields, and Mary Jeanne Verdieck. 1988. "Changing Age Distribution and Theological Attitudes of Catholic Priests, 1970–85." *Sociological Analysis* 49:264–80.

Hymer, Stephen. 1972. "The Multinational Corporation and the Law of Uneven

Development." In *Economics and World Order from the 1970's to the 1990's,* ed. Jagdish Bhagwati, pp. 113–40. New York: Macmillan.

Iannaccone, Laurence R. 1990. "Religious Practice: A Human Capital Approach." *Journal for the Scientific Study of Religion* 29:297–314.

Johnson, Benton. 1957. "A Critical Appraisal of the Church-Sect Typology." *American Sociological Review* 22:88–92.

Johnson, Douglas W., Paul R. Picard, and Bernard Quinn. 1974. *Churches and Church Membership in the United States.* Washington, D.C.: Glenmary Research Center.

Kennedy, Eugene C., and Victor J. Heckler. 1972. *The Catholic Priest in the United States: Psychological Investigations.* Washington, D.C.: U.S. Catholic Conference.

Keyfitz, Nathan. 1973. "Individual Mobility in a Stationary Population." *Population Studies* 27:335–52.

Kim, Gertrude. 1980. "Roman Catholic Organization since Vatican II." In *American Denominational Organization: A Sociological View,* ed. Ross P. Scherer, pp. 84–129. Pasadena, Calif.: William Carey Library.

Kimberly, John R. 1976. "Organizational Size and the Structuralist Perspective: A Review, Critique and Proposal." *Administrative Science Quarterly* 21:571–97.

Kitagawa, Evelyn M., and Philip M. Hauser. 1973. *Differential Mortality in the United States: A Study in Socioeconomic Epidemiology.* Cambridge, Mass.: Harvard University Press.

Klatzky, Sheila R. 1970. "Relationship of Organizational Size to Complexity and Coordination." *Administrative Science Quarterly* 15:428–38.

Kosmin, Barry A. 1991. "The National Survey of Religious Identification, 1989–90." Unpublished report, City University of New York, Graduate School and University Center.

Küng, Hans, and Leonard Swidler (eds.). 1987. *The Church in Anguish: Has the Vatican Betrayed Vatican II?* San Francisco: Harper and Row.

Langer, Suzanne. 1961. "Life-Symbols: The Roots of Sacrament." In *Theories of Society: Foundations of Modern Sociological Theory,* vol. 2, ed. Talcott Parsons, Edward Shils, Kaspar D. Naegele, and Jesse R. Pitts, pp. 1179–88. New York: Free Press.

Lawler, Edward E., III, Allan M. Mohrman, Jr., Susan A. Mohrman, Gerald E. Ledford, Jr., Thomas G. Cummings, and Associates. 1985. *Doing Research That Is Useful for Theory and Practice.* Washington, D.C.: Jossey-Bass.

Lee, Valerie E., and Anthony S. Bryk. 1989. "A Multilevel Model of the Social Distribution of High School Achievement." *Sociology of Education* 62:172–92.

Leege, David C. 1986. "Parish Life among the Leaders." Report No. 9, Notre Dame Study of Catholic Parish Life. Notre Dame, Ind.: Institute for Pastoral and Social Ministry.

Leege, David C., and Joseph Gremillion (eds.). 1984–89. Notre Dame Study of Catholic Parish Life. Report Series 1–15. Notre Dame, Ind.: Institute for Pastoral and Social Ministry.

Lehman, Edward C., Jr. 1985. *Women Clergy: Breaking through Gender Barriers.* New Brunswick, N.J.: Transaction Books.

Levine, Charles, I. Rubin, and G. Wolohojian. 1981. *The Politics of Retrenchment: How Local Governments Manage Fiscal Stress.* Beverly Hills, Calif.: Sage.

Levinson, Daniel J. 1978. *The Seasons of a Man's Life.* New York: Ballantine Books.

Ludwig, Dean C. 1984. "Avoiding Spiraling Decline: The Effects of Reallocative Retirement Strategies on Admissions and Departures in Voluntary Organizations." Ph.D. dissertation, University of Pennsylvania, Wharton School of Finance.

Ludwig, Dean C. 1993. "Adapting to a Declining Environment: Lessons from a Religious Order." *Organization Science* 4 (Spring).

Luzbetak, Louis J. 1967. *Clergy Distribution USA.* Washington, D.C.: Center for Applied Research in the Apostolate.

Lynch, John. 1972. "Critique of the Law of Celibacy in the Catholic Church from the Period of the Reform Councils." In *Celibacy in the Church,* ed. William Basset and Peter Huizing, pp. 57–75. New York: Herder and Herder.

McCain, Bruce, Charles O'Reilly, and Jeffrey Pfeffer. 1983. "The Effects of Departmental Demography on Turnover: The Case of a University." *Academy of Management Journal* 26:626–41.

McKelvey, Bill. 1982. *Organizational Systematics: Taxonomy, Evolution, Classification.* Berkeley, Calif.: University of California Press.

McKelvey, Bill. 1988. "Organizational Decline from the Population Perspective." In *Readings in Organizational Decline: Frameworks, Research and Prescriptions,* ed. Kim S. Cameron, Robert I. Sutton, and David A. Whetten, pp. 399–410. Cambridge, Mass.: Ballinger.

McKelvey, Bill, and Howard Aldrich. 1983. "Populations, Natural Selection and Applied Organizational Science." *Administrative Science Quarterly* 28:101–28.

McNeil, Kenneth. 1978. "Understanding Organizational Power: Building on the Weberian Legacy." *Administrative Science Quarterly* 23:65–90.

Mahony, Roger. 1990. "The Good News about Priestly Vocations." *Our Sunday Visitor* (Huntington, Ind.), November 18, p. 3.

March, James G., and Johan P. Olsen. 1976. *Ambiguity and Choice in Organizations.* Bergen, Norway: Universitetsforlaget.

March, James G., and Herbert A. Simon. 1958. *Organizations.* New York: Wiley.

Matras, Judah. 1975. "Models and Indicators of Organizational Growth, Changes and Transformations." In *Social Indicator Models,* ed. Kenneth C. Land and Seymour Spilerman, pp. 301–18. New York: Sage.

Mendenhall, William, Lyman Ott, and Richard L. Schaeffer. 1971. *Elementary Survey Sampling.* Bellmont, Calif.: Wadsworth.

Menges, Robert J., and James E. Dittes. 1965. *Psychological Studies of Clergymen: Abstracts of Research.* New York: Thomas Nelson and Sons.

Meyer, Marshall W. 1972. "Size and the Structure of Organizations: A Causal Analysis." *American Sociological Review* 37:434–40.

Miles, Robert H., and Kim S. Cameron. 1982. *Coffin Nails and Corporate Strategies.* Englewood Cliffs, N.J.: Prentice-Hall.

The National Catholic Almanac. Annual. Paterson, N.J.: St. Anthony's Guild.

National Opinion Research Center (NORC). 1972. *The Catholic Priest in the United*

States: Sociological Investigations. (Andrew M. Greeley and Richard A. Schoenherr, principal investigators.) Washington, D.C.: U.S. Catholic Conference.[1]

Nouwen, Henri J. M. 1979. *Clowning in Rome: Reflections on Solitude, Celibacy,
Prayer, and Contemplation.* Garden City, N.Y.: Image Books.

O'Dea, Thomas F. 1968. *The Catholic Crisis.* Boston: Beacon Press.

The Official Catholic Directory. Annual. New York: P. J. Kenedy.

Otto, Rudolf. [1923] 1969. *The Idea of the Holy.* London: Oxford University
Press.

Ozment, Steven. 1972. "Marriage and the Ministry in the Protestant Churches."
In *Celibacy in the Church,* ed. William Basset and Peter Huizing, pp. 39–56.
New York: Herder and Herder.

Payne, Stanley G. 1984. *Spanish Catholicism: An Historical Overview.* Madison:
University of Wisconsin Press.

Perrow, Charles. 1986. *Complex Organizations: A Critical Essay.* 3rd ed. New York:
Random House.

Pettigrew, Andrew M. 1973. *The Politics of Organizational Decision-Making.* London: Tavistock.

Pettigrew, Andrew M. 1979. "On Studying Organizational Cultures." *Administrative Science Quarterly* 24:570–81.

Pettigrew, Andrew M. 1983. *The Politics of Creating Change in Organizations.*
Oxford: Basil Blackwell.

Pfeffer, Jeffrey. 1983. "Organizational Demography." In *Research in Organizational
Behavior,* vol. 5, ed. L. L. Cummings and Barry M. Staw, pp. 299–357. Greenwich, Conn.: JAI Press.

Pfeffer, Jeffrey, and Gerald Salancik. 1978. *The External Control of Organizations:
A Resource Dependence Perspective.* New York: Harper and Row.

Potvin, Raymond. 1985. *Seminarians of the Eighties: A National Survey.* Washington, D.C.: National Catholic Educational Association.

Potvin, Raymond, and Antanas Suziedelis. 1969. *Seminarians of the Sixties.* Washington, D.C.: Center for Applied Research in the Apostolate.

Pressat, Roland. 1972. *Demographic Analysis: Methods, Results, Applications.*
Trans. Judah Matras. Chicago: Aldine-Atherton.

Pugh, D. S., D. J. Hickson, C. R. Hinings, and C. Turner. 1968. "Dimensions of
Organization Structure." *Administrative Science Quarterly* 13:65–105.

Pugh, D. S., D. J. Hickson, C. R. Hinings, K. M. Macdonald, C. Turner, and T.
Lupton. 1963. "A Conceptual Scheme for Organizational Analysis." *Administrative Science Quarterly* 8:289–315.

Quinn, Bernard, Herman Anderson, Martin Bradley, Paul Goetting, and Peggy
Shriver (eds.). 1982. *Churches and Church Membership in the United States
1980: An Enumeration by Region, State and County Based on Data Reported
by 111 Church Bodies.* Atlanta, Ga.: Glenmary Research Center.

1. Andrew M. Greeley's name appears alone on the title page because of an "error" on
the part of the publishers; see the Acknowledgments for our statement of credits and "Er-
rata" insert of the publishers.

Ray, Melissa Lynn. 1991. "Blest Be the Ties That Bind: Interpretive Appropriation of External Mandates in an Organizational Culture." Ph.D. dissertation, University of Wisconsin–Madison.

Reed, Theodore L. 1978. "Organizational Change in the American Foreign Service, 1925–1965: The Utility of Cohort Analysis." *American Sociological Review* 43:404–21.

Richardson, Herbert. 1969. "The Symbol of Virginity." In *The Religious Situation, 1969,* ed. Donald R. Cutler, pp. 775–811. Boston: Beacon Press.

Riding, Alan. 1989. "Theologians in Europe Challenge Pope's Conservative Leadership." *New York Times,* July 14, section A, pp. 1, 4.

Rogot, Eugene, Paul D. Sorlie, Norman J. Johnson, Claudia S. Glover, and David W. Treasure. 1988. *A Mortality Study of One Million Persons by Demographic, Social and Economic Factors: 1979–1981 Follow-Up.* Washington, D.C.: U.S. Department of Health and Human Services, Public Health Service, National Institutes of Health.

Roof, Wade Clark, and William McKinney. 1987. *American Mainline Religion: Its Changing Shape and Future.* New Brunswick, N.J.: Rutgers University Press.

Ryder, Norman B. 1965. "The Cohort as a Concept in the Study of Social Change." *American Sociological Review* 30:843–61.

Salaman, Graeme. 1981. "Towards a Sociology of Organisational Structure." In *Complex Organizations: Critical Perspectives,* ed. Mary Zey-Ferrell and Michael Aiken, pp. 22–45. Glenview, Ill.: Scott, Foresman.

Salancik, Gerald R., and Jeffrey Pfeffer. 1974. "The Bases and Use of Power in Organizational Decision Making: The Case of a University." *Administrative Science Quarterly* 19:453–73.

Schillebeeckx, Edward. 1985. *The Church with a Human Face: A New and Expanded Theology of Ministry.* Trans. John Bowden. New York: Crossroad.

Schoenherr, Richard A. 1967. "Shape of the Pyramid and Centralization of Authority in Formal Organizations." Master's thesis, University of Chicago.

Schoenherr, Richard A. 1987a. "Power and Authority in Organized Religion: Disaggregating the Phenomenological Core." *Sociological Analysis* 47:52–71.

Schoenherr, Richard A. 1987b. *The Catholic Priest in the United States: Demographic Investigations,* Vol. 1, "Respondent Report I: Census and Registry of Incardinated Diocesan Priests, 1966–85." Private report for participating dioceses; an 86-volume set is archived at the U.S. Catholic Conference Research Office, Washington, D.C., and another at the Comparative Religious Organization Studies, Department of Sociology, University of Wisconsin–Madison, Madison, Wis.

Schoenherr, Richard A. 1988. *The Catholic Priest in the United States: Demographic Investigations,* Vol. 2, "Respondent Report II: Trends and Projections of Incardinated Diocesan Priest Population, 1966–2005." Private report for participating dioceses; an 86-volume set is archived at the U.S. Catholic Conference Research Office, Washington, D.C., and another at the Comparative Religious Organization Studies, Department of Sociology, University of Wisconsin–Madison, Madison, Wis.

Schoenherr, Richard A. Forthcoming. *Celibacy, Sacrament and Control in the Catholic Church* (tentative title). New York: Oxford University Press.

Schoenherr, Richard A., and Andrew M. Greeley. 1974. "Role Commitment Processes and the American Catholic Priesthood." *American Sociological Review* 39:407–26.

Schoenherr, Richard A., and Eleanor P. Simpson. 1978. *The Political Economy of Diocesan Advisory Councils.* Washington, D.C.: U.S. Catholic Conference.

Schoenherr, Richard A., and Annemette Sørensen. 1982. "Social Change in Religious Organizations: Consequences of Clergy Decline in the U.S. Catholic Church." *Sociological Analysis* 43:23–52.

Schoenherr, Richard A., and José Pérez Vilariño. 1979. "Organizational Role Commitment in the Catholic Church in Spain and the USA." In *Organizations Alike and Unlike: International and Interinstitutional Studies in the Sociology of Organizations,* ed. Cornelis Lammers and David J. Hickson, pp. 346–72. London: Routledge and Kegan Paul.

Schoenherr, Richard A., and Lawrence A. Young. 1990a. *The Catholic Priest in the United States: Demographic Investigations,* Vol. 3, "Final Report: National, Regional, and Local Trends and Projections of Incardinated Diocesan Priest Population, 1966–2005," with the collaboration of Tsan-Yuang Cheng. Private report for participating dioceses and all U.S. Catholic bishops; copies archived at the U.S. Catholic Conference Research Office, Washington, D.C., and at the Comparative Religious Organization Studies, Department of Sociology, University of Wisconsin–Madison, Madison, Wis.

Schoenherr, Richard A., and Lawrence A. Young. 1990b. "Organizational Demography and Structural Change in the Roman Catholic Church." In *Structures of Power and Constraint,* ed. Craig Calhoun, Marshall Meyer, and Richard Scott, pp. 235–70. New York: Cambridge University Press.

Schoenherr, Richard A., Lawrence A. Young, and José Pérez Vilariño. 1988. "Demographic Transitions in Religious Organizations: A Comparative Study of Priest Decline in Roman Catholic Dioceses." *Journal for the Scientific Study of Religion* 27:499–523.

Schoenherr, Richard A., José Pérez Vilariño, Lawrence A. Young, and Celia Muñoz-Goy. 1990. "A Cross-National Study of Structural Change in the Roman Catholic Church: Consequences of Priest Decline in Spain and the United States." Paper presented at the International Sociological Association XII World Meetings, RC 22 Religion, Madrid, Spain, July 9–13.

Scott, W. Richard. 1992. *Organizations: Rational, Natural, and Open Systems.* Englewood Cliffs, N.J.: Prentice-Hall.

Seidler, John. 1979. "Priest Resignations in a Lazy Monopoly." *American Sociological Review* 44:763–83.

Seidler, John, and Katherine Meyer. 1989. *Conflict and Change in the Catholic Church.* New Brunswick, N.J.: Rutgers University Press.

Selznick, Philip. 1957. *Leadership in Administration.* New York: Harper and Row.

Sherry, Robert. 1985. "Shortage? What Vocation Shortage?" *The Priest* 41:29–32.

Shields, Joseph J., and Mary Jeanne Verdieck. 1985. "Religious Life in the United

States: The Experience of Men's Communities." Ringbound report. Washington, D.C.: Center for Applied Research in the Apostolate.

Shryock, Henry S., Jacob S. Siegel, and Associates. 1971. *The Methods and Materials of Demography.* 2 vols. Washington, D.C.: U.S. Government Printing Office.

Simmel, George. 1950. "On the Significance of Numbers for Social Life." In *The Sociology of George Simmel,* ed. and trans. Kurt W. Wolf, pp. 77–104. New York: Free Press.

Singh, Jitendra V. 1990. *Organizational Evolution: New Directions.* Newbury Park, Calif.: Sage.

Singh, Jitendra V., David J. Tucker, and Robert J. House. 1986. "Organizational Legitimacy and the Liability of Newness." *Administrative Science Quarterly* 31:171–93.

Sipe, A. W. Richard. 1990. *A Secret World: Sexuality and the Search for Celibacy.* New York: Brunner/Mazed.

Smith, Tom W. 1984. "America's Religious Mosaic." *American Demographics* 6: 18–23.

Starbuck, William H. 1983. "Organizations as Action Generators." *American Sociological Review* 48:91–102.

Starbuck, William H., Arent Greve, and Bo L. T. Hedberg. 1978. "Responding to Crises." *Journal of Business Administration* 9:111–37.

Stark, Rodney. 1988. "How New Religions Succeed: A Theoretical Model." In *The Future of New Religious Movements,* ed. David G. Bromley and Phillip E. Hammond, pp. 11–29. Macon, Ga.: Mercer University Press.

Stark, Rodney, and William Sims Bainbridge. 1980. "Towards a Theory of Religion: Religious Commitment." *Journal for the Scientific Study of Religion* 19: 114–28.

Stark, Rodney, and William Sims Bainbridge. 1985. *The Future of Religion: Secularization, Revival and Cult Formation.* Berkeley: University of California Press.

Stark, Rodney, and Roger Finke. 1988. "American Religion in 1776: A Statistical Portrait." *Sociological Analysis* 49:39–51.

Stark, Rodney, and Roger Finke. Forthcoming. "Cultural Crises and Religious Eruptions: Contemporary Myths about American Cults and Sects." In *On Cults and Sects in America,* ed. David Bromley and Jeffrey Hadden. Greenwich, Conn.: JAI Press.

Stark, Rodney, and James C. McCann. 1989. "The Weakness of Monopoly Faiths: Market Forces and Catholic Commitment." Paper presented at a joint session of the American Sociological Association and the Association for the Sociology of Religion, San Francisco, August.

Stark, Rodney, and Lynne Roberts. 1982. "The Arithmetic of Social Movements: Theoretical Implications." *Sociological Analysis* 43:53–67.

Statistical Yearbook of the Church. Annual. Secretary of State, General Statistics Office of the Church. Vatican City: Typis Polyglottis Vaticanis.

Stevens, Carl M. 1974. "Voice in Medical-Care Markets: 'Consumer Participation.'" *Social Science Information* 13(3): 33–48.

Stewman, Shelby. 1986. "Demographic Models of Internal Labor Markets." *Administrative Science Quarterly* 31:212–47.

Stewman, Shelby, and Surresh L. Konda. 1983. "Careers and Organizational Labor Markets: Demographic Models of Organizational Behavior." *American Journal of Sociology* 88:637–85.

Stinchcombe, Arthur. 1965. "Social Structure and Organizations." In *Handbook of Organizations,* ed. James G. March, pp. 142–93. Chicago: Rand McNally.

Stinchcombe, Arthur. 1990. *Information and Organizations.* Berkeley: University of California Press.

Suenens, Cardinal Leon. 1964. "The Theology of the Diaconate." In *Council Speeches of Vatican II,* ed. Hans Küng, Yves Congar, O.P., and Daniel O'Hanlon, S.J., pp. 103–7. New York: Paulist Press.

Sullivan, Teresa A., Francis P. Gillespie, Michael Hout, and Andrew M. Greeley. 1983. "Surname versus Self-Identification in the Analysis of Hispanic Data." In *American Statistical Association 1983 Proceedings of the Social Statistics Section,* pp. 117–22. Washington, D.C.: American Statistical Association.

Szafran, Robert F. 1977. "The Occurrence of Structural Innovation within Religious Organizations." PhD. dissertation, University of Wisconsin–Madison.

Thompson, James D. 1967. *Organizations in Action.* New York: McGraw-Hill.

Troeltsch, Ernst. 1960. *The Social Teaching of the Christian Churches.* 2 vols. Trans. Olive Wyon. New York: Harper Torchbooks.

Turner, Victor W. 1969. *The Ritual Process: Structure and Antistructure.* Chicago: Aldine.

U.S. Bureau of the Census. 1974. "Estimates of the Population of the United States, by Age, Sex, and Race: April 1, 1960 to July 1, 1973." *Current Population Reports* Series P-25, No. 519. Washington, D.C.: U.S. Government Printing Office.

U.S. Bureau of the Census. 1982. "Preliminary Estimates of the Population of the United States, by Age, Sex, and Race: 1970 to 1981." *Current Population Reports* Series P-25, No. 917. Washington, D.C.: U.S. Government Printing Office.

U.S. Bureau of the Census. 1986. "Projections of the Hispanic Population: 1983 to 2080." *Current Population Reports* Series P-25, No. 995. Washington, D.C.: U.S. Government Printing Office.

U.S. Bureau of the Census. 1988. "Population Estimates by Age, Sex, and Race: 1980–1987." *Current Population Reports* Series P-25, No. 1022. Washington, D.C.: U.S. Government Printing Office.

U.S. Bureau of the Census. 1989a. "Projections of the Population of the United States, by Age, Sex, and Race: 1988 to 2080." *Current Population Reports,* Series P-25, No. 1018. Washington, D.C.: U.S. Government Printing Office.

U.S. Bureau of the Census. 1989b. "Hispanic Population Surpasses 20 Million Mark." *United States Department of Commerce News,* Release CB89-158, Oct. 12. Washington, D.C.: Public Information Office.

U.S. Bureau of Health Professions. 1987. Bureau of Health Professions Area Resource File, 1940–87. Machine-readable data file. Washington, D.C.: U.S. Department of Health and Human Services, Health Resources and Services Administration, Office of Data Statistics.

U.S. Department of Health, Education, and Welfare. 1968. *Vital Statistics of the United States, 1966,* Vol. 2. "Mortality Part A," tables 1-1 and 1-8. Washington, D.C.: National Center for Health Statistics.

U.S. Department of Health, Education, and Welfare. 1979. *Vital Statistics of the United States, 1975,* Vol. 2. "Mortality Part A," table 1-8. Hyattsville, Md.: National Center for Health Statistics.

U.S. Department of Health and Human Services. 1987a. *Vital Statistics of the United States, 1983,* Vol. 2. "Mortality Part A," section 6, "Life Tables." Hyattsville, Md.: National Center for Health Statistics.

U.S. Department of Health and Human Services. 1987b. *Vital Statistics of the United States, 1984,* Vol. 2. "Mortality Part A," tables 1-1, 1-3, and 1-8. Hyattsville, Md.: National Center for Health Statistics.

Verdieck, Mary Jeanne, Joseph J. Shields, and Dean R. Hoge. 1988. "Role Commitment Processes Revisited: American Catholic Priests 1970 and 1985." *Journal for the Scientific Study of Religion* 27:524-35.

Wach, Joachim. 1944. *Sociology of Religion.* Chicago: University of Chicago Press.

Wagner, W. Gary, Jeffrey Pfeffer, and Charles A. O'Reilly III. 1984. "Organizational Demography and Turnover in Top Management Groups." *Administrative Science Quarterly* 29:74-92.

Wallace, Ruth A. 1992. *They Call Her Pastor: A New Role for Catholic Women.* Albany, N.Y.: State University of New York Press.

Weber, Max. 1963. *The Sociology of Religion.* Trans. Ephraim Fischoff. Boston: Beacon Press.

Weber, Max. 1978. *Economy and Society.* Ed. Guenther Roth and Klaus Wittich. Berkeley: University of California Press.

Weick, Karl. 1976. "Educational Organizations as Loosely Coupled Systems." *Administrative Science Quarterly* 21:1-19.

Westhues, Kenneth. 1971. "An Alternative Model for Research on Catholic Education." *American Journal of Sociology* 77:279-92.

Whetten, David A. 1980. "Sources, Responses, and Effects of Organizational Decline." In *The Organizational Life Cycle,* ed. J. Kimberly and R. Miles, pp. 342-74. San Francisco: Jossey-Bass.

Whetten, David A. 1981. "Organizational Response to Scarcity: Exploring the Obstacles to Innovative Approaches to Retrenchment in Education." *Educational Administration Quarterly* 17:80-97.

Whetten, David A. 1987. "Organizational Growth and Decline Processes." *Annual Review of Sociology* 13:335-58.

Whitehead, Evelyn Eaton, and James D. Whitehead. 1979. *Christian Life Patterns.* Garden City, N.Y.: Doubleday.

Wilson, George B. 1986. "The Priest Shortage: The Situation and Some Solutions." *America* (May 31): 450-53.

Wilson, William J. 1987. *The Truly Disadvantaged.* Chicago: University of Chicago Press.

Windsor, Pat. 1989. "Polish Seminarian Glut Overflows to U.S." *National Catholic Reporter* (Kansas City, Mo.), September 29, pp. 9-10.

Windsor, Pat. 1990. "Attack Widely Attributed to Nicaragua Contras." *National Catholic Reporter* (Kansas City, Mo.), January 12, pp. 6-7.

Wood, James R. 1981. *Leadership in Voluntary Organizations: The Controversy over Social Action in Protestant Churches.* New Brunswick, N.J.: Rutgers University Press.

Young, Lawrence A. 1991. "Hispanic Disaffiliation from the U.S. Roman Catholic Church." Paper presented at the annual meetings of the Association for the Sociology of Religion, Cincinnati, August.

Young, Lawrence A., and Richard A. Schoenherr. 1992. "The Changing Age Distribution and Theological Attitudes of Catholic Priests Revisited." *Sociological Analysis* 53:73-87.

Young, Ruth. 1988. "Is Population Ecology a Useful Paradigm for the Study of Organizations?" *American Journal of Sociology* 94:1-24.

Zald, Mayer N. 1970. *Organizational Change: The Political Economy of the YMCA.* Chicago: Chicago University Press.

Zald, Mayer N. 1981. "Political Economy: A Framework for Comparative Analysis." In *Complex Organizations: Critical Perspectives,* ed. Mary Zey-Ferrell and Michael Aiken, pp. 237-62. Glenview, Ill.: Scott, Foresman.

Ziade, Ignatius. 1964. "Pastoral Needs of Permanent Deacons." In *Council Speeches of Vatican II,* ed. Hans Küng, Yves Congar, O.P., and Daniel O'Hanlon, S.J., pp. 98-102. New York: Paulist Press.

Name Index

417

Subject Index

Abundance: politics of, 182, 325. *See also* Scarcity

Accuracy test: applied to projections, 310. *See also* Validity test, of projections

Active population: defined, 362

Active priests: defined, 362

Actuarial processes: sick leave, 202; retirement, 237–38, 245; natural attrition, 340

Adaptiveness: organizational, 341

Adjusted projections: altered 25 percent, 38–41; and zero net migration, 187–91

Adjustments to data: and new dioceses, 382–85; and divided dioceses, 385–87. *See also* Missing values

Affluent families, percentage of: range of, illustrated, 128–29; defined, 378. *See also* Income

Africa: availability of priests in, 10; growth of priestly vocations in, 11–12

African Americans, percentage of: range of, illustrated, 191; net effect of, on net immigration, 194–95, 194*n17*, 339–40; defined, 378

Age: and ordination, 156; and immigration, 178–79; and leave and return, 198–99; and resignation, 209–11; and retirement, 246–47, 249; and death, 246, 266–67; and standardized mortality ratios, 275–79

— distribution: balanced and imbalanced,

31–32; national, 25, 30–33; regional, 49, 60–67; local, 85–89; and organizational well-being, 341

— net effect of, on: ordination, 172*n20*; preretirement mortality, 260. *See also* Older priests, percentage of; Oldest priests

Age-specific rates: resignation, 217–20; mortality, 265*n3*, 270–74; vs. numbers, 364–65; and projection assumptions, 364–65; vs. crude, 377

Aggregation procedures, 377

Aging: national, 33, 37, 40, 45–46; regional, 48–49, 61, 66–67; local, 69–70, 85–90, 91; and demographic transition stages, 94–102, 104, 106–7, 111–17, 324–25; and ordination, 156–57, 164, 172, 332, 340; and immigration, 182, 340; and resignation, 204, 207, 210, 225, 236, 332, 340; and natural attrition, 238, 241, 244–45, 247, 249–50, 261, 332, 340–41; and mortality, 262, 266, 268–70, 283; and replacement, 289, 292, 295; and clerical conservatism, 317–19; mentioned, 13, 310, 346, 348, 353

Allentown, Diocese of: high ordination rates, 58–59; aging reversed, 89; high natural attrition, 251; oldest age pyramid, 251

Analytic techniques: population studies, 7; organization demography, 13, 265–66*n4*,

Laity (*continued*)
tance of, 15; and organizational boundaries, 16–18; as service consumers, 18; and access to sacraments, 77, 79, 118, 132, 342–43; and parish decision making, 246, 325. *See also* Laypersons
Las Cruces, Diocese of: as deviant case, 186, 186n7; highest natural attrition rate, 251; newly established, 382, 384
Latin America: availability of priests in, 10; growth of priestly vocations in, 11–12; as source of U.S. clergy, 177–78, 182
Law of large numbers, 76. *See also* Diocese(s), small
Layperson-to-priest ratio: definition clarified, 77n5; growth of, 302–5, 343; religious priests included in, 303–6; and recruitment problem, 333
Laypersons: and participation in ministry, 4, 354; and ecological niche, 16–18; and church leadership, 321, 354. *See also* Laity
Lazy monopoly: Catholic church as, 138, 344; and priestly immigration, 195; and resignations, 228; and recruitment ineffectiveness, 336
Leaders, church: and organizational myopia, 345; formal and informal, 347, 350; and wait-and-see strategy, 353–54. *See also* Managers; Policymakers; Policy, management
Lean environment, 320. *See also* Ecological niche; Rich environment
Leave of absence: defined, 33–34, 174, 196, 362; national rates of, 34; national numbers of, 196–97; age at, 198–99; regional net rates of, 199–200
Liabilities of newness. *See* Diocese(s), newly established; Ecological niche; Newness, organizational
Life cycle. *See* Crisis, psychological
Life expectancy: of U.S. white males, 36; of priests, 244, 246, 262–63, 266–67, 283, 341
Life span: organizational vs. natural, 365, 376
Life table: as analytic model, 19, 93, 322, 349; and mortality assumptions, 28, 369, 374. *See also* Decrements, multiple; Increments, multiple

Little Rock, Diocese of: lowest parishioner-to-priest ratio, 70, 79, 83, 83n9, 130; low parishioner density, 83; low ordination rates, 162
Loneliness: and resignation, 222, 225, 236, 335, 337
Longevity. *See* Life expectancy
Loose coupling, 117–18, 125, 136, 316
Loosely coupled system: evidence of, discussed, 67, 126, 142–43, 173, 203; described, 117
Los Angeles, Archdiocese of: highest parishioner-to-priest ratio, 70, 79–83, 83n9, 345; highest church membership growth, 345; highest percentage of Hispanics, 345; lowest recruitment effectiveness, 345n4, 345–46; and organizational myopia, 345–46
Loyalty, organizational, 326. *See also* Exit-voice-loyalty model

Male celibate priesthood: and recruitment to, 148, 154, 164, 317, 333; as organizational form, 314–16; and process structure, 324; and sacramental tradition, 353; and gender exclusivity, 353, 355; restoration of, 354; selection and retention of, 354; costs of maintaining, 355
Male hegemony, 354. *See also* Feminist movement
Man-years of service: and rising age at ordination, 149–50; as standardization technique, 156, 349, 376; and resignation, 211; and age at retirement, 340–41; and organizational life span, 365; and projection assumptions, 365–66, 369, 374
Managers: and organizational degeneration, 344; and research, 352. *See also* Leaders, church; Policymakers; Policy, management
Margins of error, 120n7, 310n3
Marital status: and mortality ratios, 281, 342
Market, religious: Catholicism's share of, 5; described, 17–18; competition in, 140
Marriage: theological nature of, 4, 226; clergy's desire for, 222, 226–27
Married priests, 27, 27n2, 226